SHAKESPEARE AS
LITERARY DRAMATIST

In this groundbreaking study, Lukas Erne argues that Shakespeare, apart from being a playwright who wrote theatrical texts for the stage, was also a literary dramatist who produced reading texts for the page. The usual distinction that has been set up between Ben Jonson carefully preparing his manuscripts for publication, and Shakespeare the man of the theatre, writing for his actors and audience, indifferent to his plays as literature, is questioned in this book. Examining the evidence from early published playbooks, Erne argues that Shakespeare wrote many of his plays with a readership in mind and that these "literary" texts would have been abridged for the stage because they were too long for performance. The variant early texts of *Romeo and Juliet*, *Henry V*, and *Hamlet* are shown to reveal important insights into the different media for which Shakespeare designed his plays.

Lukas Erne teaches English literature at the University of Geneva, Switzerland. He is the author of *Beyond "The Spanish Tragedy": A Study of the Works of Thomas Kyd* (2001), and of a number of articles published in *Shakespeare Quarterly*, *English Literary Renaissance*, *Essays in Criticism*, *Theatre Research International*, and elsewhere.

SHAKESPEARE AS
LITERARY DRAMATIST

LUKAS ERNE

CAMBRIDGE
UNIVERSITY PRESS

CAMBRIDGE UNIVERSITY PRESS
Cambridge, New York, Melbourne, Madrid, Cape Town, Singapore, São Paulo

Cambridge University Press
The Edinburgh Building, Cambridge CB2 8RU, UK

Published in the United States of America by Cambridge University Press, New York

www.cambridge.org
Information on this title: www.cambridge.org/9780521822558

First published 2003
Fourth printing 2005
This digitally printed version 2007

A catalogue record for this publication is available from the British Library

ISBN 978-0-521-82255-8 hardback
ISBN 978-0-521-04566-7 paperback

For Katrin

Contents

Illustrations

Acknowledgments

In the writing of this book, I have incurred a considerable number of debts which it is a pleasure to acknowledge. The inception of this study goes back to the time I spent in Oxford where Emrys Jones and Don McKenzie, inspiring teachers and scholars both, infected me with a passion for matters Shakespearean and bibliographical. Emrys Jones also read and helpfully commented on a paper in which some of the ideas developed in this study first took shape. In those early days of the writing of this book, I benefited from the generosity of the Marquis de Amodio, who granted me a Berrow Scholarship to Lincoln College, Oxford, and from the Rector and Fellows of Lincoln College who provided an intellectually stimulating environment and awarded me an Andrew W. Mellon fellowship to the Huntington Library, San Marino, California.

The greatest part of this book was written during a prolonged stay at the Folger Shakespeare Library in Washington, DC for which the Swiss National Science Foundation kindly offered generous funding. The astounding quality of the human and material resources of the Folger Library have made work on my project far smoother, more pleasurable and more rewarding than it might have been otherwise. I am deeply grateful to Werner Gundersheimer, Barbara Mowat, Richard Kuhta, Georgianna Ziegler, Owen Williams, and Carol Brobeck, as well as to the entire Reading Room staff. I was fortunate in being able to participate in a Folger Seminar on "Rewriting *The Elizabethan Stage*" which allowed me to test some of my ideas while picking up plenty of others. I wish to thank the seminar leader, Susan Cerasano, as well as all participants for a most instructive seminar.

While the resources of the Folger Shakespeare Library have been essential for the writing of this study, several other libraries have also been relied upon. Accordingly, I wish to thank the staff of the following institutions: the Huntington Library, the Newberry Library, the British Library, the Bodleian Library, the English Faculty Library and Lincoln College Library, both in Oxford, the Universitätsbibliothek Freiburg i. Br., the Bibliothèque Publique et Universitaire, and the English Department Library in Geneva.

Various people have given me the opportunity to share my work in progress. Richard Strier invited me to "The Book in the Age of Theatre" conference at the University of Chicago and the Newberry Library which he co-organized with Larry Norman and Philippe Desan. I remain grateful for a splendid conference as well as for the helpful questions raised by my co-panelists David Bevington, Leah Marcus, and Steven Urkowitz. Donna Hamilton and Marshal Grossman offered me the possibility to present a paper at the Center for Renaissance and Baroque Studies of the University of Maryland. Mary Bly, Anthony Mortimer, and Margaret Tudeau-Clayton were gracious hosts on the occasion of papers presented at the University of Fordham, the University of Fribourg, and the University of Zurich. On two occasions, seminars at meetings of the Shakespeare Association of America provided a forum in which to share and discuss my ideas. I wish to thank the seminar organizers, Thomas Berger and Ann Thompson, as well as the seminar participants for their stimulating responses. Further opportunities to present and receive valued feedback on parts of this study were provided by the Cercle des Seixiémistes at the University of Geneva, by a conference of the Swiss Association of University Teachers of English, and by a conference on "Shakespeare in European Culture," organized by Balz Engler, at the University of Basel.

While I have been fortunate in having generous and responsive audiences, I have profited no less from a number of readers: Douglas Brooks, Jeremy Ehrlich, Donna Hamilton, Sonia Massai, Steven May, Kirk Melnikoff, Andrew Murphy, Stuart Sherman, Richard Strier, and Richard Waswo all read parts of my work in progress and offered incisive feedback. Neil Forsyth, M. J. Kidnie, and Sonia Massai have given generously of their time by reading the entire manuscript, and I have profited from their insightful comments. Laurie Maguire read the manuscript for Cambridge University Press and, in a painstaking report, made more useful suggestions and corrections than I would like to admit. Deborah Payne Fisk, Roslyn Knutson, and Barbara Mowat granted me access to articles of theirs prior to appearance in print; John Ripley answered a query on stage history, Thomas Merriam one on authorship attribution, and Ralph Cohen one on the performance practices of the Shenandoah Shakespeare; Donna Hamilton lent me a recently published book that had reached her before becoming available at the Folger; and Andrew Murphy, at work on his forthcoming *Shakespeare in Print* (Cambridge University Press), kindly shared his research with me and drew my attention to several relevant publications.

My thinking on aspects of this study has also benefited from conversations with Leeds Barroll, Peter Blayney, R. A. Foakes, and Paul Werstine. Others to whom I am indebted for various kindnesses are Pascale Aebischer, Dympna Callaghan, Allen Carroll, James Purkin, Michael Suarez, SJ, and Alain Veylit.

Further, I wish to express my gratitude to the editors of two journals for the permission to reproduce: an article on aspects of Part II of this book of which parts survive here in much revised form was published in *Shakespeare Jahrbuch*, 135 (1999), 66–76, while an earlier version of chapter 3 was published in *Shakespeare Quarterly*, 53 (2002), 1–20. I owe special thanks to Barbara Mowat and Gail Paster for their help and forbearance, and to *Shakespeare Quarterly*'s anonymous readers for useful advice. At Cambridge University Press, I thank the anonymous readers for their comments and criticism, and Sarah Stanton, Teresa Sheppard, Alison Powell, and Gillian Maude for their work on this book.

Finally, I wish to thank Katrin for unfailing support and encouragement. To her this book is affectionately dedicated.

Introduction

In a letter appended to his *Apology for Actors* (1612), Thomas Heywood
allows us a rare glimpse of Shakespeare's inner life. In the third edition of a miscellany called *The Passionate Pilgrim*, which had been published earlier the same year, the printer William Jaggard had added certain
pieces from Heywood's *Troia Britannica* (1608) to the poems present in
the first two editions. Yet, far from acknowledging Heywood's authorship, the title page describes the collection as "newly corrected and augmented. By W. Shakespeare." Shakespeare does not seem to have been
amused. He was, Heywood tells us, "much offended with M. *Jaggard*
that (altogether vnknowne to him) presumed to make so bold with his
name."[1] Shakespeare may well have taken the matter further. Of the two
extant copies of the 1612 *Passionate Pilgrim*, only one bears Shakespeare's
name on the title page, while the other copy omits it. Shakespeare's dis-
pleasure seems to have been such that he requested a new title page for

---

[1] Thomas Heywood, *An Apology for Actors* (London, 1612), G4^v. Heywood's letter has often been
misunderstood and deserves to be quoted at some length:

> Here likewise, I must necessarily insert a manifest iniury done me in that worke, by taking the two
> Epistles of *Paris* to *Helen*, and *Helen* to *Paris*, and printing them in a lesse volume, vnder the name
> of another, which may put the world in opinion I might steale them from him; and hee to doe
> himselfe right, hath since published them in his owne name: but as I must acknowledge my lines not
> worthy his [Shakespeare's] patronage, vnder whom he [Jaggard] hath publisht them, so the Author
> [Shakespeare] I know much offended with M. *Iaggard* (that altogether vnknowne to him) presumed
> to make so bold with his name. (G4^{r-v})

Heywood had first published the said Epistles in his *Troia Britannica* of 1608. Since they appeared in
1612 in a volume ascribed to Shakespeare, Heywood is worried that readers will mistakenly assume
that these Epistles had been unrightfully included in Heywood's earlier volume. A further mistaken
inference, Heywood fears, would be that their real author, Shakespeare, "to doe himselfe right,"
included them in his *Passionate Pilgrim* in 1612. As *The Passionate Pilgrim* contains Shakespeare's
Sonnets 138 and 144, several scholars who failed to recognize that the phrase "and hee to doe himselfe
right, hath since published them in his owne name" is syntactically subordinated to "may put the
world in opinion," have mistakenly believed that Heywood is referring to Shakespeare's publication
of his sonnets in 1609. See, for instance, Katherine Duncan-Jones, ed., *Shakespeare's Sonnets*, The
Arden Shakespeare (Walton-on-Thames, Surrey: Thomas Nelson, 1997), 2–3.

I

the unsold copies, from which Jaggard removed his name (see Figures 1 and 2).[2]

This incident presents us with a picture of an unfamiliar Shakespeare: keenly aware of what is and what is not his literary property, concerned about his reputation, proud of his name and unwilling to have it associated with lines that did not flow from his pen. The Shakespeare we are familiar with is in many ways a different figure. Building upon his article for the *Dictionary of National Biography*, Sidney Lee, in his influential biography, was instrumental in promoting the image of a Shakespeare unconscious of the quality of his work and largely uninterested in it beyond its "serving the prosaic end of providing permanently for himself and his daughters."[3] Many biographies have followed since, and few have entirely endorsed Lee's portrait of Shakespeare as a money grabber. Yet what has remained largely unchanged in our view of Shakespeare is that he allegedly had little interest in his writings as personal property and even less interest in posterity.

How inconsistent is the picture of the "much offended" Shakespeare we glimpsed above with what we gather about Shakespeare at other moments of his artistic career? Robert Greene's attack on Shakespeare in *Greene's Groatsworth of Wit* is well known: having given some advice to three of his fellow playwrights (probably Christopher Marlowe, Thomas Nashe, and George Peele), he goes on to warn them against an

upstart Crow, beautified with our feathers, that with his *Tygers hart wrapt in a Players hyde*, supposes he is as well able to bombast out a blanke verse as the best of you: and beeing an absolute *Johannes fac totum*, is in his owne conceit the onely Shake-scene in a countrey.[4]

It is possible, of course, to dismiss Greene's attack as symptomatic of his jealousy and therefore hopelessly biased. It would admittedly be foolish to argue that Greene is an altogether fair and disinterested commentator. Nevertheless, the passage may be of greater interest for what it tells us about the object of the attack than about the attacker. As early as 1592, Shakespeare had done enough to awaken a rival playwright's jealousy. He was well advanced in the first tetralogy, the most ambitious project the

---

[2] See Samuel Schoenbaum, *William Shakespeare: A Compact Documentary Life*, rev. edn (New York: Oxford University Press, 1987), 271. For a facsimile edition of the 1612 *Passionate Pilgrim* with an excellent introduction, see *The Passionate Pilgrim*, ed. Hyder Edward Rollins (New York and London: Charles Scribner's Sons, 1940).

[3] Sidney Lee, *A Life of William Shakespeare* (London: Smith, Elder & Co., 1898), 279.

[4] I quote from D. Allen Carroll's edition, *Greene's Groatsworth of Wit, Bought with a Million of Repentance (1592)*, Medieval & Renaissance Texts & Studies, 114 (Binghamton, New York: Medieval & Renaissance Texts & Studies, 1994), lines 939–43.

THE
PASSIONATE
PILGRIME,

OR

Certaine Amorous Sonnets,
betweene Venus and Adonis,
*newly corrected and aug-
mented.*

By W. Shakespere.

The third Edition.

VVhere-unto is newly ad-
ded two Loue-Epiftles, the firft
from *Paris* to *Hellen,* and
Hellens anfwere backe
againe to *Paris.*

Printed by W. Iaggard.
1612.

Figure 1. Title page of the third octavo edition of *The Passionate Pilgrim*, 1612 (*STC* 22343), attributed to Shakespeare.

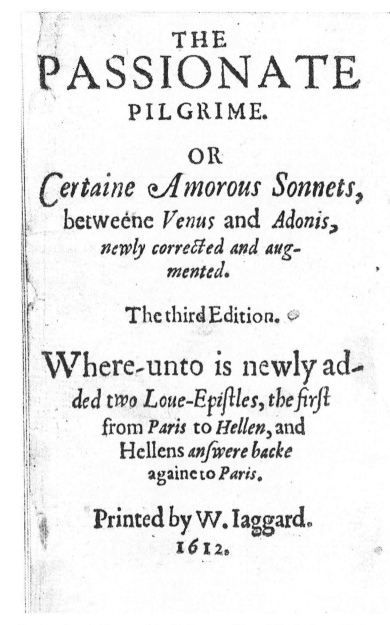

THE
PASSIONATE
PILGRIME.

OR
Certaine Amorous Sonnets,
betweéne *Venus* and *Adonis,*
newly corrected and aug-
mented.

The third Edition.

Where-unto is newly ad-
ded two Loue-Epiſtles, the firſt
from *Paris* to *Hellen,* and
Hellens *anſwere backe*
againe to *Paris.*

Printed by W. Iaggard.
1612.

Figure 2. Cancel title page of the third octavo edition of *The Passionate Pilgrim*, 1612 (*STC* 22343), with no authorship attribution.

professional stage had yet seen, which was to find its completion soon after with *Richard III*.[5] Significantly, attributing to Shakespeare a "*Tygers hart wrapt in a Players hyde*," Greene not only accuses Shakespeare of duplicity but simultaneously alludes to a line in *3 Henry VI*, probably the most recent product of Shakespeare's ambitious project. Marlowe had written a two-part play and so, it seems, had Thomas Kyd.[6] A mere player (as opposed to Greene and other university-trained gentlemen), not yet thirty years of age and still relatively new among London's playwrights, Shakespeare was not content to follow their precedent but seems to have been eager to outdo them. Shakespeare, Greene has it, "is in his owne conceit the onely Shake-scene in a countrey." There is no way of knowing how justified Greene's punning allusion to Shakespeare's alleged conceitedness was, but what we know about Shakespeare's dramatic writings at the time does suggest a fair amount of artistic ambition and self-consciousness.

Some time between Greene's attack in 1592 and Heywood's letter in 1612, Shakespeare must have written his sonnets. No reader can ignore how prominently the theme of poetry as immortalization figures in them. In fact, no fewer than twenty-eight sonnets deal with this topic.[7] Sonnet 74 will serve as an example:

> But be contented when that fell arrest
> Without all bail shall carry me away.
> My life hath in this line some interest,
> Which for memorial still with thee shall stay.
> When thou reviewest this, thou dost review
> The very part was consecrate to thee.
> The earth can have but earth, which is his due;
> My spirit is thine, the better part of me.
> So then thou hast but lost the dregs of life,
> The prey of worms, my body being dead,
> The coward conquest of a wretch's knife,
> Too base of thee to be rememberèd.
> The worth of that is that which it contains,
> And that is this, and this with thee remains.

The poem sharply distinguishes between "that" (the perishable body) and "this" (the poetry we are reading), poetry being "the better part of me" which

---

[5] Note, however, that not all scholars agree today that the three parts of *Henry VI* were written by Shakespeare alone. See below, page 193.

[6] See Lukas Erne, " 'Enter the Ghost of Andrea': Recovering Thomas Kyd's Two-Part Play," *English Literary Renaissance*, 30 (2000), 339–72, rpt. and rev. in *Beyond "The Spanish Tragedy": A Study of the Works of Thomas Kyd*, Revels Plays Companion Library (Manchester University Press, 2001), 14–46.

[7] J. B. Leishman, *Themes and Variations in Shakespeare's Sonnets* (London: Hutchinson, 1961), 21–22. Sonnet 74 and, unless stated otherwise, all following quotations are from Stanley Wells and Gary Taylor, gen. eds., *William Shakespeare: The Complete Works* (Oxford: Clarendon Press, 1986).

survives after death. J. B. Leishman rightly pointed out that Shakespeare's repeated insistence on his writings as that which will transcend his mortal existence ("My life hath in this line some interest") is not easily squared with his alleged indifference to the afterlife of his writings: "so far as I am aware, no writer on the Sonnets has remarked upon the fact that [Shakespeare], who is commonly supposed to have been indifferent to literary fame and perhaps only dimly aware of the magnitude of his own poetic genius, has written both more copiously and more memorably on this topic [i.e. poetry as immortalization] than any other sonneteer."[8] It is true, of course, that others had voiced similar ideas before Shakespeare. In Sonnet 69 of his *Amoretti*, Edmund Spenser writes that "this verse vowd to eternity" is an "immortall moniment."[9] Elsewhere, Michael Drayton speaks of "my World-out-wearing Rimes."[10] More examples could be given, going all the way back to Ovid.[11] Yet Leishman counters the objection that Shakespeare was simply drawing upon a well-known *topos*: "It seems to be generally assumed, in a vague sort of way, that most, perhaps all, sonneteers, English, French and Italian, perhaps even from Petrarch onwards, had written a great deal about their own poetry, and that Shakespeare was merely saying the sort of things they had said, but saying them better: this... is far from the truth."[12] Leishman suggests that, in his sonnets, Shakespeare, more than any of his predecessors or contemporaries, seems to have been obsessed with the transcendence of his own poetry.

Toward the end of the sixteenth century, an English poet's hopes that his verse would live on after his death were probably more likely to come true than ever before. More than a century after William Caxton had established the first printing press in England, print had become widespread. Elizabethan England was in many ways "a printing age" in which "reading was no longer the prerogative of a few."[13] In the last two decades of the sixteenth century, an average of about 280 titles per year were published

---

[8] Ibid., 22.

[9] Lines 9–10. I quote from *Edmund Spenser's Amoretti and Epithalamion: A Critical Edition*, ed. Kenneth J. Larsen (Tempe, AZ: Medieval & Renaissance Texts & Studies, 1997), 96.

[10] Line 7, sonnet 44 (in the final order first printed 1599) in *Idea's Mirror*. I quote from *The Works of Michael Drayton*, ed. J. William Hebel, corr. edn, 5 vols. (Oxford: Shakespeare Head Press, 1961), 11.332.

[11] See, for instance, Laurie E. Maguire, "Composition/Decomposition: Singular Shakespeare and the Death of the Author," in *The Renaissance Text: Theory, Editing, Textuality*, ed. Andrew Murphy (Manchester University Press, 2000), 135–53, and Leishman's study.

[12] Leishman, *Themes and Variations*, 22.

[13] H. S. Bennett, *English Books & Readers, 1558 to 1603* (Cambridge: At the University Press, 1965), 2, 4. For the impact of print on early modern culture, see Elizabeth L. Eisenstein, *The Printing Press as an Agent of Change: Communications and Cultural Transformations in Early Modern Europe*, 2 vols. (Cambridge and New York: Cambridge University Press, 1979); Lucien Febvre and Henri-Jean

in England.[14] While the output of what we now call "literature" remained below that of religious texts throughout the sixteenth century, the number of literary titles was increasing and reached more than a quarter of the total output by the end of the century. The years 1500 and 1550 saw the publication of fourteen and twenty-one "literary" titles respectively, but no fewer than eighty-four of them were published in the year 1600.[15] By the time Shakespeare started writing poetry and plays, the printing press had made the creation and perpetuation of literary fame a distinct possibility.

It is one of the great paradoxes of English literary history that even though print had become an agent of greatest importance in the construction of literary reputation by the late sixteenth and the early seventeenth century, scholarship has long taught us that Shakespeare and many of his con-temporary dramatists remained largely unaffected by these developments. Writing about Shakespeare and his contemporaries in the theatrical world, Andrew Gurr only perpetuates what others said before him when holding that "Except for a few poets, nobody gave a thought to posterity."[16] Julie Stone Peters has pertinently identified this wide-spread belief as "One of those lies so convenient to the history of progress: that Renaissance drama-tists were unconcerned with the circulation of their work on the page; that the press kept aloof from the stage and the early stage kept aloof from the press." Her impressive study shows that, on the contrary, in England as well as in the rest of Western Europe, the institutions of the printing press and the modern theater "grew up together." Whereas a performance critic like William Worthen believes that "Shakespeare's works were perhaps not viewed as textual in his era,"[17] Peters amply demonstrates that, by the end of the sixteenth century, "Drama was understood to play itself out in two arenas – on the stage and on the page."[18]

Martin, *The Coming of the Book: The Impact of Printing 1450–1800*, trans. David Gerard, eds. Geoffry Nowell-Smith and David Wootton (London: NLB, 1976); Roger Chartier, *Cultural Uses of Print*, trans. Lydia G. Cochrane (Princeton University Press, 1987) and "Texts, Printing, Reading," in *The New Cultural History*, ed. Lynn Hunt (Berkeley and Los Angeles: University of California Press, 1989), 154–75; and Adrian Johns, *The Nature of the Book: Print and Knowledge in the Making* (Chicago and London: University of Chicago Press, 1998).

[14] I owe this figure to the website at http://cbsr26.ucr.edu/ESTCStatistics.html, which presents "Some Statistics on the Number of Surviving Printed Titles for Great Britain and Dependencies from the Beginnings of Print in England to the year 1800," by Alain Veylit.

[15] Edith L. Klotz, "A Subject Analysis of English Imprints for Every Tenth Year from 1480 to 1640," *Huntington Library Quarterly*, 1 (1937–38), 417–19, 418.

[16] Andrew Gurr, *The Shakespearean Stage 1574–1642*, 3rd edn (Cambridge University Press, 1992), 46.

[17] William B. Worthen, "Drama, Performativity, and Performance," *PMLA*, 113 (1998), 1093–107, 1099.

[18] Julie Stone Peters, *Theatre of the Book, 1480–1880: Print, Text, and Performance in Europe* (Oxford and New York: Oxford University Press, 2000), 1, 4–5, 8.

One way to perpetuate the belief in Shakespeare's indifference to the publication and afterlife of his playbooks is to argue that, while the influence of the printing press had spread by the late sixteenth and early seventeenth centuries, modern notions of individuality, authorship, and copyright had not. It is true that a copyright law in the modern sense did not exist before the eighteenth century. Copyright in Shakespeare's time, Lyman Ray Patterson rightly points out,

> was a private affair of the company. The common-law courts had no part in its development, for it was strictly regulated by company ordinances. The Stationers' company granted the copyright, and since it was developed by and limited to company members, it functioned in accordance with their self-interest... Authors, not being members of the company, were not eligible to hold copyright, so that the monopoly of the stationers meant that their copyright was, in practice and in theory, a right of the publisher only. Not until after the Statute of Anne [of 1709] did the modern idea of copyright as a right of the author develop.[19]

In so far as the legal aspect of copyright is concerned, this is an excellent summary upon which I cannot hope to improve. The argument that "the modern idea of copyright as a right of the author" did not develop until the eighteenth century is problematic, however. It fosters precisely the impression of the Renaissance writer who has no sense of having any moral rights to his works. In fact, the *idea* of copyright as the right of the author was very much present in Shakespeare's time, though it was not anchored in the law until the eighteenth century.[20]

In the early seventeenth century, several writers show keen awareness of what they perceived as the stationers' usurpation of their rights. In his petition for a patent for his *Paraphrase upon the Psalmes*, George Sandys wrote that, "whereas the Company of Stationers have an order, that no Printer shall print any booke but for one of their own Societie, thereby to ingrosse to themselves the whole profit of other mens Labours; He humbly desireth, that your Majestie wilbe pleased to grant him a Patent of Priviledge for these his Paraphrases."[21] When George Wither was involved in a dispute

---

[19] Lyman Ray Patterson, *Copyright in Historical Perspective* (Nashville: Vanderbilt University Press, 1968), 5. On the subject of copyright, see also chapter 5 of Marjorie Plant, *The English Book Trade: An Economic History of the Making and Sale of Books* (London: George Allen & Unwin Ltd., 1939), 98–121; Mark Rose, *Authors and Owners: The Invention of Copyright* (Cambridge, Mass.: Harvard University Press, 1993); and Joseph Loewenstein, *Ben Jonson and Possessive Authorship* (Cambridge University Press, 2002).

[20] This point has recently been well made by Brian Vickers (*English Renaissance Literary Criticism*, ed. Vickers (Oxford University Press, 1999), 29).

[21] Bodleian MS Bankes 11/62, dated 1635, printed in W. W. Greg, *Companion to Arber* (Oxford: Clarendon Press, 1967), 321.

with the Stationers' Company over a patent for his *Hymns and Songs of the Church* in the 1620s, he tells us that he "humbly peticioned the Kings most excellent Maiestie" so that "according to the lawes of nature, I might enioy the benefit of some part of myne owne labours." Authorial copyright is here not a modern notion that is anachronistically imposed upon a time and a society in which it did not yet apply, but one which, as Wither tells us, should always apply "according to the lawes of nature." Wither explains that "by an vniust custome... the Stationers haue so vsurped vpon the labours of all writers, that when they [the writers] haue consumed their youth and fortunes in perfiting some laborious worke, those cruell Bee-masters burne the poore Athenian bees for their hony, or else driue them from the best part thereof."[22] Like others before and after him (including Heminge and Condell in the prefatory material to Shakespeare's First Folio), Wither is scandalized by the interference of stationers who "take vppon them to publish bookes contriued, altered, and mangled at their owne pleasures, without consent of the writers: nay and to change the name sometyms, both of booke and Author (after they haue been ymprinted)."[23] He concludes that "it is high tyme to seeke a remedie, and a remedy (I hope) wil shortly be prouided in due place."[24] A copyright that protected stationers but not authors seems to have been thought of by many writers as a historically contingent "vniust custome" that was defying "the lawes of nature."

Nor did the sixteenth and seventeenth-century practice of protecting stationers but not authors apply to all books. King James and his successor granted a series of patents to authors who were thereby allowed to derive a profit from the sale of their books. Samuel Daniel was granted a patent for his *History of England*, Fynes Moryson for his *Itinerary*, Caleb Morley for "a book invented by him for the helpe of memory and grounding of Schollars in severall languages," Joseph Webb "for the teaching the languages after a newe sorte by him devised, and alsoe the printing of the bookes and selling

---

[22] George Wither, *The Schollers Purgatory* (London, 1624), A3^r. A facsimile edition is available in "The English Experience" series (Amsterdam: Theatrum Orbis Terrarum, 1977). For the original text of the royal "privilege" and for some of the other surviving legal documents, see Greg, *Companion to Arber*, 212–18. On Wither's dispute with the Stationers' Company, see Norman E. Carlson, "Wither and the Stationers," *Studies in Bibliography*, 19 (1966), 210–15; Jocelyn C. Creigh, "George Wither and the Stationers: Facts and Fiction," *Publications of the Bibliographical Society of America*, 74 (1980), 49–57; and James Doelman, "George Wither, the Stationers' Company and the English Psalter," *Studies in Philology*, 90 (1993), 74–82. For a previously unknown reply to Wither that presents the stationers' point of view, see Allan Pritchard, "George Wither's Quarrel with the Stationers: An Anonymous Reply to *The Schollers Purgatory*," *Studies in Bibliography*, 16 (1963), 27–42.

[23] Wither, *Schollers Purgatory*, A5^v–A6^r.   [24] Ibid., A6^r.

them." Many more could be added.[25] The growing number of patents that allowed authors to reap the benefits of their inventions testifies to the fact that the *idea* of copyright as the right of the author was not absent from Renaissance England.

Unlike many poets of his own time, however, Shakespeare was first and foremost a playwright. Providing the company in which he was also an actor and shareholder with scripts, Shakespeare was a participant in an entertainment industry that needed plays to make money. As in today's movie industry, novelty was often the key to commercial success. While poets may well have hoped to create an "immortall moniment," many playwrights knew they were producing little more than theatrical fast food. Yet, to understand the Elizabethan and Jacobean plays that have come down to us as mere products and unlikely survivors of an entertainment industry that only produced to the moment does less than full justice to the status these plays had. For their very existence bears witness to the fact that, during Shakespeare's time, many plays started having more than one kind of public existence: on stage *and* on the page; at the Globe, the Rose, or the Fortune *and* in St. Paul's Churchyard; produced by players *and* by printers. During Shakespeare's lifetime, *The First Part of Henry IV* would not only have been watched by a great number of spectators, but also read by all those who bought the printed playbooks that appeared in no fewer than six editions. Shakespeare's attitude toward the emergent printed drama, the place his plays occupy within it, and the way in which it may have affected the composition of his plays are at the center of this book.

Before introducing the nine chapters in which I propose to develop these issues, it is necessary to deal with the broader question of the status of printed playbooks in Renaissance England. Today, Elizabethan and Jacobean drama occupies a central position in the English literary canon. The drama of Shakespeare, in particular, has been turned into a literary and cultural monument that has little to do with the prestige it enjoyed

---

[25] I quote from the list of "Printing Patents Granted by James the First and His Successor," in Edward Arber, ed., *A Transcript of the Registers of the Company of Stationers of London, 1554–1640*, 5 vols. (London: Privately Printed, 1875–94), 5.lvii–lviii. The fullest treatment this topic has received is Arnold Hunt's "Book Trade Patents, 1603–1640," in *The Book Trade and Its Customers: Historical Essays for Robin Myers*, eds. Arnold Hunt, Giles Mandelbrote, and Alison Shell (Winchester, Hampshire: St. Paul's Bibliographies, 1997), 27–54. Hunt shows that James and his son granted more than seventy patents, more than half of which did not go to members of the Stationers' Register (27–28). Hunt presents convincing evidence that suggests that the increase of the number of patents to authors in the early seventeenth century was due to "authorial dissatisfaction with the restrictions imposed by the system of publisher's copyright" (31). See also Phoebe Sheavyn, *The Literary Profession in the Elizabethan Age*, 2nd edn, rev. by J. W. Saunders (Manchester University Press, 1967), 76–77.

in Elizabethan and Jacobean England. It is important to recognize that, to a large extent, the cultural capital that Shakespeare, Jonson, Marlowe, and their contemporary dramatists possess today is a product of later times. "Shakespeare," as Michael Dobson and Margreta de Grazia have shown, is in many ways a product of the late seventeenth and the eighteenth centuries.[26] Scholarship has thus rightly insisted on how later ages turned the drama of Shakespeare and his contemporaries into literary and cultural entities that are substantially different from what they were in their own time. What this insistence may have led to, however, is a scholarly climate that underestimates the legitimacy printed playbooks were starting to acquire in Renaissance England.

Students of Elizabethan drama have often been told that early quarto playbooks represented mere ephemera, to be read and discarded. Fredson Bowers is among those who have argued that "plays were not regarded as 'literature' but as relatively ephemeral entertainment reading on no higher plane than, say, a novel made from the script of a popular moving picture."[27] In order to support the claim that printed plays were not considered literature in Shakespeare's lifetime, critics usually refer to Sir Thomas Bodley's injunction not to include any such "riff raff Books" in the great library which he began gathering in 1598: "I can see no good Reason, to alter my Opinion, for excluding such Books, as Almanacks, Plays, and an infinite Number, that are daily Printed, of very unworthy matters."[28] It is necessary to raise the question, however, of just how representative Bodley is.

The composition of libraries in Shakespeare's time was in a state of flux. At the beginning of the sixteenth century, most libraries were attached to ecclesiastical institutions, and their collections had generally confined themselves to the four principal fields of medieval learning: theology, law, medicine, and philosophy. The dissolution of the monasteries led to the rise of private and university libraries in the course of the sixteenth century, and the early seventeenth century saw the advent of new institutional libraries such as the Bodleian library – which opened in 1602 – and the first independent town library, founded in Norwich in 1608. One of the results of this development was that the collections generally became much

---

[26] See Michael Dobson, *The Making of the National Poet: Shakespeare, Adaptation and Authorship, 1660–1769* (Oxford: Clarendon Press, 1992), and Margreta de Grazia, *Shakespeare Verbatim: The Reproduction of Authenticity and the 1790 Apparatus* (Oxford: Clarendon Press, 1991).
[27] Fredson Bowers, "The Publication of English Renaissance Plays," in *Elizabethan Dramatists*, ed. Fredson Bowers, Dictionary of Literary Biography, 62 (Detroit: Gale Research Company, 1987), 414.
[28] *Reliquiae Bodleianæ; Or Some Genuine Remains of Sir Thomas Bodley* (London, 1703), 82, 278.

more varied and open to previously unacceptable printed matter, including playbooks.[29] As has been shown, the acquisition of printed plays seemed worthwhile "perhaps not to Bodley but certainly to many early modern men and women."[30] Bodley's exclusion of playbooks is, in fact, exceptional rather than the norm.

The library of Sir John Harington (1561–1612), godson of Queen Elizabeth and translator of Ariosto's *Orlando Furioso*, presents a very different picture from that suggested by Bodley. Harington purchased, bound and catalogued the great majority of all the playbooks published in the first decade of the seventeenth century, including no fewer than eighteen copies of Shakespeare's plays.[31] His extant writings suggest that he not only purchased, but was intimately acquainted with, the playbooks he owned. For instance, in his Rabelaisian *Metamorphosis of Ajax*, which, along with other satires, led to his banishment from court, he writes: "For the shrewd wife, reade the booke of taming a shrew, which hath made a number of us so perfect, that now every one can rule a shrew in our countrey, save he that hath her."[32] Harington's ironic promise of a fictional lesson that seemingly instructs only to prove useless in actual life highlights and intelligently reenacts the final twist of the dramatic Sly-frame present in *A Shrew* (published in 1594) but absent from *The Shrew* (not published until 1623):

> TAPSTER. Ay marry, but you had best get you home,
> For your wife will course you for dreaming here tonight.
> SLY. Will she? I know now how to tame a shrew.
> I dreamt upon it all this night till now[33]

Harington does not seem to have considered it below himself to read widely and carefully among the printed playbooks of his time.

Nor was Harington an exception. A book-list of *c.* 1625 shows that Sir Roger Townshend, Bacon's grandson, was in possession of several

[29] Heidi Brayman Hackel, " 'Rowme' of Its Own: Printed Drama in Early Libraries," in *A New History of Early English Drama*, eds. John D. Cox and David Scott Kastan (New York: Columbia University Press, 1997), 113–30, 114. Hackel's essay provides an excellent survey, demonstrating that "vernacular drama – if not yet granted the security it has found at the Folger Shakespeare Library – was beginning to find 'rowme' in private libraries" (127).

[30] See Hackel, " 'Rowme' of Its Own," 127.

[31] See F. J. Furnivall, "Sir John Harington's Shakespeare Quartos," *Notes and Queries*, 7th series, 9 (1890), 382–83.

[32] John Harington, *The Metamorphosis of Ajax*, ed. Elizabeth Donno (New York: Columbia University Press, 1962), 153–54.

[33] Scene 15, lines 14–17. I quote from *The Taming of a Shrew*, ed. Stephen Roy Miller, The New Cambridge Shakespeare: The Early Quartos (Cambridge University Press, 1998).

playbooks, including Jonson's *Volpone* and Chapman's *All Fools*.[34] A list of books in the possession of Frances Egerton, Countess of Bridgewater (dated 1633) included Jonson's *The New Inn*, a volume of "Diverse plays by Shakespeare" and several others volumes of "diverse plays,"[35] while another list of books owned by Scipio le Squyer (1579–1659), Deputy Chamberlain of the Exchequer (1620–59), includes Shakespeare's *Romeo and Juliet*, Fletcher's *Faithful Shepherdess*, Middleton's *A Game at Chess*, Jonson's *Volpone*, and Kyd's *Spanish Tragedy*.[36] Sir Edward Dering, first baronet, of Surrenden in Kent (1598–1644) recorded the purchase of no fewer than 225 playbooks in the years 1619 to 1624.[37] A list of books purchased by Sir Thomas Barrington, baronet, from 1635 to 1639 includes many works of theology and philosophy, but also a copy each of the two parts of Shakespeare's *Henry IV*.[38] In the 1660s, Henry Oxinden (1608–1670) inherited a collection that had been formed decades earlier which included some seventy playbooks printed between 1590 and 1616.[39] Humphrey Dyson (d. 1633), son-in-law of Thomas Speght who edited the 1598 Chaucer *Works*, drew up a "Catalogue of all such Bookes touching aswell the State Ecclesiastical as Temporall of the Realme of England w[hi]ch were published vpon seuerall occasions." He found nothing inappropriate about including six play quartos published between 1591 and 1613, among them Shakespeare's *Troilus and Cressida* (1609).[40] The library of Robert Burton contained a great many "comedies, tragedies, poetry, and comic works," and marginal comments in books in his library suggest his familiarity with *Hamlet* and *Henry IV*.[41] One of the largest seventeenth-century family collections, the Bridgewater

---

[34] See R. J. Fehrenbach, gen. ed., *Private Libraries in Renaissance England: A Collection and Catalogue of Tudor and Early Stuart Book-Lists* (Binghamton, NY: Medieval & Renaissance Texts & Studies, 1992), 81–82, 85, 134.

[35] See Hackel, " 'Rowme' of Its Own," 125.

[36] F. Taylor, "The Books and Manuscripts of Scipio le Squyer, Deputy Chamberlain of the Exchequer (1620–59)," *Bulletin of the John Rylands Library*, 25 (1941), 137–64, esp. 157–58.

[37] See Fehrenbach, gen. ed., *Private Libraries*, 141. Dering also staged private theatricals, including *1* and *2 Henry IV* of which a manuscript version of 1623 that cuts down the two parts to one play survives in the Folger Shakespeare Library (V.b.34). See Laetitia Yaendle, "The Dating of Sir Edward Dering's Copy of 'The History of King Henry the Fourth,' " *Shakespeare Quarterly*, 37 (1986), 224–26, and T. N. S. Lennam, "Sir Edward Dering's Collection of Playbooks, 1619–1624," *Shakespeare Quarterly*, 16 (1965), 145–53.

[38] Mary Elizabeth Bohannon, "A London Bookseller's Bill: 1635–1639," *The Library*, 18, 4th Series (1938), 417–46.

[39] W. W. Greg, *A Bibliography of the English Printed Drama to the Restoration*, 4 vols. (London: Bibliographical Society, 1939–59), III.1314.

[40] See Alan Nelson's home page at http://socrates.berkeley.edu/~ahnelson/winess.html. Dyson's "Catalogue" is preserved in the Codrington Library of All Souls' College, Oxford (MS 117).

[41] Nicolas K. Kiessling, *The Library of Robert Burton* (Oxford: Bibliographical Society, 1988), 43, 87, and Hackel, " 'Rowme' of Its Own," 120.

House library included plays by Shakespeare, Marlowe, and many of their contemporaries.[42] Edward 2nd Viscount Conway (1594–1665) owned an astounding 350 English playbooks.[43] William Drummond of Hawthornden drew up lists of "Bookes red be me" for the years 1606 to 1614. The list for 1606 contains forty-two titles of which eight are plays: "Orlando Furioso, comedie," "Romeo and Julieta, tragedie," "Loues Labors Lost, comedie," "The Malcontent, comedie," "A Midsommers Nights Dreame, comedie," "Doctor Dodipol, comedie," "Alphonsus historie, comed.," and "The Tragedie of Locrine."[44] Extant books that had been in Drummond's possession – like his copies of *Romeo and Juliet* and *Love's Labour's Lost*, now in the library of the University of Edinburgh – show Drummond's careful overlinings of witty and poetic passages.[45] In Drummond's lists, plays appear alongside "Knox, Chronicles," "The Holie Loue of Heuinlie Wisdome," and Sir Thomas Hoby's translation of Castiglione's *Book of the Courtier*, which indicates that he found nothing inappropriate about juxtaposing playbooks with "serious" books. Far from indicating that playbooks were read and discarded like modern newspapers or other ephemera, the extant evidence suggests that playbooks started being read, collected, bound, and catalogued from the beginning of the seventeenth century.

For many adherents to the now omnipresent performance criticism, the basic premise underlying their approach to Shakespeare is the claim that his plays were written in order to be performed.[46] I will argue that this view needs to be reconsidered. In a sense, what is particular about the time of Shakespeare's active involvement with the theater in London is that plays stopped having a public existence that was confined to the stage. The

[42] Hackel, " 'Rowme' of Its Own," 122.

[43] T. A. Birrell, "Reading as Pastime: the Place of Light Literature in some Gentlemen's Libraries of the 17th Century," in Robin Myers and Michael Harris, eds., *Property of a Gentleman: The Formation, Organisation and Dispersal of the Private Library 1620–1920* (Winchester: St. Paul's Bibliographies, 1991), 113–31, 124. See also Arthur Freeman and Paul Grinke, "Four New Shakespeare Quartos?," *The Times Literary Supplement*, 5 April 2002, 17–18.

[44] I quote from David Laing, ed., *Extracts from the Hawthornden Manuscripts* (Edinburgh, 1831–32), 17–18. Seven of the thirty-one plays listed under "Bookes red anno 1609" are also plays: "No Body, comedy," "Sir Gyles Gooscape, comedie," "A Mad World, comedie," "The Ile of Fooles, comedie," "Liberalitie and Progidalitie, comedie," "Parasitaster, by Marston." For the mistaken assumption (perpetuated by Greg, Chambers, and Prouty and still in evidence in the latest edition of Harbage's *Annals*) that Peele's lost "Hunting of Cupid," which Drummond also read in 1609, is a play, see John P. Cutts, "Peele's *Hunting of Cupid*," *Studies in the Renaissance*, 5 (1958), 121–32.

[45] See R. H. MacDonald, *The Library of Drummond of Hawthornden* (Edinburgh University Press, 1971), 140.

[46] See, for instance, Herbert R. Coursen, *Shakespearean Performance as Interpretation* (Newark: University of Delaware Press; London: Associated University Presses, 1992), 15.

previous age, the first generation, as it were, of the London commercial stage between, say, the opening of the Red Lion in 1567 and the end of the 1580s, has left isolated traces of plays of which we might rightly say that they only had a public life on stage: "Lady Barbara, Clorido and Radiamanta, Predor and Lucia, Panecia, Perseus and Andromeda, Phedrastus, Timoclea at the Siege of Thebes, King Xerxes, The Painter's Daughter, The Red Knight, The History of Error, The Cruelty of a Stepmother, The Three Sisters of Mantua, Murderous Michael, and Felix and Philiomena."[47] Dozens more could be added. These plays were clearly popular and deemed worthy to be performed at Court in the 1570s and 1580s. Yet nothing is known about them except their titles, suggesting that with a very few exceptions even the best plays of the time had an existence on stage but not yet on the printed page.

Things radically changed in the early 1590s, in the very years in which Shakespeare was making himself a name as an "upstart Crow" among London's playwrights. Social historians have described this period as one in which literacy was higher than ever before, a factor that may have contributed to the emergence of printed drama on an unprecedented scale.[48] It is true that according to Peter Blayney, printed playbooks did not account for a "significant fraction of the trade in English books."[49] Yet, if we concentrate on the twenty years from 1594 to 1613, the years most relevant for Shakespeare as they coincide with his years with the Lord Chamberlain's and King's Men, a slightly different picture presents itself. For, as a detailed analysis of the available data makes clear, it is during these years that the publication of playbooks was at its peak, with more than double the number of titles appearing in the twenty years between 1594 and 1613 than in the same number of years from 1584 to 1593 and from 1614 to 1623 (see Appendix A). During the twenty years of Shakespeare's active involvement with the company in which he was player, playwright, and shareholder, a total of 246 playbook titles was published, more than twelve per year. The total number of titles published in London in these years being

[47] The titles of these plays are quoted from Alfred Harbage's *Annals of English Drama, 975–1700*, rev. by Samuel Schoenbaum (London: Methuen, 1964), 42–48.

[48] Arguing that "The reign of Elizabeth saw a solid improvement in literacy among tradesmen and craftsmen in all parts of England," David Cressy has tried to measure and describe in considerable detail the "surge toward literacy" in that period (*Literacy and the Social Order: Reading and Writing in Tudor and Stuart England* (Cambridge University Press, 1980), 153). Predictably, illiteracy in London was scarcer than elsewhere. For instance, Cressy shows that illiteracy of tradesmen and craftsmen in the diocese of London from the 1590s to the 1630s dropped to approximately 30 percent, considerably less than in other parts of the country (146).

[49] Peter Blayney, "The Publication of Playbooks," in *A New History of Early English Drama*, eds. Cox and Kastan, 385.

close to 375 per year, playbooks account for approximately 3.3 percent, or one title in thirty. This may not sound like much, but we need to remember that the other twenty-nine titles comprise genres as varied as history, law, politics, science, education, and religious controversy; plague bills and other official documents; tales of travel and adventure; bibles, psalms, and sermons; and ballads and other ephemera. Since "literature," as pointed out above, constituted only about a quarter of the total number of titles, printed playbooks accounted for approximately one-seventh of all literary titles, including translations from the classics, books of verse, countless tales of chivalry and romance, miscellanies and anthologies, academic and closet drama, euphuistic and other prose works, besides many ballads. Whether this is a "significant" fraction or not may depend on one's point of view, but it seems fair to say that the fraction was much larger then than it is today. To look at it from a different angle, for a stationer who invested considerably more time and money into one Latin law book in folio than into a dozen playbooks in quarto, printed plays must have remained of little significance.[50] Yet, for potential customers with an interest in literature and for aspiring poets and dramatists such as Shakespeare, printed playbooks became a conspicuous presence in St. Paul's Churchyard.

In the early 1630s, William Prynne, author of the bulky anti-theatrical *Histrio-mastix*, complains that more than 40,000 playbooks have been printed and sold in the last two years, a figure which conforms well with what we can gather from Greg's *Bibliography of Early Printed Drama* about play publications during the years in question.[51] If we apply the same arithmetic to the time of Shakespeare's active presence in London, similar figures present themselves: in the year 1594 alone – the year in which Shakespeare joined the Lord Chamberlain's Men and first attained a position of professional stability – some 20,000 copies of playtexts written for the commercial stage were printed, more than in the 1570s and the 1580s altogether. In addition, in the three years 1598, 1599, and 1600 a total of about 50,000 copies of playbooks must have been printed.[52] Moreover, playbooks adopted

---

[50] Even this statement may deserve some qualification. The stationer Thomas Creede was commercially involved in the making of no fewer than thirty-five playbook editions from 1594 to 1616, Edward Allde in thirty-six from 1584 and 1624, and Valentine Simmes in twenty-five from 1597 to 1611. It seems reasonable to assume that "publishing plays would not usually have been seen as a shortcut to wealth" (Blayney, "Publication of Playbooks," 389), but the careers of the above stationers does not suggest that they considered playbooks as commercially insignificant.

[51] See Hackel, " 'Rowme' of Its Own," 116.

[52] For the number of editions upon which I base my count, see Appendix A. For edition sizes, see Blayney, "Publication of Playbooks," 412–13.

roman typography earlier than most other literary genres, suggesting that the market for printed plays was catering to an educated and progressive readership.[53] During the 1590s, stage plays began to enjoy a second existence of a kind and scope which we would be unwise to ignore.

The claim that Shakespeare's quarto playbooks would have been considered sub-literary material also deserves to be reconsidered on other accounts. In an anthology that gathers excerpts from a number of English poets, we read:

> Rude was his garment, and to rags all rent,
> No better had he, ne for better carde:
> With blistered hands among the cynders brent,
> And fingers filthy, with long nayles vnpared,
> Right for to rend the food on which he fared.
> His name was Care; a black Smyth by his trade:
> That neither day nor night from working spared.
> But to small purpose yron wedges made,
> Those be vnquiet thoughts, that woful minds inuade.
>
> *Ed. Spencer.* [*sic*]

> Care keepes his watch in euery olde mans eye,
> And where Care lodges, sleepe will neuer lie:
> But where vnbruiz'd youth with vnstuft braine
> Doth couch his limbs, there golden sleepe doth raine.
>
> *W. Shakespeare.*

At first, there seems nothing extraordinary about this juxtaposition. Here we have two thematically related passages, correctly attributed to two of England's greatest poets. Both excerpts will be recognized quite easily by those well versed in English literature. The first, is a stanza taken from *The Faerie Queene* (4.5.35) which describes the blacksmith Care, forger of "vnquiet thoughts" which invade the mind of Scudamor after Ate makes him suspect the loyalty of Britomart and Amoret. The second is part of the Friar's moralizing admonitions to the male protagonist in *Romeo and Juliet* (2.2.35–38). What is noteworthy about these passages is when the anthology containing them was published. The copy in the Folger Shakespeare Library bears the (probably genuine) manuscript signature "Wm Wordsworth" on the title page, and we would perhaps not be greatly surprised if the anthology

---

[53] See Mark Bland, "The Appearance of the Text in Early Modern England," *TEXT: An Interdisciplinary Annual of Textual Studies*, 11 (1998), 106; and Heidi Brayman Hackel, "The 'Great Variety' of Readers and Early Modern Reading Practices," in *A Companion to Shakespeare*, ed. David Scott Kastan (Oxford: Blackwell, 1999), 145.

were more or less contemporary with Lamb's *Specimens of English Dramatic Poets*. Called *England's Parnassus, or, The choycest flowers of our moderne poets*, the anthology was printed as early as 1600, however, less than halfway through Shakespeare's dramatic career.

The juxtaposition of passages from Shakespeare plays and recognized literary masterpieces such as Spenser's *Faerie Queene* in an anthology of 1600 calls into question the view promoted by Bowers and others about the (lack of) prestige of plays in Shakespeare's time: "the key to understanding their original status is the recognition that in their own day they were not highly regarded except as entertainment, without literary value."[54] It seems on the contrary, as Barbara Mowat has suggested, that "the printing and selling of plays for readers made the boundary between theatres and literary culture increasingly porous."[55] It is true that Shakespeare's plays were consumed as part of an entertainment industry in which many writers had no literary pretensions. Yet excerpts from the same plays were also consumed as poetry amid the "choysest Flowers" of contemporary writers.

Anyone who is aware of T. W. Baldwin's *Smalle Latine and Lesse Greeke* and Geoffrey Bullough's *Narrative and Dramatic Sources* knows that Shakespeare must have been an avid reader of books.[56] So is it plausible to assume that Shakespeare remained unaware of an anthology such as *England's Parnassus*? And, if not, can we expect that the writer who expressed the hope that poetry would outlive "the guilded monument" with greater insistence than anyone else remained unaffected by the fact that passages from his own dramatic writings started appearing in anthologies along with the recognized literary masterpieces of Spenser and Sidney? The recent recognition that Shakespeare may have revised several of his plays clearly does nothing to discourage a view of Shakespeare as a self-conscious artist.

Yet how could Shakespeare – as a participant in an entertainment industry in which competition was fierce – have afforded to be mindful of more than the immediate needs of the business in which he was a player? In a reaction to earlier views of Shakespeare that removed him from the material pressures of the stage business in which he was involved, scholars

[54] Bowers, "Publication," 415.

[55] Barbara Mowat, "The Theater and Literary Culture," in *A New History of Early English Drama*, eds. Cox and Kastan, 217.

[56] See T. W. Baldwin, *Smalle Latine and Lesse Greeke*, 2 vols. (Urbana: University of Illinois Press, 1944) and Geoffrey Bullough, ed., *Narrative and Dramatic Sources of Shakespeare*, 8 vols. (London: Routledge, 1957–75).

habitually portray him as one among many playwrights writing for the public stage under similar circumstances. What may be disregarded from such a perspective is the extent to which Shakespeare, as a shareholder in his company, was what Susan Cerasano has called a "privileged playwright."[57] While we do not know how much Shakespeare was paid for the plays he furnished his company, it is clear that the greatest part of the handsome fortune Shakespeare had started to amass as early as the 1590s came from his share in the profits of his company rather than from his plays. For Shakespeare's contemporary playwrights, the situation must have been altogether different. Henslowe's diary and his other papers yield a good picture of the pressures and constraints under which the playwrights employed by him worked. The series of payments of ten or twenty shillings paid to playwrights such as Henry Chettle, Thomas Dekker, John Day, William Haughton, Samuel Rowley, Anthony Munday, Michael Drayton, and Robert Wilson bespeaks people in immediate need of the money they earn by writing plays. The extant letters written from Robert Daborne to Henslowe in 1613 show the playwright repeatedly begging for further installments in partial payment of the (now lost) play *Machiavel and the Devil* which he is in the process of composing.[58] While the original agreement stipulates that Henslowe is to pay 6 pounds in advance, 4 pounds upon completion of three acts and a final payment of 10 pounds "vpon delivery in of yᵉ last scean perfited," Henslowe ends up making several small advance payments to meet Daborne's immediate needs. Dated April 17, 1613, the agreement dictates that the playwright "shall before yᵉ end of this Easter Term deliver in his Tragoedy," an extremely tight schedule which Daborne fails to meet.[59] All in all, Henslowe's diary and papers give evidence of a tightly run business in which playwrights would have neither the time nor the financial resources to produce more than was necessary. Nor does Henslowe seem to have been willing to pay for more than was necessary. That many of Shakespeare's plays are of a length that exceeds those of his contemporaries (Ben Jonson excepted) may well have much to do with

---

[57] In a Folger Institute Seminar taught by her at the Folger Shakespeare Library in spring 2001. Deborah Payne Fisk has suggested that something similar may apply to Dryden who appears to have written inventive, daring and, consequently, partly unsuccessful plays while he was a shareholder. Once he had sold his share and consequently depended upon the play's commercial success for his profit, he seems to have become more anxious to please the crowds (see "'Betwixt Two Ages Cast': Theatrical Dryden," in *"An Old Age is Out": A New Century of Dryden Studies*, eds. Maximillian E. Novak and Jayne Lewis (Toronto: University of Toronto Press, forthcoming).

[58] W. W. Greg, ed., *Henslowe Papers: Being Documents Supplementary to Henslowe's Diary* (London: A. H. Bullen, 1907), 67–83.

[59] Ibid., 67.

the different material situations within which they operated. I will argue that Shakespeare, "privileged playwright" that he was, could afford to write plays for the stage *and* the page.

Considering the current climate in Shakespeare studies, this study advances its case for a "literary Shakespeare" in the hope that it may constitute a timely intervention. Since the inception of the "Shakespeare revolution" which J. L. Styan, in 1977, both diagnosed and accelerated with the book of that title, performance has become a central component of Shakespeare studies.[60] Publications in the last two decades make this abundantly clear. Multi-volume editions such as the Arden (third generation), the New Cambridge or the Oxford have been giving ample space to the theatrical dimension as evidenced not only in copious stage histories but, increasingly, throughout the introduction and the annotations. The longest part of R. A. Foakes's excellent introduction to his Arden *King Lear*, for instance, is about "Reading and Staging *King Lear*."[61] To give another example, Ernst Honigmann, in his introduction to the Arden *Othello*, raises a series of questions any director of the play may want to address, and he allows his own response to the play to be informed by its stage history. Accordingly, where Honigmann engages in character criticism, it is not so much to offer an interpretation as to show how that character can and has been played and understood.[62] In contrast, most volumes of the previous Arden generation did not even include stage histories. Other recent series such as the Globe Quartos, the Arden Shakespeare Playgoer's series and the Arden Shakespeare at Stratford series specifically target the theatrically interested reader.[63] The aim of the "Shakespeare in Production" series of Cambridge University Press is to offer "the fullest possible stage histories of individual Shakespearean texts,"[64] while the "Shakespeare in Performance" series of Manchester University Press wants to assist performance criticism "by describing how certain of Shakespeare's texts have been realised in

[60] J. L. Styan, *The Shakespeare Revolution: Criticism and Performance in the Twentieth Century* (Cambridge University Press, 1977).

[61] R. A. Foakes, ed., *King Lear*, The Arden Shakespeare (Walton-on-Thames, Surrey: Thomas Nelson, 1997).

[62] E. A. J. Honigmann, ed., *Othello*, The Arden Shakespeare (Walton-on-Thames, Surrey: Thomas Nelson, 1997).

[63] The Globe Quartos series, published by Nick Hern and Theatre Arts Books/Routledge in association with Globe Education, makes available non-Shakespearean plays of which there have been performances or staged readings at the New Globe in London.

[64] The general editors of the "Shakespeare in Production" series are J. S. Bratton and Julie Hankey. The words I quote appear on page iv of the various volumes.

production."[65] Shakespeare journals have also registered and participated in the theatrical turn. In the late 1970s, *Shakespeare Quarterly* started publishing theatre reviews, and the early eighties saw the beginning of the heavily theater-oriented *Bulletin of the New York Shakespear* [*sic*] *Society*, later renamed *Shakespeare Bulletin: A Journal of Performance Criticism and Scholarship*. Philip Brockbank, Russell Jackson, and Robert Smallwood have given a voice to "Players of Shakespeare."[66] Others, like Barbara Hodgdon and William Worthen, have brought greater theoretical sophistication to performance studies.[67] A great number of monographs have also contributed their share to the field, as have various collections, for instance Philip C. McGuire and David A. Samuelson's *Shakespeare, the Theatrical Dimension* or, more recently, Lois Potter and Arthur F. Kinney's *Shakespeare, Text and Theater*, Grace Ioppolo's *Shakespeare Performed*, and a New Casebooks volume on *Shakespeare in Performance*.[68] The same applies, more generally, to the work of such critics as Bernard Beckerman, John Russell Brown, H. R. Coursen, Alan Dessen, Jay L. Halio and Marvin Rosenberg, to name only a few.

Mentioning these various instances of Shakespearean performance criticism since the late 1970s, I do no more than scratch the surface of what is perhaps the most important development in Shakespeare studies of the last century, and this without addressing the rapidly expanding field of Shakespeare on film, a powerful offshoot of the "Shakespeare revolution." While Styan could write in 1977 that, "The call for a stage-centred study

---

[65] Margaret Shewring, *King Richard II*, Shakespeare in Performance (Manchester University Press, 1996), xi. Some twenty volumes have appeared in this series since 1984. The general editors are J. R. Mulryne and J. C. Bulman.

[66] *Players of Shakespeare: Essays in Shakespearian Performance by Players with the Royal Shakespeare Company*, ed. Philip Brockbank (Cambridge University Press, 1985); *Players of Shakespeare 2, 3: Further Essays in Shakespearian Performance by Players with the Royal Shakespeare Company*, ed. Russell Jackson and Robert Smallwood (Cambridge University Press, 1988, 1993); and *Players of Shakespeare 4: Further Essays in Shakespearian Performance by Players with the Royal Shakespeare Company*, ed. Robert Smallwood (Cambridge University Press, 1998).

[67] Barbara Hodgdon, *The Shakespeare Trade: Performances and Appropriations* (Philadelphia: University of Pennsylvania Press, 1998); William B. Worthen, "Deeper Meanings and Theatrical Technique: The Rhetoric of Performance Criticism," *Shakespeare Criticism*, 40 (1989), 441–55, *Shakespeare and the Authority of Performance* (Cambridge University Press, 1997), and "Drama, Performativity, and Performance," *PMLA*, 113 (1998), 1093–107.

[68] Philip C. McGuire and David A. Samuelson, eds., *Shakespeare, the Theatrical Dimension* (New York: AMS Press, 1979); Lois Potter and Arthur F. Kinney, eds., *Shakespeare, Text and Theater: Essays in Honor of Jay L. Halio* (Newark: University of Delaware Press; London: Associated University Presses, 1999); Grace Ioppolo, ed., *Shakespeare Performed: Essays in Honor of R. A. Foakes* (Newark: University of Delaware Press; London: Associated University Presses, 2000); Robert Shaughnessy, ed., *Shakespeare in Performance*, New Casebooks (Basingstoke: Macmillan, 2000).

of Shakespeare" has not been "fully answered," this no longer holds true today.[69]

The greatest part of performance-oriented Shakespeare criticism has been salutary and beneficial, and this book has no quarrel with it. What does need to be questioned, however, are some of the more dogmatic claims that have been made about the importance of performance for our understanding of Shakespeare's plays. When performance critics claim, for instance, that "the stage expanding before an audience is the source of all valid discovery" and that "Shakespeare speaks, if anywhere, through his medium," they are simply ignoring one of the two media in which Shakespeare's plays exist and existed.[70] Statements such as "These plays were scripts originally, and remain so today" or "A play has to be seen and heard in order to be understood" also miss part of a more complex truth.[71] Trying to justify his opinion that Shakespeare's plays need to be approached as scripts, H. R. Coursen writes: "A script involves a process and is not, like 'literature,' a finished product. As R. B. McKerrow says, a Shakespearean 'manuscript... was not a literary document at all. It was merely the barebones of a performance on the stage, intended to be interpreted by actors skilled in their craft.'"[72] McKerrow was correct, but Coursen is not. For a Shakespeare play has come down to us not in the form of a manuscript but as a printed play which stationers considered enough of a finished product to believe in its commercial viability.

Similarly, some performance critics have approved of and promoted the view of what Styan calls "text-as-score."[73] The analogy with music may be tempting, but it is also false. For, while musical scores are usually intended for performers, a printed play generally is not, but is (and was) meant for readers instead. In fact, when "Stage-centred criticism... does not admit critical opinion as fully valid without reference to the physical circumstances of the medium,"[74] it imposes upon itself a disabling restriction that cannot

[69] Styan, *Shakespeare Revolution*, 6.
[70] Ibid., 235. In the passage from which I quote, Styan is paraphrasing and agreeing with John Russell Brown. For those who feel that *The Shakespeare Revolution* is a dated study by now, it may be well to quote from Styan's more recent *Perspectives on Shakespeare in Performance* (New York: Peter Lang, 2000) to show that the rhetoric has not much changed: "we must allow Shakespeare himself to decide what must be studied. Throw out those learned introductions to the text. We are to learn by doing, and the insights of actors are more likely to be right than those of scholars" (17).
[71] H. R. Coursen, *Reading Shakespeare on Stage* (Newark: University of Delaware Press; London: Associated University Presses, 1995), 46; John Russell Brown, *William Shakespeare: Writing for Performance* (New York: St. Martin's Press, 1996), viii.
[72] Coursen, *Reading Shakespeare on Stage*, 45.   [73] Styan, *Shakespeare Revolution*, 235.
[74] Ibid., 72.

be justified by how plays existed in Shakespeare's lifetime nor, I will argue, by how Shakespeare intended them to exist.

In his commendatory poem to his collaborator John Fletcher prefacing their *Faithful Shepherdess* (n.d., *c.* 1610), Francis Beaumont refers to the printed play as a "second publication" which allows readers to become aware that the playtext is with "much wit and art adornd."[75] Shakespeare and his contemporaries were aware that, as John Marston put it, "the life of these things consists in action," but they also realized that reading a play allowed valuable insights into other, more literary, aspects of their art.[76] The same applies to the reception of Shakespeare's plays today. R. A. Foakes has summed up this debate with concision and lucidity: "Plays have a double life, in the mind as read, and on the stage as acted; reading a play and seeing it acted are two different but equally valid and valuable experiences."[77]

If we have erred in the last thirty years or so, we have erred on the side of performance and at the expense of the text. While the New Critical obsession with close readings that turned plays into poems needed a corrective, this corrective may have led some to consider Shakespeare's plays exclusively as scripts to be performed, a view that is not justified by the double existence these plays had in the late sixteenth and early seventeenth centuries. It may be time, that is, for the pendulum to swing back, not to return us to the days of New Criticism, nor to undo the beneficial work undertaken by performance critics. Rather, our work may profit from an increased awareness of the fact that, from the very beginning, the English Renaissance plays we study had a double existence, one on stage and one on the printed page.

This recognition would call for a reception that takes into account the respective specificities of the two media. To simplify matters, performance tends to speak to the senses, while a printed text activates the intellect. As I will attempt to demonstrate in the second part of this study, some of the Shakespearean playbooks bear signs of the medium for which they were designed. For instance, the long texts of plays such as *Hamlet* (Q2, 1604 and Folio, 1623) and *Henry V* (Folio 1623), I will argue, tend to function according to a "literary" logic, while the short texts of the same plays (*Hamlet* Q1, 1603; *Henry V*, Q1, 1600) reflect their oral, theatrical provenance.

---

[75] Fredson Bowers, gen. ed., *The Dramatic Works in the Beaumont and Fletcher Canon*, 10 vols. (Cambridge University Press, 1966–96), III.491. Etymologically, "to publish" derives, of course, from "making public" – see the *OED*.

[76] I quote from the prefatory address "To my equall Reader," Q1 *Parasitaster, or The Fawn* (1606), A2ᵛ.

[77] Foakes, ed., *King Lear*, 4. See also Richard Levin, "Performance Critics vs Close Readers in the Study of English Renaissance Drama," *Modern Language Review*, 81 (1986), 545–59.

Such a view might go some way toward explaining the aversion to performed Shakespeare on the part of many Romantic critics and poets, an aversion which, fortunately, few with a real interest in Shakespeare would share today. Nevertheless, several of their comments about the stage suitability of some of Shakespeare's plays may be more to the point than we have been willing to grant. For instance, in his essay "On the Tragedies of Shakspeare [*sic*], Considered with Reference to Their Fitness for Stage Representation," Charles Lamb wrote: "I cannot help being of opinion that the plays of Shakspeare are less calculated for performance on a stage, than those of almost any other dramatist whatever."[78] Goethe, similarly, called Shakespeare's plays "more epic and philosophic – than dramatic."[79] Two centuries later, we are likely to disagree. Yet, in fairness to Lamb, Goethe and their contemporaries, it should be remembered that their Shakespeare was essentially the writer of the great tragedies, of *Hamlet*, *King Lear*, and *Othello*, of extremely long plays, that is, whose "original copy" is very likely to contain substantially more than what would have been performed by Shakespeare and his fellows. Lamb and Goethe may have been right insofar as several of the versions that have come down to us were in fact intended for the page.

In a recent book on Shakespeare's language, Frank Kermode points out that "the fact that [Shakespeare] was a poet has somehow dropped out of consideration." Objecting to today's "commonplace that only in performance can the sense of Shakespeare's plays be fully apprehended," Kermode writes: "Members of an audience cannot stop the actors and puzzle over some difficult expression, as they can when reading the play. The action sweeps you past the crux, which is at once forgotten because you need to keep up with what is being said, not lose the plot by meditating on what has passed. Following the story, understanding the tensions between characters, is not quite the same thing as following all or even most of the meanings."[80] While it is not the purpose of this study to probe into the complexity of Shakespeare's language, my book does go some way toward justifying such an approach, suggesting that a close, "readerly," attention to the play's text is not a modern aberration.

While Kermode's vindication is only incidental to his study of Shakespeare's language, the case for the "writtenness" of Shakespeare's texts

---

[78] *Lamb's Criticism*, ed. E. M. W. Tillyard (Cambridge: At the University Press, 1923), 37.
[79] "[M]ehr episch und philosophisch – als dramatisch" (diary entry of September 21, 1815, in *Briefe, Tagebücher und Gespräche, Sämtliche Werke*, 40 vols. (Frankfurt: Deutscher Klassiker Verlag, 1986), XXXIV.515).
[80] Frank Kermode, *Shakespeare's Language* (New York: Farrar, Straus and Giroux, 2000), vii, 3, 4, 5.

has been fully argued by Harry Berger, Jr. Having the courage to "state the case against the stage-centered approach," Berger, like Kermode, is very much swimming against the current today.[81] Berger's writings raise the important question, left unanswered by much performance criticism, of how to deal with "a text which is overwritten from the standpoint of performance and the playgoer's limited perceptual capacities."[82] Berger's eloquent and sophisticated defense of a readerly approach to Shakespeare would be even stronger, however, if he were less willing to throw history overboard:

Perhaps Harriett Hawkins is right to insist that Shakespeare "showed no interest in publishing the text," or perhaps, if the text was company property, he wasn't able to publish it . . . Perhaps he did expect that at some point readers would be able to "study the script," to "read – and re-read – it to ponder its subtleties." Or perhaps not . . . I think the rules of the game change when the Age of Reading makes the plays available in the same medium as the sonnets.[83]

When Shakespeare's sonnets were published, the majority of the plays Shakespeare had written up to that date *were* available in print. Consequently, Shakespeare did not only expect that at some point in the future people would "read – and re-read" his plays. He could not help knowing that his plays were being read and reread, printed and reprinted, excerpted and anthologized as he was writing more plays. Not only "the Age of Reading" but also Shakespeare's friends and fellow actors John Heminge and Henry Condell recommended that we "Reade him, therefore; and againe, and againe."[84] As for the beliefs that Shakespeare "showed no interest in publishing the text" or "wasn't able to publish it," I will show in chapter 3 on what slender foundations this time-honored assumption has been built. One of the aims of this study is thus to provide a historicist dimension to Harry Berger's Shakespeare who "knows how to write successful plays while still indulging his indomitable zest for literary *jouissance*, and, like many other authors, takes pride in that double accomplishment."[85]

Chapter 1 investigates the publication of printed playbooks during Shakespeare's lifetime. I argue that printed playbooks became respectable

---

[81] Harry Berger, Jr., *Making Trifles of Errors: Redistributing Complicities in Shakespeare*, ed. Peter Erickson (Stanford University Press, 1997), 100.

[82] Harry Berger, Jr., *Imaginary Audition: Shakespeare on Stage and Page* (Berkeley and Los Angeles: University of California Press, 1989), 29–30.

[83] Ibid., 23.

[84] I quote from Heminge and Condell's address "To the Great Variety of Readers," in the 1623 Folio edition of *Mr. William Shakespeares Comedies, Histories, & Tragedies* (A3ʳ), commonly referred to as "the First Folio."

[85] Berger, *Imaginary Audition*, 18.

reading matter earlier than we have hitherto supposed, early enough for Shakespeare to have lived through and to have been affected by this process of legitimation. Chapter 2 examines how Shakespeare became "Shakespeare," a dramatic author whose name was counted upon to sell books and whose plays began being excerpted in anthologies next to passages from Spenser's *Faerie Queene* and other literary masterpieces as early as 1600.

While chapters 1 and 2 locate the primary agency for the legitimation of printed drama and the emergence of the "Shakespeare" label in St. Paul's Churchyard, chapter 3 turns to Shakespeare himself. Drawing on recent work by Peter Blayney, I argue that the assumption of Shakespeare's indifference to the publication of his plays is a myth. Scholars have often taken for granted that the playing companies and Shakespeare were basically opposed to the publication of their plays. Those plays that were published during Shakespeare's lifetime have thus generally been accounted for as alleged "breaches" such as the need for cash during a period of plague. More economic reasoning can account for the publication history of Shakespeare's plays if we assume that, after joining the Lord Chamberlain's Men in 1594, Shakespeare and his fellows had a coherent strategy of trying to get his plays published approximately two years after they first reached the stage. The following chapters complement this argument by focusing on the publication history of Shakespeare's plays after his company had become the King's Men (chapter 4), and by addressing some of the documents that have traditionally been taken to imply the players' opposition to print (chapter 5).

Chapter 6 argues that Shakespeare's interest in a readership may account for the fact that he – "privileged playwright" that he was – wrote a significant number of plays that are considerably too long ever to have been performed in anything close to their entirety. In the light of this thesis, I examine a variety of dramatic documents including the plays of Shakespeare, of his contemporaries, and of his successors Beaumont and Fletcher, the extant manuscript plays, and Restoration players' quartos and promptbooks. Chapter 7 investigates the implications this argument has for modern editorial practices, particularly of Shakespeare's plays. Specifically, I subject to scrutiny the groundbreaking Oxford Shakespeare edition, which took as its project the alleged recovery "of Shakespeare's plays as they were acted in the London playhouses." I suggest that, rather than presenting the plays as they would have been performed in Shakespeare's time, such an editorial practice actually recovers conflations of theatrical scripts and reading texts.

In chapters 8 and 9, I turn to the three plays Shakespeare wrote for the Lord Chamberlain's Men for which "long" and "short" versions are extant: *Romeo and Juliet*, *Henry V*, and *Hamlet*. Drawing on recent revisionary work on the so-called "bad" quartos, I will argue that the short and long texts do not represent provincial and London versions, as is often argued, nor are they simply "good" and "bad," "authentic" and "corrupt" (chapter 8). Rather, I believe, they represent "literary" and "theatrical" versions whose respective distinctiveness allows us important insights into Shakespeare's theatrical *and* literary art (chapter 9).

PART I

Publication

The legitimation of printed playbooks in Shakespeare's time

When were printed playbooks first considered literature? When did playwrights first become authors? What are the cultural and material forces that shaped these processes? Scholarship has investigated these questions and proposed answers or, more often, taken certain answers for granted. In this chapter, I am going to suggest that these answers need to be refined or, in some cases, corrected.

The standard critical argument in the past has been that the concept of dramatic authorship emerges in the early seventeenth century with the advent of a new kind of scholarly writer, the first "self-crowned laureate," to use Richard Helgerson's designation, who was also a dramatist.[1] He was neither a professional writer of the sort of Robert Greene, who scraped a living with his pen, nor a writer in the service of a nobleman, like Samuel Daniel or Michael Drayton, nor a courtier or a gentleman writing to please his own private circle, like Sir Philip Sidney. Instead, he was a scholar interested in writing and bringing a new kind of self-confidence to the profession. In the more sweeping version of this argument, his advent in print is first signaled by the publication of Jonson's *Workes* in 1616. Commenting on the "conception of the nature and status of drama," one scholar has written that:

One man can be said to have ... changed literary history abruptly. This man, Ben Jonson, deserves his place in English cultural history not just for his brilliant hard-edged comedies, but also for his insistence that a play is literature. The moment that changed the conception of the nature and status of drama came in 1616. In that year Jonson published a folio of about a thousand pages containing nine of his plays, eighteen of his masques and entertainments, and a substantial body of his epigrams, panegyrics, and verse letters; he called this miscellany of traditional literary forms and dramatic texts *The Works of Benjamin Jonson*.[2]

---

[1] See Richard Helgerson, *Self-Crowned Laureates: Spenser, Jonson, Milton and the Literary System* (Berkeley and Los Angeles: University of California Press, 1983).

[2] John W. Velz, "From Authorization to Authorship, Orality to Literature: The Case of Medieval and Renaissance Drama," *TEXT: An Interdisciplinary Annual of Textual Studies*, 6 (1994), 204.

Another recent scholar has constructed a similarly smooth dichotomy between two situations, one before the publication of Jonson's Folio (when plays were on a level with pamphlets and ballads) and one after (when plays were included in *Works*):

Elizabethan dramatists enjoyed little prestige for their work; even the printed plays were regarded as ephemeral, as the linking of "pampheletes, playes and balletes" indicates in a 1559 parliamentary bill on press censorship. This was the situation which Jonson, determined to advance the dignity of playwriting, finally overturned by including his plays in the 1616 collection of his *Works*.[3]

Scholars who adhere to the more refined version of this argument resist this *fiat lux* account. They hold instead that dramatic authorship becomes visible gradually in such key documents as the title-page of *Every Man Out of His Humour* (Q1, 1600) or the address "To the Reader" in the 1605 quarto of *Sejanus*. The latter famously points out that the text contains "more than hath been Publickely Spoken or Acted," while the former states that "this Booke, in all numbers, is not the same with that which was acted on the publike Stage."[4] According to this view, the publication of the *Workes* in 1616 is only the culmination of what Jonson had begun at the turn of the century.[5]

---

[3] Gordon Williams, *Shakespeare, Sex and the Print Revolution* (London and Atlantic Highlands, N.J.: Athlone, 1996), 7–8.

[4] For readings of the Q1 *Every Man Out of His Humour* title page, see David Riggs, *Ben Jonson: A Life* (Cambridge, Mass.: Harvard University Press, 1989), 65; Jonas Barish, *The Antitheatrical Prejudice* (Berkeley, Los Angeles: University of California Press, 1981), 136–37. For *Sejanus*, see Philip Ayres, "The Iconography of Jonson's *Sejanus*, 1605: Copy-text for the Revels Edition," in *Editing Texts: Papers from a Conference at the Humanities Research Centre, May 1984*, ed. J. C. Eade (Canberra: Humanities Research Centre, Australian National University, 1985), 47–53, and John Jowett, "Jonson's Authorization of Type in *Sejanus* and Other Early Quartos," *Studies in Philology*, 44 (1991), 254–65. For Jonson's play quartos, see Robert S. Miola, "Creating the Author: Jonson's Latin Epigraphs," *Ben Jonson Journal*, 6 (1999), 35–48. See also Loewenstein, *Ben Jonson and Possessive Authorship*.

[5] The provocation the term "Workes" represented for a volume consisting mostly of stage plays, and the reactions it triggered have been well documented. It may be indicative of how problematic a word it remained with regard to plays that when an octavo collection of Marston's plays was published in 1633 as "The Workes of Mr. Iohn Marston, Being Tragedies and Comedies," it was reissued later the same year as "Tragedies and Comedies." For the publication of Jonson's Folio, see Barish, *Antitheatrical Prejudice*, 138–40; Richard C. Newton, "Jonson and the (Re-)Invention of the Book," in *Classic and Cavalier: Essays on Jonson and the Sons of Ben*, eds. Claude J. Summers and Ted-Larry Pebworth (University of Pittsburgh Press, 1982), 31–58; Joseph Loewenstein, "The Script in the Marketplace," *Representations*, 12 (1985), 101–15; Timothy Murray, *Theatrical Legitimation: Allegories of Genius in Seventeenth-Century England and France* (New York and Oxford: Oxford University Press, 1987), chs. 3 and 4; Jennifer Brady and W. H. Herendeen, eds., *Ben Jonson's 1616 Folio* (Newark: University of Delaware Press; London and Toronto: Associated University Presses, 1991); Arthur Marotti, *Manuscript, Print, and the English Renaissance Lyric* (Ithaca: Cornell University Press, 1995), 238–47; Mark Bland, "William Stansby and the Production of *The Workes of Beniamin Jonson*, 1615–1616," *The Library*, 20 (1998), 1–34; Douglas A. Brooks, *From Playhouse to Printing House: Drama and Authorship in Early Modern England*, Cambridge Studies in Renaissance Literature and Culture, 36 (Cambridge University Press, 2000), 104–39.

As a result of these accounts, it is often assumed that the gap between the printed text that has come down to us and what was performed did not start opening up before these Jonsonian publications. John Jowett, for instance, has argued that "*Every Man Out of His Humour* stands apart from all previously printed drama" and that "the gambit of offering a *non-theatrical* text had not been tried before."[6] I argue that the "evolving history of interaction between performance and print" does not begin with Jonson, but can be traced back at least as far as the 1590 octavo edition of Marlowe's *Tamburlaine*.[7]

As early as the 1590s, we can witness a process of legitimation of dramatic publications leading to their establishment as a genre of printed texts in its own right rather than as a pale reflection of what properly belongs to the stage. Similarly, the dramatic author who, as Michel Foucault has taught us, was not born but made, was in the making considerably earlier than is often presumed.[8] Just as the legitimation of printed lyric poetry can be traced through a number of key publications[9] – from *Tottel's Miscellany* in 1557 to the 1633 editions of the poems of Donne and Herbert – so the publication of Jonson's and Shakespeare's plays in folio in 1616 and 1623 have a complex pre-history. When Shakespeare started working as a playwright, playtexts were not considered literary artifacts, written by an author, with a life on the stage *and* the page. Such a summary statement no longer applies half way through his career, however, and is even less true at the moment of his death.

I argue that the first people who had a vested interest in the rise of dramatic authorship were not the playwrights themselves but the London printers, publishers, and booksellers eager to render respectable and commercially profitable what was initially an enterprise with little or no prestige.[10] A comparison with the printed poetry of the age is instructive. Much of it was published in popular miscellanies. If we recall that all but two of the Elizabethan miscellanies seem to have been collected under the supervision of a publisher or printer, we realize just how central their agency was in the formation of Elizabethan poetic taste and practice.[11] Addressing the difficulty of legitimizing printed playbooks, Wendy Wall writes:

---

[6] Jowett, "Jonson's Authorization of Type," 256.   [7] Ibid., 264.

[8] Michel Foucault, "What Is an Author?," trans. Catherine Porter, in *The Foucault Reader*, ed. Paul Rabinow (New York: Pantheon Books, 1984), 101–20.

[9] See Marotti, *English Renaissance Lyric*, especially ch. 4 on "Print and the Lyric," 209–90.

[10] For the sake of clarity, I am using the word "publisher" to refer to the person who commissioned and financed a book project, a use that is anachronistic considering the *OED* dates 1654 the earliest occurrence of the word with this meaning.

[11] Elizabeth W. Pomeroy, *The Elizabethan Miscellanies: Their Development and Conventions* (Berkeley and Los Angeles: University of California Press, 1973), 20.

Theatrical texts were even more unauthorized than poetic texts, for exactly opposite reasons: they were seen as illegitimate and vulgar trivial events rather than as elite but trivial noble "sport." ... Legitimating the authority of the theatrical book was an even more arduous task than the business of legitimating the private forms of printed poetry. For the theatrical script was not only subject to multiple sites of production and protean textual practices, but it was also associated with a socially suspect cultural domain.[12]

The social cachet of plays was low, their aim mere entertainment and their realization by nature collaborative and subject to constant change. Transferring them from the playhouse to the printing house and supplying them with an authorizing author and a stabilizing single text was no easy undertaking. The performance of this task, rather than any authorial transgressions, brought about the formation of the dramatic author.[13] In this sense, the rise of dramatic authorship actively fostered by playwrights after the turn of the century is, I argue, only part of a trajectory which presupposes a shift in the making of and attitude toward dramatic publications before Jonson's plays started being printed.

I thus situate in the late sixteenth century rather than in the early seventeenth century the moment when published playbooks first legitimate themselves by emphasizing their non-theatrical features and by tying themselves to an authorizing originator. It could be objected that the difference between earlier accounts and mine is minor and of little consequence. Only a decade separates the first quarto of *Every Man Out of His Humour* from the earliest edition of *Tamburlaine*, and even Jonson's *Workes* are published only a quarter of a century after Marlowe's two-part play. So does the difference matter? I believe that, in the crucial case of Shakespeare, it does. In one account, Shakespeare is a passive figure in the emergence of dramatic authorship, uninvolved in and indifferent to it, in direct opposition to the innovator Ben Jonson. In the other account, Shakespeare is aware of, affected by, and an active participant in the theater's gradual emancipation from an existence that is confined to the stage. I argue that the traditional narrative that diametrically opposes Shakespeare and Jonson, the former indifferent to print, the latter loathing the stage, needs to be interrogated.[14] In

---

[12] Wendy Wall, *The Imprint of Gender: Authorship and Publication in the English Renaissance* (Ithaca: Cornell University Press, 1993), 89.

[13] See Foucault's well-known arguments that "Texts, books, and discourses really began to have authors ... to the extent that authors became subject to punishment, that is, to the extent that discourses could be transgressive" ("What Is an Author?," 103).

[14] For two relatively recent formulations of this narrative, see Richard Dutton, *Ben Jonson, Authority, Criticism* (Basingstoke: Macmillan, 1996), 44, and David Scott Kastan, *Shakespeare After Theory* (New York and London: Routledge, 1999), 75–77.

chapter 3, I demonstrate that, contrary to what we have often been made to believe, Shakespeare was far from indifferent to the publication of his plays. This chapter establishes the cultural forces that are likely to have contributed to Shakespeare's attitude toward the existence of his plays not only on stage but also on the page.

One of the purposes of the present chapter is to refine and supplement some of the earlier work upon which it builds. Jeffrey Masten, in particular, has provided an incisive treatment of how dramatic authorship was negotiated, produced, and contested in Renaissance Drama.[15] Yet, it seems to me that Masten and others underestimate the extent to which the process that turned collaboratively produced theatrical scripts into authorized literary drama was already under way. In particular, I take issue with Masten's assertion that "play-text quartos printed early in the late sixteenth and early seventeenth centuries generally did not record the presence of an author or authors."[16] As we will see, this statement is too sweeping when applied to the whole period, and simply wrong as far as the early seventeenth century is concerned. Masten's argument that the early quartos "pass themselves off as representation of a theatrical event" also seems to me to hide a more complex truth. The claim on the title page of *Tamburlaine* according to which the two parts are printed "as they were sundrie times shewed vpon Stages in the Citie of London," is immediately contradicted by the publisher's address "To the Gentlemen Readers." Similarly, while the first quarto of *Hamlet does* promise a play "As it hath beene...acted," the second quarto *does not*, announcing instead "the true and perfect Coppie." From very early on, the apparatus of early quarto playbooks enacts a tension between the playhouse and the printing house as stationers simultaneously try to capitalize on the popularity of stage plays and appropriate them to their own medium.

The first section of this chapter is an introductory consideration of the evolving concept of dramatic authorship in Shakespeare's London. While its aim is to provide the basis for the following discussion in this and the next chapter, readers familiar with the scholarship on the topic may wish to skip it and pass directly to the second section. In it, I investigate how the title pages of printed playbooks in the late sixteenth and the early seventeenth

---

[15] See Jeffrey Masten, *Textual Intercourse: Collaboration, Authorship, and Sexualities in Renaissance Drama*, Cambridge Studies in Renaissance Literature and Culture, 14 (Cambridge University Press, 1997), especially chs. 1 and 4. See also de Grazia, *Shakespeare Verbatim*, and Leah S. Marcus, *Puzzling Shakespeare: Local Readings and Its Discontents* (Berkeley and Los Angeles: University of California Press, 1988).

[16] Masten, *Textual Intercourse*, 113.

century negotiate the rise of dramatic authorship. Finally, I concentrate on
the 1590 edition of *Tamburlaine* and the 1592 edition of *The Spanish Tragedy*
as early examples of printed playbooks that open a gap between a play's two
forms of existence, in the theater and in print.

In sixteenth- and seventeenth-century London, title pages were more than
front covers. The speaker of John Davies of Hereford's *Paper's Complaint*
derides those who "pester Poasts, with Titles of new bookes."[17] Similarly, in
an address prefacing *The Terrors of the Night* (1594), Thomas Nashe complains that "a number of you there bee, who consider neither premisses
nor conclusions, but piteouslie torment Title Pages on euerie poast, neuer
reading farther of anie Booke, than Imprinted by Simeon such a signe."[18]
Title pages were thus put up on posts and elsewhere, serving publishers
as crucial tools for the marketing of books. As Philip Gaskell pointed out,
the type for title pages was often kept standing after the printing of the
book, allowing for easy reuse if additional advertising was needed.[19] The
title page, contrary to the text it announces, is thus usually the publisher's
rather than the writer's.[20] McKerrow called it "an explanatory label affixed
to the book by the printer or publisher."[21] The term "explanatory" hardly
covers the uses to which title pages were put, however, and needs to be
supplemented by "panegyric" considering they often praise books in the
most laudatory terms. The provenance and aim of title pages also explains
the many inaccuracies they contain of which the notorious "Mariana" –
instead of "Marina" – in Q1 *Pericles* is only the most famous example.
Clearly, accuracy about a book's contents mattered less to publishers than
the promotion the title page guaranteed. As Janette Dillon has put it suc-
cinctly: "Title pages are devised in order to sell books, not to make precise

---

[17] Line 97, quoted from *The Complete Works of John Davies of Hereford*, ed. Alexander B. Grosart,
2 vols. (London: Privately Printed, 1875–77, rpt. New York: AMS Press, 1967), II.76.

[18] Sig. A4, quoted from *The Works of Thomas Nashe*, ed. Ronald B. McKerrow, 5 vols. (London:
Oxford University Press, 1904–10), I.343. The examples could be multiplied: Jonson, addressing the
bookseller in the third epigram of his Folio (1616), instructs him to have his book "lye vpon thy stall,
till it be sought; / Not offer'd, as it made sute to be bought; / Nor haue my title-leafe on posts, or
walls, / Or in cleft-sticks, aduanced to make calls / For termers, or some clarke-like seruing-man, /
Who scarse can spell th'hard names" (*The Works of Ben Jonson*, eds. C. H. Herford and Percy and
Evelyn Simpson, 11 vols. (Oxford: Clarendon Press, 1925–52), VIII.28). The practice was still current
in the eighteenth century: see Pope's *Epistle to Doctor Arbuthnot*, lines 215–16 and *The Dunciad*, line
40.

[19] Philip Gaskell, *A New Introduction to Bibliography* (Oxford: Clarendon Press, 1972), 116.

[20] On printers' copy for title pages, see also Peter W. M. Blayney, *The Texts of "King Lear" and Their
Origin: Nicholas Okes and the First Quarto* (Cambridge University Press, 1982), 259–62.

[21] Ronald B. McKerrow, *An Introduction to Bibliography for Literary Students* (Oxford: Clarendon Press,
1927), 91.

scholarly statements about the texts they preface."[22] Being at the crossroads of the books' fictional contents and their economic reality, they thus allow inferences about the dynamics of the marketing of printed playbooks in Elizabethan England.

A comparison of the original title pages of Christopher Marlowe's *Tamburlaine* and Ben Jonson's *Volpone* yields instructive insights. The title page of *Tamburlaine* contains type that is spread out over a total of twenty lines, making up a disorderly whole that requires substantial attention for a full appreciation. The title page of *Volpone*, in contrast, is of classicist simplicity, generously spaced out and easily appreciable. The main part of the title page, taking up the upper two-thirds, is occupied by no more than seven words, the five important ones (Ben Ionson, Volpone, The Foxe) in big roman capital letters, the other two in smaller, lower-case type. The far more unruly bulk of language on *Tamburlaine*'s title page seems to change somewhat randomly not only from one size to another, but also from italicized to non-italicized and from roman to black letter (see Figures 3 and 4).[23]

If we try to distinguish the kind of information the two title pages contain, other differences can be pointed out. The front page of *Tamburlaine* communicates information of a variety of kinds, notably about:

- the title: "Tamburlaine the Great"
- the play's contents: "Who, from a Scythian Shephearde, by his rare and woonderfull Conquests, became a most puissant and mightye Monarque. And (for his tyranny, and terrour in Warre) was termed, The Scourge of God. Deuided into two Tragicall Discourses"
- performance, more specifically where the play was performed: "as they were sundrie times shewed vpon Stages in the Citie of London," and by whom: "By the right honorable the Lord Admyrall, his seruantes"

---

[22] Dillon, "Is There a Performance in This Text?," *Shakespeare Quarterly*, 45 (1995), 79.

[23] Note that black-letter type was growing old-fashioned by the end of the sixteenth century and was superseded by Roman type which had been introduced to the London trade in 1509 by Richard Pynson (see D. F. McKenzie, "Printing in England from Caxton to Milton," in *The Age of Shakespeare*, ed. Boris Ford, The New Pelican Guide to English Literature, 2, rev. edn (Harmondsworth: Penguin, 1982), 211). Mark Bland has argued that black letter "remained the predominant English language typeface until a combination of Italianate fashion, economic prosperity and type replacement finally changed the typography of literary publications in the years between the Armada of 1588 and the plague of 1593" ("Appearance of the Text," 94). If we bear in mind the relationship between typography and meaning to which a number of scholars have recently paid attention, the mixture of roman and black-letter type on the 1590 title page is in itself a resonant source of meaning. See, for instance, Harry Graham Carter, *A View of Early Typography up to about 1600* (Oxford: Clarendon, 1969) and W. C. Ferguson, *Pica Roman Type in Elizabethan England* (Aldershot and Brookfield, Vt.: Ashgate, 1989). For early modern playbooks and the shift from black-letter to roman type, see Bland, "Appearance of the Text," 105–7, and Blayney, "Publication of Playbooks," 414–15.

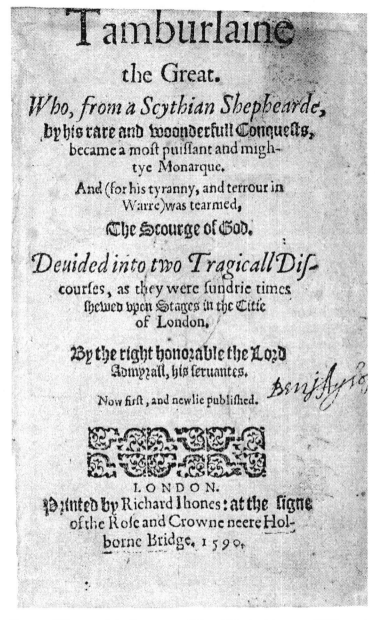

Figure 3. Title page of the first octavo edition of *Tamburlaine*, 1590 (*STC* 17425), published anonymously.

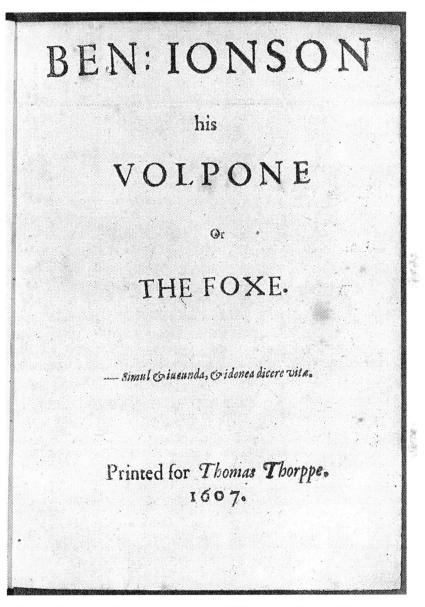

BEN: IONSON

his

VOLPONE

Or

THE FOXE.

—— *simul & iueunda, & idonea dicere vitæ.*

Printed for *Thomas Thorppe.*
1607.

Figure 4. Title page of the first quarto edition of *Volpone*, 1607 (*STC* 14783), attributed to Ben Jonson.

– publication, in particular which edition: "Now first, and newlie published"; the place of publication: "LONDON"; the publisher: "Printed by Richard Ihones"; the precise place of publication and sale: "at the signe of the Rose and Crowne neere Holborne Bridge"; and the date of publication: "1590."[24]

The wealth of information on the title page of *Tamburlaine* is perhaps as surprising for a modern reader as the information it withholds. For what is conspicuously absent, of course, is any indication of the play's author.[25] Indeed, by using the word "author," I am imposing a concept that would not have applied to the text of a public stage play in 1590. What authorizes Marlowe's play according to its original title page is emphatically not its writer (or "author") but rather a variety of other figures: Tamburlaine, coming first on the title page in type substantially bigger than what follows; the players – patronized by the Lord Admiral – who had performed the play; and the publisher Richard Jones. This fascinating authorizing conglomerate thus ranges from the English aristocracy via the London playhouse and printing houses to a Scythian shepherd and conqueror turned fictional character.

What is the marketing strategy discernible behind the title page of *Tamburlaine*? What seems to have been supposed to whet a customer's appetite was the exotic and extravagant protagonist. That the play was performed "sundrie times," on not just one but several stages by one of the leading companies of the day, the Lord Admiral's Men, was further counted on to boost sales.[26] Reminiscences of a live performance of what was clearly

---

[24] The book could of course have been bought in many different bookshops. What the indication on the title pages does is "to inform *retailers* where a book could be purchased *wholesale*" (Blayney, "Publication of Playbooks," 390). Blayney has shown that Greg was instrumental in entrenching the mistaken belief that the sale of a book was restricted to one exclusive retailer (390).

[25] By the most conservative standards of cataloguing, *Tamburlaine* would in fact have to be regarded as an anonymous play. The first unambiguous attribution, some forty-five years after the play's composition, is in Robert Henderson's *The Arraignment of the Whole Creature, At the Barre of Religion, Reason, and Experience* (1632) (*STC* 13538.5; here and below, *STC* refers to A. W. Pollard and G. R. Redgrave, comp., *A Short-Title Catalogue of Books Printed in England, Scotland and Ireland, and of English Books Printed Abroad*, 1475–1640, 2nd edn [London: The Bibliographical Society, 1976–1991]) followed by ascriptions in the catalogues of Francis Kirkman (1671), and Gerard Langbaine (1687); see J. S. Cunningham, ed., *Tamburlaine*, The Revels Plays (Manchester University Press, 1981), 7–8.

[26] Recent performance seems to have been of importance for the marketability of an early playtext. In 1584, when Lyly went into print with plays which had only just been performed before the Queen, they went through two (*Sappho and Phao*) or even three (*Campaspe*) editions in the same year, while the four plays by Lyly printed in 1591/92, after performance at Paul's had stopped, remained without further reprints until Blount's collection *Six Court Comedies* of 1632. Moreover, in the address "To the Reader" in the first quarto of *The Family of Love* (1608), an anonymous playwright – Middleton's authorship has been convincingly disputed by MacDonald P. Jackson in *Studies in Attribution:*

one of the early potboilers in London's theaters could also be expected to recommend the book to customers. These customers were clearly not expected to buy *Tamburlaine*, however, because they knew about Marlowe, had seen or read plays they knew to be his, had enjoyed them and wanted more.[27]

The contrast to the title page of *Volpone* could hardly be more obvious. Not only is the author's name present, but it is printed first and biggest, the capital letters extending from the very left to the very right of the page. The play, the other information deemed worthy of presence, is quite literally subordinate to the author's name, coming second and in smaller type though also in capitals. While the concept of authorship does violence to the original title page of *Tamburlaine*, it does justice to that of *Volpone*. Indeed, "the author and his work" is what the title page suggests. Little else beside remains: year of publication, the publisher, and the motto in the language of learning, suggesting that the transaction proposed is from a scholarly author to an educated reader. Accordingly, no mention is made of players and playhouses.

Before the beginning of Shakespeare's dramatic career, the playwright's name, like Marlowe's in the 1590 edition of *Tamburlaine*, is typically absent from the title page of a printed playbook. Long after the rise of dramatic authorship and the canonization of a good many dramatists, most emphatically Shakespeare himself who, to a large extent, has come to stand for what exactly an author is, such a situation may seem surprising. That the seemingly timeless concept of authorship was not only renegotiated in Shakespeare's, but remains subject to change in our own time, is perhaps best illustrated by a comparison that can simultaneously shed light on the artistic status of playwrights before Shakespeare's time. Modern screenwriters, like sixteenth-century playwrights, are known by insiders and experts but ignored by the multitude. There is a general awareness that they exist, but little curiosity about their specific contribution to the final product. As playwrights in the sixteenth century and screenwriters in the twentieth century are little known and their achievements little appreciated, so prominent actors (the "Puppets...that spake from [their] mouths" to quote

---

Middleton and Shakespeare, Salzburg Studies in English Literature (Salzburg: Universität Salzburg, 1979), 103–9 – complains that the play is published: "Too late, for that it was not published when the general voice of the people had seald it for good, and the newnesse of it made it much more desired, then at this time: For Plaies in this Citie are like wenches new falne to the trade, onelie desired of your neatest gallants, whiles the'are fresh: when they grow stale they must be vented by Termers and Cuntrie chapmen" (quoted from Greg, *Bibliography*, III.1207).

[27] McKerrow (*Bibliography for Literary Students*, 93) has pointed out that the mention of an author's earlier work on title pages did not begin, some exceptions granted, until the eighteenth century.

Robert Greene's fit of jealousy) have fame in abundance.[28] A particularly eloquent document to illustrate the relative prominence of actor and playwright is the play *A Knack to Know a Knave*, performed by the Lord Strange's Men in 1592 and published in 1594.[29] The play is not only "anonymous" (and has remained so),[30] but the title page points out that it "hath sundrie tymes bene played by Ed. Allen and his Companie. With Kemps applauded Merrimentes." While the playwright authors what the actors speak, Edward Alleyn and William Kempe, two of the most famous actors of the 1590s, here serve to authorize the playtext an anonymous playwright has produced. This ironic reversal finds its modern equivalent in the marketing of spin-off novels based on recent box-office hits which appeal to the potential customer with a picture of the star actor(s) or actress(es) on the front cover.

Comparing the repertory systems in Elizabethan theater and Hollywood cinema, G. K. Hunter writes that "The Elizabethan system, like the Hollywood one, put [the writers] at the bottom of the pile."[31] The *auteur* theory in the fifties and early sixties promoted by François Truffaut and others further accentuated the view that it was the director, not the writer, who was the author of a film.[32] If screenplays by F. Scott Fitzgerald, William Faulkner, Nathanael West, Aldous Huxley, and Graham Greene have been studied in depth, this is precisely because their authors were not first and foremost screenwriters. Even the screenplay for the 1999 Academy-Award-winning *Shakespeare in Love* – which was published by Faber and Faber and boasted impressive sales figures – owed much of the attention it attracted to its dramatist co-author Tom Stoppard. It is true that the Dictionary of Literary Biography series has recently published two volumes on American screenwriters, but what their editor says does nothing to refute the suggested parallel between Elizabethan playwrights and modern screenwriters: "The American screenwriter has received very little serious study. Even among film scholars, emphasis has most often been placed on the director

---

[28] *Greene's Groatsworth of Wit*, ed. Carroll, line 934. The Hollywood equivalent of Greene's view of the players, the "Hollywood-as-destroyer legend" (3), is the subject of Richard Fine's *West of Eden: Writers in Hollywood 1928–1940* (Washington D.C.: Smithsonian Institution Press, 1993).

[29] E. K. Chambers, *The Elizabethan Stage*, 4 vols. (Oxford: Clarendon Press, 1923), IV.24–25.

[30] Of course, the very word "anonymous" is anachronistic, anonymity being an attribute of people, not of texts, in the late sixteenth and early seventeenth century (see Masten, *Textual Intercourse*, 12–13, and Emma Smith, "Author v. Character in Early Modern Dramatic Authorship: The Example of Thomas Kyd and *The Spanish Tragedy*," *Medieval and Renaissance Drama in England*, 11 (1999), 133).

[31] G. K. Hunter, "The Making of a Popular Repertory: Hollywood and the Elizabethans," in *Shakespearean Continuities: Essays in Honour of E.A.J. Honigmann*, eds. John Batchelor, Tom Cain, and Claire Lamont (London: Macmillan, 1997), 249.

[32] Fine, *West of Eden*, 6–7.

rather than the writer," Randall Clark writes.[33] The important number of "anonymous" printed playbooks in Elizabethan England suggests a similar lack of interest in playwrights in the late sixteenth century. Yet, as the status of printed playbooks underwent an emancipation during Shakespeare and Jonson's lifetime, so that of the screenplay may currently be changing. On the same page, Clark writes, on the one hand, "Although it is a written work, the screenplay is not composed to be read. It is not meant to exist apart from the motion picture," and, on the other hand, "over the past decades, the status of the screenwriter has changed, and the screenplay has emerged as a new form of literature."[34] The contrast between the two statements is instructive, for the publication of playbooks in the late sixteenth and the early seventeenth centuries reveals the same ambivalence toward their status. In the following, it may be well to keep in mind the contradictory attitude of seeing as "not composed to be read" what has nevertheless emerged, or is emerging, "as a new form of literature."

In the years between the publication of *Tamburlaine* and *Volpone*, publishers seem to have increasingly realized that another way of turning playtexts into more respectable printed matter was by naming the author on the title page. As Wendy Wall has pointed out, playtexts were "unruly bulks of language, whose collaborative process of creation complicated their states as marketable commodities."[35] Associating plays with a single source of origin and authority meant legitimating plays by dissociating them from the disreputable commercial playhouses where players, shareholders, theatrical entrepreneurs, and playwrights collaborated. Significantly, the Puritan pamphleteer William Prynne used the designation "playhouse books" throughout his antitheatrical *Histrio-mastix*, thus attempting to discredit playtexts by linking them to the playhouse rather than to their authors.

The fact that many of the plays were not only collaboratively staged and produced but also collaboratively written, complicated this process of authorization. In fact, only slightly more than one out of three plays paid for by Henslowe for the Lord Admiral's Men was not written collaboratively.[36]

[33] Robert E. Morsberger, Stephen O. Lesser, and Randall Clark, eds., *American Screenwriters*, Dictionary of Literary Biography, 26 (Detroit: Gale Research Company, 1984), and Randall Clark, ed., *American Screenwriters*, 2nd series, Dictionary of Literary Biography, 44 (Detroit: Gale Research company, 1986). I quote from volume 26, page ix.

[34] Morsberger, Lesser, and Clark, eds., *American Screenwriters*, ix.

[35] Wall, *Imprint of Gender*, 89.

[36] Carol Chilington Rutter, ed, *Documents of the Rose Playhouse*, 2nd edn, The Revels Plays Companion Library (Manchester University Press, 1999), 128. A comprehensive examination of the collaborative writing of playtexts is Masten, *Textual Intercourse*. See also Masten's "Authorship and Collaboration,"

Acknowledging the extent of collaboration on title pages would no doubt have failed to convey the impression of authorship publishers tried to foster. Some simple figures confirm this: for the three-year period from the autumn of 1597 to the summer of 1600, collaborated plays accounted for nearly 60 percent (thirty out of fifty-two) of the plays written for the Lord Admiral's Men.[37] Yet of the thirty-two playbooks published during the same years, thirteen are said to be by a single author, nineteen are published anonymously, while not a single one acknowledges multiple authorship on the title page.[38] For the total forty-year period from 1584 to 1623, only 13 of the III plays attributed to a playwright or playwrights acknowledge multiple authorship, that is less than 12 percent (see Appendix A).

The extent to which the creation of the dramatic author in early printed playbooks preceded the creation of the dramatic author in the playhouse can be inferred from a letter dated March 4, 1698, in which Dryden comments on a playbill for a performance of Congreve's *The Double Dealer*. What Dryden is particularly interested in is the seemingly unremarkable fact that the playbill contains the words: "Written by Mr Congreve." Dryden points out that "the printing an Authours name, in a Play bill, is a new manner of proceeding, at least in England."[39] Unless we want to argue that Dryden is mistaken, this indicates that, while as early as the turn of the sixteenth and seventeenth centuries the majority of title pages bore the dramatists' names, it took another century until playbills started acknowledging the playwrights. Throughout the seventeenth century, the documents advertising printed playbooks, on the one hand, and those announcing theatrical performances, on the other, thus seem to have a significantly different attitude toward the playwright. Playbills keep reflecting the theatres' communal enterprise in which the playwright(s) do(es) not occupy a privileged position. From the 1590s, title pages, in contrast, show the stationers' effort to tie playbooks to a playwright who authorizes the playtext much as a poet authorizes a book of poetry.

in *A New History of Early English Drama*, eds. Cox and Kastan, 357–82; Brooks's chapter "'What Strange Production Is At Last Displaid': Dramatic Authorship and the Dilemma of Collaboration," in *Playhouse to Printing House*, 140–88; and Heather Hirschfeld, "Early Modern Collaboration and Theories of Authorship," *PMLA*, 116 (2001), 609–22.

[37] Neil Carson, *A Companion to Henslowe's Diary* (Cambridge University Press, 1988), 57–58.

[38] It seems significant that Robert Allot, in his anthology *England's Parnassus* (1600), attributed all passages from plays written in joint authorship to one of the playwrights only, often to the most famous one (see Robert Allot, comp., *England's Parnassus*, ed. Charles Crawford (Oxford: Clarendon Press, 1913), xxxii).

[39] John Dryden, *Letters*, ed. Charles E. Ward (Durham, N.C.: University of North Carolina Press, 1942), 113. For a list and illustrations of some of the earliest British playbills, see Ifan Kyrle Fletcher, "British Playbills Before 1718," *Theatre Notebook*, 17 (1962–63), 48–50.

This process of authorization was gradual and dependent upon dramatic genre. From very early on, certain kinds of dramatic publications acknowledged the writers' identity and were published with the usual trappings of more respectable publications, with dedications, in collections, even as part of "works."[40] These plays, however, had not been written for and performed on the public stage. Among these belong: academic Latin dramas such as William Gager's *Meleager* (1592) and *Ulysses Redux* (1592); the translations of Seneca's plays by Jasper Heywood, Alexander Neville, John Studley, Thomas Nuce, and Thomas Newton, published first separately and subsequently in a collection between 1559 to 1581; translations of other ancient plays such as Maurice Kyffin's version of Terence's *Andria* (1588); translations of modern continental plays like Anthony Munday's *Fedele and Fortunio* (1585) – from Luigi Pasqualigo's *Il Fedele* (1576) – or Thomas Kyd's and the Countess of Pembroke's renderings of Garnier's *Cornélie* and *Antoine*; other closet tragedies such as Samuel Daniel's *Cleopatra* (1594); Inns of Court tragedies like Thomas Hughes's *Misfortunes of Arthur* of 1587; and George Gascoigne's *Supposes* and *Jocasta* which were part of the quarto collections of 1573, 1575, and 1587. Gascoigne's and Daniel's plays were even included in collections entitled "Works" long before Jonson's publication with the same title of 1616.[41] What all of these dramatic texts have in common is that they were associated neither with the disreputable acting profession nor with the stigma of commerce.

As for plays of the commercial stage, sixteen plays performed before paying audiences – public and private theaters together – were published between 1584 and 1593 in a total of twenty-three editions. Only one of these plays indicates the playwright's full name, not on the title page, but at the end of the text, in the so-called "explicit": *Edward I* by "George Peele Maister of Artes in Oxenford." The title pages of Robert Wilson's plays (*The Three Ladies of London* and *The Three Lords and Three Ladies of London*) bear the playwright's initials. All other playbooks (Lyly's *Sapho and Phao*, *Campaspe*, *Endimion*, *Galathea*, and *Midas*, Peele's *The Arraignment of Paris*, Marlowe's *Tamburlaine*, Kyd's *The Spanish Tragedy* and *Soliman and Perseda*, and *The Rare Triumphs of Love and Fortune*, *The Troublesome*

---

[40] For dedications prefacing printed playtexts, see Virgil B. Heltzel, "The Dedication of Tudor and Stuart Plays," *Wiener Beiträge zur Englischen Philologie*, 65 (1957), 74–86.

[41] Gascoigne's "Works" were published in 1575. See Marotti, *English Renaissance Lyric*, 223–25, for a fine discussion of the 1573 and 1575 editions of Gascoigne, the first suggesting a gathering of miscellanies, the second the works of an author. Daniel's *Cleopatra* was included in collected editions in 1594, 1595, 1598, 1599, 1601–2, 1605, 1607, 1611, and 1623, which were similarly called "Works" from 1601 to 1602. For other collections of dramatic texts printed in the first third of the seventeenth century, see Brooks, *Playhouse to Printing House*, 197–98.

Raigne of King John, Arden of Faversham, and *Fair Em*) were published anonymously.

It is hardly by chance that Peele is the only playwright whose authorship is acknowledged before 1594. His Oxford degree, duly mentioned, gave him the social respectability which most people associated with the commercial stage lacked. As early as 1582, Peele contributed commendatory verses to Thomas Watson's *Hekatompathia,* and, three years later, he seems to have been called upon to write the annual Lord Mayor's show of which two pageants have survived.[42] In 1589, Nashe called Peele "the chiefe supporter of pleasance nowe liuing, the *Atlas* of Poetrie, & *primus verborum Artifex*: whose first encrease, the arraignement of *Paris,* might pleade to your opinions his pregnant dexterity of wit, and manifold varietie of inuention; wherein (*me iudice*) he goeth a steppe beyond all that write."[43] When *Edward I* was published in 1593 with his name on the title page, Peele was clearly an established figure.

An unprecedented number of plays was printed at the end of a period of plague in 1594 of which eighteen had been written for and performed before a paying audience. While only one of the sixteen playbooks printed during the previous ten years indicate the playwright's full name, the proportion rises to seven out of eighteen for the plays published in 1594.[44] The playwrights nominally mentioned are Marlowe (*Edward II* and *The Massacre at Paris*), Marlowe and Nashe (*Dido, Queen of Carthage*), Robert Wilson (*The Cobler's Prophecy*), Thomas Lodge (*The Wounds of Civil War*), Robert Greene (*Friar Bacon and Friar Bungay*), and Lodge and Greene (*A Looking-Glass for London and England*). With the exception of two of Marlowe's plays, all title pages add an indication of rank to the author's name, again suggesting that a claim to social respectability served to legitimize the authorship of stage plays.[45] That Marlowe is an exception may well be significant: after his recent death, Marlowe was a figure of some

---

[42] Charles Tylor Prouty, ed., *The Life and Work of George Peele,* 3 vols. (New Haven: Yale University Press, 1952), 1.71.

[43] The "Preface" to Greene's *Menaphon* (1589) is quoted from McKerrow, ed., *Works of Thomas Nashe* III.323.

[44] The eleven plays that were published anonymously are Shakespeare's *Titus Andronicus; The First Part of the Contention,* a "bad" quarto of Shakespeare's *2 Henry VI; The Taming of a Shrew,* a "bad" quarto, a source play, or an adaptation of Shakespeare's *Taming of the Shrew;* Lyly's *Mother Bombie; Orlando Furioso, The Wars of Cyrus, The True Tragedy of Richard III, The Battle of Alcazar, Selimus, The Life and Death of Jack Straw,* and *A Knack to Know a Knave.*

[45] The same applies for the legitimation of poetic miscellanies. For instance, even though substituting initials for names, *The Phoenix Nest* of 1593 mentions the contributors' rank after the initials. Note, though, that not all indications of rank need have been correct, and that some publishers did not shy away from attributing to the authors they published a social status they did not have. Several title pages added the title of "gentleman" to Thomas Nashe's name as he himself points out in *Strange*

notoriety which the publishers may well have tried to profit from by mentioning his name.[46]

The process of authorizing printed plays by providing them more and more often with named authors continued after 1594 in much the same way. During the last years of the century, the ratio of "anonymously" published plays was only just over 50 percent, swiftly falling below in the early years of the seventeenth century. Between 1601 and 1616, there is not a single year in which the majority of printed playbooks failed to attribute the plays to their authors. By the second decade of the seventeenth century, playbooks published without any indication of authorship had become exceedingly rare, totaling less than 10 percent. The claim that "play-text quartos printed early in the late sixteenth and early seventeenth centuries generally did not record the presence of an author or authors" thus does hardly justice to the gradual establishment of the concept of dramatic authorship during Shakespeare's lifetime.[47] In spite of what critics have held, the early publication history of Elizabethan drama suggests that the rise of the dramatic author did not have to wait until Ben Jonson clamorously announced his agency in the publication of his plays.

Nor do we have to wait until the advent of Ben Jonson to witness the first printed playbooks that present themselves as readerly rather than as theatrical. Far from apologizing for the medium in which they appear, printed playbooks thereby start vindicating their existence in print and as books. To illustrate this, I will return to the 1590 edition of *Tamburlaine*, more specifically to Richard Jones's address "To the Gentlemen Readers: and others that take pleasure in reading Histories":

Gentlemen, and curteous Readers whosoever: I haue here published in print for your sakes, the two tragical Discourses of the Scythian Shepheard, *Tamburlaine*, that became so great a Conquerour, and so mightie a Monarque: My hope is, that they wil be now no lesse acceptable vnto you to read after your serious affaires and studies, then they haue bene (lately) delightfull for many of you to see, when the same were shewed in London vpon stages: I haue (purposely) omitted and left out

Newes (1592): "it hath pleased M. Printer, both in this booke and *pierce Pennilesse*, to intaile a vaine title to my name, which I care not for, without my consent or priuitie I here auouch" (McKerrow, ed., *Works of Thomas Nashe*, 1.311–12; see also III.128). To give another example, Robert Wilson, who seems to have been an actor as well as a playwright, is a gentleman according to the title page of *The Cobler's Prophecy* of 1594, though it is doubtful that he was indeed of that rank.

[46] That the 1594 Marlowe publications may have had something to do with the playwright's death and its notoriety is also suggested by the now lost elegy by Nashe on the death of Marlowe which seems to have been part of some copies of the first quarto of *Dido, Queen of Carthage*.

[47] Masten, *Textual Intercourse*, 113.

some fond and friuolous Iestures, digressing (and in my poore opinion) far vnmeet for the matter, which I thought, might seeme more tedious vnto the wise, than any way els to be regarded, though (happly) they haue bene of some vaine cōceited fondlings greatly gaped at, what times they were shewed vpon the stage in their graced deformities: neuertheles now, to be mixtured in print with such matter of worth, it wuld prooue a great disgrace to so honorable & stately a historie: Great folly were it in me, to commend vnto your wisedomes, either the eloquence of the Authour that writ them, or the worthinesse of the matter it selfe; I therefore leaue vnto your learned censures, both the one and the other, and my selfe the poore printer of them vnto your most curteous and fauourable protection; which if you vouchsafe to accept, you shall euermore binde mee to imploy what trauell and seruice I can, to the aduauncing and pleasuring of your excellent degree.

> Yours, most humble at commaundement,
> R. I. Printer[48]

The address contains a sharp dichotomy: on the one hand, there are the "fond and friuolous Iestures" (the spelling of the last word being an obsolete variant of "gestures," but perhaps also containing the additional idea of "jests" with its low-comedy implications) "gaped at" by "vaine cōceited fondlings" (foolish persons, perhaps with the additional suggestion of groundlings); on the other hand, there are the "honorable & stately" histories or "tragical Discourses," written by an "Authour," to be read by "Gentlemen, and curteous Readers" after their "serious affaires and studies," and submitted to their "learned censures." Much of the rhetoric Jonson was to employ later on is already present here.

Jones goes out of his way to stress that the play on stage does not correspond to the play in print. His address from "The Printer to the Reader" prefacing his edition of *Promos and Cassandra* had already shown awareness of the respective specificity of print and stage twelve years earlier. Yet, while the address of 1578 contains an implied apology (piece out with your imagination what print, as opposed to the stage, cannot supply), the address of 1590 offers a solution (I have purposely omitted crude stage action which would have disgraced the printed playtext).

Commentators disagree whether the omissions concern comic material (by Marlowe or someone else) of the kind extant in *Doctor Faustus* or only interpolations by actors who "speak...more than is set down for them."[49] Bowers believed that the additions originated in the playhouse and were very successful so that Jones – who did not have access to this material – felt the need to invent a reason for not including them.[50] Fuller has added

[48] Greg, *Bibliography*, III.1196.　　[49] *Hamlet*, 3.2.39.
[50] Fredson Bowers, ed., *The Complete Works of Christopher Marlowe*, 2 vols. (Cambridge University Press, 1973), 1.75.

that at 2,508 and 2,532 lines, the two parts seem too long to have contained lengthy additional comic scenes of the kind in *Faustus*.[51] Una Ellis-Fermor believed that some comic fragments of the kind referred to by Jones survive in the extant text (for instance 2.4.28–35 and 3.3.215–27 in Part One).[52] Ethel Seaton shared this view and suggested that the misnumbering of scenes in the first edition may indicate the cutting of entire comic scenes.[53] Recent work that takes into account Richard Jones's working methods during his entire career considerably strengthens the view that, interventionist publisher that he was, Jones may well have applied the scissors himself.[54] Whatever Jones is referring to, what is important in this context is that he distinguishes between material for the stage and material for the page. The idea of some performance critics that playtexts are scripts that are solely designed for, or even reflect, performance would have seemed wholly strange to him. The passages that were "greatly gaped at" are precisely omitted in print. While Marotti, analyzing the passage from manuscript to printed poetry, has identified a "recoding of social verse as primarily *literary* texts in the print medium," Jones's preface announces a first recoding of a playtext as a primarily *literary* text in the print medium.[55] It is significant that the first distinct attempt to drive a wedge between stage and page as early as 1590 is that of a publisher. It suggests that the printers' and publishers' commercial strategies thus preceded, and quite possibly helped bring about, the playwrights' artistic self-consciousness as writers – later even "authors" – of playtexts that could be printed and read.[56]

Jones's address and title page call the two parts of *Tamburlaine* "tragical Discourses." David Bevington suggested that Marlowe may have written the "prologue" at Jones's request (announcing a "stately" tragedy "with high astounding terms").[57] If we further recall Jones's reference to comic material in the original performances, we realize that his intervention may have considerable generic consequences. Would a theater audience in the

---

[51] David Fuller, ed., *Tamburlaine the Great Parts 1 and 2*; and Edward J. Esche, ed., *The Massacre at Paris with the Death of the Duke of Guise* (Oxford University Press, 1998), xlix. The prologue to *Tamburlaine* is quoted from Fuller's edition.

[52] *Tamburlaine the Great* (London: Hesperides Press, 1930), 104, 134.

[53] See Seaton's review of Ellis-Fermor's edition in *The Review of English Studies*, 8 (1932), 469.

[54] See Kirk Melnikoff, "Richard Jones (fl. 1564–1613): Elizabethan Printer, Bookseller, and Publisher," *Analytical & Enumerative Bibliography*, 12 (2001), 153–84.

[55] Marotti, *English Renaissance Lyric*, 218.

[56] See also Robert Weimann's fine analysis of the competing claims of "pen" and "voice" in Jones's address (*Author's Pen and Actor's Voice: Playing and Writing in Shakespeare's Theatre*, edited by Helen Higbee and William West, Cambridge Studies in Renaissance Literature and Culture, 39 (Cambridge University Press, 2000), 59–62).

[57] See Bevington, *"Mankind" to Marlowe*, 200–2.

late 1580s have thought of *Tamburlaine* as a tragedy, as a history, or rather as something generically more mixed? While Jones considered the comic bits as "digressing," the spectators who "greatly gaped" at them may well have thought differently. Generic descriptions were notoriously loose at the time: *Troilus and Cressida*, for instance, was variously called a comedy (address in the 1609 quarto), a tragedy (First Folio), or a history (title page of the 1609 quarto). Nevertheless, it may be well to recall that the entry in the Stationers' Register on August 14, 1590 has "twooe commical discourses of TOMBERLEIN the Cithian shapparde."[58] The generic categories within which *Tamburlaine* was placed by Jones in 1590 and has been placed by critics since may reflect a *Tamburlaine* for the page as opposed to the stage.

The publication history of Shakespeare's plays suggests that comedies were less popular reading matter than tragedies or histories. Five comedies – *Love's Labour's Lost*, *A Midsummer Night's Dream*, *The Merchant of Venice*, *The Merry Wives of Windsor*, and *Much Ado about Nothing* – found their way into print during his lifetime.[59] Of these, only *Love's Labour's Lost* was reprinted before Pavier and Jaggard tried to publish a collection of Shakespeare plays in 1619. The tragedies and histories fared very differently: *1 Henry IV* went through six, *Richard III* through five editions in Shakespeare's lifetime, and both had an additional edition before the publication of the Folio. *Richard II* received five, *Hamlet* four, and *Romeo and Juliet*, *Titus Andronicus*, *The First Part of the Contention* (*2 Henry VI*), *Richard Duke of York* (*3 Henry VI*), and *Henry V* three editions before 1623.[60] As we will see below, there is considerably more evidence suggesting that tragedies and histories were deemed more respectable reading matter than comedies or generically mixed plays.[61] This may lend further

[58] Arber, *Transcript*, II.558.
[59] Three explanations need be added: firstly, I here adopt what seems today the majority view that *The Taming of a Shrew* (published 1594) is to be treated as an independent play and does not derive from Shakespeare's *The Taming of the Shrew*; secondly, I do not, contrary to Heminge and Condell, count *Troilus and Cressida* among the comedies, though with the single edition of 1609, it, too, would conform to the point I am making; thirdly, I here exclude Shakespeare's "*Love's Labour's Won*," which may have been an independent play of whose only edition no copy has survived (see chapter 3, page 82).
[60] *2 Henry IV* is in fact the only one of the twelve histories or tragedies printed during Shakespeare's lifetime which appeared in a single edition before the First Folio. I here assume, with the Oxford editors, that the fourth, undated quarto of *Hamlet* was published before 1623 (see Stanley Wells and Gary Taylor, with John Jowett and William Montgomery, *William Shakespeare: A Textual Companion* (Oxford: Clarendon Press, 1987), 396). My count assumes that the undated fourth quarto of *Romeo and Juliet* was printed before 1623. Note, though, that Lynette Hunter has recently argued that it may have appeared in any year between 1618 and 1626 ("The Dating of Q4 *Romeo and Juliet* Revisited," *The Library*, 7th series, 2 (2001), 281–85).
[61] See chapter 6, pages 142–43.

credibility to the argument that Jones's editorial intervention rather than the script Marlowe originally wrote for the stage is responsible for the play's genre as modern criticism – following the "tragic glass" in the prologue and the "tragicall discourses" of the title page – has understood it.

Contrary to what we might think today, Jones's edition of *Tamburlaine* – even though the play was a potboiler in the theater – was a commercially risky undertaking.[62] The publication of commercial plays performed by adult companies in public playhouses had been an extremely rare phenomenon before 1590, suggesting that there had been little demand. In fact, only two of them had found their way into print, Robert Wilson's *The Three Ladies of London* (1584) and the anonymous *Rare Triumphs of Love and Fortune* (1589). Clearly there was no established readership for commercial plays when Jones went into print with *Tamburlaine* in 1590. It is all the more remarkable that Jones published a quarto edition of Robert Wilson's *The Three Lords and Three Ladies* the same year.[63] Jones's address "To the Gentlemen Readers," and the fact that he felt the need to insert one, betray some of his anxieties. In many ways, it reads like an aggressive advertisement for a product that is not yet established on the market. Its rhetoric is gropingly ambivalent: "many of you" have enjoyed the play, so I hope it "will be now no less acceptable unto you to read." Yet, at the same time as Jones asserts an expected overlap between audience and readership, he also stresses their social difference: the "conceited fondlings" in the playhouse, the "Gentlemen, and curteous readers" at the bookstalls. Jones clearly expected that the social flattery would not be lost on potential customers. On the other hand, aiming at gentlemen only might have been an unnecessary restriction limiting the number of customers who feel addressed. So Jones's address is "To the Gentlemen Readers: *and others that take pleasure in reading Histories*" (my emphasis).[64] Jones is walking cautiously on what is clearly new ground.[65]

---

[62] Having recently disposed of the myth that "plays in quarto . . . must have sold like hot cakes" and that "A publisher lucky enough to acquire a play . . . would confidently expect to make a quick profit" ("Publication of Playbooks," 384), Blayney has persuasively argued that publishing playbooks remained commercially risky throughout the early modern period (see in particular his estimations of the publisher's costs and his expected profits (ibid., 405–13)).

[63] See Scott McMillin and Sally-Beth MacLean, *The Queen's Men and their Plays* (Cambridge University Press, 1998), 155–56, for a fine analysis of the "defining moment in 1590" with "playgoers standing before a London bookstall" (155) faced with two generically very different plays published by Jones, one of the earliest blank verse tragedies and a late morality play.

[64] The later pioneers Heminge and Condell, publishing the first folio edition consisting of nothing but playtexts in 1623, similarly tried to be as catholic as possible in their address to "The great Variety of Readers. From the most able to him that can but spell."

[65] Jones, interestingly, also appears to have had business with other contemporary playwrights: in 1589 he published Thomas Lodge's *Scillaes metamorphosis: enterlaced with the vnfortunate loue of*

Jones's conditional promise that "if you vouchsafe to accept [this history], you shall euermore binde mee to imploy what trauell and seruice I can" is more than mere publishers' rhetoric. It reflects a genuine uncertainty about whether printing a playbook will be a commercial failure or a profitable undertaking opening up new opportunities for the future. The latter proved to be the case. Within the next three years, more than twenty playtexts found their way into print and three plays, *The Three Ladies of London* (first published 1584), *Tamburlaine*, and *The Spanish Tragedy*, were even reprinted. At least one publication shows the specific influence of Jones's 1590 *Tamburlaine*: in 1591, a quarto entitled *The Troublesome Raigne of King John* was published. Though only slightly longer than Shakespeare's *King John*, the anonymous play was printed in two parts in an attempt to profit from the popularity of the two parts of *Tamburlaine*.[66] The address "To the Gentlemen Readers" (reproducing in itself Jones's device in *Tamburlaine*) explicitly establishes a connection to the publication of the previous year:

> You that with friendly grace of smoothed brow
> Have entertained the Scythian Tamburlaine,
> And given applause unto an Infidel:
> Vouchsafe to welcome (with like curtesie)
> A warlike Christian and your Countreyman.[67]

Jones's 1590 edition of *Tamburlaine* was a groundbreaking publishing venture that seems to have been understood as such in its own time.

Another huge stage success which, following *Tamburlaine*, recommended itself for commercial recycling in print, *The Spanish Tragedy* was published one year after *The Troublesome Raigne*. Its early printing history – unusually well documented owing to the records of the court of the Stationers' Company – suggests that printers and publishers were growing more confident of the commercial viability of playtexts. For not one but two publishers

---

Glaucus (*STC* 16674) and George Peele's "An eglogue. Gratulatorie. Entituled: to the honourable shepheard of Albions arcadia: Robert earle of Essex" (*STC* 19534); and in 1590 he published George Peele's "Polyhimnia describing, the honourable triumph at Tylt" (*STC* 19546). For his active role in the constitution and publication of miscellanies, see Pomeroy, *Elizabethan Miscellanies*, 8–20, and Marotti, *English Renaissance Lyric*, 217–18.

[66] Even before the two-part publication of *Tamburlaine* was imitated in the printing house, the play had received the honor of several stage imitations. See Peter Berek, "*Tamburlaine's* Weak Sons: Imitation as Interpretation Before 1593," *Renaissance Drama*, n.s. 13 (1982), 55–82, and "*Locrine* Revised, *Selimus*, and Early Responses to *Tamburlaine*," *Renaissance Opportunities in Renaissance Drama*, 22 (1980), 33–54. For other early reactions to the play and its hero, see Richard Levin, "The Contemporary Perception of Marlowe's Tamburlaine," *Medieval and Renaissance Drama in England*, 1 (1984), 51–70.

[67] I quote *Troublesome Raigne* from Bullough, ed., *Sources of Shakespeare*, IV.72.

printed Kyd's play in 1592. Though only Abel Jeffes had acquired the rights to the play, Edward White, too, had secured a text and was preparing an edition. Jeffes entered his copy in the Stationers' Register by paying a fee of 4 pence, thereby protecting his rights.[68] When White, undeterred, piratically published his edition, he was fined, and the copies of his edition were confiscated "to thuse of the poore of the companye."[69] Ironically, no copy of Jeffes's legitimate edition has survived, while White's surreptitious publication is the one on which modern editions of Kyd's plays are normally based. White thus took what he must have known to be a considerable risk in his attempt to secure an edition of *The Spanish Tragedy*. He rightly guessed that the play, a "stately" tragedy in "high astounding terms" like *Tamburlaine*, would be deemed good reading matter. It went through no less than eleven editions by 1633, more than any other play except for the anonymous *Mucedorous*.[70] It unashamedly advertises its Senecan ancestry and, despite its spectacular theatricality, has long narrative passages that are undeniably literary: Andrea's prologue (1.1.1–85), the General's report of the battle with Portugal (1.2.22–84), or Hieronimo's fourteen-line Latin dirge (2.5.67–80).[71] Like *Tamburlaine*, it self-confidently advertises its genre: where *Tamburlaine* has the prologue ("From jygging vaines..."), *The Spanish Tragedy* has Hieronimo's

> Fie, comedies are fit for common wits:
> But to present a kingly troop withal,
> Give me a stately-written tragedy,
> *Tragedia cothurnata*, fitting kings,
> Containing matter, and not common things.
>
> (4.1.157–61)

Like Jones's edition of *Tamburlaine*, the playbook contains a publisher's note suggesting that the printed text is not simply a record of a performance

---

[68] On the often misunderstood subject of "entrance," see Blayney, "Publication of Playbooks," 400–5.

[69] I quote from W. W. Greg's introduction to *The Spanish Tragedy* (1592), Malone Society Reprints (London: Oxford University Press, 1948), x. For full discussions and for the records of the court of the Stationers' Company, see Greg, ed., *The Spanish Tragedy*, vi–xiii; Greg, "*The Spanish Tragedy* – A Leading Case?," *The Library* 4th Series, 6 (1926), 47–56; and Leo Kirschbaum, "Is *The Spanish Tragedy* a Leading Case? Did a Bad Quarto of *Love's Labours Lost* Ever Exist?," *Journal of English and German Philology*, 37 (1938), 501–12; see also Erne, *Beyond "The Spanish Tragedy,"* 57–66.

[70] *The Spanish Tragedy* was published in 1592 (twice), 1594, 1599, 1602, 1603, 1610, 1615, 1618, 1623, and 1633. In a recent publication, Emma Smith ("Author v. Character," 129) has mistakenly asserted that *The Spanish Tragedy* "was published in *ten* separate editions between *1594* and *1613*" (my emphasis).

[71] I refer to and quote from Philip Edwards's Revels edition (London, 1959). Given the literary inflection of Kyd's play, it may be significant that it contributed substantially to the poetic miscellany *Belvedere, or the Garden of the Muses* (1600). See Charles Crawford, "*Belvedere*, or *The Garden of the Muses*," *Englische Studien*, 43 (1910–11), 198–228.

but a document that has been specifically prepared for readers. Before the bloody playlet with which Hieronimo brings about his revenge, the readers are told (4.3.10.1–4):

> Gentlemen, for this play of HIERONIMO in sundry languages, was
> thought good to be set down in English more largely,
> for the easier understanding to every
> public reader.

There is no reason to doubt that Hieronimo's *Soliman and Perseda* was performed in "sundry languages." The protagonist suggests multilingual performance at the beginning of act four and quickly overcomes Balthazar's resistance (4.1.172–94). During the playlet, the King ignores what role Lorenzo plays even though Balthazar-as-Soliman has just pointed it out, suggesting that the King does not understand Balthazar's words (4.4.28–34). At the end of the deadly spectacle, Hieronimo's words are equally unambiguous: "Here break we off our sundry languages / And thus conclude I in our vulgar tongue" (4.4.74–75). So clearly, there was a multilingual playlet performed on stage but an English play-within-the-play in the printed editions.

The multilingual playlet on stage can be a powerful moment of drama as linguistic and ontological confusions coalesce to bring about the play's holocaust. For a spectator, the enacted linguistic confusion is more important than a literal understanding of the characters' lines (which Hieronimo has already summarized at the beginning of the last act anyway – see 4.1.110–26). The effect of the playlet upon an audience is thus similar to that of a dumb show in which linguistic content gives way entirely to the performed spectacle. For a reader, however, the Babel-like confusion seems difficult if not impossible to convey. While Richard Jones's edition of *Promos and Cassandra* of 1578 apologized for what gets lost in the transfer from one medium to another, from the stage to the page, editions of *Tamburlaine* and *The Spanish Tragedy* in the early 1590s adapt the playtext so as to make them suitable for reading.

Intriguingly, Hieronimo's *Soliman and Perseda* can be shown to draw upon the tale of "Soliman and Persida" in Henry Wotton's novella collection *A Courtlie Controuersie of Cupid's Cautels* (1578).[72] The same novella was Kyd's chief source for his full-length play *Soliman and Perseda* which

---

[72] This was first pointed out by Gregor Sarrazin in *Thomas Kyd und sein Kreis* (Berlin, 1892), 42. For Wotton's *Courtlie Controuersie*, see Erne, " 'Throughly ransackt': Elizabethan Novella Collections and Henry Wotton's *Courtlie Controuersie of Cupid's Cautels* (1578)," *Cahiers Elisabéthains*, forthcoming.

was published the same year.[73] Kyd himself, that is, seems to have been responsible both for the "sundry languages" version, which conforms to a theatrical logic, and for the English version, which was inserted into the print publication to make it conform to a readerly logic. In other words, as early as 1592, a playwright may well have altered a script he had written for the stage in order to make it more suitable for a readership.

One part in the publisher's note is particularly puzzling: "this play of HIERONIMO in sundry languages," the note says, is "set down in English more largely." Why more largely? A possible, and perhaps the most likely, explanation is that the multilingual playlet was kept short, shorter than the fifty lines that make up the English text. The implication would be that while a reader cannot well appreciate the enacted confusion on stage, he has fuller access to the lines' referential content which it is therefore worthwhile to convey "more largely."[74] A different, no less interesting, interpretation should not be excluded, however. *Soliman and Perseda* was in fact printed "more largely" very shortly after White's edition of *The Spanish Tragedy*. It is possible to determine with some certainty that White must have published his edition of *The Spanish Tragedy* in the second half of 1592.[75] Now *Soliman and Perseda* was entered to the very same Edward White on November 20, 1592. Arthur Freeman's analysis of the printing of *The Spanish Tragedy* even suggests that *The Spanish Tragedy* and *Soliman and Perseda* were printed simultaneously.[76] If the play which it "was thought good to be set down in English more largely" is Kyd's full-length *Soliman and Perseda*, then White would seem to have tried to advertise the fuller version of *Soliman and Perseda* at the beginning of the play-within-the-play in *The Spanish Tragedy*. Whichever of the two interpretations is correct, White's 1592 edition of *The Spanish Tragedy* reveals an author and a printer contributing to a text that is aimed at "the easier understanding to every public reader."

Tamburlaine, *The Spanish Tragedy* and the like not only taught Shakespeare how to write plays, but their early publication history also showed him that a market for good reading material was coming into existence.

---

[73] For Kyd's authorship of *Soliman and Perseda*, see Erne, *Beyond "The Spanish Tragedy,"* 160–62.

[74] Note that the specific meaning of "largely" as the word is used in the present instance is that described by the *OED* as "Of discourse: (At great) length, in full, fully. Obs[olete] or arch[aic]."

[75] For the events surrounding the publication of *The Spanish Tragedy* in 1592, see Greg, ed., *The Spanish Tragedy*, v–xiii.

[76] Arthur Freeman, "The Printing of *The Spanish tragedy* [*sic*]," *The Library*, 24, 5th series (1969), 187–99, esp. 197.

CHAPTER 2

The making of "Shakespeare"

This chapter tries to answer the question when and through what process Shakespearean dramatic authorship first acquired visibility. My contention is that this process started early enough for Shakespeare to have lived through and to have been affected by it. I will pay special attention to Shakespeare's early play quartos and to the possible impact of Meres's "canonization" of Shakespeare in *Palladis Tamia*, before considering how the presence of excerpts from playtexts in poetical miscellanies at the turn of the century comments upon and participates in shaping the changing status of plays. I will conclude this chapter by considering what possible impact the emergence of dramatic literature and authorship may have had on Shakespeare's writing.

From early on, Shakespeare was a writer of plays that could be read in print as well as witnessed on stage. This is perhaps best illustrated if we divide the forty plays of which Shakespeare wrote a substantial part (adding *Edward III*, *Pericles*, *The Two Noble Kinsmen*, and the lost *Cardenio* to the thirty-six plays in the First Folio) into two chronological halves, the first half ending with *Much Ado about Nothing* (1598) and *Henry V* (1598–99). By 1600, fifteen or all but five of the first twenty plays were in print, and more than half of them had reached at least a second edition.

In the course of the 1590s, the title pages of Shakespearean playbooks underwent some transformation. What is prominent on one of the earliest is the summary of the plot's most salient features. The play that came later to be called *The Second Part of Henry VI* was printed in 1594 as:

THE First part of the Contention betwixt the two famous Houses of Yorke and Lancaster. With the death of the good Duke Humphrey: And the banishment and death of the Duke of Suffolke, and the Tragicall end of the proud Cardinall of Winchester, with the notable Rebellion of Iacke Cade, And the Duke of Yorkes first claime vnto the Crowne.

Titus Andronicus, the other Shakespeare play printed in 1594, gives unusually detailed information about the play's company connections: "As it was

Plaide by the Right Honourable the Earle of Darbie, Earle of Pembrooke, and Earle of Sussex their Seruants." Neither text published in 1594 contains any indications about the playwright's name, nor does the "bad" quarto (in fact: octavo) of *3 Henry VI*, the only Shakespeare play printed in 1595. By 1597, quarto/octavo editions of seven of Shakespeare's plays had been published, all giving information about the plot, or evidence of performance, or both, but all lacking any indication about their author.[1]

In *From Playhouse to Printing House: Drama and Authorship in Early Modern England*, Douglas A. Brooks has recently tried to account for the emergence of Shakespeare's name on title pages of his printed plays. Highlighting the words "Written by William Shakespeare" on the title page of the first quarto of *2 Henry IV* (1600), Brooks claims that it is "extraordinarily significant that the first title page to attribute the writing of a play to Shakespeare belongs to a play which appears after its prequel, *1 Henry IV*, had recently embroiled our playwright in something of a political – and perhaps religious – scandal."[2] The assertion that the title page of *2 Henry IV* contains "the first instance of an unambiguously authorial attribution to Shakespeare on the title page of an early modern play" is so central to Brooks's argument that he repeats it no fewer than six times.[3] According to Brooks, the construction of Shakespeare's authorship is thus a direct result of the quarrel over *Henry IV* resulting in the renaming of Sir John Oldcastle as Falstaff. In Brooks's neat narrative – into which even Foucault's argument that the author comes into existence qua transgression fits – "the author-function comes to lodge itself where previously the martyr-function served to individualize and embody England's national consciousness."[4]

There would be no need to rehearse Brooks's argument at such length if its publication by a reputed press did not grant it wide circulation. For his narrative is as tempting as it is mistaken. The quarto edition of *2 Henry IV* of 1600 is in fact not the first, as Brooks claims, but the sixth edition of a playtext that gives evidence of Shakespeare's authorship on the title page. Even if we discount the 1598 quarto of *Love's Labour's Lost* and the 1599 quarto of *1 Henry IV*, which ambiguously assert that they have been "Newly corrected and augmented / By W. Shakespere" and "Newly corrected by W. Shakespeare," we are still left with the second quarto of *Richard III* and the second and third quartos of *Richard II*, published in 1598, which are unambiguously said to be "By William Shake-speare." Brooks has simply

---

[1] *Love's Labour's Lost* had also been published by 1597 (see below, p. 85), but since we have no information about the title page of the non-extant edition, I exclude the play from this count.
[2] Brooks, *Playhouse to Printing House*, 73.
[3] Ibid., 71, and repeated on pages 73, 79–80, 95, 99, 103, and 133.   [4] Ibid., 95.

failed to consult any edition of Shakespeare's early quartos except the first (see Figures 5 to 8).

Brooks's oversight is all the more serious as it is precisely the replacement of an anonymous edition by an authored one that is unusual and in need of explanation. A good many Elizabethan and Jacobean playbooks were either published anonymously or with the author's name on the title page. For an anonymously published play to be ascribed to a playwright in a later edition was an extremely rare phenomenon, however. *Mucedorous* went through sixteen editions by 1668, *The Spanish Tragedy* through eleven by 1633, *The First Part of If You Know Not Me You Know Nobody* through eight by 1639, and *Tamburlaine* through four by 1606. What they have in common is that all editions were equally silent about the identity of their author. Most title pages slavishly followed that of the preceding edition: the eighth quarto edition of *1 Henry IV* (1639) still announces, like the edition of 1599, that it is "Newly corrected, By William Shakespeare." How little the wording changed can also be gathered from the fact that up to the third edition (1611), *Doctor Faustus* is said to be "Written by Ch. Marl.," while the fourth (1616) and all the following editions until the tenth (1663) has "Written by Ch. Mar." Apart from *Richard II*, *Richard III*, and *1 Henry IV*, there are hardly any exceptions – and none during Shakespeare's lifetime as far as I am aware – to the rule that once a play had been published anonymously, it remained so in the following editions.[5]

So *pace* Brooks, it was in 1598 that things suddenly changed with no fewer than four editions featuring Shakespeare's name on the title page. Only one edition, the first extant quarto of *1 Henry IV*, was published anonymously, though a year later, when the following edition appeared, it was (incorrectly) said to be "Newly corrected by W. Shakespeare."[6] In 1600, another five plays were published, four of which (*2 Henry IV*, *A Midsummer Night's Dream*, *The Merchant of Venice*, and *Much Ado about Nothing*) announced

---

[5] This obviously does not apply to collections such as the Shakespeare Folios. There are only a few exceptions of which I am aware: The fourth, undated quarto of *Romeo and Juliet* (*c*. 1618–26) is the first to assert Shakespeare's authorship, though only some of the extant copies do so. The other exceptions are even later: Q1613 of *The Knight of the Burning Pestle* is anonymous, while the second quarto of 1635 is said to be "Written by Francis Beaumont and John Fletcher, Gent." Similarly, Q1607 of *The Woman Hater* bears no author ascription, while Q1648 has "Written by John Fletcher Gent.," and Q1649 "Written by Francis Beaumont and John Fletcher Gent." Q1607 of *Bussy D'Ambois* was published anonymously; the second edition of 1641 was reissued three times, the third of 1657 being the first to bear Chapman's name on the title page. Another, non-dramatic, exception is Shakespeare's *The Rape of Lucrece*: not before the ninth edition of 1616 did the title page assert Shakespeare's authorship.

[6] There had been an earlier edition of *1 Henry IV* of which only a fragment of a single copy is extant. It has traditionally been referred to as Q0, though Wells and Taylor (*Textual Companion*, 329) prefer to call it Q1. As the title-page of the mostly lost edition is not extant, I retain the earlier convention, thus calling the first fully extant edition "Q1."

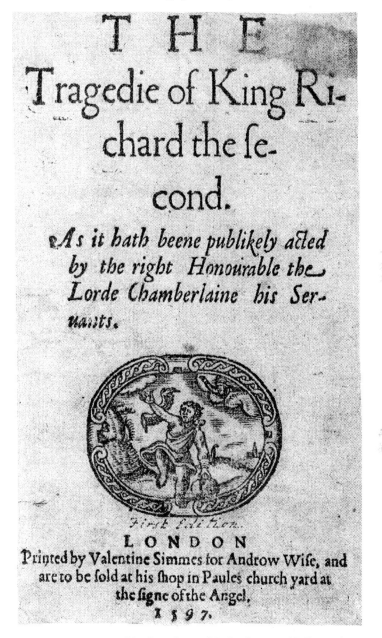

Figure 5. Title page of the first edition of *Richard II*, 1597 (*STC* 22307), published anonymously.

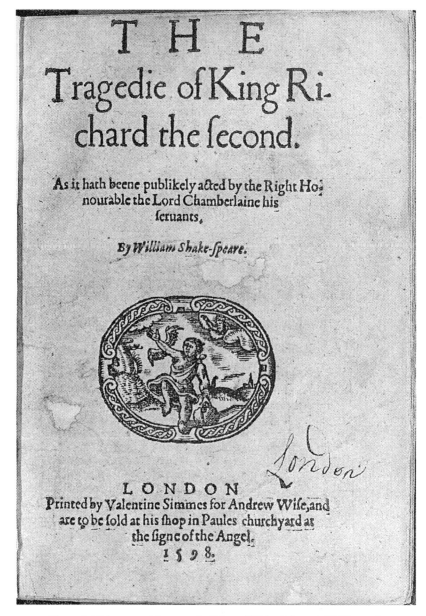

Figure 6. Title page of the second edition of *Richard II*, 1598 (*STC* 22308),
attributed to Shakespeare.

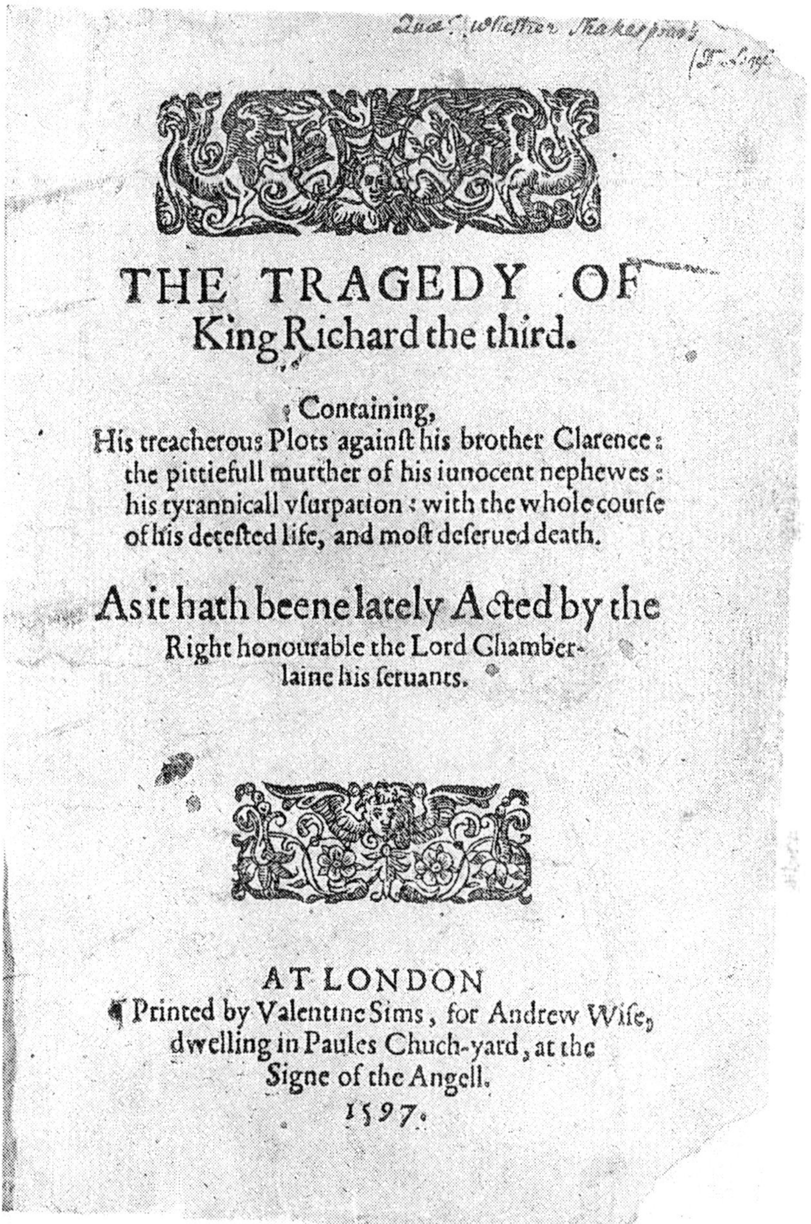

THE TRAGEDY OF
King Richard the third.

Containing,
His treacherous Plots againſt his brother Clarence:
the pittiefull murther of his iunocent nephewes:
his tyrannicall vſurpation: with the whole courſe
of his deteſted life, and moſt deſerued death.

As it hath beene lately Acted by the
Right honourable the Lord Chamberlaine his ſeruants.

AT LONDON
Printed by Valentine Sims, for Andrew Wiſe,
dwelling in Paules Chuch-yard, at the
Signe of the Angell.
1597.

Figure 7. Title page of the first edition of *Richard III*, 1597 (*STC* 22314),
published anonymously.

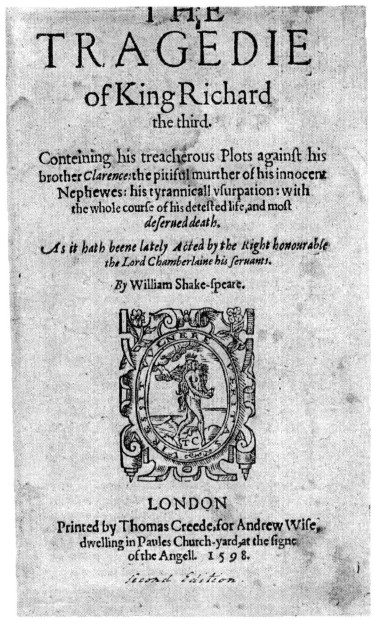

THE
TRAGEDIE
of King Richard
the third.

Conteining his treacherous Plots againſt his
brother *Clarence:* the pitiful murther of his innocent
Nephewes: his tyrannicall vſurpation : with
the whole courſe of his deteſted life, and moſt
deſerued death.

*As it hath beene lately Acted by the Right honourable
the Lord Chamberlaine his ſeruants.*

By William Shake-ſpeare.

LONDON

Printed by Thomas Creede, for Andrew Wiſe,
dwelling in Paules Church-yard, at the ſigne
of the Angell. 1 5 9 8.

ſecond Edition.

Figure 8. Title page of the second edition of *Richard III*, 1598 (*STC* 22315),
attributed to Shakespeare.

Shakespeare's authorship on the title page. Only the first quarto of *Henry V* (a so-called "bad" quarto) was published anonymously. In the same year, Shakespeare's name appears for the first time in the Stationers' Register: according to an entry dated August 23, 1600, *Much Ado about Nothing* was "Wrytten by master Shakespere." More than two decades later, the publisher Thomas Walkley wrote in the preface to the first quarto of *Othello* (1622) that "the Authors name is sufficient to vent his worke" (A2^r). The comment to be made about this assertion is not so much, it seems to me, that "this was not true at the end of the sixteenth century," than that the various title pages bearing Shakespeare's name suggest that to a certain, admittedly lesser, extent it already *was* true.[7] If we consider the suddenness and the frequency with which Shakespeare's name appears on title pages of printed playbooks from 1598 to 1600, it is no exaggeration to say that in one sense, "Shakespeare," author of dramatic texts, was born in the space of two or three years at the end of the sixteenth century.[8]

Shakespeare was by no means the only playwright whose early progress toward authorship is reflected in the early publication history. Marlowe's *Tamburlaine* appeared anonymously in 1590, yet, in 1594, *The Massacre at Paris* was "Written by Christopher Marlow," *Edward the Second* was "Written by Chri. Marlow Gent," and *Dido, Queen of Carthage* was "Written by Christopher Marlowe, and Thomas Nashe. Gent." Lyly had to wait longer until the first printed playtext acknowledged his dramatic authorship: six plays in a total of eleven editions had appeared anonymously before the 1597 quarto edition of *The Woman in the Moon* was acknowledged to be "By Iohn Lyllie maister of Artes." The publication of Peele's plays shows a development in four steps: the title page of the 1584 quarto of *The Arraignment of Paris* is silent about the play's authorship. So is the title page of the 1593 quarto of *Edward I*, but the explicit has "By George Peele Maister of Artes in Oxenford." The title page of *The Old Wives Tale* of 1595 at least contains the playwright's initials: "Written by G. P." The 1599 quarto of *David and Bethsabe*, finally, announces on its title page that it was "Written by George Peele."

---

7 Berger and Lander, "Shakespeare in Print," 405. Notice that Berger and Lander's "Chronology of publication" table (411), purporting to list the publications of Shakespeare's works from 1593 to 1640, fails to list the second editions of *The First Part of the Contention* (2 *Henry VI*) and of *Richard Duke of York* (3 *Henry VI*), both of 1600, the third edition of *Richard Duke of York* of 1619, and the fifth edition of *Richard III* of 1612.

8 It is perhaps a coincidence worth noting that, while 1598 began the making of "Shakespeare," the dramatic author, the same year, owing to the publication of Speght's *Works*, was also crucial for the making of "Chaucer." See Tim William Machan, "Speght's *Works* and the Invention of Chaucer," *TEXT: An Interdisciplinary Annual of Textual Studies*, 8 (1995), 145–70.

With several playwrights of the next generation, a similar picture emerges, though the number of anonymous plays diminishes. The example of Dekker will suffice here: *The Shoemaker's Holiday* was published anonymously in 1600. The same year, *Old Fortunatus* appeared mentioning the name of "Tho. Dekker" in the explicit. *Satiromastix* (1602), finally, was published as "By Thomas Dekker," as were *The Whore of Babylon* (1607) and *If It Be Not Good, the Devil Is in It* (1612). Many of England's early dramatic authors, it appears, were born within a few years of 1600.

As we have seen, the dramatic authorship of Lyly, Peele, and Dekker emerged rather slowly. In fact, no playwright's name appears as suddenly and as often as Shakespeare's does between 1598 and 1600. In 1597, a purchaser of books in St. Paul's Churchyard could have been aware of an author of two narrative poems called Shakespeare. Yet only three years later, browsing in the bookshops would have made it clear that publishers and booksellers now expected the name "Shakespeare" to sell plays. The evidence suggests that around the year 1598 something happened that changed the marketability of Shakespeare's name.

In the search for a cause, we first need to eliminate what I think are two false leads. Shortly before 1598, Falstaff seems to have had tremendous success on stage. Yet there is little evidence suggesting that his popularity was generally associated with Shakespeare. It may be well to remember that Tamburlaine and Hieronimo were tremendously popular characters but that hardly anyone in the late sixteenth and early seventeenth century seems to have associated them with Marlowe and Kyd. Another explanation we might be tempted to advance for the advent of Shakespeare's name on the title page of playbooks is the playwright's social mobility. Shakespeare had become a gentleman of means by 1598. Late in 1596 or in 1597, the Shakespeares had acquired a coat of arms. William could now refer to himself as a gentleman. That Shakespeare was wealthy can be gathered from the only extant letter addressed to Shakespeare, dated October 25, 1598. It is a request from his Stratford acquaintance Richard Quiney for a loan of £30, a request Shakespeare seems to have agreed to meet.[9] Yet, even though there was a relationship between dramatic authorship and social status in

---

[9] See Schoenbaum, *William Shakespeare*, 238–40. The following quotation may serve to shed some light on how much this amount corresponds to: "It has been estimated that during the last part of the sixteenth century a schoolmaster earned between £12 and £20 annually which probably did not include other perquisites such as board or lodging. A workman made sixpence a day with food, and ten pence without. Wages at this latter rate for a six-day week over a full year would amount to between £12 and £13. At the other end of the social scale, Thomas Lodge estimated that a gentleman could live comfortably on £40 a year. Allowing for inflation, therefore, we might suppose that in

the late sixteenth century, Shakespeare's social mobility does not seem to account for the appearance of his name on title pages from 1598. In fact, it was not until 1619, when the Pavier quarto of *1 Contention* was said to be "Written by W. Shakespere, Gent.," that a title page gives evidence of Shakespeare's gentlemanly status.

What seems more significant is that 1598 is the year in which Francis Meres's *Palladis Tamia* was published. Its "Comparatiue Discourse of our English Poets with the Greeke, Latine, and Italian Poets" is often quoted, and phrases such as "our best for Tragedie" (283^r) or "his sugred Sonnets among his priuate friends" (281^v–282^r) have long earned Meres immortality. It has received little attention as a whole, however, and its author is often disparaged.[10] Samuel Schoenbaum called him "a writer of disarming witlessness,"[11] and C. S. Lewis wrote that the "Comparatiue Discourse" bears "about the same relation to real criticism as Fluellen's comparison of Macedon and Monmouth bears to real geography."[12] Of course, it is not "real criticism," nor was it meant to be. Though it consists of little more than a succession of comparisons (as the ancient . . . so we English . . .), it is a fascinating attempt at the formation of an English literary canon *avant la lettre*.

Meres's "Comparatiue Discourse" falls into three parts. In the first, Meres treats the English writers of the past, in particular Chaucer, "the God of English poets" (314). The last part is little more than an appendix, commenting on the different genres in past and present literature. Between the two comes the part that is best known today, consisting of a series of comparisons between contemporary or near-contemporary English poets and Greek, Latin, or Italian poets. Six English poets are singled out for special praise, Sidney, Spenser, Daniel, Drayton, Warner, and Shakespeare, all of them being given several paragraphs. Although Schoenbaum called Meres "a remarkably undiscriminating panegyrist,"[13] the five poets in Shakespeare's company are a reasonable choice at the time it was made. The mention of Sidney, the paragon of his age, and Spenser, whose *Faerie Queene* had

---

1600 an income of £15 a year would have been considered equivalent to a working-class wage, and that to live like a 'gentleman' would require two or three times that amount" (Carson, *Companion to Henslowe's Diary*, 66).

[10] For a fully, though not always reliably, annotated edition, see Don Cameron Allen, ed., *Francis Meres's Treatise "Poetrie": A Critical Edition*, University of Illinois Studies in Language and Literature (Urbana: University of Illinois Press, 1933). I quote from Arthur Freeman's more easily accessible *Palladis Tamia: Wits Treasury* (New York: Garland, 1973).

[11] Schoenbaum, *William Shakespeare*, 192.

[12] *Poetry and Prose in the Sixteenth Century*, Oxford History of English Literature, 4 (originally numbered 3) (Oxford: Clarendon Press, 1954), 430.

[13] Schoenbaum, *William Shakespeare*, 192.

been published in 1590 (in three books) and in 1596 (in six books), needs no lengthy explanation. If we remember that the sixteenth century did not yet separate poetry and history the way later centuries did, the presence of Daniel, Drayton, and Warner stops being surprising. Samuel Daniel was a prestigious courtly poet and may well be the poet of superior genius referred to in Shakespeare's Sonnet 80.[14] Of his works had appeared not only the highly esteemed sonnet collection *Delia* (1592) and the closet tragedy *Cleopatra* (1594), but also the first four books of his *Civil Wars*, a verse epic on the Wars of the Roses (1595). The first edition of his collected works was to be published only three years after *Palladis Tamia*. Michael Drayton had had a series of verse histories published (even though his *Poly-Olbion* was not to be printed for another fourteen years): *Peirs Gaveston* (n.d., entered December 3, 1593, rpt. 1595 and 1596), *Robert, Duke of Normandy* (1596), and *Mortimeriados* (1596). *England's Heroical Epistles* had appeared in 1597 and were to go through five editions within as many years. These had been preceded by volumes of pastoral eclogues modeled on Spenser's *Shepheardes Calender* (*Idea. The Shepheardes Garland*, 1593), short lyrics (*Ideas Mirrour*, 1594), narrative poetry (*Endimion and Phoebe*, 1595), and a secular saint's life (*Matilda*, 1594). Though little read today, Drayton was much appreciated and published in 1598, and had acquired a considerable reputation.[15] His portrait painted in 1599 (now in the National Portrait Gallery) shows him with the poet's laurel wreath. Finally, William Warner's then famous and influential verse chronicle *Albion's England* had been published in four books in 1586, and enlarged in the editions of 1589, 1592, and 1596 to six, nine, and twelve books respectively. How reasonable choices Daniel, Drayton, and Warner were can also be gathered from the poetic anthology *England's Parnassus* published in 1600. Of the more than fifty poets quoted from, only Spenser (386) has more passages than Drayton (225), Warner (171), and Daniel (140).[16]

---

[14] "O how I faint when I of you do write, / Knowing a better spirit doth use your name" (Sonnet 80.1–2), "better spirit" being glossed as "a poet of superior genius" by G. Blakemore Evans in his New Cambridge Shakespeare edition (Cambridge University Press, 1996), 186. Hyder Rollins's *New Variorum Edition of Shakespeare: The Sonnets*, 2 vols. (Philadelphia and London: Lippincott, 1944) sums up the arguments for the various contenders (11.277–94).

[15] Drayton's reputation remained high in the following century: "In late-seventeenth-century estimates of literary stature, Michael Drayton ranks only slightly below Sir Philip Sidney, Edmund Spenser, and Ben Jonson" (Jean R. Brink, "Michael Drayton," in *Seventeenth-Century British Nondramatic Poets*, ed. M. Thomas Hester, 1st series (Detroit: Gale Research Company, 1992), 97–109).

[16] With ninety-five passages, Shakespeare is quoted less often not only than Spenser, Drayton, Warner, and Daniel, but also than Sir John Harington (all quotations from *Orlando Furioso*), Joshua Sylvester, and Thomas Lodge. Sidney, surprisingly, only received fifty-seven passages. See Allot, comp., *Englands Parnassus*, xliii.

Meres thus places Shakespeare, "the most excellent in both kinds for the stage" (282ʳ), amidst the literary giants of his own time. Though this may not be surprising from the vantage point of literary history, it must have been at the end of the sixteenth century. While Meres has been called "a gossip and a somewhat derivative critic,"[17] the importance he gives to Shakespeare at a time when his name had not appeared on a single title page seems more prophetic than derivative. Only *Venus and Adonis* (1593) and *The Rape of Lucrece* (1594) had been published under Shakespeare's name before 1598.[18] Few surviving documents bear witness to an earlier rise of Shakespeare's reputation. Biographers have liked to believe that Chettle's reference of 1592 to a playwright that is esteemed by "diuers of worship" and of whom he praises the "facetious grace in writting" is to Shakespeare, though it seems more likely that the reference is in fact to Peele.[19] Earlier the same year, Greene had placed Shakespeare among the players, the "rude groomes," "Apes," and "Puppets... that spake from our mouths."[20] That Shakespeare's social standing suffered from his acting is not only suggested by *Greene's Groatsworth of Wit*. In 1611, John Davies of Hereford addressed Shakespeare in his Epigram 159:

> Some say good *Will* (which I, in sport, do sing)
> Had'st thou not plaid some Kingly parts in sport,
> Thou hadst bin a companion for a *King*;
> And, beene a King among the meaner sort.[21]

Shakespeare himself seems to suggest something similar in Sonnet 111:

> O, for my sake do you with Fortune chide,
> The guilty goddess of my harmful deeds,
> That did not better for my life provide
> Than public means which public manners breeds.
> Thence comes it that my name receives a brand,
> And almost thence my nature is subdued
> To what it works in, like the dyer's hand.   (1–7)

If we remind ourselves of the reputation Shakespeare – player and provider for the stage – had had and, to a certain degree, continued to have, we

---

[17] R. H. MacDonald, *The Library of Drummond of Hawthornden* (Edinburgh University Press, 1971), 138.

[18] Note that, although Shakespeare's name did not appear on the earliest title pages, it was printed at the end of the dedications.

[19] See my "Biography and Mythography: Rereading Chettle's Alleged Apology to Shakespeare', *English Studies*, 79 (1998), 430–40. Quotations are from *Kind-Hartes Dreame*, ed. G. B. Harrison, The Bodley Head Quartos, 4 (London: John Lane, 1923), 6.

[20] I quote from *Greene's Groatsworth of Wit*, ed. Carroll, lines 951, 945, 934.

[21] I quote from *Complete Works*, ed. Grosart, 11.26.

realize that Shakespeare's appearance alongside Sir Philip Sidney, Edmund Spenser, and other literary worthies of his age in 1598 comes as much out of nowhere as the massed appearance of Shakespeare's name on the title pages of his plays starting the same year.

Palladis Tamia was entered in the Stationers' Register by Cuthbert Burby on September 7, 1598. Q1 *Richard III* and Q1 *Richard II* (both dated 1597) must have been, and Q1 *1 Henry IV* (dated 1598 and entered by Andrew Wise on February 25, 1598 (new style)) is likely to have been, published earlier. Q2 and Q3 *Richard II*, Q2 *Richard III*, and Q1 *Love's Labour's Lost* (all four dated 1598) may have been, Q2 *1 Henry IV* (1599) must have been, published later. If we remember that the former texts were published anonymously and that the latter were not, it seems possible that Meres's promotion of Shakespeare to the top of the canon of recent and contemporary English poets is responsible for his name's appearance on the title pages of his plays.

It seems unlikely that Wise, in 1598, had both editions of *Richard II* printed *after* the appearance of *Palladis Tamia*. It may well be, however, that Wise found out about *Palladis Tamia* and Shakespeare's role in it before its appearance. After all, it would have been in the publishers' and booksellers' best interest to be aware as early as possible of a text which, by dealing with literary reputation, might have an effect upon their customers' future demand. The printer Peter Short may well have provided Wise with the necessary information. Short not only printed *Palladis Tamia* for Burby, but also did business with Wise for whom he printed a part of Q1 *Richard III* in 1597, John Racster's *Book of the Seven Planets* (1598 – *STC* 20601), and both editions of *1 Henry IV* in 1598. The latter play had been entered as early as February 1598, however, probably too early for Short to have had knowledge of *Palladis Tamia* when printing the play without mentioning Shakespeare's authorship. Later in the year, however, Short may well have been in a position to tell Wise about *Palladis Tamia*. It seems a distinct possibility that the emergence of "Shakespeare," the dramatic author, in 1598 owed something to Meres's *Palladis Tamia*.

What lends further credibility to the theory that *Palladis Tamia* turned "Shakespeare" into a name with which publishers expected to make money is the 1599 publication of *The Passionate Pilgrim*. Containing Shakespeare's sonnets 138 and 144, three sonnets from *Love's Labour's Lost* and fifteen non-Shakespearean poems, this collection, published by William Jaggard, was ascribed to Shakespeare on the title page.[22] Meres had famously praised

---

[22] It may be interesting to note that not all of Shakespeare's contemporaries were taken in by the attribution of the entire collection to Shakespeare. The following year saw the publication of

Shakespeare's "sugred Sonnets" a few months earlier.[23] Like Wise and Burby (the publisher of *Love's Labour's Lost*), Jaggard may well have tried to cash in on the promotion Meres had provided. The strategy would seem to have been successful considering two editions of *The Passionate Pilgrim* were published in 1599.[24]

Within the next ten years, four non-Shakespearean plays with title pages bearing his name or initials show evidence of further attempts to make money with his name: "THE True Chronicle Historie of the whole life and death of Thomas Lord Cromwell. As it hath beene sundrie times publikely Acted by the Right Honorable the Lord Chamberlaine his Seruants. Written by W. S." (1602); "THE LONDON Prodigall. As it was plaide by the Kings Maiesties seruants. By William Shakespeare" (1605); "THE PVRITAINE OR THE WIDDOVV of Watling-street. Acted by the Children of Paules. Written by W. S." (1607); and "A YORKSHIRE Tragedy. Not so New as Lamentable and true. Acted by his Maiesties Players at the Globe. Written by W. Shakespeare" (1608).[25] Meres's *Palladis Tamia* and the Shakespearean playbooks of 1598 seem to have initiated a whole series of attempts to capitalize on the name of Shakespeare.[26]

At a surprisingly early time, then, Meres lists Shakespeare, the dramatic author, among the greatest contemporary poets. This surely poses a problem if we believe that playbooks had to await the publication of Jonson's *Workes* until anyone started taking them seriously as dramatic *literature*. We may be tempted to argue that Meres simply noticed Shakespeare's greatness, a greatness that seems so obvious to anyone today that there would seem to

---

England's Helicon, a miscellany that reprints five of the poems in *Passionate Pilgrim*, attributing only one of them, correctly, to Shakespeare. See *England's Helicon*, ed. Hyder Edward Rollins, 2 vols. (Cambridge, Mass.: Harvard University Press, 1935), 11.31, 114–15, 117, 186–87, 189–90.

[23] See John Roe, ed., *The Poems*, New Cambridge Shakespeare (Cambridge University Press, 1992), 54–55.

[24] See Joseph Quincy Adams, ed., *The Passionate Pilgrim* (New York: Charles Scribner's Sons, 1939), xi–xxxvi.

[25] The second quarto of *The Troublesome Raigne of King John* (1611), "Written by W. Sh." and the third edition of *The Passionate Pilgrim* (1612), "By W. Shakespeare," are further attempts to profit from Shakespeare's name, as are Q2 *Thomas Lord Cromwell* (1613), the "Pavier quartos" of *A Yorkshire Tragedy* and *Sir John Oldcastle* (1619), and the third quarto of *Troublesome Raigne* (1622). So is, perhaps, *A Funerall Ellegye in memory of the late vertuous Maister William Peter*, "By W. S." See Brian Vickers, *Counterfeiting Shakespeare: Evidence, Authorship, and John Ford's "Funerall Elegye"* (Cambridge University Press, 2002).

[26] As Blayney has rightly pointed out, the fact that Shakespeare's name was so used should not blind us to the fact that the drawing power of Shakespeare's name toward the end of the playwright's career remained quite low. The two quartos which give special prominence to his name on their title-page, the 1608 *History of King Lear* and the 1609 *Shakespeare's Sonnets*, were not quickly succeeded by further editions. *King Lear* was not reprinted until 1619 and even then only as part of a collection. *Shakespeare's Sonnets* was not reprinted until 1640 (see Blayney, *Texts of "King Lear,"* 82–83).

be nothing surprising about Meres having been aware of it in 1598. Such a view, however, is clearly in danger of being anachronistic. It may then be that Meres put Shakespeare among the literary worthies of his time because there was nothing inherently implausible about considering playbooks as literature as early as 1598.

Edmund Bolton's "Enumeration of the best Authors for written English," which also predates Shakespeare's death and the publication of Jonson's *Workes*, corroborates such a view. It is somewhat more difficult to denigrate Bolton as a half-wit than Meres. Having been at Trinity Hall, Cambridge, and the Inner Temple, Bolton later became a respected and well-published historian with access to the King. His design for a royal academy or college, an order of men of science and literature whose tasks would have included the superintendence of all books of secular learning printed in England, found King James's support. Its accomplishment appears only to have been prevented by the King's death and his son's relative indifference to it. Clearly, Bolton was an influential person of learning who had precise ideas about secular literature. He wrote that "hee who would penn our affaires in English, and compose unto us an entire body of them, ought to have a singular care ther of," but "fewe there be who have the most proper graces thereof." Bolton goes on to give his list of what the title calls "the best Authors for written English":[27]

the books . . . out of which wee gather the most warrantable English are not many . . . But among the cheife, or rather the cheife, are in my opinion these.
Sʳ Thomas Moore's works
*   *   *   *
George Chapmans first seaven book of Iliades.
Samuell Danyell.
Michael Drayton his Heroicall Epistles of England.
Marlowe his excellent fragment of Hero and Leander.
Shakespere, Mʳ Francis Beaumont, & innumerable other writers for the stage;
    and presse tenderly to be used in this Argument.
Southwell, Parsons, & some fewe other of that sort.

Despite its Catholic inflection,[28] Bolton's is arguably a very discerning canon, even though the omission of Jonson is surprising. The chief

---

[27] Bolton's "Enumeration of the best Authors for written English" is among the Rawlinson manuscripts in the Bodleian Library in Oxford. I quote from C. M. Ingleby, comp., *The Shakespeare Allusion-Book*, 2 vols. (London: Chatto & Windus, 1909), 1.213.

[28] The composition of this list of names, headed by More and concluded by Southwell and Parsons, leads one to suspect that Bolton was a Catholic, a suspicion which the *Dictionary of National Biography* confirms (11.787–89). Note that Bolton wrote a life of Henry II that was originally intended to be included in an edition of Speed's *Chronicle* but was rejected on the grounds that

importance of Bolton's list in this context, however, is that the inclusion of Shakespeare and Beaumont besides "innumerable other writers for the stage" again suggests that playbooks were not considered sub-literary ephemera.

I have tried to suggest that the social *cachet* of printed playbooks increased well before the advent of Ben Jonson and the publication of his *Workes* in folio in 1616. The gradual advent of plays as literature is signaled, firstly, by the interventions of publishers such as Richard Jones and Edward White who, as early as the beginning of the 1590s, shape dramatic texts in such a way as to adapt them for the needs of readers; secondly, by the increasing frequency with which dramatic texts that have been spoken on the public stage are authorized in their printed form by the appearance of the playwright's name on the title page, and, thirdly, by the emergence of "Shakespeare" not only on the title pages of playbooks but also in literary canons such as Meres's and Bolton's.

In the Introduction, I briefly touched upon an early literary anthology and its inclusion of passages from Shakespeare's plays. I still need to establish fully, however, how these anthologies comment upon the respectability printed plays in general and printed "Shakespeare" in particular had reached by the turn of the century. Two literary anthologies were published in 1600, *England's Parnassus*, compiled by Robert Allot, and *Belvedere, or the Garden of the Muses*, edited by "A. M." (probably Anthony Munday). In *England's Parnassus*, Allot compiles an important number of verse passages, chiefly from Elizabethan poets, Spenser and Sidney, Daniel and Drayton, Harington and Warner, among many others. In keeping with this, the title page announces "The choysest Flowers of our Moderne Poets." It may then be surprising to notice that there are no fewer than twenty-three plays among the works quoted. One of them is an Inns of Court tragedy (Gascoigne and Kinwelmarshe's *Jocasta*) and four others are either closet tragedies (Daniel's *Musophilus* and *Cleopatra*) or a translation (Munday's *Fedele and Fortunio*) or both (Kyd's *Cornelia*). The remaining seventeen plays were written for the public stage, however. Eight playwrights are represented: four who were dead by 1600 (Marlowe, Greene, Peele) or had ceased writing for the stage (Lodge), three who were beginning to outgrow their years as hack writers for Henslowe (Jonson, Chapman, and Dekker),

the life provided too favorable an account of Thomas of Canterbury (see Sir Leslie Stephen and Sir Sidney Lee, eds., *The Dictionary of National Biography* (henceforth: *DNB*), 22 vols. (Oxford: Smith, Elder, & Co., 1885–1901), 11.787).

and Shakespeare. The following list summarizes the number of quotations from the various commercial plays in Allot's anthology:[29]

Chapman, George, *The Blind Beggar of Alexandria*	I
Dekker, Thomas, *Old Fortunatus*	13
Greene, Robert, *Orlando Furioso*[30]	6
Friar Bacon and Friar Bungay	2
James IV of Scotland	3
Selimus	6
and Th. Lodge, *A Looking Glass for London and England*[31]	5
Jonson, Benjamin, *Every Man in his Humour*	2
Every Man out of his Humour	7
Marlowe, Christopher, *The Massacre at Paris*	I
Peele, George, *David and Bethsabe*	3
The Battle of Alcazar	2
Shakespeare, William, *Love's Labour's Lost*	3
Richard II	7
Richard III	5
1 Henry IV	2
Romeo and Juliet	13

With five plays and a total of thirty passages (of eighty-one in all), Shakespeare's plays are more generously represented than those of any other playwright. Rather unexpectedly, even though *Dido, Queen of Carthage, Edward II*, *The Massacre at Paris*, and *Tamburlaine* had all been published, only *The Massacre at Paris* among Marlowe's plays is quoted, and even that play only once. Marlowe's portion of *Hero and Leander*, in contrast, is made use of no fewer than thirty-two times.

---

[29] All but one of the plays from which Allot quotes had been published in the 1590s or in 1600 (*Every Man out of his Humour*). It should be noted, however, that Jonson's *Every Man in his Humour* was not printed until 1601 and that, consequently, the passages in the anthology seem to have been copied from a manuscript. Note that *Selimus* and *The Battle of Alcazar* were published anonymously and that Greene's authorship of the former and Peele's of the latter – which chiefly rely upon Allot's attribution of the various passages in *England's Parnassus* – are not always accepted.

[30] *Orlando Furioso* was published anonymously, but the 1592 pamphlet *A Defence of Coney-Catching* establishes Greene's authorship: "Maister R. G. would it not make you blush – if you sold Orlando Furioso to the queenes players for twenty nobles, and when they were in the country, sold the same play to Lord Admiral's men, for as much more? Was not this plain coney-catching, M. G.?" (quoted from Evelyn May Albright, *Dramatic Publication in England, 1580–1640: A Study of Conditions Affecting Content and Form of Drama* (London: Oxford University Press, 1927), 222–23).

[31] Note that the passages from *A Looking Glass for London and England*, which the title page of the first quarto attributes to Greene and Lodge, are attributed either to Greene or to Lodge. Nothing suggests that Allot's attributions are more than conjectures.

Allot's excerpts are consistently (and in general correctly) attributed to authors. It is then understandable that when passages were selected, the presence on the title page of an author to whom the passages could be attributed was a criterion for inclusion in Allot's compilation. As we have seen, a majority of the plays written for the public stage and printed before the turn of the century was published anonymously. Less than one in three of the plays published in the 1580s and 1590s bears the playwright's (or playwrights') name on the title page (see Appendix A). In contrast, when it comes to the plays in *England's Parnassus*, fifteen of the seventeen plays Allot quotes from had been published by the time the compilation was printed. Twelve of these – or three in four – had been attributed to an author or, in the case of Greene and Lodge's *A Looking-Glass for London and England*, to authors.[32] The difference could hardly be more conspicuous. While passages from a number of stage plays were included among "The choysest Flowers of our Moderne Poets" as early as 1600, the legitimation thus bestowed upon early modern playbooks was clearly facilitated by the presence of an author's name on the title page.

In *England's Parnassus*, nothing suggests that while the poetical worthies of the Elizabethan age were considered respectable, playwrights were not. Regular playgoers and readers with well-trained memories must have noticed that verses they had read in authorized editions of some of England's greatest poets occurred side by side with lines they had heard at the Rose, the Fortune or, more recently, the Globe. Various passages Allot compiled on the subject of "Grief" contain excerpts from Spenser's *Faerie Queene*, Sidney's *Arcadia*, Harington's translation of *Orlando Furioso*, but also an excerpt from Lady Capulet's admonition to Juliet that "Some grief shows much of love, / But much of grief shows still some want of wit" (3.5.72–73). The texts from which passages on the topic of "Words" are taken include Edward Fairfax's *Godfrey of Bulloigne*, a translation of Tasso's *Gerusalemme Liberata*, Warner's *Albion's England*, *The Faerie Queene*, *A Mirror for Magistrates* and Shakespeare's *Richard III* (4.4.126–31). Not only Drayton's *Civil Wars*, Daniel's *Cleopatra*, and *Albion's England*, but also Shakespeare's *Richard II* (3.2.54–57) are drawn upon to illustrate the subject of "Kings," while lines from Sidney's *Astrophil and Stella*, Drayton's *Mortimeriados*, *A Mirror for Magistrates* along with Shakespeare's *1 Henry IV* (5.2.9–11) illustrate the subject of "Treason."[33]

---

[32] Note that, while the title page of *Old Fortunatus* does not mention Dekker's authorship, the play is signed "Tho. Dekker" in the explicit.

[33] Allot, comp., *England's Parnassus*, 97, 228–29, 119–21, 214–15.

That Shakespeare's and other plays should have a place in a poetical anthology of 1600 may not seem extraordinary from our modern vantage point. It bears repeating then what students of English Renaissance drama have long been told. For instance, in "The Publication of English Renaissance Plays" (1987), Fredson Bowers, one of the most influential twentieth-century scholars in the field, wrote that "plays were not regarded as 'literature' but as relatively ephemeral entertainment reading on no higher plane than, say, a novel made from the script of a popular moving picture."[34] This is in line with the opinion of many others who, like Andrew Gurr, believe that Elizabethan playwrights, typically, never "gave a thought to posterity."[35] Yet it seems difficult to imagine passages from "the script of a popular moving picture" in a modern literary anthology. Bowers insists, however, that "the key to understanding [the] original status [of English Renaissance plays] is the recognition that in their own day they were not highly regarded except as entertainment, without literary value."[36] An awareness of the extent to which the place of "Shakespeare" and "English Renaissance Drama" in the literary canon is the product of later ages is admittedly important for any student of English literature. Yet the insistence with which this point appears to have been made has clouded the fact that these dramatic texts were not considered quite so trivial and sub-literary after all.

Like *England's Parnassus*, *Belvedere, or the Garden of the Muses* was published in 1600. The two anthologies resemble each other in that both promise to gather the choicest flowers of English poets under various subject headings (in this resembling commonplace books). While the passages in *England's Parnassus* are attributed to their authors, however, and can be of some length (usually one to ten lines with some going up to as many as sixty), *Belvedere* only prints unattributed snippets of one or two lines. Thanks to the astounding scholarship of Charles Crawford, more than half of these snippets were identified long before the existence of electronic databases.[37]

When it comes to the inclusion of stage plays, the findings are similar to those in *England's Parnassus* even though the two anthologies are not textually related. (For instance, the second, "good" quarto of *Romeo*

---

[34] Bowers, "Publication," 414.   [35] Gurr, *Shakespearean Stage*, 46.

[36] Bowers, "Publication," 415.

[37] See Crawford, "*Belvedere*," 198–228, and Charles Crawford, "Appendix D: J. Bodenham's *Belvedere*," in Ingleby, comp., *The Shakespeare Allusion-Book*, 11.489–518. *Belvedere* is in many ways an important volume for the evaluation of poetic reputations and taste at the end of sixteenth century. It is regrettable that it has not been edited since 1875, and that no attempt seems to have been undertaken since the advent of large databases such as the Chadwyck-Healey to analyze its make-up more fully.

and Juliet was used for *England's Parnassus*, while the first, "bad" quarto underlies the passages present in *Belvedere*.) Fourteen stage plays are represented in *Belvedere*, quoted 165 times all in all. With five plays (six if we include *Edward III*) and eighty-nine (112 including those from *Edward III*) passages, Shakespeare is again drawn upon more often than any other playwright, Kyd (28 passages), the anonymous author of *Arden of Faversham* (10), Marlowe (7), Jonson (6), and Lyly (2).[38] Excerpts from these plays are again placed alongside Sidney, Spenser, Brandon's *Vertuous Octavia*, and Harington's *Ariosto*. Bowers and others have long told us that plays written for the public stage belonged to a subliterary genre in Shakespeare's time. However, the anthologies *England's Parnassus* and *Belvedere* – beside much other evidence outlined above – suggest that dramatic texts were on the way to becoming part of the English literary canon well before Jonson and Shakespeare's plays were published in prestigious folio editions.

For most of the twentieth century, the relationship between Shakespeare and the stationers was seen as antagonistic. Greedy publishers, often of dubious reputation, and disconcertingly incompetent printers eagerly collaborated with other corrupters and pirates to deprive Shakespeare's manuscripts of the perfection they had had and which it was the editors' task to restore as best they could. This view, I have argued, is in need of revision. I have argued that it would be more accurate to say that the stationers in some ways *made* Shakespeare (or "Shakespeare") or, to the extent that they did not make him, catalytically enabled his (or: its) making. Not that this had been the stationers' intention: their considerations, understandably, were economic. At a time when the Stationers' Company was unsuccessfully striving to restrict the proliferation of printing presses, attempts to open up new markets must have been welcome.[39] Ironically, this attempt was crowned with little success in the case of the publication of playtexts. Despite what earlier scholars (thinking that Elizabethan drama *must* have sold well) believed, a publisher did not make a significant profit unless there was a second edition. Of the 371 plays printed between 1583 and 1642, only 150, that is roughly 40 percent, reached a second edition within twenty-five

---

[38] The plays by Kyd, Marlowe, Jonson, and Lyly are: *The Spanish Tragedy* (20), *Soliman and Perseda* (8), *The Case Is Altered* (4), *Every Man in His Humour* (2), *Edward II* (7), and *The Woman in the Moon* (2).

[39] See Cyndia Susan Clegg, "The Stationers' Company of London," in *The British Literary Booktrade 1475–1700*, eds. James K. Bracken and Joel Silver, Dictionary of Literary Biography, 170 (Detroit: Gale Research Company, 1996), 275–91, esp. 283–84.

years of their appearance.[40] Nonetheless, it may be no exaggeration to say that, without the explosion of playtext publications in the 1590s and the evolution of the concept of dramatic authorship as mirrored in the title-pages of the 1590s, the foundations on which Jonson's self-assertion of dramatic authorship rested would have been missing. And it seems fair to assume that, without Jonson's Folio, there would have been no folio edition of the dramatic works of Shakespeare either.

When Shakespeare arrived in London, there was no market for printed playbooks. Halfway through his active career, however, a large part of his plays had been published. While his earliest play to reach print was "Plaide by the Right Honourable the Earle of Darbie, Earle of Pembrooke, and Earle of Sussex their Seruants," several plays published in 1598 were "By William Shake-speare." The sudden emergence of "Shakespeare" at the end of the sixteenth century may prompt us to reconsider the view that "The privileging and hypostatisation of the authorial function is, of course, a retrospective anachronism."[41] Whatever violence the reduction to a single author may do to the communal enterprise of the public stage, "anachronism" is hardly the right word if we take into account emergent publication practices in early modern London.

At the pace he had been seeing his plays get into print up to 1600, Shakespeare had good reasons to expect that the plays he went on to write early in the seventeenth century, especially the great tragedies, would soon reach a readership. As it turned out, only another five plays were printed during Shakespeare's lifetime, and the majority of those written after the turn of the century were not published before 1623. Yet those that were printed reinforce the impression that Shakespeare's plays find in print an adequate form of publication: the second quarto of *Hamlet* (1604/5) stresses on its title page that it was printed "according to the true and perfect Coppie" and gives no evidence of performance. Contrary to Shakespeare's previous plays, the title page of Q1 *King Lear* (1608) has Shakespeare's name come first and in substantially bigger letters than the rest.[42] The prefatory address in Q1 *Troilus and Cressida* (1609) addresses an "Eternall reader" who

---

[40] See Blayney, "Publication of Playbooks," 387, 412–13. "Masques, pageants and entertainments, closet and academic plays, Latin plays and translations published as literary texts" (Blayney, "Publication of Playbooks," 384) are excluded from this count.

[41] *The Tragicall Historie of Hamlet Prince of Denmarke*, eds. Graham Holderness and Bryan Loughrey, Shakespearean Originals: First Editions (Hemel Hempstead: Harvester, 1992), 16.

[42] The prominence of Shakespeare's name on the title page of Q1 *King Lear* may well owe something to the title pages of Jonson's previously published plays. In particular, the title page of *Volpone* – which had appeared the preceding year – resembles that of *King Lear* in having the dramatist's name come first and in letters of a similarly impressive size.

is assured of having "heere a new play, neuer stal'd with the Stage, neuer clapper-clawd with the palmes of the vulger."[43] Long before the First Folio and with Shakespeare still alive and active, we can witness a far-reaching emancipation of Shakespeare's text from the stage. The playtexts no longer render what such-and-such a company has performed in a medium that fails to do the play full justice, but they present what the dramatist William Shakespeare has originally written and is now offered to the reader. Authority, in other words, has shifted from the dramatic company to the dramatist, from the stage to the page.

In the address "To the Judicious Reader" in *The Devil's Law-Case* published in the year of the appearance of Shakespeare's First Folio, Webster wrote that "A great part of the grace of this (I confess) lay in action; yet can no action ever be gracious, where the decency of the language, and ingenious structure of the scene, arrive not to make up a perfect harmony."[44] Webster's apology for the play's appearance in print reveals a double-edged attitude – neither anti-theatrical nor hostile to print, blind to the virtues of neither medium. Despite the modern orthodoxy that Shakespeare was only interested in one form of publication for his plays, namely that on stage, I believe that Webster's words give us a more likely version of what Shakespeare's attitude was, granting the grace of stage action yet also aware that a certain artistic ingenuity survives better on the page than the stage. As my next chapter will make clear, to argue, as Harold Love and others have done, for "Shakespeare's disdain, as a dramatist, for the typographical medium"[45] therefore seems to me misguided.

[43] I agree with Berger and Lander's comment on the title page of Q2 *Hamlet*: "The stage has given way to the study, the action to the work," and on the epistle prefacing the text of Q1 *Troilus and Cressida*: "The movement from stage to page, from print as record of a performance to print as separate from and superior to performance, offers a striking conclusion to those plays of Shakespeare that appeared in print in his lifetime" ("Shakespeare in Print," 402–3).

[44] Elizabeth M. Brennan, ed., *The Devil's Law-Case*, The New Mermaids (London: Ernest Benn, 1975), 7.

[45] Harold Love, *Scribal Publication in Seventeenth-Century England* (Oxford: Clarendon Press, 1993), 146.

CHAPTER 3

Shakespeare and the publication of his plays (I): the late sixteenth century

In what Samuel Schoenbaum has called Pope's "most influential contribution to Shakespearean biography," the eighteenth-century poet and critic wrote:

> Shakespear, (whom you and ev'ry Play house bill
> Style the divine, the matchless, what you will)
> For gain, not glory, wing'd his roving flight,
> And grew Immortal in his own despight.[1]

Pope's lines were no doubt instrumental in reinforcing the opinion, soon to be frozen into dogma, that Shakespeare only cared for that form of publication – the stage – which promised an immediate payoff, while being indifferent to the one that eventually guaranteed his immortality – the printed page. Pope, who counted on his writings, in particular the *Iliad* and *Odyssey* translations, to earn him gain *and* glory, may well have taken comfort in the fact that his motives, compared to what he took to be Shakespeare's, were relatively noble. Yet Schoenbaum's suspicion that Pope's lines may tell us more about his own than about Shakespeare's attitude has not kept us from perpetuating Pope's opinion. To argue, as Thomas L. Berger and Jesse M. Lander have done as recently as 1999, that Shakespeare "never showed the least bit of interest in being a dramatic author while he lived" is still the accepted view.[2]

---

[1] "The First Epistle of the Second book of Horace, Imitated" (1737), in *Imitations of Horace*, ed. John Butt, *The Twickenham Edition of the Poems of Alexander Pope*, vol. 4, 2nd edn (New Haven: Yale University Press, 1953), 199. For Schoenbaum's comment on Pope, see Samuel Schoenbaum, *Shakespeare's Lives*, new edn (Oxford: Clarendon Press, 1991), 91.

[2] Berger and Lander, "Shakespeare in Print," 409. Brooks similarly believes that "Shakespeare seems to have been reluctant to see his plays published" (*Playhouse to Printing House*, 9). See also George Walton Williams's affirmation that "performance was the publication that Shakespeare sought for his plays, and with it he seems to have been entirely content" ("The Publishing and Editing of Shakespeare's Plays," in *William Shakespeare: His World, His Work, His Influence*, ed. John F. Andrews, 3 vols. (New York: Charles Scribner's Sons, 1985), III.589).

What is at stake in Shakespeare's alleged indifference to the publication of his plays is more, I believe, than a biographical issue. Spelling out the premises which inform the way we read and edit Shakespeare today, John Jowett has recently written:

One large assumption... is that we are interested in Shakespeare as a dramatist who wrote for the theatre, and who took relatively little if any interest in seeing his plays in print. This viewpoint is often articulated in general introductions as a matter of historical interest, but it is bound up with editorial practices as well.[3]

With the rise of performance criticism over the last twenty-five years or so, the premise that Shakespeare was indifferent to the publication of his plays has come to inform editorial policy and criticism more than ever before.

Although the view that Shakespeare took little interest in a publication of his plays beyond the stage is widely accepted, a dissenting voice tried to make itself heard as long ago as 1965, when Ernst Honigmann suggested that we revise "the modern myth of [Shakespeare's] complete indifference to the printing of his plays."[4] If Honigmann's suggestion – in contrast to other theories of his such as the "early start" chronology, the "lost years" in Catholic Lancashire, and authorial revision – has failed to provoke much debate, this may be because Shakespeareans have not taken seriously what is after all a central component in the publication of playbooks. As Gerald D. Johnson has pointed out, "The economics of the book-trade have been largely ignored by analytical bibliographers and textual critics, whose primary interest is to recover the text of Shakespeare and other key literary figures from the vicissitudes of the printing houses of the period."[5] Now that Peter Blayney has taken a fresh look at a series of bibliographical *idées reçues* that had been gathering dust for most of the twentieth century, we may be equipped to carry out the project for which Honigmann fruitlessly pleaded several decades ago.[6]

The belief "that acting companies usually considered publication to be against their best interests" is included by Blayney among the "unfounded myths" that have bedeviled Shakespeare scholarship ever since the 1909 publication of Pollard's *Shakespeare Folios and Quartos*.[7] It may thus be useful to reconsider the publication of Shakespeare's plays without the usual *parti pris* that the company opposed such publication. After this introduction,

[3] John Jowett, "After Oxford: Recent Developments in Textual Studies," in *The Shakespearean International Yearbook, 1: Where Are We Now in Shakespearean Studies?*, eds. W. R. Elton and John M. Mucciolo (Aldershot: Ashgate, 1999), 73.

[4] E. A. J. Honigmann, *The Stability of Shakespeare's Text* (London: Edward Arnold, 1965), 190.

[5] Gerald D. Johnson, "Thomas Pavier, Publisher, 1600–25," *The Library*, 14 (1992), 13.

[6] Blayney, "Publication of Playbooks," 383–422.   [7] Ibid., 383–84.

I examine the twelve plays that may have been the first written by
Shakespeare for the Lord Chamberlain's Men (whom Shakespeare joined
in 1594).[8] Their publication history suggests, I argue, that the Lord
Chamberlain's Men had a coherent strategy to try to get their playwright's
plays into print. Toward the end of this chapter, I will inquire into what
can or cannot be inferred from Shakespeare's alleged involvement (as with
the narrative poems) or noninvolvement (with the plays) in the publication
of his writings.

Four of the plays Shakespeare wrote for the Lord Chamberlain's Men in
the 1590s present special problems: *Romeo and Juliet*, *The Merry Wives of
Windsor*, *Henry V*, and, perhaps, *Love's Labour's Lost* appeared first in what,
since Pollard, have usually been labeled "bad" quartos. Each had been set
up from a text of which Shakespeare, we may assume, would have preferred
the fuller and, in some ways, better version. It may be tempting to argue
that, because the earliest editions of *Romeo and Juliet*, *Hamlet* (written
c. 1601), and, possibly, *Love's Labour's Lost* were followed by fuller and
"better" versions, this is in itself strong evidence that the Lord Chamberlain's
Men and their playwright did care and did intervene.[9] The evidence is more
complex, however. In the case of *Romeo and Juliet*, John Danter seems to
have licensed but not entered the play before printing the 1597 edition.[10]
By 1599, Cuthbert Burby – who had published the (allegedly) "Newly
corrected and augmented" *Love's Labour's Lost* a year earlier – appears
to have acquired the rights to *Romeo and Juliet* (even though the extant
records of the Stationers' Company nowhere mention this)[11] and was in the
possession of a "good" manuscript which he went on to print (though also
without entering it). What exactly led to this unusual succession of events
will never be fully understood. Yet if, as seems likely, the Lord Chamberlain's

[8] It should be noted that I do not follow the Oxford editors in counting *The Comedy of Errors*
among the plays written for this company (Wells, Taylor, et al., *Textual Companion*, 116–17). It has
traditionally been ascribed to an earlier date on good grounds. R. A. Foakes, in his Arden 2 edition,
plausibly argued for "between 1590 and 1593," while T. S. Dorsch, in the New Cambridge edition,
suggested "the summer or autumn of 1591" (Foakes, ed. (London: Methuen, 1962), xxiii; Dorsch,
ed. (Cambridge University Press, 1988), 6).

[9] See, for instance, Honigmann, *Stability*, 190; Andrew Gurr, ed., *King Henry V*, The New Cambridge
Shakespeare (Cambridge University Press, 1992), 217; and W. W. Greg, *The Editorial Problem in
Shakespeare: A Survey of the Foundations of the Text*, 3rd edn (Oxford: Clarendon Press, 1954), 17.

[10] Blayney has shown that there was nothing illegal about having a text licensed without paying for the
"insurance policy" which entrance in the Stationers' Register provided ("Publication of Playbooks,"
400–5, 404).

[11] That Burby was later considered the rightful owner of the rights to *Romeo and Juliet* is born out by
the fact that on January 22, 1607, *Romeo and Juliet* was transferred to Nicholas Ling "with consent
of Master Burby" (Arber, ed., *Transcript*, III.337).

Men sold the manuscript to Burby, this might well have happened before Danter published his edition rather than because the Lord Chamberlain's Men, troubled by the printing of what modern scholarship has labeled a "bad" quarto, approached a stationer in order to have it superseded by a "good" text.

Similarly, that the "good" manuscript underlying the second quarto of *Hamlet* (1604/5) had changed hands before the "bad" first quarto appeared (1603) is a strong, indeed the strongest, possibility. The play had been entered to James Roberts on July 26, 1602.[12] Q1, however, was "printed [by Valentine Simmes] for N[icholas]. L[ing]. and Iohn Trundell," whereas Q2 was "Printed by I[ames]. R[oberts]. for N[icholas]. L[ing]." While various scenarios have been proposed to account for this, only one is uncomplicated, fits all the evidence, and is consistent with normal book-trade practice: Ling and Trundle seem to have licensed but not entered their manuscript and had it printed without anyone realizing that Roberts had once entered a different version. Having found out about Ling and Trundle's unintentional breach, Roberts could have caused them trouble but preferred to negotiate an advantageous deal with his neighbors in Fleet Street, selling to Ling and Trundle his longer and better manuscript and having them pay him to print it.[13]

As for *Love's Labour's Lost*, it is far from clear that the first extant edition really did supersede a "bad" one. It is true that the title page of the 1598 quarto describes the text as "Newly corrected and augmented," suggesting that, like Q2 *Romeo and Juliet* and *Hamlet*, it superseded a "bad" text. While this has been the traditional view,[14] it has been forcefully argued in more recent times that this edition may well have followed (and indeed have been set up from) a "good" edition. What supports this view is that similar title page advertisements exist where nothing has been corrected or augmented.[15] Furthermore, according to Paul Werstine's study of the practices in William White's printing house, typographical evidence suggests that Q1 *Love's Labour's Lost* was set up from printed rather than from manuscript copy, and, consequently, that it was a reprint of the textually "good" Q0.[16] Thus, while the evidence is not unambiguous in any of the three cases, it seems more likely that in each case the Lord Chamberlain's

[12] Arber, ed., *Transcript*, III.212.
[13] In this paragraph, I am indebted to a private conversation with Peter Blayney.
[14] See, for instance, Greg, *Editorial Problem*, 17; and Honigmann, *Stability*, 190.
[15] See Wells, Taylor, et al., *Textual Companion*, 270, Woudhuysen, ed., *Love's Labour's Lost*, 301–4, and Leo Kirschbaum, "Leading Case," 501–12.
[16] Paul Werstine, "The Editorial Usefulness of Printing House and Compositor Studies," in *Play-Texts in Old Spelling: Papers from the Glendon Conference*, eds. G. B. Shand and Raymond C. Shady (New

Men sold a "good" manuscript before the publication of the first edition than that there was an active attempt on their behalf to supersede a "bad" text with a "good" one.

On the other hand, when it comes to the two "bad" texts that were not superseded by "good" ones (or at least not until 1623), it will not do to claim that "nothing was done during Shakespeare's lifetime to replace the bad texts of *Henry V* and *The Merry Wives of Windsor*."[17] This is more than we know. *Merry Wives* – first printed in a particularly corrupt text, even by the standards of other "bad" quartos – was not reprinted until the publication of the Pavier quartos in 1619. This suggests that this play sold rather poorly. Thus, even if the players had approached the play's publisher, Arthur Johnson, with a good text, he would have had no reason to print it and invest in a second edition as long as he had not sold the copies of the first.

Of eight other plays Shakespeare is likely to have written for his company from 1594 until close to the turn of the century, two need to be first addressed: a now lost play called *Love's Labour's Won* may or may not have existed and been printed. Since no copy is extant, it is impossible to say anything about this hypothetical edition except that it would have appeared before 1603.[18] *King John* was not printed until the First Folio in 1623, for reasons that may have had nothing to do with reluctance on the part of the Chamberlain's Men. *The Troublesome Raigne of Iohn King of England*

York: AMS Press, 1984), 35–64. Werstine's article is discussed in some detail in Woudhuysen's edition (305–6).

[17] Michael J. B. Allen and Kenneth Muir, eds., *Shakespeare's Plays in Quarto* (Berkeley and Los Angeles: University of California Press, 1981), xviii.

[18] On *Love's Labour's Won*, see T. W. Baldwin, *Shakespeare's "Love's Labor's Won": New Evidence from the Account Books of an Elizabethan Bookseller* (Carbondale, Ill.: Southern Illinois University Press, 1957); Wells, Taylor, et al., *A Textual Companion*, 117; and *William Shakespeare: The Complete Works* Wells and Taylor, gen. eds. (Oxford: Clarendon Press, 1986), 349. I believe that the case for the earlier existence of a now lost play is not as strong as Baldwin and the Oxford editors have it. Meres mentions "Love's Labours Won" in 1598 and a 1603 list of printed plays in the account books of an Elizabethan bookseller similarly contains the title. While it had long been believed that "Love's Labors Won" was simply an alternative title for a comedy Shakespeare had written by 1598, Baldwin's discovery and discussion of the 1603 list seemed to make this position untenable. This need not be so. As neither Baldwin nor the Oxford editors have pointed out, not all the titles in the bookseller's list reproduce the title of the printed play. *Edward IV*, published in 1599 as *The First and Second Parts of King Edward the Fourth* and reprinted in 1600 under the same title, is referred to as "Jane shore." To call this a "shortened title," as Baldwin does, will not quite do, as "Jane Shore" is not part of the full title. *Edward IV* is also referred to as "Jane Shore" in *The Knight of the Burning Pestle* (1607) (see Chambers, *Elizabethan Stage*, IV.11). *Edward IV*, in other words, seems to have been commonly called "Jane Shore," just as *Henry VIII* usually seems to have been referred to as "All is True" prior to 1623. "Love's Labors Won" may thus have been a popular title for *Much Ado about Nothing*, the only play that fulfills all the necessary conditions: the title is not mentioned by Meres, the play had been published by 1603, and it may have been performed before *Palladis Tamia* was entered on September 7, 1598. I am indebted to a conversation with Peter Blayney about this issue.

had been published in 1591 by Sampson Clarke, who would no doubt have considered any edition of *King John* to which he had not consented a breach of his rights. As Blayney explains, "The owner of a copy had not only the exclusive right to reprint the text, but also the right to a fair chance to recover his costs. He could therefore seek the Company's protection if *any* book – not necessarily a reprint or plagiarism of his own copy – threatened his ability to dispose of unsold copies of an existing edition."[19] *Troublesome Raigne* was not reprinted until 1611, when, significantly, it was attributed to "W. Sh." When Heminge and Condell wanted to include *King John* (and *The Taming of the Shrew*) in the First Folio, they first had to obtain the consent of the owners of *Troublesome Raigne* (and *The Taming of a Shrew*). The fact that *King John* was not printed until 1623 thus provides no evidence for the players' alleged reluctance to have their plays printed.

The six remaining plays – *Richard II*, *A Midsummer Night's Dream*, *The Merchant of Venice*, *1 Henry IV*, *2 Henry IV*, and *Much Ado About Nothing* – were all printed between 1597 and 1600. Whether or not we believe that Shakespeare and his company were responsible for selling the manuscripts to the publishers will partly depend on our assessment of the nature of printer's copy. In the cases of *Richard II* and *The Merchant of Venice*, it appears to be difficult to determine whether copy was provided by an authorial manuscript or a faithful transcript of one, while *1 Henry IV* may well have been set up from a scribal transcript of an authorial manuscript.[20] Copy for the first quartos of *A Midsummer Night's Dream*,[21] *2 Henry IV*,[22] and *Much Ado about Nothing*,[23] on the other hand, has generally been believed to have come from Shakespeare's own manuscripts. As my fuller discussion of this issue below will make clear, it is true that the canons of

[19] Blayney, "Publication of Playbooks," 399.
[20] David Bevington, ed., *The Complete Works of Shakespeare*, updated 4th edn (New York: Longman, 1997), A-4, A-10–11; G. Blakemore Evans, gen. ed., *The Riverside Shakespeare*, 2nd edn (Boston and New York: Houghton Mifflin Company, 1997), 57–58; Stephen Greenblatt, gen. ed., *The Norton Shakespeare* (New York and London: W. W. Norton & Company, 1997), 950, 1089, 1155; Wells, Taylor, et al., *Textual Companion*, 306, 323, 329.
[21] Bevington, ed., *Complete Works*, A-4; Greenblatt, gen. ed., *Norton Shakespeare*, 812; Wells, Taylor, et al., *Textual Companion*, 279; Peter Holland, ed., *A Midsummer Night's Dream*, The Oxford Shakespeare (Oxford University Press, 1994), 113.
[22] See Bevington, ed., *Complete Works*, A-11; Greenblatt, gen. ed., *Norton Shakespeare*, 1302; Wells, Taylor, et al., *A Textual Companion*, 351; René Weis, ed., *Henry IV, Part 2*, The Oxford Shakespeare (Oxford University Press, 1998), 90; Giorgio Melchiori, ed., *The Second Part of King Henry IV*, The New Cambridge Shakespeare (Cambridge University Press, 1989), 53.
[23] See Bevington, ed., *Complete Works*, A-5; Greenblatt, gen. ed., *Norton Shakespeare*, 1387; Wells, Taylor, et al., *Textual Companion*, 371. Note, however, that Sheldon P. Zitner less categorically believes that "The 1600 Quarto [of *Much Ado*] was set from the author's manuscript or a transcription of it" (Zitner, ed., *Much Ado About Nothing*, The Oxford Shakespeare (Oxford University Press, 1993), 80).

bibliographical proof are currently being subjected to scrutiny. It would indeed be unwise, in the light of recent pleas for greater bibliographical agnosticism, to pretend to be able to determine the precise origin and nature of these manuscripts. Nevertheless, nothing seems to contradict the interpretation that any one of them may (though not necessarily all of them must) have been in the possession of the Lord Chamberlain's Men and/or their playwright before being sold to a stationer.

What emerges is the probability that the Lord Chamberlain's Men did not try to have Shakespeare's plays printed immediately after they had been written. If we consider the likely dates of composition and the dates of entrance in the Stationers' Register, a fairly consistent pattern presents itself: as a rule, roughly two years seem to have elapsed between the former and the latter. *Richard II*, normally dated 1595,[24] was entered in the Stationers' Register on August 29, 1597. *1 Henry IV* and *The Merchant of Venice*, both probably of 1596/97,[25] were entered on February 25, 1598 (new style) and July 22, 1598 respectively. *2 Henry IV*, composed late in 1597 or early 1598,[26] and *Much Ado about Nothing*, probably written in late 1598 or early 1599,[27] are first mentioned in the Stationers' Register in August 1600. Little seems to have changed when we come to *Troilus and Cressida* and *King Lear*, the two remaining plays (aside from the corrupt text of *Pericles*) printed during Shakespeare's lifetime. *Troilus and Cressida*, which was entered on February 7, 1603 (though not printed until 1609), has been conjectured by Ernst Honigmann and, more recently, David Bevington to have been written in 1601.[28] *The History of King Lear*, finally, is usually dated *c.* 1605–6[29] and was entered on November 26, 1607. For the sake of completeness, it should be added that *Antony and Cleopatra*, usually dated 1606/07,[30] was

---

[24] This date is favored by Bevington, ed., *Complete Works*, A-10; in *Riverside Shakespeare*, gen. ed. Evans, 81; by Wells, Taylor, et al., *Textual Companion*, 117–18; and by Andrew Gurr, ed., *King Richard II*, The New Cambridge Shakespeare (Cambridge University Press, 1984), 1.

[25] See Bevington, ed., *Complete Works*, A-4, A-10–11; Evans, ed., *Riverside Shakespeare*, 82; and Wells, Taylor, et al., *Textual Companion*, 119–20.

[26] See Bevington, ed., *Complete Works*, A-11–12; Evans, ed., *Riverside Shakespeare*, 82–83; and Wells, Taylor, et al., *Textual Companion*, 120.

[27] See Bevington, ed., *Complete Works*, A-5; Evans, ed., *Riverside Shakespeare*, 83; and Wells, Taylor, et al., *Textual Companion*, 120–21.

[28] Honigmann, "The Date and Revision of *Troilus and Cressida*," in *Textual Criticism and Literary Interpretation*, ed. Jerome J. McGann (Chicago and London: University of Chicago Press, 1985), 38–54; David Bevington, ed., *Troilus and Cressida*, The Arden Shakespeare (Walton-on-Thames: Thomas Nelson, 1998), 11.

[29] Bevington, ed., *Complete Works*, A-17; Wells, Taylor, et al., *Textual Companion*, 128.

[30] Bevington, ed., *Complete Works*, A-18; Evans, ed., *Riverside Shakespeare*, 86; Wells, Taylor, et al., *Textual Companion*, 129–30; Michael Neill, ed., *The Tragedy of Anthony and Cleopatra*, The Oxford Shakespeare (Oxford University Press, 1994), 20–21.

entered on May 20, 1608, though the play was not printed before the First Folio.

If presented too rigidly, my argument is in danger of circularity. The traditional dating of at least some plays is likely to be infected with exactly those assumptions about the publication of Shakespeare's plays which I am arguing against here. If scholars mistakenly believed, for instance, that the players reluctantly (if at all) released a manuscript only once a play had lost its drawing power on stage, a date of composition too close to the play's appearance in print (or in the Stationers' Register) would clearly not have recommended itself. On the other hand, the date of composition of several plays can be determined with relative precision independently of any assumptions about publication. *Richard II*, for example, is probably indebted to Daniel's *Civil Wars* (1595) and may have been performed at the House of Sir Edward Hoby on December 9, 1595. The topical allusion to the Spanish vessel called the St. Andrew in the opening scene of *The Merchant of Venice* would very likely have been made soon after news of its capture reached England in July 1596. While other comparable examples could be given, it must be admitted that for some of the plays, such as *A Midsummer Night's Dream*, there is nothing beyond style to suggest a particular date. Therefore, much of the above is necessarily conjectural. Yet where evidence is available regarding a play, it indicates an interval of roughly two years between composition and entrance.

Whatever manuscript the lost edition was based on, *Love's Labour's Lost* – probably written about 1594–95[31] and apparently first published in 1597[32] without having been entered in the Stationers' Register – appears not to have markedly departed from the established pattern. All we know about *Romeo and Juliet* is that it may well have been written *c.* 1595,[33] that the "bad" edition was published in 1597, and that it was followed by the "good" edition in 1599. Whether or not Q1 anticipated Shakespeare and his fellows'

---

[31] Evans, ed., *Riverside Shakespeare*, 80–81; and Wells, Taylor, et al., *Textual Companion*, 117. In the introduction to the play in *The Complete Works*, Wells and Taylor unaccountably disagree with themselves, this time suggesting "1593 or 1594" (315). Bevington, more cautiously, considers dates as wide apart as 1588 and 1597 (*Complete Works*, A-2–3).

[32] The existence of the first, lost edition of *Love's Labour's Lost*, which has long been inferred from the title page of the second edition, has recently found support in a piece of documentary evidence. The library catalogue of Edward, 2nd Viscount of Conway (1594–1655) refers to "Loves Labours Lost by W: Sha: 1597," thus settling the question of the date of the first edition which previously could only be narrowed down to the years between composition (1594/95) and the first extant edition (1598). See Arthur Freeman and Paul Grinke, "Four New Shakespeare Quartos?," *The Times Literary Supplement*, April 5, 2002, 17–18.

[33] See Bevington, ed., *Complete Works*, A-14; Evans, ed., *Riverside Shakespeare*, 81; and Wells, Taylor, et al., *Textual Companion*, 118.

sale of the manuscript underlying Q2, the time lapse is again one of approximately two years. As for *Henry V*, if the Lord Chamberlain's Men
had intended to sell a "good" manuscript some two years after the play
was first performed, they may have been anticipated by whoever sold the
non-authorial manuscript that served as copy for the first, "bad," edition.
Significantly, the time lapse between composition and sale to a stationer
seems in this case to have been far less than two years: probably written
in 1599, *Henry V* is mentioned in the Stationers' Register in August 1600
among a list of "thinges formerlye printed" suggesting that it had appeared
relatively early that year.[34]

Something similar may have happened with *The Merry Wives of Windsor*.
While scholars had long dated the play *c.* 1600–1,[35] Leslie Hotson's
Shakespeare Versus Shallow suggested in 1931 that the play was written specifically for the Garter Feast at Westminster on April 23, 1597, a theory that
was later elaborated by William Green and, until recently, was generally endorsed (despite the fact that Meres does not mention the play).[36] In recent
years, however, it has been shown that the early date has little to recommend
itself and had mainly become orthodoxy "because it ha[d] been repeated so
many times."[37] Elizabeth Schafer and, especially, Giorgio Melchiori have
now discredited Hotson's suggestion, and Melchiori has convincingly argued that the play was written "not before late 1599 or 1600."[38] Whoever
was responsible for selling to John Busby the manuscript that was entered
in the Stationers' Register on January 18, 1602 (new style) and published
the same year may thus have anticipated the Lord Chamberlain's Men's
attempt to sell the play some two years after it first reached the stage.

To sum up: of the first dozen or so plays Shakespeare wrote for the Lord
Chamberlain's Men, not a single one that could legally have been printed
remained unprinted by 1602. As a rule, the Lord Chamberlain's Men (if they
had not been anticipated by someone else, or if legal constraints did not

---

[34] Arber, ed., *Transcript*, III.169. For the date of *Henry V*, see Bevington, ed., *Complete Works*, A-12–13;
Evans, ed., *Riverside Shakespeare*, 83; and Wells, Taylor, et al., *Textual Companion*, 121.

[35] See, for instance, E. K. Chambers, *William Shakespeare: A Study of Facts and Problems*, 2 vols.
(Oxford: Clarendon Press, 1930), I.270.

[36] Leslie Hotson, *Shakespeare Versus Shallow* (London: Nonesuch Press, 1931). See especially the chapter
on "The Date of the *Merry Wives of Windsor*," III–22. William Green, *Shakespeare's "Merry Wives
of Windsor"* (Princeton University Press, 1962).

[37] Elizabeth Schafer, "The Date of *The Merry Wives of Windsor*," *Notes and Queries*, 236, n.s. 38 (1991),
57–60, 60.

[38] Giorgio Melchiori, ed., *The Merry Wives of Windsor*, The Arden Shakespeare (Walton-on-Thames:
Thomas Nelson, 2000), 18–30, 20. See also Melchiori, *Shakespeare's Garter Plays: "Edward III" to
"Merry Wives of Windsor"* (Newark: University of Delaware Press; London and Toronto: Associated
University Presses, 1994), 92–112.

make printing impossible) seem to have sold Shakespeare's manuscripts to a publisher approximately two years after the plays reached the public stage. If the composition date of *c.* 1595–96, which has been favored in recent times, is correct, then *A Midsummer Night's Dream*, not entered until October 8, 1600, is an exception, the *only* exception.[39] Scholars have hitherto argued that Shakespeare and his company were indifferent, if not opposed, to the publication of his plays, and have tried to find various explanations for all those plays that were published. I suggest that more economical reasoning can account for the publication of his plays if we assume, on the contrary, that the Lord Chamberlain's Men and their playwright actively supported the publication of his plays. Consequently, it is the absence rather than the presence of an early edition of a Shakespeare play that requires explanation.

If, as I have argued, the Lord Chamberlain's Men developed a coherent strategy to get Shakespeare's plays into print, the number and the identity of the stationers involved might also reflect a certain coherence. As Blayney has pointed out, "since the overall demand for plays was unimpressive it is likely that many of those that saw print were offered to, rather than sought out by, their publishers" ("The Publication of Playbooks," 392). It seems then reasonable to assume that Shakespeare and his fellows would not have approached a different stationer every time they wanted to sell a manuscript but that they built up and entertained commercial relationships with a small number of them. One stationer whom Shakespeare and/or his fellows appear to have approached repeatedly seems an obvious choice: James Roberts entered *The Merchant of Venice* (July 22, 1598), the Lord Chamberlain's Men's *A Larum for London* (May 29, 1600),[40] *Hamlet* (July 26, 1602), and *Troilus and Cressida* (February 7, 1603). Having been granted the exclusive privilege of printing playbills – "which were set up on posts in conspicuous places up and down the city and probably also at the play-house doors"[41] – from May 31, 1594 until October 29, 1615,[42] he must have had regular dealings with the theater companies.[43] Andrew Wise, who

---

[39] If, in the case of *A Midsummer Night's Dream*, not only two but an exceptional four to five years elapsed between composition and entrance, several explanations might be advanced. The supply of playbooks often having exceeded the demand, no stationer may have been willing to invest. Perhaps *A Midsummer Night's Dream* was originally written for a specific wedding and did not reach the public stage until later. Alternatively, it would not be greatly surprising if Shakespeare and his fellows had not adhered to their own custom with absolute regularity.

[40] The anonymous play was published in 1602 "As it hath been playde by the right Honorable the Lord Charberlaine [*sic*] his Seruants."

[41] Chambers, *Elizabethan Stage*, II.547. [42] Arber, ed., *Transcript*, II.651–52, III.575.

[43] Even though Henslowe's diary and papers do not seem to contain any specific references to payments for the printing or posting of playbills, it can be inferred that a considerable number of them must have existed. William Jaggard had applied for the patent for playbills as early as 1593 when his hopes

entered *Richard II* (August 29, 1597), and *Richard III* (October 20, 1597), *1 Henry IV* (February 25, 1598), *2 Henry IV* (August 23, 1600), and *Much Ado About Nothing* (August 23, 1600), is a far less obvious choice. Wise had been a bookseller in London since 1589 and appears to have taken over John Perrin's bookshop – The Angel – in St. Paul's Churchyard after Perrin's death in *c.* 1592.[44] Wise's activities as a publisher were minimal. Apart from Shakespeare's plays, all he published before the end of the century are two sermons by Thomas Pleyfere.[45] A meager total of four non-Shakespearean publications followed before he transferred his copyrights to Matthew Law on June 25, 1603 and disappeared from all records.[46] Wise, in other words, was everything but an established publisher. If members of the Lord Chamberlain's Men approached him several times with manuscripts between 1597 and 1600, this would seem to require explanation. What can most plausibly account for the connection is, I believe, the commercial dealings Wise had with Roberts, the playbill printer. As early as 1593, Wise had functioned as retail seller of Nashe's *Christ's Tears over Jerusalem* (*STC* 18366), the rights to which Roberts had acquired by marrying the widowed Alice Charlewood.[47] More specifically, in 1597, the year in which Wise entered and published the first two Shakespearean playbooks, Roberts functioned as printer for the two sermons Wise owned. As a printer, Roberts's fortunes depended of course upon publishers who regularly commissioned work from him. If some time in 1597, Shakespeare and his fellows, willing to sell the manuscripts of *Richard II* and *Richard III*, asked Roberts for advice and if Roberts was unwilling to take the risks of purchasing the manuscripts himself, he would have had good reasons to recommend Andrew Wise.[48]

The third and last stationer with whom the Lord Chamberlain's Men repeatedly seem to have done business is Cuthbert Burby. As early as 1594, Burby had published Greene's *Orlando Furioso*, Robert Wilson's *The Cobler's Prophecy*, and Lyly's *Mother Bombie*. Toward the end of the following year,

were frustrated by the marriage of John Charlewood's widow to James Roberts. In 1602, he agreed to pay Roberts four shillings per month for the right to "the printinge of the billes for the company of stage players – apperteyninge to the right honorable the Erle of Worcester" (William A. Jackson, *Records of the Court of the Stationers' Company* (London: The Bibliographical Society, 1957), 1. I have expanded the contractions). A single company thus seems to have ordered enough playbills for Jaggard to make a profit despite his monthly payments to Roberts.

[44] See R. B. McKerrow, gen. ed., *A Dictionary of Printers and Booksellers in England, Scotland and Ireland, and of Foreign Printers of English Books 1557–1640* (London: The Bibliographical Society, 1910), 214, 296.

[45] See *STC* 20014, 20014.3, 20014.5, 20015, 20016, 20020, 20021.

[46] See *STC* 4543, 16916.3, 17671a, 19154.   [47] See McKerrow, *Dictionary*, 66.

[48] That the choice of printer seems to have depended on who one knew has also been suggested in Laurie Maguire, "The Craft of Printing (1600)," in *A Companion to Shakespeare*, ed. Kastan, 436.

Burby entered the Lord Admiral's Men's *A Knack to Know an Honest Man* as well as *Edward III* and both appeared in print in 1596. Burby further seems to have obtained the "good" manuscript of *Romeo and Juliet* from which the second quarto of 1599 was set up as well as the manuscript to which the earliest extant quarto edition of *Love's Labour's Lost* ultimately goes back. Finally, Burby, along with Walter Burre, also entered *Every Man in his Humour* on August 14, 1600. Jonson's play was published the following year "As it hath beene sundry times publickly acted by the right Honorable the Lord Chamberlaine his seruants," according to the title page.

Burby thus accounts for *Edward III* (which Shakespeare seems to have (co-)written before joining the Lord Chamberlain's Men),[49] the "good" second edition of *Romeo and Juliet*, and the second (though first extant) edition of *Love's Labour's Lost*. Roberts and Wise account for eight of the nine plays Shakespeare wrote for the Lord Chamberlain's Men that were first published in "good" editions during Shakespeare's lifetime, *A Midsummer Night's Dream*, entered by Thomas Fisher on October 8, 1600 being the only exception. Fisher's appearance among London's publishers is even briefer and more perfunctory than Wise's, with only Breton's *Pasquil's Mistress* of 1600 and the two parts of Marston's *Antonio and Mellida* of 1602 besides *A Midsummer's Night's Dream* to his credit. It seems impossible to recover what led to Fisher publishing a text that seems likely to have been set up from Shakespeare's manuscript. All the other plays that first appeared in "good" editions, however, go back to three stationers only – of whom one was the playbill printer, and another one commercially related to the playbill printer. This consistency does not discourage the view that a coherent strategy informed the Lord Chamberlain's Men's publication of Shakespeare's plays.

What can account for the approximate two-year lapse between composition and initial performance, on the one hand, and sale to and entrance by a publisher in the Stationers' Register on the other? In other words, why, if the Lord Chamberlain's Men supported rather than opposed the publication of Shakespeare's plays, did they wait rather than sell the manuscripts as quickly as possible? A possible reason is that as long as a play was relatively new, the Lord Chamberlain's Men hoped to profit from a more prestigious and lucrative form of publication than print. Harold Love believes that "Shakespeare may well have put work into circulation through the agency of scribes." He explains that "The sale or presentation to a wealthy patron

[49] See *King Edward III*, ed. Giorgio Melchiori, The New Cambridge Shakespeare (Cambridge University Press, 1998), 3–17.

of a manuscript of a favorite play would have offered an opportunity for additional income."[50] Introducing the 1647 "Beaumont and Fletcher" Folio, Humphrey Moseley wrote: "Heretofore when Gentlemen desired but a Copy of any of these *Playes*, the meanest piece here...cost them more then foure times the price you pay for the whole *Volume*."[51] Blayney has estimated that an unbound copy of the Shakespeare First Folio cost 15s. approximately.[52] The "Beaumont and Fletcher" Folio, printed twenty-four years later, may have cost about the same or slightly more. In other words, Moseley's "Gentlemen" paid a lot of money for a manuscript playbook, perhaps as much as three or four pounds.[53] They may well have been unlikely to order a manuscript copy if the playwright was not able to boast – as Middleton does in a dedication to William Hammond on one of the extant manuscripts of *A Game at Chess* – that the play was not available in print, that no "Stationers Stall can Showe" the play.[54] There is no evidence that such a practice was at all common during Shakespeare's lifetime. Nevertheless, it is possible that Shakespeare's company chose to postpone the publication of a play during the first two years of its existence in the expectation that certain gentlemen would order and pay a handsome sum for a scribal copy.[55]

This, however, is perhaps not the most likely explanation for the delayed publication of Shakespeare's plays. Discussing the wave of playbook publication in 1594, shortly after the playhouses reopened, Blayney has argued:

> If we assume that the players thought of performance and publication as mutually exclusive alternatives, it would indeed seem likely that the closure, rather than the reopening, caused the glut. But if we decline to make that assumption, there is a perfectly plausible reason why the reopening itself might have prompted the players to flood the market with scripts. The strategy is known today as "publicity," or "advertising."[56]

In other words, the companies viewed two of a play's forms of publication – performance and print, the stage and the page, the playhouse and the printing house – not only compatible but synergetic. If this was so, it may

---

[50] Love, *Scribal Publication*, 67–88.   [51] I quote from Greg, *Bibliography*, III.1234.

[52] *The First Folio of Shakespeare* (Washington DC: Folger Library Publications, 1991), 26.

[53] Love gives further evidence suggesting that a manuscript presented by its author would have sold for about three or four pounds, two or three times as much, that is, as a stationer paid for a manuscript. See *Scribal Publication*, 67.

[54] See the Bodleian Library manuscript Malone 25.

[55] See Appendix C for a brief discussion of the possibility that (some of) Shakespeare's plays were sold and circulated in manuscript.

[56] Blayney, "Publication of Playbooks," 386.

explain why it was in the Lord Chamberlain's Men's interest to postpone print publication. When a play first reached the stage, it was likely to attract an important number of spectators simply because it was new. This is demonstrated by the figures in Henslowe's diary, which are consistently much higher for new than for old plays. In the prefatory address "To the Reader" in the 1612 quarto of *The White Devil*, Webster complains of playgoers who "resemble those ignorant asses (who visiting Stationers shoppes their vse is not to inquire for good bookes, but new bookes)." Furthermore, in the address "To the Reader" in *The Famelie of Love* (1608), the author points out that "Plaies in this Citie are like wenches new falne to the trade, onelie desired of your neatest gallants, whiles the'are fresh: when they grow stale they must be vented by Termers and Cuntrie chapmen" (A1^v). A new play, then, did not need extra publicity. On the other hand, selling a manuscript to a publisher may have been a way of securing free promotion for a revival when a playbook would have been sold in bookshops and advertised with title pages put up on posts in London.[57] Considering that only a small fraction of the playwrights' output reached print, published playbooks may well have recommended plays to theatergoers.[58]

---

[57] See Gaskell, *Introduction to Bibliography*, 116. The precise documentation of the performances and printings of Molière's plays allows us to gather that his company did use print publication to promote a revival. Contrary to most other Molière plays (which were printed within a few months of their first performance), *Le Mariage Forcé*, staged as early as 1664, was only entered and published in 1668. In 1664, *Le Mariage Forcé* had been relatively unsuccessful. Attendance diminished rapidly and performances stopped after May 13, 1664. The play was revived some four years later, the first performance taking place on February 24, 1668. Four days earlier, the play had been entered. It was printed immediately, the date of the "achevé d'imprimer" being March 9 (Albert-Jean Guibert, *Bibliographie des Oeuvres de Molière Publiees au XVIIe Siècle*, 2 vols. (Paris: Centre national de la recherche scientifique, 1961) I.231). What these dates suggest is that theatrical and print publications, performance and print, clearly constituted a concerted effort, carefully timed so as to enhance the marketability of both. Print performance appears to have been relied upon to recommend the play to potential spectators, whereas stage performances of Molière's *Mariage Forcé* appear to have been trusted to increase sales of the printed play.

[58] It should be noted that on the one occasion when a company did intervene to avoid (or postpone) the publication of a play, that play was brand new and ended up being printed from what seems to have been a "good" manuscript three years later. As Henslowe's diary shows, *Patient Grissell* was written by Chettle, Dekker, and Haughton late in 1599. The diary next records a payment for "a grey gowne for gryssell" late in January 1600. The play is likely to have reached the stage soon after. On March 18, Henslowe's diary records a payment of 20s. to one of the Lord Admiral's Men "to geue vnto the printer to staye the printing of patient gresell." This printer appears to have been Cuthbert Burby who entered the play in the Stationers' Register ten days later without proceeding to prepare an edition. This suggests that Henslowe and the Lord Admiral's Men successfully thwarted someone else's attempt to publish without their agreement what may have been a "bad" text. What is equally significant, however, is that the play did end up in print in 1603, published by Henry Rocket who had been Burby's apprentice until 1602. The printed text is of a quality that made Bowers believe that "Henslowe paid forty shillings to stay the printing of a 'bad quarto' and later supplied a good text" (*The Dramatic Works of Thomas Dekker*, ed. Fredson Bowers, 4 vols. (Cambridge University

What evidence can be adduced in support of the theory that theatrical companies in the 1590s considered print publication favorable rather than damaging to the plays' destiny on the public stage? There is the fact that the first quarto of *Romeo and Juliet*, printed in 1597, would have been on sale in 1598 when (as we know thanks to John Marston's *Scourge of Villanie*) the play was performed at the Curtain.[59] There is also the fact that the second edition of *Tamburlaine* (1593) would have been available in London's bookshops when the Lord Admiral's Men revived the play on August 30, 1594.[60] Additionally, *Titus Andronicus*, printed 1594, was revived by the joint Chamberlain's and Admiral's Men in June 1594.[61] *The Taming of a Shrew*, acted on June 13, 1594, had been entered in the Stationers' Register on May 2, 1594 and was printed the same year. *A Knack to Know an Honest Man*, entered in the Stationers' Register on November 26, 1595 and published in an edition dated 1596, remained in the Lord Admiral's Men's repertory between October 23, 1594 and November 3, 1596. The octavo edition of *The Massacre at Paris* is undated but in all probability belongs to 1594, the year when the play was performed ten times by the Admiral's Men between June 21 and September 27. *The Spanish Tragedy*, finally, belonged to the Lord Strange's Men's repertory when the play was first published and, going through eleven editions between 1592 and 1633, could be found both in the London bookstalls and playhouses. The above evidence suffices to make clear that the stage and the printed page did not necessarily represent two rival forms of publication.

I have so far concentrated on the first dozen plays Shakespeare wrote after joining the Lord Chamberlain's Men in 1594. But what of the plays Shakespeare wrote before joining the Lord Chamberlain's Men in 1594? According to standard chronologies, eight First Folio plays and *Edward III* seem likely to have been written before the Lord Chamberlain's Men came into existence in 1594. The plays published in the 1623 Folio are the three parts of *Henry VI*, *The Two Gentlemen of Verona*, *The Comedy of Errors*, *The Taming of the Shrew*, *Titus Andronicus*, and *Richard III*.[62]

Press, 1953–61), 1.210; see also Cyrus Hoy, *Introductions, Notes, and Commentaries to Texts in "The Dramatic Works of Thomas Dekker" Edited by Fredson Bowers*, 4 vols. (Cambridge University Press, 1980), 1.129–31). What Henslowe and the Lord Admiral's Men thus objected to was not publication per se but publication over which they had no control.

[59] *Scourge of Villainy*, entered September 8, 1598: "what's playd to day? . . . *Iuliet* and *Romeo*." I quote from G. B. Harrison's edition (New York, 1966), 107.

[60] This and the following items of information concerning performance dates is taken from R. A. Foakes and R. T. Rickert, eds., *Henslowe's Diary* (Cambridge University Press, 1961).

[61] This, in any case, is the majority view. Some critics, including Jonathan Bate in his Arden3 edition (London: Routledge, 1995), 69–79, argue that *Titus Andronicus* was new in 1594.

[62] See, for instance, Evans, ed., *Riverside Shakespeare*, 78–80.

Shakespeare's company connections up to 1594 are shrouded in obscurities. The years 1592 to 1594 were a period of severe plague in London, entailing a major reorganization among the theatrical companies with players and plays moving from one company to another. Shakespeare himself has been conjecturally linked to the Lord Strange's Men (who became Derby's on the death of Henry Stanley and the succession of Ferdinando Stanley, Earl of Derby, on September 25, 1593), the Earl of Pembroke's Men, and the Queen's Men, but there is no unambiguous evidence to confirm any of these cases.[63] Shakespeare's possible co-authorship with other playwrights of several of the earliest plays attributed to Shakespeare further complicates matters. We can be fairly confident that the twelve plays I discussed above were written by one playwright for one company and remained in the possession of that company. In contrast, we know very little about the origins and the ensuing history of several of the plays Shakespeare wrote – or wrote a substantial part of – before joining the Lord Chamberlain's Men. Once Shakespeare had released his plays to a company, he did not necessarily keep control over their subsequent fate. It should therefore not surprise us if no easily recognizable pattern emerges from the publication history of these plays.

Depending on whether we consider *The Taming of a Shrew* as a Shakespearean or non-Shakespearean version of *The Taming of the Shrew*, five or six of Shakespeare's earliest nine plays were in print by 1597. Here is a summary of their early publication history:

Title	Date	Entrance	Publisher	Company/Companies on title page
Titus	1594	2/6/1594	John Danter	Derby's, Pembroke's, Sussex's
2 Henry VI	1594	3/12/1594	Thomas Millington	none
A Shrew	1594	5/2/1594	Peter Short	Pembroke's
3 Henry VI	1595	no entry	Thomas Millington	Pembroke's
Edward III	1596	12/1/1595	Cuthbert Burby	no company
Richard III	1597	10/12/1597	Andrew Wise	Chamberlain's

Hardly anything can be gathered about what led to the publication of the first four of these plays. *Titus Andronicus* and *2 Henry VI* were entered before

---

[63] For Shakespeare's possible company affiliations up to 1594, see McMillin and MacLean, *The Queen's Men and Their Plays*; Schoenbaum, *William Shakespeare*, 159–83; G. M. Pinciss, "Shakespeare, Her Majesty's Players and Pembroke's Men," *Shakespeare Survey*, 27 (1974), 129–36; and Mary Edmond, "Pembroke's Men," *The Review of English Studies*, n.s., 25 (1974), 129–36.

the Lord Chamberlain's Men came into existence, but it seems impossible to determine who sold the manuscripts to Danter and Millington. *A Shrew* may or may not have anything to do with Shakespeare. Finally, all that can be said about the 1595 edition of *3 Henry VI* is that the title page mentions the Earl of Pembroke's rather than the Lord Chamberlain's Men, which does not suggest that Shakespeare and his fellows were involved in its publication.

All we thus know about the publication history of *2* and *3 Henry VI*, *Titus Andronicus*, and *The Taming of a Shrew* is that someone had managed to bring about their publication by 1595 and that the Lord Chamberlain's Men were thus unable to do so themselves. The same does not apply to the two remaining plays Shakespeare may well have written before mid-1594. As we have seen above, manuscripts of *Edward III* (entered by Cuthbert Burby) and *Richard III* (entered by Andrew Wise) were sold to stationers with whom the Lord Chamberlain's Men also did business on other occasions. The absence of auspices on the title page of the earliest edition of *Edward III*, Shakespeare's possible co-authorship of the play and its absence from the First Folio makes the case for the Lord Chamberlain's Men's publication of *Edward III* no more than tentative. The publication of *Richard III* – entered by the stationer who went on to publish *Richard II*, *1 Henry IV*, and *Much Ado about Nothing* – is likely, however, to have been brought about by Shakespeare and his fellows.

This leaves us with three of Shakespeare's early plays, *1 Henry VI*, *The Two Gentlemen of Verona*, and *The Comedy of Errors*, and the question of why they were not published during Shakespeare's lifetime. Even though the First Folio presents a trilogy about the reign of Henry VI, *1 Henry VI* seems to have originated as a play independent of parts two and three. Henslowe's diary records a performance on March 3, 1592 of what appears to have been *1 Henry VI*, but shows no evidence of *2* and *3 Henry VI*. Furthermore, long after E. K. Chambers's apparent rebuttal of the disintegrators,[64] recent scholarship takes seriously the possibility that Shakespeare was only one among several playwrights who wrote *1 Henry VI*.[65] It seems likely that *1 Henry VI* became part of the repertory of the Lord Chamberlain's Men, though it is by no means certain. Even if it did, it is possible that the play

---

[64] See E. K. Chambers, *The Disintegration of Shakespeare* (London: Published for the British Academy, 1924).

[65] See Gary Taylor, "Shakespeare and Others: The Authorship of *Henry VI, Part I*," *Medieval and Renaissance Drama in England*, 7 (1995), 145–205. Note that Edward Burns, editor of *1 Henry VI* in the Arden3 series, is in basic agreement with Taylor (Burns, ed., *King Henry VI, Part 1* (London: Thomson Learning, 2000), 73–84).

did not become "Shakespearean" until after Shakespeare's death, and that Shakespeare never thought of it as his own rather than as a play – perhaps like *Sir Thomas More* – to which he had made a contribution.

The stage history of *The Two Gentlemen of Verona* prior to the eighteenth century is a blank. Accordingly, very little can be gathered about the reasons for its non-publication during Shakespeare's lifetime. Meres's mention in 1598 suggests that the play was known and thought of as Shakespearean. It seems impossible to know whether Shakespeare considered it an immature play whose publication he did not promote, whether the Lord Chamberlain's Men had a different policy toward the publication of the plays Shakespeare had written for different companies or whether other reasons kept the play out of print.

Finally, *The Comedy of Errors*, like *King John*, may well not have been published for reasons of copyright. Plautus's *Menaechmi*, translated by William Warner, was entered in the Stationers' Register in June 1594 and published in 1595. Plautus's play is the main source for *The Comedy of Errors*, and Shakespeare followed it quite closely in the dramatization of the confusion arising from twins. *Gesta Grayorum*, the records of Gray's Inn, contain an account of the revels on December 28, 1594, according to which "a Comedy of Errors (like to *Plautus* his *Menechmus*) was played by the Players."[66] As explained above, copyright within the Stationers' Company protected a publisher not just against someone else reprinting or plagiarizing his own copy but also against the publication of any text that was "like to" it. *Henry V* is probably less "like to" *The Famous Victories of Henry the Fifth* than *The Comedy of Errors* to Plautus's *Menaechmi*. The fact that the publishers of *Henry V* had to seek the consent of Thomas Creede, who had published *Famous Victories* in 1598,[67] thus supports the possibility that *The Comedy of Errors* could not easily have been published in the 1590s even if Shakespeare and his fellows had tried to sell it to a stationer.

Contrary to the Lord Chamberlain's Men plays written from 1594, the plays Shakespeare wrote for other companies prior to that date do not conform to a publication history with an easily discernible pattern. Yet this is what we should expect. Too various are the agencies that may have been involved in the transmission and the publication of these texts. What seems clear, however, is that the Lord Chamberlain's Men did not come into the possession of a number of Shakespeare plays which they then tried to keep out of print.

---

[66] See *Gesta Grayorum*, ed. W. W. Greg (London: Oxford University Press, 1914), 22–24.
[67] See Blayney, "Publication of Playbooks," 399.

The fact that there is no evidence that Shakespeare saw any of his plays into print has been instrumental in strengthening the opinion that Shakespeare lacked interest in or was opposed to their publication. I would argue that, in fact, it provides little evidence of this kind. The assumption that Shakespeare could very well have supervised the printing of his plays had he only cared to and, *ex negativo*, that his failure to do so reveals his indifference relies, I believe, on a set of mistaken premises. As shareholder, player, and "ordinary poet" of the Lord Chamberlain's Men, writing an average of two plays a year, studying his parts or rehearsing in the morning, playing in the afternoon, going to Stratford at least once a year and probably for longer periods when playing was suspended by outbreaks of plague, Shakespeare can hardly be blamed for not having spent his time in printing houses. It may be tempting to imagine that when printers were busy working on some of the world's finest plays, they were more than happy to deliver proofs to the Fortune or the Globe, or to Shakespeare's home in Bishopsgate, Southwark, or Cripplegate, patiently awaiting their return after the play-wright had time to examine them. The reality, however, was very different. Single plays published in quarto or octavo format sold for roughly 6d. They were considered unimportant publications and comparatively little effort went into their printing. Type usually had to be distributed for reuse soon after a sheet was printed off,[68] which means that an author supervising the printing of his text would have to invest a considerable amount of time. For the 1608 quarto of *The History of King Lear*, for example, twenty-one proof-sheets would have been printed and corrected at twenty-one different stages of the printing.[69] Shakespeare cannot reasonably be expected to have envisaged supervising the printing of his playbooks even if he was interested in their publication.

Since the texts of *Venus and Adonis* and *The Rape of Lucrece* are remarkably clean by comparison with those of the quarto playtexts, it is often believed – indeed taken for granted – that Shakespeare supervised their printing. This is another myth we will do well to discard and, with it, the reasoning that if Shakespeare saw the poems into print, but not the plays, then surely he did not care about the publication of his plays. London printers produced work of highly variable quality; the textual quality of *Venus and Adonis* and *The Rape of Lucrece* reflects Richard Field's printing rather than William Shakespeare's proofreading. As John Roe, editor of the narrative poems in

[68] See Gaskell, *Introduction to Bibliography*, 116.
[69] For the most thorough analysis of the proof-reading, revising, and press-correcting of the first quarto of *King Lear*, see Blayney, *Texts of "King Lear*," 188–218.

the New Cambridge Series, shows, "Once [Shakespeare's] carefully prepared manuscript was in the hands of the printer he most likely entrusted
the enterprise to the professional competence of others, pausing over the
printed copy only long enough to make sure that all was well with the dedication page."[70] It may be well to recall that even Ben Jonson supervised
only part of the printing of his First Folio: the plays but not the masques
and entertainments; the *Epigrammes* but not *The Forrest*.[71]

Even Middleton, who prepared *A Game at Chess* for publication, producing himself a transcript that served as printer's copy and partly revising
the play in the process, "did not proofread the sheets or supervise correction
of the text."[72] Middleton's attitude toward *A Game at Chess* in 1624 may
not have been so different from Shakespeare's toward his plays. Owing to
the existence of no fewer than six manuscripts (two of which are wholly
[Trinity] or partially [Bridgewater–Huntington] in his hand) and two substantive printed editions (one of which set up from another manuscript
in Middleton's hand), the playwright's involvement in the textual history
of his play is quite fully documented. On the one hand, Middleton appears to have adapted the play for the theater. On the other hand, after the
stage run, he was very involved in the play's dissemination, transcribing
it for patrons and preparing it for publication without, however, worry-
ing about the quality of the manuscripts or seeing it through the press.
Howard-Hill points out that "all the surviving manuscripts of *A Game at
Chess* are grossly defective, with the acquiescence of the author" and that
"Middleton's concern for his play stopped at the printing-house door."[73]
Clearly, there was nothing inconsistent for Middleton about interest in his
play's afterlife in print and manuscript and involvement in its dissemination

---

[70] John Roe, ed., *The Poems*, The New Cambridge Shakespeare (Cambridge University Press, 1992), 291.

[71] See Douglas A. Brooks, " 'If he be at his book, disturb him not': The Two Jonson Folios of 1616," *Ben Jonson Journal*, 4 (1997), 81–103, rpt. and rev. in *Playhouse to Printing House*, 104–39. Moreover, the second quarto of Marston's *Parasitaster, or The Fawn* was, according to its title page, "corrected of many faults, which by reason of the Authors absence, were let slip in the first edition." Marston claims in a note added to the second edition that "I have perused this copy to make some satisfaction for the first faulty impression" (A2ᵛ). As bibliographical investigations have shown, however, Marston was not present in the printing house when the second quarto was in press, but simply marked up a copy of the first edition (David A. Blostein, ed., *Parasitaster or The Fawn*, The Revels Plays (Manchester University Press, 1978), 42–52, esp. 49). As Donald Foster has pointed out, "Renaissance authors assisted in reading the proofs far less often than has usually been supposed in past criticism. It was the exception, rather than the rule, for a writer in Shakespeare's London to make a thorough inspection of his proofs, since this was a labor that took at least several days, and sometimes months, to complete" (*Elegy By W. S.: A Study in Attribution* (Newark: University of Delaware Press; London and Toronto: Associated University Presses, 1989), 228–29).

[72] Howard-Hill, "Scribe or Reviser," 315.   [73] Ibid., 314–15.

on the one hand and relative carelessness about the quality of the texts on the other.

David Scott Kastan is among those who have argued that Shakespeare "displayed . . . no obvious desire to see his plays in print at all." Yet his argument that Shakespeare "might well have brought [his plays] to his townsman Field, as he apparently did with the narrative poems, but he did not" seems to rely on another misapprehension, this one concerning printing-house practices.[74] Richard Field produced approximately three-hundred books, among them many theological works, educational textbooks, editions of the classics, the 1591 edition of John Harington's translation of *Orlando Furioso*, and the 1598 collection of Sidney's works (for William Ponsonby); but Field did not publish a single play written for the public playhouse. As an apprentice, he served six of the seven years with the Huguenot printer Thomas Vautrollier (1579–85), whom he later succeeded and whose widow he married in 1590.[75] Field seems to have been of a conviction that made playbooks unsuitable matter for his printing house. Other printing houses would have been far more hospitable. Andrew Wise, for example – publisher of *Richard III* (1597), *Richard II* (1597), *1 Henry IV* (1598), *2 Henry IV* (with William Aspley, 1600), and *Much Ado About Nothing* (with Aspley, 1600) – and the playbill printer James Roberts – who entered *The Merchant of Venice* (1598), *Hamlet* (1602), *Troilus and Cressida* (1603) – seem reasonable choices if Shakespeare and his company were trying to have some of their plays published.

It is true, of course, that Shakespeare provided dedications for his narrative poems but for none of his plays. This, however, simply reflects the conventions of his time. While Shakespeare, unlike Jonson, did nothing to change the conventions of play publication, it does not follow that Shakespeare was indifferent to the fate of his plays in print. In the fullest study of "The Dedication of Tudor and Stuart Plays" to date, Virgil B. Heltzel has pointed out that "not all types of Elizabethan literature were equally suitable for dedication to a patron . . . Satires, controversial pamphlets, humorous and other trivia, and common stage plays either sought no patrons or were dedicated only in exceptional circumstances."[76] While Latin dramas and translations of ancient or modern dramas often did contain dedications, plays written for and performed on the public stage, as

[74] *Shakespeare After Theory*, 77.
[75] See A. E. M. Kirwood, "Richard Field, Printer, 1589–1624," *The Library*, 4th series, 12 (1931), 1–39; *DNB*, VI.1276, and McKerrow, gen. ed., *Dictionary*, 102.
[76] Heltzel, "The Dedication of Tudor and Stuart Plays," 74.

Heltzel shows, were an entirely different matter: "the commercialization to which ordinary stage plays had been subjected after the establishment of the London theaters placed upon all such works the stigma of trade," and thus made them unfit for dedication to patrons.[77] Heltzel's exhaustive survey demonstrates that "during the entire reign of Queen Elizabeth and for some years after, the ordinary stage play was not thought worthy of patronal favor and none was dedicated."[78] The first dramatist to dedicate a play that had been performed in front of a paying audience was George Chapman, who furnished his *Charles, Duke of Byron* (printed in 1608) with a dedication to Sir Thomas Walsingham and his son.[79] What the evidence thus suggests is that the dedication of printed playtexts remained nearly nonexistent until the end of Shakespeare's career.[80]

In their address "To the great Variety of Readers" which prefaces the First Folio, Heminge and Condell – who must have known more about Shakespeare's attitude toward print than we ever will – say nothing to convey the impression that Shakespeare had been indifferent to his works' afterlife: "It had bene a thing, we confesse, worthie to haue bene wished, that the Author himselfe had liu'd to haue set forth, and ouerseen his owne writings." While Heminge and Condell do not positively assert that it was Shakespeare's intention to prepare the folio edition of his plays, these friends and fellow-actors imply that he might well have "set forth, and ouerseen his owne writings" if he had lived.

Heminge and Condell's assumption makes it seem all the more surprising that we have so long refused to believe that Shakespeare did care about the publication of his plays. His investment, I have argued in this chapter, is visible in the publication history of the plays Shakespeare wrote after 1594.

---

[77] Ibid.   [78] Ibid.

[79] As Heltzel points out, "Chapman may have been encouraged in this by Jonson's dedicatory epistle dated February 11, 1607, and prefixed to *Volpone*, in which he undertakes to defend despised dramatic poetry and with boldness to place the stamp of respectability upon his play by addressing it 'to the most noble and most aequall sisters, the two universities'" ("Dedication," 82). Even earlier, Jonson appears to have provided presentation copies of his plays with (printed or autograph) dedications. There are extant copies of *Cynthia's Revels*, printed 1601, with inserted dedications to Jonson's old schoolmaster William Camden and to the Countess of Bedford, and two copies of *Sejanus*, printed 1605, with inscriptions to Francis Crane and to Sir Robert Townshend (see Heltzel, "Dedication," 80–81).

[80] That Shakespeare was not as indifferent to print as is often claimed has also been suggested by Katherine Duncan-Jones, who has argued that the publication of the 1609 *Shakespeare's Sonnets* was authorial. See Duncan-Jones, ed., *Shakespeare's Sonnets*, 1–13, and "Was the 1609 *Shakespeares Sonnets* really unauthorized?" *The Review of English Studies*, 34 (1983), 151–71. Donald W. Foster has also argued that Shakespeare himself was behind the publication of his sonnets in 1609 (*Elegy by W. S.*, 227–32).

I have shown that what may well have been the first twelve plays Shakespeare wrote for the Lord Chamberlain's Men conform to a consistent pattern insofar as all those plays that could be published had appeared in quarto editions by 1602, usually about two years after they were first performed. This pattern seems too regular to be accidental. It is with these findings in mind that we now need to consider the evolving publication history of Shakespeare's plays in the following years.

CHAPTER 4

Shakespeare and the publication of his plays (II): the early seventeenth century

The number of publications of Shakespearean playbook declined after 1600. All in all, only five plays were published from 1601 to 1616, as opposed to thirteen plays between 1594 and 1600.[1] The seven years before 1600 saw a total of twenty-four editions of Shakespearean playbooks, that is more than three per year.[2] In contrast, there were only nineteen editions in the sixteen years preceding Shakespeare's death, slightly more than one per year (see Appendix A). *The Merry Wives of Windsor*, of which a "bad" text was published in 1602, is the only comedy that found its way into print; and though four comedies had been printed from 1598 to 1600, none was reprinted within Shakespeare's lifetime. Apart from *Richard II, Richard III*, and *1 Henry IV*, which had been popular with readers in the late sixteenth century and remained so in the early seventeenth, only *Hamlet* and *Pericles* appeared in more than one edition between the turn of the century and Shakespeare's death.

These are the surprising figures with which I intend to grapple in this chapter. It may be well to state at the outset that the data resist straightforward explanation. I have argued in the preceding chapter that the publication history of the plays Shakespeare wrote between joining the Lord Chamberlain's Men and the turn of the century conforms to a recognizable pattern which bespeaks a coherent strategy. This is not the case for the plays Shakespeare wrote after the turn of the century. Accordingly, the conclusions I arrive at in this chapter are altogether more tentative.

What, then, are the possible reasons for the decrease in the number of Shakespearean playbook publications? One reason, as Blayney has suggested, is that the market for playbooks was temporarily glutted in the early

---

[1] *Love's Labour's Won* is excluded from this count as the evidence does not make clear whether the play, if there was an edition of which no copy has survived, was printed before or shortly after the turn of the century.

[2] This includes the lost edition of *Love's Labour's Lost* and the first edition of *1 Henry IV* of which only few leaves of one copy have been preserved.

seventeenth century. No fewer than twenty-seven plays had been entered in the Stationers' Register between May 1600 and October 1601. As the supply would temporarily exceed the demand, several publishers delayed the printing of their plays for several years.[3] In such a situation, a stationer would think twice before investing in a new playbook. The sale of few play-books repaid the initial investment within the first few years. In the early seventeenth century, expectations to make a profit with a newly published playbook would have been particularly low. Of the Shakespeare plays pub-lished in 1600 or after, *Hamlet* and *Pericles* (both going through three edi-tions within roughly ten years) were a commercial success. *The Merchant of Venice*, *Much Ado About Nothing*, *A Midsummer Night's Dream*, *The Merry Wives of Windsor*, *The History of King Lear*, and *Troilus and Cressida* – none of which was reprinted until the collected editions of 1619 or 1623 – were not.

Another reason for Shakespearean playbooks' diminished popularity in the early years of the seventeenth century is the 1599/1600 revival at St. Paul's and Blackfriars' of children's companies, which constituted an important transformation of London's theatrical landscape. The Lord Chamberlain's and the Lord Admiral's Men had enjoyed a virtual monopoly on London's stages since 1594, a monopoly which had been formalized by the Privy Council in 1597.[4] With the return of the children's companies, a number of self-confident and ambitious dramatists (among whom Jonson, Marston, Chapman, Dekker, and Webster) started writing plays in a new and so-phisticated style. They catered to the contemporary taste for satire, thereby constituting a conscious and temporarily successful challenge to the adult companies. As R. A. Foakes has convincingly argued, "during the decade following their revival, the children's theatres and the dramatists who wrote for them formed a major influence in determining the course English drama was to take."[5] The children's companies played to more sophisticated and wealthier spectators than the adult companies, spectators with the money and education to purchase and to read printed playbooks. In the early sev-enteenth century, the children's companies, in terms of dramatic fashion, were the latest hit. It may then be understandable that a disproportionate number of the plays written for children's companies found their way into print, and that, consequently, the number of other printed plays, including plays by Shakespeare, dwindled.[6]

---

[3] Blayney, "Publication of Playbooks," 385.   [4] See Chambers, *Elizabethan Stage*, 11.6–7.

[5] R. A. Foakes, "Tragedy at the Children's Theatres after 1600: A Challenge to the Adult Stage," in *The Elizabethan Theatre, 2*, ed. David Galloway (Toronto: Macmillan of Canada, 1970), 39.

[6] In their highly useful statistical analysis of the marketing of early modern playbooks, Alan B. Farmer and Zachary Lesser point out that the custom of advertising printed plays with a mention of the

These pressures may explain why *As You Like It* was not printed before 1623. That a manuscript had been sold to a stationer is suggested by an entry in the Stationers' Register of August 4, 1600, "staying" the printing of "*muche A doo about nothinge,*" "*HENRY the FFIFT*" (in fact *2 Henry IV*),[7] "*as yow like yt,*" and "*Every man in his humour.*"[8] Some scholars have believed that this "staying entry" provides evidence for the Lord Chamberlain's Men's alleged reluctance to have Shakespeare's plays printed.[9] It has been convincingly argued, however, that it had nothing to do with an attempt by the players to "preclude unauthorized publication by establishing prior copyright," but rather indicates that the license "lacked ecclesiastical authorization."[10] Three of the four plays were regularly entered within twenty days and published the same or the following year in texts that seem to be based on authorial manuscripts. This fact is difficult to reconcile with the reading that sees in the "staying entry" an abortive attempt on behalf of the Lord Chamberlain's Men to prevent publication. It is thus more likely that the Lord Chamberlain's Men somehow failed to have *As You Like It* published than that they tried but failed to prevent the publication of *Much Ado About Nothing*, *2 Henry IV*, and *Every Man In His Humour*. Considering no fewer than three romantic comedies of Shakespeare reached print in 1600 – which, as a potential publisher perhaps anticipated, more than met the demand for the years to follow – it may not be surprising that *As You Like It* remained unpublished until 1623.

The publication history of *Troilus and Cressida* also deserves separate attention. The play had been entered on February 7, 1603 to "master Robertes," "for his copie in full Court holden this day to print when he hath gotten sufficient aucthority for yt, That booke of '*TROILUS and CRESSEDA*' as yt is acted by my lord Chamberlens Men."[11] The six-year gap between entrance and publication, the two title pages, and the

commercial playhouse at which they had been acted began when the boys' companies resumed playing. They show that the first fourteen playbooks thus advertised, published from 1601 to 1607, had been performed by the two children's companies at Paul's and Blackfriars ("Vile Arts: The Marketing of English Printed Drama, 1512–1660," *Research Opportunities in Renaissance Drama*, 39 (2000), 77–165, 87).

7 In an unpublished paper, Blayney has convincingly argued that the present reference must be to *2 Henry IV* rather than to *Henry V*. The argument is summarized in Cyndia Susan Clegg, "Liberty, License, and Authority: Press Censorship and Shakespeare," in *A Companion to Shakespeare*, ed. David Scott Kastan (Oxford: Blackwell, 1999), 478–79.

8 Arber, ed., *Transcript*, III.37. The "Staying Entry" of 4 August 1600 has attracted much scholarly discussion. For a full survey, see Richard Knowles, ed., *As You Like It*, A New Variorum Edition of Shakespeare (New York: MLA, 1977), 353–64.

9 See, for example, Richard Dutton's "Birth of the Author," in *Licensing, Censorship and Authorship in Early Modern England: Buggeswords* (Houndmills, Basingstoke, Hampshire; New York: Palgrave, 2000), 95. Dutton's essay has appeared in three slightly differing versions – see the bibliography.

10 Clegg, "Liberty, License, and Authority," 478.   11 Arber, ed., *Transcript*, III.226.

counterfactual assertion in the 1609 prefatory address that the play has never been performed have understandably puzzled critics and occasioned much debate.[12] So has the comment in the same address that readers should "thank fortune for the scape it hath made amongst you. Since by the grand possessors wills I beleeue you should haue prayd for them rather then beene prayd." Dutton has suggested that "the point of the epistle is that it announces a *reading version* of the play, new to a print readership and superior to what had doubtless been performed in a cut text by the King's Men at the Globe."[13] This plausible suggestion finds support in the publication of *Hamlet* Q2 a few years earlier. Its title page announces that it is "Newly imprinted and enlarged to almost as much againe as it was, according to the true and perfect Coppie." As the long Q2 *Hamlet* would have been new (though *Hamlet* was not), so the long reading text of *Troilus and Cressida* had never been offered to the public before even though a stage version had been "*acted by my lord Chamberlens Men.*"

Dutton's subsequent point that the difference between reading and acting version "may well have been what got the publishers their license" is more doubtful.[14] The very entrance in the Stationers' Register shows that Roberts had had his copy licensed, the entrance (for which he would have had to pay 4d.) recording the payment of the license fee of 6d.[15] So what Roberts was still lacking after entering the play in the Stationers' Register was not the license (which guaranteed him the Stationers' Company's protection against other stationers' infringements of his rights in the licensed copy), but the ecclesiastical authorities' "allowance" or "authority" whose purpose it was "to prevent the publication of unacceptable material and to justify the punishment of anyone who overstepped the line."[16]

Even substituting "allowance" or "authority" for "license," Dutton's claim remains questionable. That the printing of a book was to be stayed "until [the publisher] hath gotten sufficient authority for it" was neither rare nor a sign that the publisher need have had any problems obtaining the necessary authority for the printing of the playbook if he had tried.[17] Roberts entered several plays which had not been allowed, suggesting that he had not attempted to obtain the right to print the plays before entering them. As playbill printer, Roberts had regular dealings with the players, from which he seems to have profited by purchasing manuscripts at an advantageous price. As he did not want to run the financial risk of publishing the plays himself, he resold the rights to them to fellow publishers, perhaps making

[12] Greg, *Bibliography*, iii.1208.   [13] Dutton, "Birth of the Author," 103.
[14] Ibid.   [15] See Blayney, "Publication of Playbooks," 398–404.
[16] Ibid., 397.   [17] For a list of examples, see Chambers, *Elizabethan Stage*, iii.169.

a handsome profit on the deal or, as in the case of *The Merchant of Venice*, securing the right to print the play. Understandably, then, Roberts did not need to pay 10d. in order to have plays allowed which he did not intend to publish.[18]

The publication history of *Troilus and Cressida* does not indicate, therefore, that two different manuscripts passed into the stationers' hands, an acting version into Roberts's in 1603 which he did not succeed in getting allowed, and a reading version, six years later, into Bonian and Walley's.[19] Rather, Roberts seems to have acquired a manuscript from the Lord Chamberlain's Men and later sold it to Bonian and Walley. The same happened with *The Merchant of Venice*: the play was entered to Roberts on July 22, 1598 and transferred to Thomas Heyes on October 28, 1600, who published the play the same year.

In its first state, the title page of the 1609 quarto of *Troilus and Cressida* announces the text "As it was acted by the Kings Maiesties seruants at the Globe." Yet, in its second state, this phrase is omitted and the prefatory address claims that the play was "neuer stal'd with the Stage, neuer clapper-clawd with the palmes of the vulger." What can account for the contradictory evidence? A possible explanation is that the play was performed (as suggested by Stationers' Register) though only privately (and so was "neuer stal'd with the Stage, neuer clapper-clawd with the palmes of the vulger"). According to the Stationers' Register entry in February 1603, the play "is acted by my lord Chamberlens Men." If these words were copied from the title page of Roberts's manuscript, Bonian and Walley may have tried to update them (substituting "Kings Maiesties seruants" for "lord Chamberlens Men"), but mistakenly took for granted – as they realized before the end of the printing – that the play had been performed at the Globe.[20]

---

[18] On May 29, 1600 *"the Allarum to London"* was entered to Roberts's name, "PROVIDED that yt be not printed without further Aucthoritie" (Arber, ed., *Transcript*, III.161). The play was printed in 1602 by Edward Allde for William Ferbrand (*STC* 16754) and is said to have been "playde by the right Honorable the Lord Chamberlaine his seruants." On May 27, 1600, a different entrance to his name reads: *"A morall of Clothe breches and veluet hose, As yt is Acted by my lord Chamberlens servantes.* PROVIDED that he is not to putt it in prynte Without further and better Aucthority" (Arber, ed., *Transcript*, III.161). The play was never printed. On July 26, 1602, "A booke called *'the Revenge of* HAMLETT PRINCE *[of] Denmarke'* " was also entered to Roberts, though again he did not publish the play himself (see above).

[19] Dutton's point that Bonian and Walley "may well have convinced the licenser, William Segar, that what they were printing was different in kind from the acting version" ("Birth of the Author" (1996), 85) is unconvincing considering the Stationers' Company's license granted a protection "far beyond the limits of a specific text" (Blayney, "Publication of Playbooks," 399). In the revised versions of his article (1997, 2000), Dutton formulates this point more tentatively.

[20] I am indebted to Peter Blayney for the suggestion in this paragraph.

In the isolated cases of *As You Like It* and *Troilus and Cressida*, possible reasons for their delayed publication can be found. The more general question of the decrease of Shakespeare playbook publications remains to be answered, however. If we want to have a more detailed picture of the evolving publication history of Shakespeare's playbooks during his lifetime, it may be useful to list the relevant entries in the Stationers' Register:

February 6, 1594	Danter	*Titus Andronicus*
March 12, 1594	Millington	*2 Henry VI*
December 1, 1595	Burby	*Edward III*
August 29, 1597	Wise	*Richard II*
October 20, 1597	Wise	*Richard III*
February 25, 1598	Wise	*1 Henry IV*
July 22, 1598	Roberts	*Merchant of Venice*
August 4, 1600	"to be staied"	*Much Ado about Nothing,*
		As You Like It, 2 Henry IV
August 14, 1600	Pavier	*Henry V*
August 23, 1600	Wise, Aspley	*2 Henry IV*
August 23, 1600	Wise, Aspley	*Much Ado about Nothing*
October 8, 1600	Fisher	*Midsummer Night's Dream*
January 18, 1602	Busby	*Merry Wives of Windsor*
July 26, 1602	Roberts	*Hamlet*
February 7, 1603	Roberts	*Troilus and Cressida*
November 26, 1607	Butter, Busby	*King Lear*
May 20, 1608	Blount	*Antony and Cleopatra*
May 20, 1608	Blount	*Pericles*

Entries continue with relative regularity until February 1603, when Shakespeare and his fellows seem to have sold a manuscript of *Troilus and Cressida* to Roberts. That entry is followed by a break of almost five years until Butter and Busby have *King Lear* recorded at the end of November 1607. Moreover, the manuscript Butter and Busby purchased resulted in what is in many ways the most problematic of the "good" quartos. Long believed to be set up from a shorthand report or a memorial reconstruction, Q1 *King Lear*, published in 1608, contains much prose printed as verse and verse printed as prose, a considerable amount of mislineation, less punctuation than usual and an important number of mistakes of which some seem to point to oral/aural origins. What can be inferred about the quality of the manuscripts from which Shakespeare's "good" quartos have been set up is generally compatible with my argument that Shakespeare was not indifferent to the publication of his plays. Mistakes of the kind present in Q1 *Merchant of Venice* or Q2 *Hamlet*, to give only two examples, can be accounted for either by printing-house mistakes or by the assumption that Shakespeare's expectations of textual accuracy had little to do with the standards prevalent in a post-Enlightenment period. What appears to have been the state of the manuscript from which *King Lear* was set up does pose a problem, however, if we wanted to assume that Shakespeare cared about its publication.[21]

When we move on to the last entry in the Stationers' Register that bears witness to the sale of Shakespearean manuscript playbooks to a stationer, it seems even more doubtful that Shakespeare and the King's Men were involved in the publication. While the entry in the Stationers' Register records Edward Blount's rights to *Pericles*, it appeared in the following year as "Imprinted...for Henry Gosson." Since there is no record indicating that Blount had sold the rights to Gosson, Greg believed that "It was apparently not in pursuance of this entry [of May 20, 1608] that the play was printed the following year."[22] It is perhaps not entirely clear what Greg means by "in pursuance of this entry," but the fact that Gosson went on to publish a second edition the same year seems to indicate that he was not acting in contravention of Blount's rights. If Gosson had acquired from Blount the manuscript of and the rights to *Pericles* before publishing the play in 1609, it seems unlikely that Shakespeare and his fellows were involved in the publication of the "bad" text of *Pericles*.

I have outlined above what evidence there is to suggest that the attitude of Shakespeare and his fellows toward publication did not necessarily change in a fundamental way. A temporary glut in the playbooks market and the resurrection of the children's companies may have led to a drop in the number of playbooks publications. While this number may have dropped it did not necessarily stop as long as we assume that the King's Men were responsible for the *King Lear, Pericles,* or *Antony and Cleopatra* entries in

---

[21] A possibility that has perhaps not been given its due in the debate over the texts of *King Lear* is that quarto copy may have been a private transcript, or even a transcript of a private transcript at more than one remove from Shakespeare. The following three facts may support such a view: firstly, the publication of Q1 *Lear* occurs at a moment when the Lord Chamberlain's/King's Men may well have stopped or interrupted their previously regular dealings with a small group of stationers. Secondly, the text is of inferior quality compared to those of the other "good" quartos. Thirdly, contrary to all other title pages of "good" Shakespearean quartos, that of *King Lear* makes performance at court a selling point. Court records show that the play was performed at court on December 26, 1605 and requests for private transcripts may have followed the court performance. Note that Fredson Bowers suggested that the private transcript of *The Woman's Prize* – which had also been previously performed at court – was commissioned by someone who attended the court performance (*Beaumont and Fletcher Canon,* IV.6). I am indebted to a conversation with Leeds Barroll for my thinking on this issue.

[22] Greg, *Bibliography,* 1.419.

the Stationers' Register. On the other hand, considering it cannot be taken for granted that the publication (or attempted publication) of any of these plays was authorized by the King's Men, it seems possible that their strategy in publishing Shakespeare's plays did significantly change some time after February 1603. For greater clarity, it may be useful to distinguish between three chronologically distinct groups of plays and their publication history. Shakespeare wrote roughly a dozen plays for the Lord Chamberlain's Men from *c.* 1594 to 1599. As discussed in chapter 3, these plays seem to have been published by Shakespeare and his fellows unless special circumstances prevented them. The following group consists of the five plays Shakespeare wrote next according to the standard chronology:[23] *Julius Caesar, As You Like It, Hamlet, Twelfth Night,* and *Troilus and Cressida.* Insofar as the plays' publication history is concerned, this group may be called "mixed." Shakespeare and his fellows appear to have supported the publication of *Hamlet* and *Troilus and Cressida* – as mirrored by Roberts's entries in 1602 and 1603 – and possibly desired the publication of *As You Like It* – staged on August 4, 1600. There are no indications, however, that they ever attempted to have *Julius Caesar* and *Twelfth Night* published. Nothing else seems to have been printed previously which would have made their publication difficult or impossible (as in the case of *King John*). Considering all of Shakespeare's earlier plays written for the Lord Chamberlain's Men had been published, *Julius Caesar* and *Twelfth Night* appear to be the first exceptions among the first seventeen plays Shakespeare wrote for his company.

Following after a group of plays that were, as a rule, published a couple of years after their composition and a second group of plays partly published and partly not, the third group of plays consists of all of Shakespeare's remaining plays. As a rule, these plays were not published before Shakespeare's death: *Measure for Measure* (1603), *Othello* (1603–4), *All's Well That Ends Well* (1604–5), *Timon of Athens* (1605), *King Lear* (1605–6), *Macbeth* (1606), *Antony and Cleopatra* (1606), *Pericles* (1607), *Coriolanus* (1608), *The Winter's Tale* (1609), *Cymbeline* (1610), *The Tempest* (1611), *Cardenio* (probably with Fletcher, 1612–13), *Henry VIII* (with Fletcher, 1613), and *The Two Noble Kinsmen* (with Fletcher, 1613–14). Of these fifteen plays, only two were published during Shakespeare's lifetime (and one entered), and in both cases the nature of the text raises doubts about Shakespeare's involvement in the transactions that led to the publications.

If we believe that these figures suggest that Shakespeare and his fellows' attitude toward the publication of Shakespeare's plays must have drastically

---

[23] See, for instance, Wells, Taylor, et al., *Textual Companion*, 69–109.

changed, what might account for this change and what may their new attitude have been? It is certainly striking that the entries in the Stationers' Register continue with regularity until shortly before Queen Elizabeth's death on March 24, 1603, but become very rare during the years of King James's reign. Yet, to claim that the change of reign and patron had in and of themselves anything to do with what may have been a new attitude toward the publication of Shakespeare's plays seems far-fetched and is not supported by any firm evidence. What may also invite speculation is the prominence of the plague during the first years of James's reign. As Leeds Barroll has shown in his study, *Politics, Plague and Shakespeare's Theatre*, London's public theaters may have been closed roughly three months out of four between March 1603 and December 1610.[24] If publicity was the players' major motive for print publication, it may have seemed pointless to sell manuscripts at a time when conditions remained precarious and playing was impossible most of the time.

What argues against this interpretation is the number of other plays published during the same years (see Appendix A). It is true that few plays were printed in the year of the Queen's death (*Hamlet* is in fact one of only two plays first published that year) and in the following year (only four). Yet the four-year period from 1605 to 1608 saw the publication of no fewer than fifty-two plays written for the commercial stage, more than in any other four-year period during Shakespeare's life. While Shakespeare's plays account for more than 18 percent of all the (commercial) plays printed in the ten years prior to 1603, that figure is down to less than 4 percent for the ten years after 1603. If Shakespeare and the King's Men had refrained from publishing Shakespeare's plays because the London playhouses were closed more often than not, this would not have corresponded to what seems to have been the practice of other playwrights and companies.

In search for other possible explanations for the turn the publication history of Shakespeare's plays takes around the year 1603, another path one may be tempted to explore is the number of "bad" editions that appeared around that time. Q1 *Merry Wives of Windsor*, a text that is bad even in comparison with the other "bad" quartos, was published in 1602. In the same year, the "bad" text of *Henry V* reached a second edition. The following year, finally, the "bad" quarto of *Hamlet* appeared. At the same

---

[24] Leeds Barroll, *Politics, Plague and Shakespeare's Theatre: The Stuart Years* (Ithaca: Cornell University Press, 1991). See page 173 for a convenient summary of "Theatrical Conditions in London: 1603–1613." According to Barroll's table, the theaters were closed during sixty-three, open during twenty, and partly open and partly closed during eleven of the ninety-four months from March 1603 to December 1610.

time, the "good" texts of *Hamlet* and *Troilus and Cressida* the company probably sold to Roberts in July 1602 and February 1603 did not appear until 1604 and 1609 respectively. The assumption that Shakespeare and his fellows changed their attitude toward print publication because of the massed appearance of "bad" and the delayed appearance of "good" texts is not unproblematic, however. The fact that the second edition of *Henry V* is a reprint of the first, "bad" edition rather than a corrected and enlarged edition does nothing to suggest that the company had been troubled enough to intervene. More importantly, an early sale of a maximum number of play manuscripts rather than a temporary reluctance to sell them would reduce the risk of "bad" texts such as Q1 *Pericles* getting published.

It seems that Jonson started to prepare the folio edition of his works as early as 1612, and may have entertained plans to do so considerably earlier, plans which Shakespeare might well have been familiar with.[25] As long as we go on believing that Shakespeare's attitude toward the publication of his plays is the very opposite of Jonson's, it will seem preposterous to assume that Shakespeare likewise came to entertain the idea of having his plays published in a collected edition. Once we realize, however, that he and his fellows consistently published his first dozen plays written for the Lord Chamberlain's Men unless *force majeure* prevented it, the speculation may seem less implausible.

While Jonson's and Shakespeare's folios broke new ground by publishing plays that had been performed in front of paying audiences, other collections before theirs had also contained dramatic material. *Seneca his Tenne Tragedies* of 1581 republished several translations that had first appeared separately in the 1560s. In 1601/02, shortly before Shakespeare and his fellows may have stopped, or interrupted, the publication of Shakespeare's plays, Samuel Daniel, often believed to be the "rival poet" Shakespeare compares himself to in Sonnets 76–86 published the folio edition of his *Works* which included the closet tragedy *Cleopatra*. William Alexander's *Monarchick Tragedies*, first published in 1604 and "Newly enlarged" in 1607, gathered four closet tragedies in a quarto volume. To follow up these collections with an edition of Shakespeare's plays may have started to seem less preposterous once Shakespeare's company had come under royal patronage, and Ben Jonson may have started thinking about a collected edition that would include some of his plays.

Furthermore, it may be well to recall that in the early years of the seventeenth century, Shakespeare was able to look back upon a brief but extremely successful career in print. He had become the best-published dramatist with

[25] See Jonson, *Works*, eds. Herford and Simpson, 1.64, IX.14.

far more title page ascriptions than any other English playwright dead or alive. He had been promoted to the top of the canon of recent or contemporary English writers by Meres in 1598, and a great number of excerpts from his plays and poems had been published in two miscellanies of 1600 alongside passages from Spenser's *Faerie Queene* and Fairfax's Tasso among others. He had further had the honor of having his initials and his name taken in vain, the former in the 1602 quarto edition of *Thomas Lord Cromwell*, the latter on the title page of *The Passionate Pilgrim* in 1599. Shakespeare, in other words, was in many ways the rising star of the English literary scene during the final years of Queen Elizabeth's reign. Few writers beside him would have been in a better position to contemplate the possibility of an ambitious collected edition of their writings.

The role William Herbert, the third Earl of Pembroke, may have played in the history of Shakespeare's company is of some importance. As Leeds Barroll has shown, Pembroke appears to have had a particular interest in the theater, and is likely to have been the force that secured royal patronage for Shakespeare and his company in 1603.[26] We further know that Pembroke entertained a personal relationship with Richard Burbage. In a letter written in June 1619, Pembroke wrote that "all the company are at the play, which I being tender-hearted could not endure to see so soon after the loss of my old acquaintance Burbage."[27] Despite what Pembroke's words might lead one to suppose, Burbage had been dead for some three months suggesting that Pembroke's attachment to Burbage had been considerable. This is not the place to repeat the arguments for and against the identification of "Mr. W. H.," "THE ONLY BEGETTER" of Shakespeare's Sonnets, with William Herbert. Suffice it to say that while there is little if any chance that a definitive answer to the question posed by the 1609 quarto edition of *Shakespeare's Sonnets* will ever be found, Pembroke has generally been considered the most plausible candidate, an opinion that is strengthened by a recent statistical analysis of rare words by one of the leading practitioners in the field.[28]

---

[26] See Barroll, *Plague*, 37–41.

[27] Quoted in R. C. Bald, *John Donne: A Life* (Oxford University Press, 1970), 351; and in Barroll, *Plague*, 39. I am grateful to Leeds Barroll for drawing my attention to this point.

[28] MacD. P. Jackson, "Vocabulary and Chronology: The Case of Shakespeare's Sonnets," *The Review of English Studies*, 52 (2001), 59–75. Jackson argues that Shakespeare worked on the sonnet sequence well into the seventeenth century. He believes that "As recipient of Sonnets 1–17, [William] Herbert, eventual earl of Pembroke, notoriously unwilling to accept as bride Elizabeth Carey in 1595–6, Bridget Vere in 1597, or a niece of Charles Howard in 1599, and even in 1600–1 refusing to marry Mary Fitton, whom he had made pregnant, would – if we are willing to believe that there is any sort of biographical base to the sonnets' cast of characters – provide a much better chronological fit" than Southampton, the other chief candidate (74). Similarly, Katherine Duncan-Jones has come to the conclusion that "Once it is accepted that the publication of Q was authorized by Shakespeare, and

When it comes to the publication of Shakespeare's plays, the First Folio is of course dedicated to Pembroke and his brother, the Earl of Montgomery. Heminge and Condell praise the two aristocrats for having "beene pleas'd to thinke these trifles some-thing, heeretofore" and for having "prosequuted both them [the plays], and their Authour liuing, vvith so much fauour" (A2ʳ). These suggestive words do nothing to rule out the possibility that Pembroke and his brother had been for some time Shakespeare's most important readers. These readers would have been of an importance that might have prompted Shakespeare and his fellows to change their publication strategy from print for a relatively wide readership to manuscript presentation copies for a small group of influential patrons.

Pembroke's role in the publication history of Shakespeare's plays in print is not confined to that of dedicatee. Four years before the publication of the First Folio, he intervened on behalf of the King's Men by writing a letter to the Stationers' Company. The actual letter is lost, but an entry in the Records of the Court of the Stationers' Company dated May 3, 1619 specifies that "vppon a lēr from the right hoᵇˡᵉ the Lo. Chamberlayne It is thought fitt & so ordered That no playes that his Maᵗʸᵉˢ players do play shalbe printed wᵗʰout consent of soɱe of them."[29] The date of Pembroke's letter coincides with Pavier's aborted Shakespeare collection, and its abortion is in all probability due to Pembroke intervention. Pembroke's highly unusual intervention in 1619 suggests both that Heminge and Condell were planning Shakespeare's Folio and that Pembroke's cared enough about the King's Men and the forthcoming publication to further their cause.

In other words, it is perhaps unwise not to take seriously Heminge and Condell's regrets at Shakespeare's inability to supervise the printing of his collected edition. In *The Shakespeare First Folio*, Greg wondered when the idea of the Folio had first been entertained:

Jonson was preparing his works for the press about the time Shakespeare left London for Stratford, and Shakespeare must surely have known of it. It is foolish to suppose that Shakespeare was indifferent to the fate of his own works. . . . In the quiet evening of his days at New Place, did Shakespeare ever discuss the possibility of printing with the cronies who visited him there? According to tradition, Ben Jonson himself was of their number; and Chambers sees "no reason to reject this report."[30]

that it was in the Jacobean period that he put the sequence into its final form, an identification of Pembroke as the dedicatee and addressee of *Sonnets* becomes overwhelmingly attractive" (Duncan-Jones, ed., *Shakespeare's Sonnets*, 69).

[29] Jackson, *Records*, 110.

[30] W. W. Greg, *The Shakespeare First Folio: Its Bibliographical and Textual History* (Oxford: Clarendon Press, 1955), 2–3.

Stanley Wells has recently concurred: "We do not know where the plan originated, but Shakespeare himself may well have encouraged it in his last years. It is surely significant that the only three colleagues mentioned in his will are Richard Burbage, who died in 1619, and John Heminges and Henry Condell, who appear to have taken the prime responsibility for putting the book together."[31] I agree with Greg and Wells that Shakespeare may well have conceived of a collected edition of his plays, though I am not sure that it necessarily happened after his retirement.

Anyone who argues that Shakespeare died unmindful of his plays' after-life and that plans for a folio edition of his plays did not take shape until after his death would have to account for all those texts which were not simply set up from "good" quarto editions.[32] After all, it would have been easy enough to base plays like *Hamlet*, *Troilus and Cressida*, and *2 Henry IV* on the "good" printed editions. It is surely suggestive that the hand of a "literary editor" can be detected in the Folio text of *2 Henry IV*, or that differences between the quarto and the Folio texts of *Richard II* shows "revision... in the light of historical knowledge."[33] Moreover, a play like *Antony and Cleopatra* contains fuller stage directions than earlier plays, which has led to the speculation that Shakespeare may already have been contemplating retirement in 1607.[34] It seems more likely that *Antony and Cleopatra* reflects a literary text that Shakespeare prepared for future readers: "Enter Pompey, Menecrates, and Menas, in warlike manner" (Through Line Numbering [hereafter TLN] 614–15, 2.1.1); "Enter Ventidius as it were in triumph" (TLN 1494, 3.1.1); "Enter Cæsar... with his Counsell of Warre" (TLN 3108–09, 5.1.1); "Enter the Guard rustling in" (TLN 3574, 5.2.313). These are descriptive stage directions that seem directed at readers rather than at the bookkeeper. In sum, the textual make-up of the First Folio corroborates the contention that Shakespeare was not unmindful of a future readership of his plays.

The documentary record is too sketchy to allow a straightforward explanation for the uneven publication history of Shakespearean playbooks. What can be asserted with some confidence is that Shakespeare and his fellows had regular dealings with a small groups of stationers from 1595 to 1603,

---

[31] Stanley Wells, "Foreword," in Anthony James West, *The Shakespeare First Folio: The History of the Book, Volume I, An Account of the First Folio Based on Its Sales and Prices, 1623–2000* (Oxford University Press, 2001), v. See also Katherine Duncan-Jones, *Ungentle Shakespeare*, The Arden Shakespeare (London: Thomson Learning, 2001), 264.

[32] The seven years between Shakespeare's death and the publication of the First Folio have seemed to some an inordinately long time, but it should be borne in mind that "preparations for the collection started before the end of 1620" (Greg, *First Folio*, 4).

[33] Ibid., 269, 236.   [34] Ibid., 398.

the period during which Shakespeare acquired a remarkable reputation in print. We further know that these dealings were stopped, interrupted, or significantly reduced after the company had secured royal patronage. Finally, the Lord Pembroke intervened on behalf of the King's Men in 1619 to protect the publication of their plays at the time when Pavier's collection was threatening the commercial viability of the First Folio. What the total picture thus suggests is, I believe, not Shakespeare and his fellows' indifference to the publication of Shakespeare's plays during the years of James's reign. Such an indifference would be difficult to account for after a policy of regular and systematic publication from 1595 to 1603. Rather, print publication seems to have been postponed, possibly in lieu of manuscript presentation copies for influential patrons. Whatever other reasons there may have been for this postponement – restricted playing owing to the plague, disgust over the kind of editions Pembroke complains about in his letter to the Stationers' Company, a glut in the market of printed playbooks, or more specifically the great number of copies of "Shakespeare" playbooks which remained unsold in the early years of the seventeenth century – the time may well have come when Shakespeare and his fellows projected a collected edition and therefore refrained from publishing in cheap quartos. All things considered, the likelihood is that Shakespeare, late in his career, believed that the publication of his plays had been interrupted, not ended.

CHAPTER 5

The players' alleged opposition to print

I have argued above that Shakespeare and his fellows, far from being opposed to print publication, had a coherent strategy of trying to get Shakespeare's plays into print. In this chapter, I will attempt to anticipate objections by addressing a number of arguments that have fostered belief in the players' opposition to the publication of their plays.

The narratives that have long served to account for the players' alleged reluctance to publication in print – a reluctance that was only overcome by dire financial needs occasioned by the closure of the theaters owing to the plague – usually follow one of two lines. As for the first, the following statement can serve as a representative example: "it was in the companies' interests that their plays should not get into print, when they could be acted by rival companies."[1] As Blayney, Roslyn L. Knutson, and Richard Dutton have shown, there is no evidence that anything of the sort happened in London except in a couple of exceptional cases.[2] The Master of the Revels' licence conferred not on any but only on a specific company the right to perform a play. Furthermore, companies are known to have commissioned plays on subjects on which a different version was already in print. Ben Jonson, for instance, was paid for a play on King Richard III ("Richard Crookback") in the same year as Shakespeare's *Richard III* appeared in print. Henslowe could have saved the money he paid Jonson if acting other companies' plays had been an option. Knutson has disposed of the belief

---

[1] "General Introduction," in Shakespeare, *Complete Works*, gen. eds. Wells and Taylor, xxx. See also Chambers: "the danger was not so much that readers would not become spectators, as that other companies might buy the plays and act them" (*Elizabethan Stage*, 111.183).

[2] Blayney, "Publication of Playbooks," 386; Roslyn L. Knutson, "The Repertory," in *A New History of Early English Drama*, eds. Cox and Kastan, 461–80; Dutton, "Birth of the Author," 91–94. The most famous instance of a theatrical "theft" was the appropriation of "Jeronimo" by the Children of the Chapel, causing the King's Men to retaliate by performing *The Malcontent* ("Why not Malevole in folio with us, as Jeronimo in decimo-sexto with them?" Induction to *The Malcontent*, ed. George K. Hunter, The Revels Plays (London: Methuen, 1975), lines 78–79). For the circumstances leading to this incident, see Erne, *Beyond "The Spanish Tragedy,"* 14–46, esp. 21–23.

that players kept plays out of print lest rival companies perform them as "A canard of old theater histories."[3]

The other reason which allegedly kept the companies from having their plays printed is that the availability of a printed text might reduce attendance at the playhouse:

> Under solvent conditions, the acting companies stored licensed scripts in their archives and withheld them from publication. The theatrical companies believed that the value of a stage play was enhanced by this process, since the surprise and delight of a play's performance would not be diminished by the text's having been widely circulated beforehand. Because printed plays released by the companies were the exception, printers usually acquired manuscripts from dishonest players who reconstructed the text from memory, from patrons the company favored with private transcripts, or even from the authors, who lacked legal authority over the manuscripts they had submitted to the players.[4]

From the licensed manuscripts carefully stored in archives to the dishonest players surreptitiously reconstructing the text and selling them to publishers, the passage provides a version of what Blayney has called the "stirring melodrama" Pollard first invented in 1909 which critics have been reluctant to abandon ever since.[5] Fredson Bowers similarly believed that "if the play continued to be popular, the company could withhold it entirely in order to maintain the curiosity of the public."[6] Even Dutton thought "It is possible that those who had paid good money for a play were less certain than I can now be that publication would not reduce its value."[7] The problem with this argument is that, apart from scholarly tradition, there are no solid grounds on which to base it. It seems on the contrary that a play that fared well in the printing house, like *The Spanish Tragedy*, also remained exceptionally popular on stage. That the players should not wish to have their plays offered to a stationer by someone else seems plausible enough. That publication at one moment might not be as desirable as publication at another moment also makes sense. It does not follow,

---

[3] Knutson, "Repertory," 469–70.

[4] Murray, *Theatrical Legitimation*, 35. Even Murray's point that authors had no legal rights over the texts they had sold to the players is incorrect. Unless a contract specifically forbade playwrights to have their plays published, what the acting company acquired from the author was the exclusive right to *perform* the play rather than a copyright in anything resembling its modern sense.

[5] Blayney, "Publication of Playbooks," 383. When inquiring into the reasons why players sold manuscripts to stationers, Loewenstein is similarly trapped in Pollard's "stirring melodrama": "surely [these sales] always constituted efforts on the part of the acting companies to forestall the printing of corrupt copies, texts pirated by actors" ("Script in the Marketplace," 105). As Loewenstein's footnotes make clear, Pollard's now outdated *Shakespeare's Fight with the Pirates* is his principal authority for "the various possible motives for a company's printing plays" (112).

[6] Bowers, "Publication," 406.   [7] Dutton, "Birth of the Author," 94.

however, that publication per se was detrimental to the players' interests. Even Blayney "knows of no evidence that any player ever feared that those who bought and read plays would consequently lose interest in seeing them performed."[8]

Richard Dutton's article on "The Birth of the Author," which has been said to "shed much new light on the ties that may have bound Shakespeare to the playhouse and kept him out of the printing house,"[9] has recently explored the question "Why did Shakespeare not print his own plays?" Dutton suggests, following Bentley, that "it was the works of contracted 'ordinary poets' that companies were particularly anxious to keep out of print."[10] With regard to Shakespeare and the Lord Chamberlain's Men, the question this raises is why their strategy would have had so little success. Shakespeare seems to have written an average of about two plays per year, so even allowing for revivals, a good many other plays must have been composed by other playwrights for the Lord Chamberlain's Men. In his diary, Henslowe's list of performances by the Lord Admiral's Men features a play that is marked as new (the accepted interpretation of "ne") about every two or three weeks. Even though Henslowe also appears to have applied this designation to revised and revived plays ("new or marketably new" plays, in Roslyn Knutson's words), the number of new plays was important.[11] Even if the Lord Chamberlain's Men did not commission as many new plays as the Lord Admiral's Men did, Shakespeare cannot have produced more than a fraction of the amount of new dramatic material his company needed. There are only eight non-Shakespearean plays, however, which we know were written for the Lord Chamberlain's Men between 1594 and 1603 that reached print: Ben Jonson's *Every Man in his Humour* (Q1601) and *Every Man out of his Humour* (Q1600), Dekker's *Satiromastix* (Q1602), and the anonymous *Mucedorous* (Q1598), *A Warning for Fair Women* (Q1599), *A Larum for London* (Q1602), *Thomas Lord Cromwell* (Q1602), and *The Merry Devil of Edmonton* (Q1608).[12] In comparison, no fewer than twelve of Shakespeare's plays written in the same period had appeared in print by 1603. If the Lord Chamberlain's Men were "particularly anxious" to keep the plays of their "ordinary poet" out of print, their endeavors were a spectacular failure.

[8] Blayney, "Publication of Playbooks," 386.   [9] Brooks, *Playhouse to Printing House*, 56.

[10] Gerald Eades Bentley, *The Profession of Dramatist in Shakespeare's Time 1590–1642* (Princeton University Press, 1971), 264–92; and Dutton, "Birth of the Author," 90, 95.

[11] Knutson, "Repertory," 467.

[12] See Roslyn L. Knutson, "Shakespeare's Repertory," in *A Companion to Shakespeare*, ed. Kastan, 346–61. See also Knutson's *The Repertory of Shakespeare's Company, 1594–1613* (Fayetteville, Ark.: University of Arkansas Press, 1991).

Anyone who argues that the actors were opposed to the publication of playbooks must somehow account for those plays which were printed during Shakespeare's lifetime. The first quartos of *Romeo and Juliet, Henry V, The Merry Wives of Windsor*, and *Hamlet* (traditionally counted among the "bad" quartos) are editions whose publication Shakespeare is unlikely to have supported. Even if we discount them, however, we are still left with no fewer than thirteen substantive texts printed between 1597 and 1609 which go back to "good" manuscripts. Despite their large number, these texts have often been considered as exceptions to the rule – or as specific "breaches," to employ Dutton's term – for which various explanations can be found.[13] Chambers, for instance, believed that "so long as the companies were prosperous, they kept a tight hold on their 'books,' and only let them pass into the hands of the publishers when adversity broke them up, or when they had some special need to raise funds." More specifically, he attributed the spate of plays published in 1600 to "the call for ready money involved by the building of the Globe in 1599 and the Fortune in 1600."[14]

Dutton, too, avails himself of an alleged "breach" to account for the publication of *Richard III, Love's Labour's Lost*, and *1 Henry IV* in 1597/98. These plays were published, Dutton argues, only because the players "faced a financial crisis when unable to use either the Burbages' new Blackfriars venue or the Theater."[15] This argument needs to be questioned. The financial gain from the sales would have been insignificant. Blayney estimates that a stationer paid approximately 30s. for a manuscript.[16] In fact, the most precious property a company owned was not play manuscripts but costumes. In 1605, the estimated value of Edward Alleyn's "share of apparell" was £100.[17] Neil Carson's analysis of Henslowe's diary makes abundantly clear that companies spent several times more on costumes and staging than on plays.[18] If Shakespeare and his colleagues had needed some money in 1598, there would have been easier ways of securing it than by selling manuscripts.

---

[13] Dutton, "Birth of the Author," 99.   [14] Chambers, *Elizabethan Stage*, III.184.

[15] Dutton, "Birth of the Author," 99.

[16] Blayney, "Publication of Playbooks," 398. Greg pointed out long ago that "The few shillings that a publisher would have paid for a manuscript can have been no matter of consequence to a thriving company" (*Editorial Problem*, 44). On payments for playtexts, see also Roslyn L. Knutson, "The Commercial Significance of the Payments for Playtexts in *Henslowe's Diary*, 1597–1603," *Medieval and Renaissance Drama in England*, 5 (1991), 117–63.

[17] Chambers, *Elizabethan Stage*, II.298.

[18] "A particularly startling feature of the picture the diary reveals, therefore, is the apparent extravagance of the staging. Compared to £5–00–0 or £8–00–0 paid out for a play, the actors would spend £20–00–0, £30–00–0, or even more on production" (Carson, *Companion to Henslowe's Diary*, 78). See also Ann Jones and Peter Stallybrass, *Renaissance Clothing and the Materials of Memory* (Cambridge University Press, 2001), especially part III on "Staging Clothes."

We can be fairly confident that Shakespeare and his fellow shareholders were far from bankrupt in 1598. Theirs had been a thriving business since 1594, especially as the Lord Admiral's Men had been virtually the only company they had to compete with.[19] Even though hired players probably remained fairly poor, company shareholders did not. Burbage seems to have left more than £300 to his heirs, and Shakespeare had amassed a handsome fortune before the turn of the century.[20] In 1598, Shakespeare was wealthy enough to help a Stratford acquaintance, who, in the only extant letter addressed to Shakespeare, asked for a loan of £30.[21] If Shakespeare's plays really did "take on an almost fetishistic significance" and "were, so to speak, the company's family silver, not to be traded in by any of the sharers,"[22] it is not clear why Shakespeare and his fellow shareholders should have sold three plays for less than five pounds at a time when Shakespeare himself could spare substantially more.[23]

Being simultaneously shareholder, actor, and "ordinary poet" of the Lord Chamberlain's and King's Men, primarily interested in the economics of his company though hardly indifferent to the texts he had composed, Shakespeare occupied a position – in particular vis-à-vis the publication of his plays – that seems extraordinary if not unique and thus difficult to compare to anyone else's. Yet there is, of course, another famous seventeenth-century actor and playwright, heading a leading company, with stakes in both the economics of the company and the texts he has written. Like Shakespeare, he is accused of plagiarism soon after his arrival in the capital.[24] Like Shakespeare he gets into trouble with the authorities with one of his most popular plays by offending Puritan sympathies. As in Shakespeare's case, the protagonist's name ended up being changed.[25] Without denying the respective specificities of the place and time they lived in, the material conditions in which Shakespeare and Molière wrote and acted contain so

---

[19] See Gurr, *Shakespearean Stage*, 41–49.
[20] For Burbage, see Chambers, *Elizabethan Stage*, 11.308.
[21] See Schoenbaum, *William Shakespeare*, 238–40.   [22] Dutton, "Birth of the Author," 98.
[23] Blayney ("Publication of Playbooks," 386–87) has disposed of other alleged breaches to the players' unwillingness to have their plays published. Looking into the publications of 1594 – which have often been attributed to the closing of the theaters owing to a period of plague – Blayney has argued that the "suggestion that the players were motivated by financial hardship is less compelling, partly because the peak period happened *after* rather than during the closure and partly because the sums involved would have been relatively small" (386).
[24] See the "Préface" to Baudeau de Somaise's *Les Véritables précieuses* (Paris, 1660), printed in Georges Mongrédien, ed., *Recueil de textes et de documents du XVIIe siècle relatifs à Molière*, 2 vols. (Paris: CNRS, 1965), 1.117.
[25] The name of Hal's companion in *Henry IV* was famously changed from Oldcastle to Falstaff, while the "querelle" over Molière's *Tartuffe* resulted in the protagonist's name change to Panulphe (see Roger Duchêne, *Molière* (Paris: Fayard, 1998), 484–86).

many similarities that a comparison may yield instructive insights. Julie Stone Peters' *Theatre of the Book: Print, Text, and Performance in Europe, 1480–1880* and Roger Chartier's *Publishing Drama in Early Modern Europe* have recently demonstrated what can be gained from investigations that do not confine themselves to one country.[26] In particular, a brief look at the publication history of Molière's plays can throw light on the reasoning that has shaped belief in Shakespeare and his fellows' alleged indifference or opposition to print publication.

Only some thirty years separate the end of Shakespeare's career and the beginning of Molière's. Nevertheless, the documentary record Molière has left behind is considerably fuller, giving us access to hard figures where the absence of records leaves Shakespeareans guessing. Specifically, a good deal more is known about the publication history of Molière's plays than about that of Shakespeare's. In 1658, Molière and his fellows returned to Paris after thirteen years in the provinces, secured the patronage of Philippe d'Orléans, the king's only brother, and started to perform regularly at the Hôtel de Bourgogne. Despite his initial protests that his plays were written in order to be performed, he soon takes to having them published not long after they first reached the stage, a practice he did not relinquish until his death.[27] Most of Molière's plays were entered and printed within a year of their first performance.[28] Some of them reached print very quickly indeed, *L'Ecole des maris* less than two months and *Les Précieuses ridicules, Sganarelle ou le Cocu imaginaire, L'Ecole des maris, La Critique de "L'Ecole des femmes,"* and *Les*

---

[26] Chartier, *Publishing Drama in Early Modern Europe*, Panizzi Lectures, 14 (London: The British Library, 1999). For Peters, see above, page 7.

[27] See the "Préface" to the *editio princeps* of *Les Précieuses ridicules* (1660):

comme une grande partie des grâces qu'on y a trouvées dépendent de l'action et du ton de voix, il m'importait qu'on ne les dépouillât pas de ces ornements; et je trouvais que le succès qu'elles avaient eu dans la représentation, était assez beau pour en demeurer là. J'étais résolu, dis-je, de ne les faire voir qu'à la chandelle, pour ne point donner lieu à quelqu'un de dire le proverbe; et je ne voulais pas qu'elles sautassent du théâtre de Bourbon dans la Galerie de Palais [where publishers congregated]. Cependant je n'ai pu l'éviter, et je suis tombé dans la disgrâce de voir une copie dérobée de ma pièce entre les mains des libraires, accompagnée d'un privilège obtenu par surprise. J'ai eu beau crier: "O temps! Ô moeurs," on m'a fair voir une nécessité pour moi d'être imprimé ou d'avoir un procès; et le dernier mal est encore pire que le premier. Il faut donc se laisser aller à la destinée, et consentir à une chose qu'on ne laisserait pas de faire sans moi. (Mongrédien, ed., *Recueil*, 1.120)

By the time of the publication of *L'Ecole des maris* the following year, Molière admits having instigated the play's publication himself ("le premier ouvrage que je mets de moi-même au jour"), a practice he regularly repeated in the following years.

[28] All of the following plays were available in print less than a year after they first reached the stage: *Les Précieuses ridicules, Sganarelle ou le Cocu imaginaire, L'Ecole des maris, Les Fâcheux, L'Ecole des femmes, La Critique de "L'Ecole des femmes," L'Amour médecin, Le Médecin malgré lui, Le Misanthrope, Le Sicilien ou l'Amour peintre, Amphitryon, L'Avare, George Dandin ou le Mari confondu, Monsieur de Pourceaugnac, Le Bourgeois gentilhomme, Les Fourberies de Scapin, Psyché,* and *Le Malade imaginaire.*

Fourberies de Scapin less than three months after they first reached the stage. Clearly, Molière and his company found nothing counterproductive about having plays become available in print at a moment when their drawing power on stage had not yet been exhausted.

When Molière refrained from having one of his plays printed, he usually had good reasons for doing so. *Dom Juan* was not printed during Molière's lifetime because the outrage the play provoked led to its suppression after the fifteenth performance.[29] *L'Impromptu de Versailles* was not printed until after the author's death probably because Molière did not want to fan the "war of the theatres" in which he was then engaged.[30] The publication of *Tartuffe*, first performed in 1664, was delayed until 1669 because of the trouble into which Molière got with his play. In fact, the play did not receive its first officially allowed public performance until February 5, 1669, after which the play soon appeared in print.[31] *Les Amants magnifiques*, a "comédie-ballet," was not printed because it had only been performed at court, while *Mélicerte* and *Dom Garcie de Navarre* were not published by Molière because they had very little success on stage.[32]

Charles Varlet de la Grange's "registre," in which a fellow actor of Molière's recorded in Henslowe-like fashion performances and receipts for the period from 1659 to 1685, allows us to evaluate with some precision what influence stage and print publications exerted upon each other.[33] Even though printed soon after its first performance, *Sganarelle ou le Cocu imaginaire* reached a total of one hundred and twenty performances during Molière's lifetime. Similarly, *L'Ecole des femmes* did very well on stage throughout 1663, during which year it also went through no fewer than six editions.[34] *L'Ecole des maris* and *Les Fâcheux* were also performed more than a hundred times while being published a few months after their first performances and reprinted several times within two or three years. Far from discouraging attendance at playhouses, the speed with which plays were printed and the number of reprints they received seem to have been fairly reliable indicators of the plays' popularity on stage in Molière's Paris. Even though Molière is not Shakespeare and Paris is not London, there are reasons to believe that the situation was not altogether different in Shakespeare's London.

---

[29] See Guibert, *Bibliographie*, 413.   [30] See Duchêne, *Molière*, 349.

[31] Guibert, *Bibliographie*, 1.257–60.   [32] Ibid., 1.396, 1.422, 1.430.

[33] For the best edition of de la Grange's diary, see Bert Edward Young and Grace Philputt Young, eds., *Le Registre de la Grange, 1659–1685*, 2 vols. (Paris: Droz, 1947).

[34] See René Bray, *Molière, homme de théâtre* (Paris: Mercure de France, 1954), 107.

The argument for the players' opposition to print publication has not simply sprung up *ex nihilo*, but has been taken to find support in a number of key documents which I need to address before the end of this chapter. One such document is the only contract between a playwright and a theater company of which we have detailed knowledge. Though not extant, its terms are laid out in a Requests Proceedings Bill of Complaint of February 12, 1640 by the Queen Henrietta's Company against Richard Brome, and in Brome's answer dated March 6, 1640. Without rehearsing the complex story that led to the company taking legal action against Brome,[35] what is important in the present context is that the second contract Brome signed stipulated "that hee should not suffer any playe made or to bee made or Composed by him . . . to bee printed by his Consent or knowledge, priuitye, or dirreccō without the Licence from the said Company or the Majoʳ *p*te of them."[36] Brome's contract plays a central role in Bentley's influential account of the publication of playbooks.[37] From Bentley to Dutton, the reasoning has been that Shakespeare seems to have been bound by a contract similar to Brome's and that these contracts "commonly seem to have put an embargo on the printing of corporately-owned playbooks." Dutton concludes that "Shakespeare must have felt massively restricted" owing to "the inviolability of the 'ordinary poet's' plays."[38]

Independently of whether Brome's contract really allows inferences about the arrangements Shakespeare may have had with the Lord Chamberlain's/ King's Men – Shakespeare, after all, was also actor and shareholder whereas Brome was only a contracted poet – it seems important that Brome's contract nowhere forbids publication. The wording, on the contrary, appears to presuppose publication, though leaving the company the right to veto it at any given moment. In other words, what the company (like the Lord Chamberlain's Men) seems to have wanted to have a say about is the moment when – rather than the question whether – the play would be offered for publication.

The address from "A neuer writer, to an euer reader" in Bonian and Walley's quarto edition of *Troilus and Cressida* has sometimes been understood as referring to the King's Men withholding the play from publication: "thanke fortune for the scape it hath made amongst you. Since by the grand possessors wills I beleeue you should haue prayd for them rather

---

[35] See Ann Haaker, "The Plague, the Theater, and the Poet," *Renaissance Drama*, n.s. 1 (1968), 283–306. Haaker paraphrases, interprets, and transcribes the two documents that allow a relatively detailed reconstruction of the relationship between Brome and Queen Henrietta's Company.
[36] Quoted from Haaker, "Plague," 298.   [37] See Bentley, *Profession of Dramatist*, 264–92.
[38] Dutton, "Birth of the Author," 97–98.

then beene prayd."[39] It is not clear whether the words "grand possessors" are really meant to refer to the King's Men, but even if they are, we should beware of taking the statement at face value. After all, a manuscript seems to have changed hands as early as 1603 when the play had been entered in the Stationers' Register, and so the King's Men cannot be expected to have had any control over the play's publication in 1609. The events surrounding the publication of *Troilus and Cressida* in 1609 are so mysterious that not much weight should be given to a preface which may well have been designed to promote sales.

Heywood's assertion in the address "To the Reader" prefacing *The English Traveller* (1633) seems at first more straightforward:

True it is, that my Playes are not exposed vnto the world in Volumes, to beare the title of *Workes*, (as others) one reason is, That many of them by shifting and change of Companies, haue beene negligently lost, Others of them are still retained in the hands of some Actors who thinke it against their peculiar profit to haue them come in Print, and a third, That it neuer was any great ambition in me, to bee in this kind Volumniously [*sic*] read.[40]

If Heywood's address is read out of context, there seems at first no reason to doubt the truthfulness of his assertion that the actors opposed publication. At a closer look, it may appear that his first reason curiously undermines the second: if many of his manuscripts were negligently lost, it would be surprising if his other manuscripts had been judged valuable enough to make it very hard to keep them out of print. More importantly, however, the passage needs to be read in the context of some of Heywood's other publications. In the address "To the Reader" prefacing *The Second Part of the Iron Age* of 1632, the last of his five plays dealing with classical mythology following *The Golden Age* (1611), *The Silver Age* (1613), *The Brazen Age* (1613), and *The First Part of The Iron Age* (1632), Heywood wrote:

If the three former Ages (now out of Print,) bee added to these (as I am promised) to make vp an handsome Volumne; I purpose (*Deo Assistente,*) to illustrate the whole Worke, with an Explanation of all the difficulties, and an Historicall Comment of euery hard name, which may appeare obscure or intricate to such as are not frequent in Poetry.[41]

Heywood's gibe in 1633 at those who have their plays "exposed vnto the world in Volumes, to beare the title of *Workes*" resonates very differently once we realize that only a year earlier, he himself had hoped to have

[39] I quote from Greg, *Bibliography*, III.1208.
[40] *The Dramatic Works of Thomas Heywood*, ed., R. H. Shepherd, 6 vols. (London, 1874), IV.5.
[41] Ibid., III.351–52.

several of his plays published in "an handsome Volumne" and intended to "illustrate the whole Worke." Between the publication of *2 Iron Age* and *The English Traveller*, Heywood seems to have realized that his project would come to nothing. The words "as I am promised" suggest that a publisher, perhaps Nicholas Okes who published *1* and *2 Iron Age*, had envisaged preparing a volume with Heywood's *Age* plays. The time may have seemed right to Heywood: the second volume of Jonson's works, again in folio, had been published in 1631, the Shakespeare Folio had received a second edition in 1632, and duodecimo and octavo collections of plays by Lyly and Marston appeared in 1632 and 1633. Granted, Heywood had long been a kind of dramatic jack-of-all-trades who had had "either an entire hand, or at the least a maine finger" in no fewer than two hundred and twenty plays.[42] In 1608 he professed himself "ever faithful to the [stage] and never guilty of the [press]" and vowed that "It hath been no custome in me of all other men... to commit my Playes to the Presse."[43] Nevertheless, his attitude to print seems to have radically changed by 1632, perhaps owing to the appearance of collected editions by several of his earlier contemporaries.

The year before he had voiced his hopes to have "an handsome Volumne" published, Heywood had stated in the preface to *The First Part of the Fair Maid of the West* that "my Plaies have not beene exposed to the publike view of the world in numerous sheets, and a large volume; but singly (as thou seest) with great modesty, and small noise."[44] Either Heywood suddenly lost his modesty during the next months or his denial of the desirability of "a large volume" again hides a thwarted desire which becomes transparent when placed against the later hopes for his own "handsome Volumne."[45] Heywood simply confirms what J. W. Saunders pointed out long ago in "The Stigma of Print": "whereas in the case of the Court poets the distaste for the publicity of print was genuine and profound, in the case of the professionals the coyness was largely assumed and superficial."[46]

---

[42] I quote from the address "To the Reader" prefacing *The English Traveller* (Shepherd, ed., *Thomas Heywood*, IV.5).

[43] Ibid., V.163.   [44] Ibid., II.259.

[45] The view that Heywood was actively seeking to develop literary authority in the early 1630s is also supported by the frequency with which he used Latin on the title pages, a frequency only surpassed by Ben Jonson (see Farmer and Lesser, "Vile Arts," 77–165, 99–100).

[46] Saunders, "The Stigma of Print: A Note on the Social Bases of Tudor Poetry," *Essays in Criticism*, 1 (1951), 150. Saunders's article needs to be read along with Steven W. May's "Tudor Aristocrats and the Mythical 'Stigma of Print,'" in *Renaissance Papers 1980*, eds. A. Leigh Deneef and M. Thomas Hester (Durham, NC: The Southeastern Renaissance Conference, 1981), 11–18, which offers an important corrective to Saunders's argument: "the substantial number of upperclass authors who published during the sixteenth century effectively discredits any notion of a generally accepted code which

When Heywood's address to the reader in *The English Traveller* is considered in the context of his other prefatory addresses, the various reasons he adduces as to why his plays have not appeared "in Volumes" are scarcely trustworthy. If Heywood's third "reason," "That it neuer was any great ambition in me, to bee in this kind Volumniously read," can be shown to be little more than a fib, we would be ill advised to place much trust in his second "reason," that some of his plays "are still retained in the hands of some actors who think it against their peculiar profit to have them come into print." That actors did retain some plays, especially recent plays, has been shown above, and Heywood may thus not be completely wrong. Nevertheless, we can safely assume that little effort went into keeping most of Heywood's two-hundred-and-twenty plays out of print. Rather than being "negligently lost," the manuscripts of many of Heywood's plays may have been thought not worth keeping. What seems to be the real reason why the volume failed to materialize, is that a publisher let him down some time between the publication of *2 Iron Age* in 1632 and that of *The English Traveller* in 1633.[47] Once we realize this, the reasons Heywood advances lose much of their authority. The publisher's decision not to publish Heywood's play in an impressive volume like Jonson's, Shakespeare's or, later, Beaumont and Fletcher's, or at least in a collection like Lyly's or Marston's, seems to have little to do with Heywood's alleged lack of ambition. Bentley points out that "Heywood's reputation among his literary contemporaries and successors in the seventeenth century...was not high."[48] Heywood himself wrote:

forbade publication, since noblemen and knights, courtiers and royalty, trafficked with the press in ever-increasing numbers" (18).

[47] The reason why the publisher withdrew from what seems to have been his earlier intention to publish a collected edition of Heywood's *Age* plays may not be too difficult to guess. After the publication of collections by Jonson, Shakespeare, Lyly, and Marston in the space of two years, the market for play collections may well have been momentarily glutted. Even Heywood's announcement in the prefatory material to *2 Iron Age* of a forthcoming collection that is to include the very same play may well have been counterproductive. Potential customers, flicking through the address "To the Reader" and learning of the projected collection, would have thought twice before buying a playbook that they might soon purchase as part of a collection. Nicholas Okes, the publisher of *1* and *2 Iron Age* may understandably not have agreed to a collection as long as he had not sold most of the copies of his recent *Iron Age* edition.

[48] G. E. Bentley, *The Jacobean and Caroline Stage*, 7 vols. (Oxford: Clarendon Press, 1941–68), IV.557. Bentley's suggestion is supported by the "Advertisement to the Reader" prefaced to Francis Kirkman's play-catalogue of 1671: "although I can find but twenty five of *Tho. Heywoods* in all Printed, yet (as you may reade in an Epistle to a Play of his, called *The English Traveller*) he hath had an entire hand, or, at least, a main finger in the writing of 220. And, as I have been informed, he was very laborious; for he not only Acted almost every day, but also obliged himself to write a sheet every day, for several years together; but many of his Playes being composed and written loosely in Taverns, occasions them to be so mean" (Greg, *Bibliography*, III.1353).

> Plays have a fate in their conception lent,
> Some so short liv'd, no sooner showed than spent:
> But born today, tomorrow buried, and
> Though taught to speak, neither to go nor stand.[49]

It may not be surprising, then, that no publisher wanted to undertake what would have been a commercially risky enterprise.[50]

Another document has been used to support the argument of the players' alleged opposition to the publication of their playbooks.[51] The "Articles of Agreement" confirmed by the sharers in the Whitefriars theater on March 10, 1607/8 stipulate:

noe man of the said company shall at any time hereafter put into print, or cause to be put into print any manner of playe booke now in use, or that hereafter shalbe sould unto them, upon the penaltie and forfeiture of ffortie pounds starlinge or the losse of his place and share of all things amongst them. Except the booke of Torrismount, and that playe not to be printed by any before twelve months be fully expired.[52]

Bentley believed that this article was evidence of a general objection to publication, but it seems important to pay attention to the precise words the article uses. As in the Brome contract, the prohibition is individual ("noe man"), not collective. Moreover, the manuscript the sharers are forbidden to put into print under the severest penalty is the "playe booke now in use." "Play book" is the designation usually employed not just for any manuscript but for the licensed playhouse copy. Andrew Gurr has recently dwelt on the special importance of these playscripts:

"playbooks"... were the papers that authorized the company to perform the play they recorded anywhere in England. Their value lay not in playhouse use as prompt copy but as play manuscripts carrying the signature of the Master of the Revels. That signature was the only thing that allowed the company to perform the play in London or anywhere else in England. As such, the "allowed book" became the source for every performance based on it, and it was treasured for the financial resource that provided.[53]

---

[49] The lines are quoted from a prologue written for the revival of Heywood's *The Rape of Lucrece* and published in 1637 in *Pleasant Dialogues and Dramas*, a collection of miscellaneous verse and playlets.

[50] Heywood's professed indifference to print has often been read uncritically, for instance by Bentley, *Profession of Dramatist*, 281–85; or, more recently, by Brooks, *Playhouse to Printing House*, 189–220. See also Benedict Scott Robinson, "Thomas Heywood and the Cultural Politics of Play Collections," *Studies in English Literature*, 42 (2002), 361–80.

[51] See Bentley, *Profession of Dramatist*, 266–67, and Chambers, *Elizabethan Stage*, 11.64–68.

[52] I quote from Evelyn May Albright, *Dramatic Publication*, 239. James Greenstreet gives the full text of the bill ("The Whitefriars Theatre in the Time of Shakespere," *Transactions of the New Shakespeare Society* (1887–92), 269–84).

[53] See also Andrew Gurr, "Maximal and Minimal Texts: Shakespeare v. The Globe," *Shakespeare Survey*, 52 (1999), 71.

The "playe booke," in other words, was "made sacred by the licensing signature on its last page."[54] Significantly, what the players produced in their defense after the scandal over Middleton's *A Game at Chess* was "the book it self subscribed... by the *M*aster of the *Reuells*."[55] Considering the commercial and legal importance of a "playe booke," it is not surprising that a company did not wish to part with it. Even if a play was not in the current repertory, it would be unwise to release a manuscript to a printing house from where it would not normally be returned and where it would be unlikely to remain undamaged.[56] What thus seems to require explanation is not why the article forbids the putting into print of playbooks, but why "the booke of Torrismount" should be an exception after "twelve months be fully expired." We can only conjecture whether it was a topical play no longer suited for performance or whether some other reason would have allowed the sharers in the Children of the King's Revels to sell the manuscript, but the fact that "Torrismount" was finally not printed is a reminder of the fact that publishers did not print just anything the players were ready to part with.

If we wish to discern the true attitudes toward publication of playbooks in the late sixteenth and early seventeenth centuries – Shakespeare's in particular – we must follow Peter Blayney's injunction to view such publication from the angle of the London stationers, publishers, and booksellers rather than from that of the actors and dramatists primarily. It is the failure to do so that has resulted in the distorted views of such eminent scholars as Chambers, Bentley, Bowers and Dutton.[57] As Blayney points out, "Everything depends on the axiom that the demand for printed plays greatly exceeded the supply – which happens to be untrue."[58] The impact of this ungrounded axiom on our understanding of Shakespearean drama can hardly be overstated. As long as we go on believing that publishers desperately wanted to acquire playtexts, we will continue to think that the acting companies more often than not tried to avoid publication. Once we realize, however, that publishers in most cases had little or nothing to gain from playbooks, we will be open to the suggestion that players and playwrights in general and the Chamberlain's/King's Men and Shakespeare in particular had no serious

---

[54] Ibid., 72.

[55] I quote from T. H. Howard-Hill, ed., *A Game at Chess*, The Revels Plays (Manchester University Press, 1993), 205.

[56] See Gurr, "Maximal and Minimal Texts," 72–73, and Blayney, "Publication of Playbooks," 392.

[57] Chambers, *Elizabethan Stage*, "The Printing of Plays," III.157–200; Bentley, *Profession of Dramatist*, ch. 10: "Publication," 264–92; Bowers, "Publication," 406–16; and Dutton, "Birth of the Author," 90–113.

[58] Blayney, "Publication of Playbooks," 384. See also the section on "Supply and Demand," 384–89.

objections to the publication of their plays and often actively supported it. It is true that Shakespeare does not seem to have been able to have his plays published without the consent of his company.[59] It does not follow that the Lord Chamberlain's/King's Men were opposed, that Shakespeare was indifferent to it. Once the contrary is granted, a whole series of other questions may appear in a new light: why did Shakespeare write plays that are far too long to be accommodated by "the two hours' traffic of our stage"? What was the relationship between performance text and the published playtext? What is the "socialized script" (Wells and Taylor) of a Shakespeare play? And what kind of text and/or performance can we imagine behind the "bad" (or "suspect," or "short") quartos? These are some of the questions the second part of this study will explore.

[59] See Dutton, "Birth of the Author," 97–99.

PART II

Texts

CHAPTER 6

Why size matters: "the two hours' traffic of our stage" and the length of Shakespeare's plays

It is a commonplace today to remark that an Elizabethan play was written in order to be performed on stage, not to be read on a page. The statement is indeed the chief premise of performance criticism, an approach which, as Thomas Clayton has put it, is so firmly entrenched at present that "there is scarcely a black sheep's bleat to be heard in dissent."[1] If we wish to investigate the basic premise of performance criticism less as a theoretical claim that entails a certain critical approach than as a historical statement, then strong supportive evidence can be derived from what is known about the number of plays that were never printed and thus (excepting the few plays that have survived in manuscript) have not come down to us. Most plays written for the public stage before 1642 had only a life on stage, and sometimes a very short one. We can be sure that the majority of them have left no trace whatsoever, not even their title. Thus making conjectures about their number is difficult. Henslowe's diary allows some informed guesswork though. Of the 280 plays it mentions, only thirty survive.[2] The estimate that about "90 per cent of the works have perished" may also apply to the companies on which Henslowe provides no information, though it seems likely that of Shakespeare's Lord Chamberlain's and King's Men, a somewhat higher ratio has survived.[3]

However, since modern criticism of Renaissance drama ultimately derives its object of study from the playtexts that were published in the late sixteenth and early seventeenth centuries, the statement that plays were written in order to be performed poses a number of problems. For the very fact that a playtext has come down to us implies that a publisher counted on a considerable number of people thinking otherwise. Edition sizes varied considerably, but it can be expected that the average number of copies was

[1] Thomas Clayton, ed., The "Hamlet" First Published (Q1, 1603): Origins, Form, Intertextualities (Newark: University of Delaware Press; London: Associated University Presses, 1992), 32.
[2] Carson, Companion to Henslowe's Diary, 82–84.   [3] Ibid., 68.

somewhere in the vicinity of one thousand.[4] It appears that the readership of those plays that did get printed was in many cases greater than the total audience of the many plays which Henslowe's diary shows to have disappeared after a brief stage run.[5] This simple fact calls into question the dogmatic statement that plays were written for the stage. With the exception of the few plays that only survive in manuscript, the plays to which we have access were not only written in order to be performed, but also printed in order to be read.[6] Certain adepts of performance criticism accuse critics who do not share their creed of anachronistically reducing the agency of a playtext to the "author" rather than to the various agents involved in preparing and performing a play. By doing so, they, in turn, are prone to favor authorial intention (the plays were written in order to be performed) at the expense of the agency of printers and publishers, *conditio sine qua non* for the study of all but "precious few" Renaissance playtexts.[7]

But of course, the argument goes, though plays were published, the printed texts reflect what was designed to be fully realized on stage. Therefore, the printed text is removed from the performance in which the play comes fully alive.[8] The text is the shadow on the wall of the cave, dimly

[4] See Bowers, "Publication," 414, and Blayney (*Texts of "King Lear*," 33–39), who presents a differentiated view of the average size of early modern editions. Analyzing the records of Cambridge University Press, D. F. McKenzie ("Printers of the Mind: Some Notes on Bibliographical Theories and Printing-House Practices," *Studies in Bibliography*, 22 (1969), 1–75), gives a variety of "figures invalidating any hypothetical norm" (14).

[5] See Carson (*Companion to Henslowe's Diary*, 40–41) for estimates of the average attendance based on the figures in Henslowe's diary.

[6] Earlier in the sixteenth century, interludes and moralities seem to have been printed specifically for acting purposes, "with casting lists to indicate how many actors are required to perform the play" (Bevington, *From "Mankind" to Marlowe*, 5). As late as 1582, the title page of the second quarto edition of *Damon and Pithias* states that the prologue has been "somwhat altered for the proper vse of them that hereafter shall haue occasion to play it, either in priuate, or open Audience" (Greg, *Bibliography*, 1.138). By the 1590s, however, the primary intention behind the printing of plays was clearly no longer to cater for the needs of players.

[7] See William B. Long, "'Precious Few': English Manuscript Playbooks," in *A Companion to Shakespeare*, ed. Kastan, 414–33, and see Appendix C below.

[8] See Timothy Murray's "From Foul Sheets to Legitimate Model: Antitheater, Text, Jonson," *New Literary History*, 14 (1983), 641–64 (reprinted in revised form in *Theatrical Legitimation*) for a formulation of this view: "Only by *performing* the author's script – in the sense of 'to complete or make up by addition of what is wanting' (*OED*) – could the players achieve a drama" ("Foul Sheets," 646). Discussing the designation "foul sheets," he claims that "Denoted by the players as 'foul' are the notions of intention and accountable authorship" (647). In fact, "foul sheets" or "foul papers" were originally opposed to the "fair copy," with "foul" and "fair" designating various degrees of clarity and tidiness rather than any "notions of intention and accountable authorship" (see Wells, Taylor, et al., *Textual Companion*, 9). W. B. Worthen's work offers an important corrective to the view advanced by Murray and others. See Worthen, "Rhetoric of Performance Criticism," *Authority of Performance*, and "Drama, Performativity, and Performance."

(if at all) reflecting the performance. To some extent, this is undeniable. When Polonius encourages the King to "Take this from this if this be otherwise" (2.2.158), his words presuppose a stage action (Polonius pointing to his head and shoulder) that is not spelled out. In an address "to the Reader" prefacing his edition of *Promos and Cassandra* (1578), the publisher Richard Jones shows awareness of what a printed text that has been removed from its context of oral delivery can lack: "if by chaunce, thou light of some speache that seemeth dark, consider of it with iudgment, before thou condemne the worke: for in many places he is driuen, both to praise, and blame, with one breath, which in readinge wil seeme hard, & in actiõ, appeare plaine."[9] By way of apology, Jones concedes that the page is at times unable to convey what the stage would provide.

The Platonic idealism of performance criticism hides, however, how little we know about what precisely was performed in, say, Shakespeare's Globe. Twentieth-century bibliography centering on such eminent scholars as Greg and Bowers has been instrumental in producing some of the tools that allow us insights into actual stage practice, though recent research suggests that the New Bibliography was too optimistic in its assessment of just how much could be bibliographically inferred.[10] What we still do not, nor perhaps ever will, know enough about, however, is the relationship those imperfectly reconstructable manuscripts bear to the play that was performed. In one sense, performance criticism thus takes for granted what really should be the starting point of any investigation. As Stephen Orgel puts it:

How do we know what the relation was between whatever texts have come down to us and what playgoers saw in Shakespeare's theater? Since our claims about the effects of Shakespearean drama are based almost entirely on the surviving printed

---

[9] Greg, *Bibliography*, III.1195.

[10] See Werstine, "Narratives About Printed Shakespeare Texts: 'Foul Papers' and 'Bad' Quartos," *Shakespeare Quarterly*, 41 (1990), 65–86, "Plays in Manuscript," in *A New History of Early English Drama*, eds. Cox and Kastan, 481–97, and "Post-Theory Problems in Shakespeare Editing," *The Yearbook of English Studies*, 29 (1999), 103–17, which, returning to the question of "foul papers," addresses "the question of precisely what has counted as evidence and what has not, and the question of how data have been constituted as evidence in the formation of one prominent editorial grand narrative" (103). In recent years, this new textual agnosticism has also resulted in a number of editions that are less confident than their predecessors about the possibility of recovering the precise origins of printer's copy. See, for instance, Jill L. Levenson's Oxford *Romeo and Juliet*, The Oxford Shakespeare (Oxford University Press, 2000), 103–25, and Woudhuysen, ed., *Love's Labour's Lost*, 305–27. A less refined version of Werstine's argument had been advanced by Leo Kirschbaum as early as 1955: "one has to be extremely careful in attributing a certain printed text to the author's foul papers or to the promptbook. There are no distinctive features of each that one cannot expect a scribe preparing a private transcript to copy" (*Shakespeare and the Stationers* (Columbus: Ohio State University Press, 1955), 155–253, 161).

texts, it would seem essential to consider this question, and not simply to assume that we can read backward from the latter to the former.[11]

It may be somewhat disquieting to notice that early accounts of performances often strikingly depart from the texts that have come down to us. There are no fewer than eight textual witnesses of Middleton's *A Game at Chess*, but two early accounts refer to stage action for which none of them accounts.[12] In fact, the gap between performance text and printed edition has hitherto remained seriously neglected.[13] The important gap that separates the page from the stage, what we have access to in early printed playbooks from the irretrievably lost play that was once acted on stage, undermines a performance criticism (as well as an editorial policy that is anchored in it) that pretends to be able to recover plays as they were performed.[14]

In what follows, I explore some of the implications of the possible gap between the performances that took place centuries ago and the dramatic texts which alone have come down to us. There are reasons to believe that,

---

[11] Stephen Orgel, "Acting Scripts, Performing Texts," in *Crisis in Editing: Texts of the English Renaissance*, ed. Randall McLeod (New York: AMS Press, 1994), 251–94, 268. Note that Janette Dillon has similarly questioned the new "orthodoxy of performance," particularly "the degree to which the printed text is capable of being used as evidence about the material practice of performance" ("Performance," 74).

[12] See T. H. Howard-Hill, "The Author as Scribe or Reviser? Middleton's Intentions in *A Game at Chess*," *TEXT: An Interdisciplinary Annual of Textual Studies*, 3 (1987), 305–18, esp. 305, 316.

[13] See Gurr, "Maximal and Minimal Texts," especially: "One feature of the early texts in particular, a characteristic of playing company practices through the whole period from the 1580s to 1642, needs better recognition than it has been given even in the intense debates of recent years. That is the inherent difference between the original company's own written playbook and the text the players performed" (70).

[14] See M. J. Kidnie's important essay "Text, Performance, and the Editors: Staging Shakespeare's Drama," *Shakespeare Quarterly*, 51 (2000), 456–73. Kidnie convincingly argues that "There is no necessary link between dramatic literature and the stage, and, consequently, not only can dramatic text be profitably studied as literature, but the script can in no sense achieve its 'realization' or 'fulfillment' in the theater" (459). In their "General Textual Introduction" to the *The Works of John Webster* (eds. David Gunby, David Carnegie, and Anthony Hammond, one volume published (Cambridge University Press, 1995)), Anthony Hammond and Doreen DelVecchio have also incisively commented on the gap between the page and the stage: "Needless to say, the experience of reading a Poem [i.e. a printed playbook] would not be the same as the experience of watching a Presentment of the Play, nor would anyone ever have thought so, had it not been for the activities of generations of editors and critics who wrote of the plays of Shakespeare and his contemporaries when they were really talking about the Poems – that is, the printed texts. This was understandable, since the Poem is editable, and available for discussion, while the Play is certainly not . . . We cannot edit the Play since too much of the necessary data has been lost in the dark backward and abysm of time; we must therefore edit the Poem, which is what everybody has been doing all along, though not always in as explicit an awareness as could have been desired that this was indeed what they were doing" (37).

in the case of many of Shakespeare's plays, this gap is particularly wide. In Part I, I suggested that Shakespeare's plays can legitimately be considered as more than scripts of or for performance. Shakespeare and his fellows, I argued, actively supported the publication of his playbooks, and these playbooks constituted somewhat more respectable and less sub-literary publications than has often been assumed. From the very beginning then, Shakespeare's plays, in other words, were designed to be not only staged performances but also printed texts.

Fresh insights can have the merit of providing explanations for data that has hitherto resisted satisfactory interpretation. If we accept the argument that Shakespeare's plays were partly designed to be and existed as reading texts, a long-standing conundrum in Shakespeare studies can profitably be approached anew. As Stephen Orgel wrote in an article published in 1988: "To observe the disparity between the performing time and the length of the surviving texts is a critical commonplace, but its implications are rarely considered and never taken into account."[15] Part II of this study will be a detailed consideration of this disparity and its implications. The problem of the length of many of Shakespeare's plays becomes soluble, I argue, once we accept that the text as it has come down to us may be more than a reflection of what would have been spoken on stage. Conversely, crucial evidence for Shakespeare's interest in a readership can be derived, I believe, from the sheer length of about a third of Shakespeare's plays.

The price we have to pay for failing to consider the disparity between performance time and text length becomes clear once we realize what assumptions underlie many of the editions through which Shakespeare's plays are mediated to us today. Stanley Wells and Gary Taylor, the general editors of the Oxford *Complete Works*, believe that "the full text" of even such Gargantuan plays as *Hamlet* and *Antony and Cleopatra* was acted.[16] Consequently, they can claim to "have devoted our efforts to recovering and presenting texts of Shakespeare's plays as they were acted in the London playhouses."[17] Having been called "certainly the most innovative and daring in its editorial decisions to have appeared this century,"[18] the Oxford *Complete Works* is all the more influential today as the Norton Shakespeare under the general editorship of Stephen Greenblatt has also adopted its texts. These and other editions influenced by them attempt to recover

[15] Stephen Orgel, "The Authentic Shakespeare," *Representations*, 21 (1988), 25.
[16] Wells, Taylor, et al., *Textual Companion*, 276.
[17] Wells, "General Introduction," in Shakespeare, *Complete Works*, gen. eds. Wells and Taylor, xxxvii.
[18] Norman Sanders, "Shakespeare's Text," in *Shakespeare: A Bibliographical Guide*, ed. Stanley Wells (Oxford: Clarendon Press, 1990), 29.

Shakespeare's plays "as they were acted in the London playhouses" without having examined their premise that Shakespeare's long plays were ever performed. In chapter 7 I argue that many of the resulting editions in fact produce conflated texts, approximations of what was acted by the Lord Chamberlain's/King's Men along with much material that was never, nor was ever intended to be, performed.

Many scholars take for granted or base upon little evidence their answer to the question of whether Shakespeare's long plays would have been performed in their entirety. Peter Holland has written: "I, like others, doubt that anything approaching a full text of *Hamlet*, either in its second Quarto or First Folio form, was ever played in the Jacobean theatre."[19] Yet Stanley Wells, Gary Taylor, and others precisely assume that the entirety of *Hamlet* and Shakespeare's other plays was performed. The matter is of such importance that it deserves to be explored in full. My investigation will proceed as follows: Firstly, I ask how the length of Shakespeare's plays relates to what we know about the length of performances in London's theaters and to the length of the plays by Shakespeare's contemporaries. Secondly, I attempt to show that the "Beaumont and Fletcher" Folio of 1647 contains important information about how Shakespeare's company treated the texts of his direct successors. The implications of this information for Shakespeare's plays are more far-reaching, I believe, than has hitherto been recognized. Thirdly, I argue that some of the best information about how much of a playbook was or was not performed can be gained not from printed texts but from extant dramatic manuscripts. Consequently, I discuss the length and abridgements of the material witnesses that have come down to us. Finally, I show that after the Restoration – at a time when theatrical practices were still shaped by traditions that go back to the pre-Civil War period – the gap between Shakespeare's texts as originally written and as performed becomes visible in an unprecedented way, both in the players' quartos and in the earliest extant prompt-books.

Anyone who has had the courage and time to sit through an uncut performance of *Hamlet* may have been awe-struck by the thought of Elizabethan groundlings standing in the pit of the Globe, realizing the same achievement on their feet. The playing time of Kenneth Branagh's uncut production for the Royal Shakespeare Company in 1993 was four hours and a quarter and his *Hamlet* film is only slightly shorter. F. R. Benson's *Hamlet* at the Lyceum

---

[19] Holland, "Measuring Performance," in *Performance*, ed. Peter Halter, Swiss Papers in English Language and Literature, 11 (Tübingen: Gunter Narr, 1999), 49.

in 1900 lasted six merciless hours (from 3.30 p.m. to 11 p.m., with an hour and a half for dinner).[20] The playing time of a recent RSC production of *King Lear*, from which four hundred lines had been cut, was three-and-a-half hours, while the 1997 Stratford production of *Cymbeline* played for nearly three hours, even though a full thousand lines were omitted. Even at the much higher speed at which the Shenandoah Express produce their plays, uncut performances of *Hamlet* or *Richard III* would last more than three hours.[21]

What makes these figures remarkable is that they are in striking contrast with what we gather from Shakespeare and his contemporaries about the length of performance of their plays. The prologue to *Romeo and Juliet* famously refers to "the two hours' traffic of our stage" (line 12). *The Two Noble Kinsmen* speaks of "two hours' travail" (Prologue, line 29) while *Henry VIII* is said to last "two short hours" (Prologue, line 13). Earlier and later non-Shakespearean references corroborate this evidence. Exasperated by the English players' disrespect of the unity of time, Sidney, in his *Apology for Poetry*, complains about all the absurd complications that were dramatized "in two hours' space."[22] As late as the 1630s, the prologue in William Davenant's *The Unfortunate Lovers* (1638) promises an acting time of "two hours."[23] It has been shown that, during the period of Shakespeare's theatrical activities in London, "Shakespeare, Jonson, Fletcher, Beaumont, Percy, Middleton, Barry, Tailor, Beeston, and Dekker all speak of 'two hours' as the time spent in the representation of a play."[24] Andrew Gurr has concluded: "Two hours was the standard time for a performance."[25]

It may well be, however, that the various references to two hours' playing time in Shakespeare and elsewhere correspond to no more than a convention

[20] See George C. D. Odell, *Shakespeare from Betterton to Irving*, 2 vols. (New York: Charles Scribner's Sons, 1920), 11.413.

[21] Since the construction of their Blackfriars Playhouse (a re-creation of Shakespeare's indoor theatre) in Staunton, Virginia, "Shenandoah Express" is the name of the theater company, the earlier name "Shenandoah Shakespeare Express" now being reserved for the touring troupe. Taking the "two hours' traffic of our stage" seriously, the company has done uncut productions of short plays such as *Macbeth*, *A Midsummer Night's Dream*, and *A Comedy of Errors* in under two hours. When doing productions of Shakespeare's long plays, the company does cut the text, though often less so than the RSC with a resulting playing time that is nevertheless considerably shorter than that of their English counterpart. I would like to thank Ralph Cohen, Executive Director of the Shenandoah Shakespeare, for providing me with information on this point.

[22] Sir Philip Sidney, *An Apology for Poetry or The Defence of Poesy*, ed. Geoffrey Shepherd (London: Thomas Nelson, 1965), 134.

[23] Line 20. I quote from Sir William D'Avenant, *The Dramatic Works*, eds. James Maidment and W. H. Logan, 5 vols. (Edinburgh, 1872–74), 111.12.

[24] Alfred Hart, *Shakespeare and the Homilies* (Melbourne University Press, 1934), 104.

[25] Andrew Gurr, "Maximal and Minimal Texts," 68.

and that no great importance must be attributed to the precise duration. Other references indeed imply that there must have been some variety. Dekker's *If It Be Not Good, the Devil Is in It* (*c.* 1611), for instance, refers to "three howres of mirth."[26] We are on firmer ground with the following non-fictional reference. In October 1594, it was agreed between George Carey, Lord Hunsdon, the future Lord Chamberlain, and the Lord Mayor of London that "where heretofore they began not their Plaies till towardes fower a clock, they will now begin at two, & haue don betwene fower and fiue."[27] In a virtually unabridged *Hamlet* at the Globe in December, the Prince would have held up Yorick's skull in utter darkness.[28] References from both fictional and non-fictional sources thus converge to suggest that the length of performance, including songs, dances, and the concluding jig, did not exceed the length of three hours.[29]

What would allow us to reconcile the length of several of Shakespeare's playtexts with the indications about the length of performance is to argue that many of Shakespeare's plays must have been heavily cut before being performed in the theatre. Recent scholars resist this suggestion, however. David Bradley objects that "it implies that Shakespeare's originals were filled out with irrelevant and tawdry material which he must have composed in the sure expectation that it would be jettisoned in performance."[30] This fits

---

[26] Epilogue, line 5. I quote from *The Dramatic Works of Thomas Dekker*, ed. Fredson Bowers, 4 vols. (Cambridge University Press, 1953–61), III.212.

[27] See Chambers, *The Elizabethan Stage*, IV.316.

[28] R. B. Graves's full survey of "Performance Times after 1594" shows that "public playhouses usually began performances anywhere from 2 p.m. to 4 p.m." Graves rightly points out that "The assumption that a complete entertainment at the theater lasted between two and three hours means that some representations finished in twilight. Even if plays began promptly at 2 p.m., a three-hour duration would push the end of the play past sunset for four months a year, from the second week in October until the third week in February. When plays began at three o'clock, the end of a three-hour play would continue past sunset for half the year, from the middle of September until the middle of March" (*Lighting the Shakespearean Stage, 1567–1642* (Carbondale and Edwardsville: Southern Illinois University Press, 1999), 77–84, 80, 83).

[29] In his 600-page study of *The Elizabethan Jig* (University of Chicago Press, 1929), Charles Read Baskerville came to the conclusion that toward the end of the sixteenth century "a typical jig was regularly performed" (107). Owing to the scarcity of evidence, what "a typical jig" would have amounted to is, to a certain extent, a matter of guesswork. C. J. Sisson printed a "short verse-play" which he thought was "beyond all question a Jig, of the kind that was acted by stage-players as an after-piece" (*Lost Plays of Shakespeare's Age* (Cambridge University Press, 1936), 129). If it is anything to go by, then jigs were more than danced epilogues. Sisson's "short verse-play" is 170 verses long and, performed with music and dance, would have taken some time to perform. See also the previously unknown jig discussed by J. M. Nosworthy which at 151 lines is of a similar length ("An Elizabethan Jig," in G. R. Proudfoot, ed., *Collections*, vol. IX (Oxford University Press, 1971 (1977)), 24–29).

[30] David Bradley, *From Text to Performance in the Elizabethan Theatre* (Cambridge University Press, 1991), 12.

badly the established image of the Lord Chamberlain's and King's Men's playwright only interested in providing his company with material for the stage. Others, like Wells and Taylor, clearly assume that "the full text" was performed in the London theaters and a cut version only on tour in the provinces. Steven Urkowitz has recently spent several pages trying to show that "even a 3,800-line *Hamlet* wouldn't strain anyone's patience."[31]

If it could be shown that a length of performance of under two-and-a-half hours would imply that playwrights consistently wrote much more than could possibly be acted, my hypothesis would seem to be highly questionable. The London theaters formed an entertainment industry with a great demand for new material with companies performing new plays as often as every three weeks or so.[32] It seems highly unlikely that professional playwrights who scraped a living by writing plays could afford the luxury of deliberately writing more than they needed to. It would be useful, therefore, to compare the length of Shakespeare's plays with the ones by his contemporaries.

In the 1930s, Alfred Hart carried out detailed research on the length of plays printed or known to have been acted between 1590 and 1616.[33] The results show that of Shakespeare's plays, eleven, nearly one in three, exceed three thousand lines. Jonson's eleven plays written before 1616 are all longer than three thousand lines. Shakespeare and Jonson being the authors who are best known and most often studied and performed, this may give the impression that "long" plays were the norm. Yet this is far from true. Shakespeare and Jonson wrote three-quarters of all plays exceeding three thousand lines. Out of the 233 extant plays acted on the public stage between 1590 and 1616 that are included in Hart's count, twenty-nine

---

[31] Urkowitz, "Back to Basics: Thinking about the *Hamlet* First Quarto," in *The "Hamlet" First Published*, ed. Clayton, 269.

[32] See the "Performance Calendar" in Carson's *Companion to Henslowe's Diary*, 85–100.

[33] "The Number of Lines in Shakespeare's Plays", *Review of English Studies*, 8 (1932), 19–28, "The Length of Elizabethan and Jacobean Plays", *Review of English Studies*, 8 (1932), 139–54, "The Time Allotted for Representation of Elizabethan and Jacobean Plays," *Review of English Studies*, 8 (1932), 395–413, rpt. in *Shakespeare and the Homilies*, 77–95, 96–118, 119–53. It may be objected that any line count is flawed as the length of a play like *Hamlet* can differ significantly depending on the edition used. Aware of this, Hart chose editions with a comparable number of prose words per line in order to increase the relevance of his line count. In my own line counts, I have tried to follow the same procedure whenever possible. Note that the line count in the appendix to Bradley's *From Text to Performance*, 229–43, is extremely irregular and therefore of no use for my purpose. According to Bradley's count, the Folio text of *Hamlet* is substantially longer than the second quarto (even though the opposite is in fact the case). *Bartholomew Fair* and *The Duchess of Malfi* are virtually the same length according to Bradley's figure even though Jonson's is about one-and-a-half times the length of Webster's play.

are longer than three thousand lines, of which only seven were not written by Shakespeare or Jonson.[34] Less than one in twenty-five of the plays written by their contemporaries exceeded this limit. "Long" playbooks, in other words, are extremely rare outside the dramatic *oeuvre* of Jonson and Shakespeare.

We have no problems understanding why Jonson's plays are inconveniently long from the point of view of the stage. Considering himself an author rather than a provider for the stage, he held the players in low esteem and, at times, explicitly wrote for a readership rather than for a theatre audience. The title-page of *Every Man Out of His Humour* (Q1, 1600) famously points out that the text contains "more than hath been Publickely Spoken or Acted." If we held that Shakespeare produced plays solely for the theatre without any considerations for their appearance in print, the length of his plays would clearly pose a problem.

We must be wary in comparing stage practices in Shakespeare's and in our own times. Acting styles may have been substantially different and it is possible that, in general, the lines were delivered at a higher speed than they are today. Yet, clowning and extemporizing seem to have been regular features and the Elizabethans' taste for pageantry as well as for songs, both taking up additional time, is reliably documented. Hart estimated that the Elizabethans performed approximately 2,300 lines in two hours.[35] This would be considerably faster than modern practice. Over the last few years, the RSC provided their customers with an average of less than nine hundred lines of Shakespearean text per hour amounting to something between 1,700 and 1,800 lines in two hours.[36] Even assuming the delivery was substantially faster as Hart's figures presuppose, the long texts of *Hamlet* and *Richard III* would still have taken three-and-a-half hours to perform.

For greater clarity, it will be useful to provide a table with the length of all of Shakespeare's plays. The plays are listed in the order and according to the generic grouping of the First Folio (I add *Pericles* to the end of the comedies):[37]

[34] Hart, *Shakespeare and the Homilies*, 83–84. Note that long plays were more or less confined to the period of Jonson and Shakespeare's time: "The supply of these Gargantuan dramas ceased almost immediately after the death of Shakespeare, and the almost simultaneous retirement of Jonson from active practice as a playwright; after 1616 such plays ceased to be written" (Hart, *Shakespeare and the Homilies*, 84).

[35] Alfred Hart, *Stolne and Surreptitious Copies: A Comparative Study of Shakespeare's Bad Quartos* (Melbourne University Press, 1942), 122.

[36] This figure is based on my own research carried out at the library of the Shakespeare Centre in Stratford-upon-Avon on a sample of twenty-five recent productions of Shakespeare plays.

[37] For the precise figures, I have drawn upon Hart, "Number of Lines," 21, and *Shakespeare and the Homilies*, 148.

The Tempest	2,015	
The Two Gentlemen of Verona	2,193	
Merry Wives of Windsor	2,634	
Measure for Measure	2,660	
The Comedy of Errors	1,753	
Much Ado about Nothing	2,535	
Love's Labour's Lost	2,651	
A Midsummer Night's Dream	2,102	
The Merchant of Venice	2,554	
As You Like It	2,608	
The Taming of the Shrew	2,552	
All's Well That Ends Well	2,738	
Twelfth Night	2,429	
A Winter's Tale	2,925	
Pericles	2,331	
King John	2,570	
Richard II	2,755	
1 Henry IV	2,968	
2 Henry IV	3,140 (Folio)	2,898/3,012[38] (Q1600)
Henry V	3,166	
1 Henry VI	2,676	
2 Henry VI	3,069	
3 Henry VI	2,904	
Richard III	3,570 (Folio)	3,389 (Q1597)
Henry VIII	2,807	
Troilus and Cressida	3,323 (Folio)	3,291 (Q1609)
Coriolanus	3,279	
Titus Andronicus	2,522	
Romeo and Juliet	2,989	
Timon of Athens	2,299	
Julius Caesar	2,450	
Macbeth	2,084	
Hamlet	3,537 (Folio)	3,668 (Q1604/5)
King Lear	2,899 (Folio)	3,092 (Q1608)
Othello	3,222 (Folio)	3,055 (Q1622)
Antony and Cleopatra	3,016	
Cymbeline	3,264	

[38] For the two issues of Q1600 *2 Henry IV*, see John Jowett and Gary Taylor, "The Three Texts of *2 Henry IV*," *Studies in Bibliography*, 40 (1987), 31–50, and René Weis, ed., *Henry IV, Part 2*, The Oxford Shakespeare (Oxford University Press, 1998), 79–84.

The figures suggest that the length of Shakespeare's plays is related to genre. In the order of diminishing length, Shakespeare's longest plays are *Hamlet*, *Richard III*, *Troilus and Cressida*, *Coriolanus*, *Cymbeline*, *Othello*, *King Lear*, *2 Henry IV*, *Henry V*, *2 Henry VI*, *Antony and Cleopatra*, *Romeo and Juliet*, and *1 Henry IV*. It is notable that comedies are not among Shakespeare's long plays, unless we are willing to credit *Troilus and Cressida* or *Cymbeline* with this generic label. In fact, without the romances and the generically problematic *Troilus and Cressida*, the average length of the comedies is 2,450 lines. Even if *The Comedy of Errors*, at 1,753 lines, is considered a special case of some sort, the remaining plays have an average of only just over 2,500 lines, ranging from 2,102 (*A Midsummer Night's Dream*) to 2,738 (*All's Well that Ends Well*). Shakespeare's comedies, in other words, are of a length that is easily compatible with the constraints of the stage and in line with the plays of Shakespeare's contemporaries.

The contrary is true for the tragedies and the histories. If we except the possibly incomplete *Timon of Athens* and the theatrically abridged *Macbeth* (see below), the tragedies have an average of 3,030 lines, over 500 lines more than the comedies. The ten history plays, similarly, have an average of only slightly less than 3,000 lines. The four longest plays, *Hamlet* with its profound philosophical and metaphysical issues, *Richard III* with its narrative ancestors by Holinshed, Hall, and More, and *Troilus and Cressida* and *Coriolanus* with their Greek and Roman subject matters would clearly be more respectable reading matter than *Twelfth Night* or *The Merry Wives of Windsor*.

The varying length of Shakespeare's plays suggests their author's awareness of the fact that, as reading matter, tragedies and histories had more social cachet than comedies. It may be significant that Jonson told Drummond in 1618/19 that half of his comedies were not in print.[39] John Marston added a note to the second edition of *Parasitaster, or The Fawn* (1606), in which he wrote that "*Comedies* are writ to be spoken, not read: Remember the life of these things consists in action; and for your such courteous suruay of my pen, *I* will present a Tragedy to you which shall boldly abide the most curious perusall."[40] Similarly, in his *Treatise on Playe*, Sir John Harington commends "stage-playes . . . well penned comedies, *and specially tragedies*" (emphasis mine).[41] Jonson, Marston, and Harington

---

[39] See *Ben Jonson's Conversations with William Drummond of Hawthornden*, ed. R. F. Patterson (London: Blackie and Son Ltd., 1924), 35.

[40] John Marston, *Parasitaster, or The Fawn* (1606), A2ᵛ. A marginal note reads: "*Sophonisba*," the title of Marston's tragedy that was published the same year.

[41] Sir John Harington, *Nugæ Antiquæ*, ed. Thomas Park, 2 vols. (London, 1804), 1.191. Note also that the anonymous writer of marginal notes in a copy of the First Folio of Shakespeare in the Kodama

corroborate what the relative length of Shakespeare's comedies, tragedies, and histories suggests: the tragedies and histories are of a length far exceeding what is necessary for a stage play because Shakespeare simultaneously conceived of them as literary drama with which he hoped to increase his reputation.

If Hart's exhaustive research into the length of plays does not seem to have had much impact on modern scholarship, this may be because his dogmatism led him to overstate his case: "if they wrote 'two hours' we have no option but to think that they meant exactly what they said."[42] Hart's literalist reading does not take into account that conventions take on their own dynamics beyond the limits of narrow facts. It is also anachronistic in its assumption that time-keeping in sixteenth- and seventeenth-century London is similar to time-keeping in the twentieth century.[43] There is no reason why the length of performances should not have varied between less than two and, say, two-and-a-half hours, perhaps slightly more in exceptional cases, excluding the final jig, inter-act music, and other additional entertainment. Hart's conclusions are similarly self-defeating when it comes to the length of dramatic texts: "all plays exceeding 2,300 to 2,400 lines in length would be liable to abridgment and usually would be abridged."[44] The truth, as will become apparent, must have been rather more complex.

Jonson himself provides a piece of unusually detailed information about performance length. In the Induction to *Bartholomew Fair*, the "Articles of Agreement" between "the Spectators or Hearers, at the Hope on the Bankside...and the Author" promise a playing time of "two houres and an halfe, and somewhat more."[45] In Jonsonian fashion, the indication is pedantically precise at a time when most people did not own watches.[46] Even by Jonsonian standards, *Bartholomew Fair*, at 4,344 prose lines, is very long.[47] In a survey of "Time Allotted for an Elizabethan Performance," David Klein has commented that "This play could very well have been done

---

Memorial Library of Meisei University annotated the tragedies and histories much more heavily than the comedies (see Akihiro Yamada, ed., *The First Folio of Shakespeare: A Transcript of Contemporary Marginalia* (Tokyo: Yushodo Press, 1998), xxvii–xxviii).

[42] Hart, *Shakespeare and the Homilies*, 104.

[43] Stuart Sherman's award-winning *Telling Time: Clocks, Diaries, and English Diurnal Form, 1660–1785* (Chicago and London: University of Chicago Press, 1996) provides a sense of how time-keeping changed after the age in which Shakespeare lived.

[44] Hart, *Stolne and Surreptitious Copies*, 122.

[45] The Induction, lines 79–80, quoted from Jonson, *Works*, eds. Herford, Simpson, and Simpson, VI.15.

[46] See Gurr, *Shakespearian Playing Companies* (Oxford University Press, 1996), 83.

[47] Hart, *Shakespeare and the Homilies*, 103.

in the time stated," an opinion I find impossible to share.[48] Performed at what I have above shown to be the average speed of the Royal Shakespeare Company, the unabridged play would take more than five hours to perform. At the higher speed at which Elizabethan players may well have delivered their lines, a performance of the full text would still have taken close to four hours. Jonson's precise indication thus suggests that when *Bartholomew Fair* was acted, performances were some seventy to eighty minutes shorter than they would have been if the play had been performed in its entirety.

If stage abridgement was a normal feature not just of plays performed on tours in the provinces but also of those acted in the London play-houses, we might hope to find evidence for this practice. Webster's *Duchess of Malfi* (printed 1623) was, according to its title-page, "with diuerse things Printed, that the length of the Play would not beare in the Presentment." With roughly three thousand lines,[49] the play is among the longest writ-ten by Shakespeare and Jonson's contemporaries, but much shorter than some of Shakespeare's plays. In a note at the end of the 1640 quarto of *The Antipodes*, the author Richard Brome announces that "You shall find in this book more then was presented upon the stage, and left out of the presentation, for superfluous length (as some of the players pre-tended). I thought good all should be inserted according to the allowed original."[50] With approximately 2,700 lines, *The Antipodes* is somewhat longer than the average play in its time, but considerably shorter than many of Shakespeare's plays. If the extant texts of *The Duchess of Malfi* and *The Antipodes* did not happen to point out that the printed versions contain more than what was performed, there would of course be no way of inferring this from the printed texts. Brome and Webster's plays thus bear the disquieting reminder that the length of a printed play need tell us very little about the length of the text the players actually performed.

This does not mean that any play that was abridged was deemed too long, nor, as Hart claimed, that the scissors would necessarily have been applied to any play that is slightly longer than the average. Plays of all lengths, including very short plays, might have passages omitted in order to have the text straightened out, lengthy speeches shortened, and superfluous bits of ingenious rhetoric and wordplay removed. In other words, when a relatively short play is abridged, we can generally assume that the players thought that the cuts would improve the play. With the longer texts, however, we should

[48] David Klein, "Time Allotted for an Elizabethan Performance," *Shakespeare Quarterly*, 18 (1967), 437.

[49] See Hart, *Shakespeare and the Homilies*, 131.

[50] Ann Haaker, ed., *The Antipodes*, Regents Renaissance Drama Series (Lincoln: University of Nebraska Press, 1966), 126.

be less confident about this. Deliberate cuts usually eliminate dramatically superfluous or even harmful material, get rid of obscure puns or wordplay, or remove passages that enlarge upon an idea that has been stated before. Cuts that are imposed upon the company by excessively lengthy texts, however, may also damage a play. As any writer knows, an article, a novel, or a screenplay can undergo some abridgement and, more often than not, is even the better for it. Yet it will not bear any amount of cutting without losing some of its essential qualities.

The title page of Webster's *Duchess of Malfi* thus suggests that the length of some English playbooks may be due to the fact that they were "with diuerse things Printed, that the length of the Play would not beare in the Presentment." In his dedication to George Harding, Baron Berkeley, Webster seems careful to distinguish his "Poem" from the abridged "Play." Anthony Hammond correctly points out that Webster "clearly thought that 'the length of the Play' was something related to the performance of the drama in the theatre: that is what a 'play' was. The printed 'perfect and exact Coppy,' then, is a copy of the 'poem.' "[51] "Poem" and "Play" differ in that the "Play" is the result of a collaborative effort that includes the company and is designed for performance on stage, while the "Poem" is what Webster claims as his own creation which lives on in print in order to be read. A crucial difference between "Poem" and "Play" seems to have been that of length. Whereas a "Poem" could have a length in excess of 4,000 lines (like *Every Man Out of His Humour*), even a text of 3,000 lines like that of *The Duchess of Malfi* had to be abridged before the play's "Presentment."

Even though it does not contain an explicit mention of performance length, John Marston's *Malcontent*, written and published in 1604, contains a passage that is not without implications for the length of performances. The play was originally performed by the Queen's Revels, one of the boys' companies that performed indoors in private theaters. When the same company appropriated Kyd's "Don Horatio," turning it into a burlesque that was printed in 1605 as *The First Part of Hieronimo*, the King's Men retaliated by playing *The Malcontent*.[52] For performance at the Globe, an induction (by Webster) plus some additions in the main text (by Marston and Webster) were written which, though absent from the first and the second edition, did appear in the third, also dated 1604.[53] In the Induction,

---

[51] Anthony Hammond, "Encounters of the Third Kind in Stage-Directions in Elizabethan and Jacobean Drama," *Studies in Philology*, 89 (1992), 72n.

[52] See page 115 note 2.

[53] For the authorship of the additions, see G. K. Hunter's Revels edition of *The Malcontent* (London: Methuen, 1975), xlvi–liii, and D. J. Lake, "Webster's Additions to *The Malcontent*," *Notes & Queries*, 228, n.s., 28 (1981), 153–58.

in which several of the King's Men appear in person, Burbage explains that the additions are not "greatly needful; only as your salad to your great feast, to entertain a little more time, and to abridge the not-received custom of music in our theatre." In other words, the original text of *The Malcontent* (1,908 lines) was too short for performance at the Globe.[54] Since the boy actors were primarily choristers, it is hardly surprising that music played an important part in their spectacles, allowing for (or necessitating) relatively short plays.[55] With the additional lines added to the main text, the play reaches some 2,531 lines, a total that is only slightly superior to the 2,494 lines that constitute the average length of a Globe play in the period from 1594–1603.[56]

The Induction to *The Malcontent* further suggests that what we know about additional entertainment in the form of music, masques, and dances needs to be taken into account. It seems likely that performances at the public playhouses during most of Shakespeare's career were played without intermission, but that when the King's Men started playing at the indoor Blackfriars playhouse, act division was marked by musical interludes.[57] This may explain why the extant text of *The Tempest* (*c.* 1610) is very short (2,015 lines), but contains references suggesting that indoor performance lasted between three and four hours:

> PROSPERO: What is the time o' the day?
> ARIEL: Past the mid season.
> PROSPERO: At least two glasses. The time 'twixt six and now
>   Must by us both be spent most preciously.   (1.2.240–42)
>
> PROSPERO: How's the day?
> ARIEL: On the sixth hour   (5.1.3–4)
>
> ALONSO: Give us particulars of thy preservation,
>   How thou hast met us here, whom three hours since
>   Were wrecked upon this shore   (5.1.137–39)
>
> BOATSWAIN: our ship,
>   Which, but three glasses since, we gave out split
>   (5.1.222–23)

---

[54] For the play's length, see Hart, *Shakespeare and the Homilies*, 130.
[55] See Chambers, *Elizabethan Stage*, II.556–57.   [56] See Hart, *Shakespeare and the Homilies*, 90.
[57] Wilfred T. Jewkes, *Act Division in Elizabethan and Jacobean Plays, 1583–1616* (Hamden, Conn.: Shoe String Press, 1958). Jewkes's most important results are conveniently summarized on pages 96–103. See also Gary Taylor, "Act Intervals," in Gary Taylor and John Jowett, *Shakespeare Reshaped, 1606–1623* (Oxford: Clarendon Press, 1993), 3–50, especially 30–32. Note, though, that G. K. Hunter has argued for act-pauses earlier in Shakespeare's career: "Were There Act-Pauses on Shakespeare's Stage?" in *English Renaissance Drama: Essays in Honor of Madelaine Doran and Mark Eccles*, eds. Standish Henning, Robert Kimbrough, and Richard Knowles (Carbondale, Ill.: Southern Illinois University Press, 1976), 15–35.

Performed at the same speed, the full text of *Hamlet* would, of course, take more than six hours to perform. Inter-act entertainment could thus take up a considerable amount of time. The prologue to *Lovers' Progress* speaks of "three short hours," yet the text in the "Beaumont and Fletcher" Folio adds up to a mere 2,472 lines, suggesting again that the additional entertainment occupied a considerable amount of time. When James Shirley's address "To the Reader," in the "Beaumont and Fletcher" Folio of 1647 refers to "the three hours spectacle, while Beaumont and Fletcher were presented," the exact wording is important. Shirley does not say that three hours was the duration of the play but of the "spectacle," which would have included music between the acts and probably before and after the play as well. So while the entertainments in the private indoor theaters were somewhat longer, it appears that the texts the players recited were not.

This chapter has suggested so far that the performance time of an Elizabethan play usually was in the proximity of two hours, though there seems to have been considerable variety. The "two houres and an halfe, and somewhat more" of Jonson's *Bartholomew Fair*, one of the longest plays of the entire period and considerably longer than any of Shakespeare's plays, is likely to indicate close to the maximal length a performance could have that was not drawn out by inter-act music or dances. What this suggests for texts performed on stage is that while there does not seem to have been a rigid standard length, plays could occasionally be deemed too short (*The Malcontent*) or, more commonly, too long (*The Duchess of Malfi* and *The Antipodes*). Stage abridgements therefore do not seem to have been an unusual feature of a play's preparation for the stage. Hart believed that plays would have a more or less uniform length of between 2,300 and 2,400 lines, but we are likely to be closer to the truth if we assume that the lengths varied from less than 2,000 to about 2,800 lines. Nevertheless, it remains true that Shakespeare's "long" plays from *Romeo and Juliet* (2,989 lines) to *Hamlet* (3,668/3,537 lines) appear to have been printed with considerably "more than hath been Publickely Spoken or Acted."

The lack of unambiguous external evidence for customary stage abridgement of Shakespeare's long plays is no doubt what has kept scholars from considering, as Orgel has urged us to do, the full implications of the length of many of Shakespeare's plays. A piece of precisely such unambiguous evidence in a document that is closely related to Shakespeare is thus of crucial importance.

The folio edition of "Comedies and Tragedies Written by Francis Beaumont and Iohn Fletcher Gentlemen" was published in 1647. As Heminge and Condell had taken an active part in the publication of the Shakespeare Folio, so members of the King's Men promoted the publication of the "Beaumont and Fletcher" Folio. Even though Francis Beaumont first composed plays for boy companies (*The Woman Hater*, *c.* 1606; *The Knight of the Burning Pestle*, *c.* 1607/10), he wrote for the King's Men in co-authorship with John Fletcher from about 1608.[58] Famously, Fletcher also collaborated with Shakespeare on *The Two Noble Kinsmen* (*c.* 1613), the lost *Cardenio* (*c.* 1612/13), and, probably, *Henry VIII* (*c.* 1612/1613). Beaumont and Fletcher, then, were Shakespeare's successors as the chief playwrights for the King's Men. Even though their collaboration only seems to have lasted until Beaumont's marriage to the heiress Ursula Isley in 1613, the label "Beaumont and Fletcher" has clung to a great number of plays owing to the Folio of 1647 which indiscriminately attributes the lot to the two playwrights. The label owes more to their close friendship before Beaumont's marriage than to bibliographical facts. As the antiquary John Aubrey wrote toward the end of the seventeenth century, Beaumont and Fletcher "lived together on the Banke Side, not far from the Playhouse, both batchelors; lay together; had one wench in the house between them, which they did so admire; the same cloathes and cloake, &c., between them."[59] Research has shown that the truth regarding the authorship of the plays in the 1647 Folio is rather more complex than the words "Beaumont and Fletcher" may lead one to suppose. While Beaumont contributed only to relatively few plays, Fletcher seems to have written some on his own and others in co-authorship with Philip Massinger, Nathan Field, Shakespeare, Thomas Middleton, and possibly John Ford and William Rowley.[60] It remains true, however, that the Folio of 1647 assembles a great body of plays written for and performed by Shakespeare's company in the years preceding and following his death.

The close relationship of the 1647 "Beaumont and Fletcher" Folio to Shakespeare's of 1623 is important if we want to understand what light it can shed on its predecessor. In some ways, it seems to be a conscious imitation of

---

[58] For the dating of these plays, I have drawn upon Alfred Harbage's *Annals of English Drama 975–1700*, revised by S. Schoenbaum, 2nd edn (London: Methuen, 1964).

[59] *Aubrey's Brief Lives*, ed. Oliver Lawson Dick (London: Secker and Warburg, 1949), 21.

[60] See Fredson Bowers, gen. ed., *Beaumont and Fletcher Canon*; for a convenient summary of tentative attributions, see x.751–52. See also Cyrus Hoy, "The Shares of Fletcher and his Collaborators in the Beaumont and Fletcher Canon," *Studies in Bibliography*, 8 (1956), 129–46; 9 (1957), 143–62; 11 (1958), 85–106; 12 (1958), 91–116; 13 (1960), 77–108; 14 (1961), 45–67; 15 (1962), 71–90. The assumptions underlying Hoy's work are subjected to criticism in Masten, *Textual Intercouse*, 16–20.

Heminge and Condell's venture some twenty-five years earlier. Like it and like no other Folio before, it confines itself to plays (besides one masque). Its number of plays (thirty-four) is very close to its Shakespearean predecessor (thirty-six). The indebtedness to the 1623 Folio is made explicit in the dedication addressed "TO THE RIGHT HONOVRABLE PHILIP Earl of Pembroke" (A2ʳ), William Herbert's brother and co-dedicatee of the Shakespeare Folio, who had become the Earl of Pembroke upon his brother's death in 1630. The dedication specifically reminds Philip Herbert that he and his recently deceased brother had formerly patronized a similar collection of plays by Shakespeare. The ten signatories, all actors of the King's Men, declare that they have been "directed by the example of some, who once steered in our qualitie, and so fortunately aspired to choose your Honour, joyned with your (now glorified) Brother, Patrons to the flowing compositions of the then expired sweet Swan of Avon SHAKESPEARE" (A2ʳ).

Both Folios make large claims for the authority of their texts. The title page of the Shakespeare Folio promises that the plays are "Published according to the True Originall Copies." Heminge and Condell's address "To the great Variety of Readers" adds the famous passage that cries down earlier publications:

where (before) you were abus'd with diuerse stolne, and surreptitious copies, maimed, and deformed by the frauds and stealthes of iniurious impostors, that expos'd them: euen those, are now offer'd to your view cur'd, and perfect of their limbes; and all the rest, absolute in their numbers, as he conceiued thē.

Moseley's address "The Stationer to the Readers" similarly emphasizes the credentials of his texts: "here is not any thing *Spurious* or *impos'd*; I had the Originalls from such as received them from the *Authours* themselves; by Those, and none other, I publish this Edition." This is reiterated in a later passage:

VVhen these *Comedies* and *Tragedies* were presented on the Stage, the *Actours* omitted some *Scenes* and Passages (with the *Authour's* consent) as occasion led them; and when private friends desir'd a Copy, they then (and justly too) transcribed what they *Acted*. But now you have both All that was *Acted*, and all that was not; even the perfect full Originalls without the least mutilation.[61]

The Shakespeare Folio only informed its readers that the plays were "Published according to the True Originall Copies" without commenting upon the relationship these copies bore to the plays that were performed in

---

[61] Moseley's address has been printed in full in Greg, *Bibliography*, III.1233–34.

London's theaters. The omission of "some *Scenes* and Passages" implies fairly drastic abridgement, and the possible implications of this for Shakespeare's plays will have to be examined in some detail. Interestingly, Moseley claims he is now presenting his texts "without the least mutilation" (implying they had been mutilated) just as Heminge and Condell promise they are now "cur'd and perfect of their limbes." Yet, while the latter compare their own texts to "stolne, and surreptitious copies," Moseley praises the quality of his texts in comparison to private transcripts.[62] What constitutes their superiority, Moseley argues, is their length as the private transcripts only contained much shortened acting versions.

The crucial importance of Moseley's address has long been acknowledged by some of the seminal voices in Shakespeare scholarship, including Sidney Lee, W. W. Greg, and, more recently, Richard Dutton, Paul Werstine, and Peter Blayney.[63] Yet what has perhaps not been investigated with sufficient attention is the evidence provided by the "Beaumont and Fletcher" plays themselves. In particular, if Moseley tells us that entire scenes and passages were omitted from at least some of these plays when they reached the stage, it will be important to know what their original length was and how it compares to that of Shakespeare's plays. Understandably, Moseley's words have led scholars to believe that Beaumont and Fletcher's plays are very long. Richard Dutton, for instance, has recently argued that they may have written "overlength plays . . . with the expectation of a print readership."[64] It may be surprising then that in comparison with Shakespeare's, the plays in the 1647 Folio are short. While the average length of Shakespeare's thirty-six Folio plays is 2,763 lines, that of the thirty-four plays in the Beaumont and Fletcher Folio is 2,419 lines. More significantly, perhaps, the longest play in Moseley's Folio, *Valentinian*, is only 2,875 lines long, shorter, that is, than no fewer than fifteen of Shakespeare's plays and significantly shorter than most of them. If the relatively short "Beaumont and Fletcher" plays were significantly abridged, how likely is it that the same company performed the full text of Shakespeare's substantially longer plays?

It is of some significance that there are reasons to doubt that all the plays in the "Beaumont and Fletcher" Folio represent what Moseley calls "the perfect full Originalls." In *Bibliographical Studies in the Beaumont & Fletcher Folio*

---

[62] See Appendix B for Heminge and Condell's "stolne, and surreptitious copies."

[63] See Lee, *Life of William Shakespeare*, 558–59; W. W. Greg, "Prompt Copies, Private Transcripts, and 'the Playhouse Scrivener,'" *The Library*, 4th series, 6 (1926), 148; Werstine, "Narratives," 85; Dutton, "Birth of the Author," 100–1; Blayney, "Publication of Playbooks," 394.

[64] Dutton, "Birth of the Author," 103. See also Brooks, *Playhouse to Printing House*, 54.

of 1647, the most comprehensive study of Moseley's publishing enterprise to date, R. C. Bald noted that the original entry in the Stationers' Register contained only twenty-five titles. He found further evidence supporting the argument that manuscripts of these plays had been in the possession of the King's Men and had been passed on to Moseley. A warrant dated August 7, 1641 from the Lord Chamberlain to the Master and Warden of the Stationers' Company contains a list of sixty plays in the King's Men's repertory which may not "bee put in Print w'hout their knowledge & consent."[65] The twenty-five plays of the entry in the Stationers' Register are listed in the same order as they are in 1641. Perhaps the King's Men had entertained the idea of a folio edition as early as 1641 and wanted to make sure that publications based on manuscripts other than those in their possession (including the private transcripts Moseley mentions) would not make such a costly volume superfluous. In any case, when the King's Men and Moseley first decided to go ahead with the Folio and entered a list of "Beaumont and Fletcher" plays in the Stationers' Register, that list contained only twenty-five of the thirty-four plays that ended up in print. While these plays seem to have been in the company's hands and are likely to be the full versions Moseley promises, the other texts, as we will see, do not seem to have reached Moseley straight from the King's Men and may well be less than the "perfect full Originalls."

It seems useful to isolate for a moment the twenty-five plays in the "Beaumont and Fletcher" Folio that were originally entered in the Stationers' Register and to provide a list that indicates their length:[66]

The Spanish Curate	2,596
The Little French Lawyer	2,443
The Custom of the Country	2,643
The Noble Gentleman	2,273
The Captain	2,829
Beggars' Bush	2,161
The Coxcomb	2,493
The Chances	1,857
The Loyal Subject	2,806
The Lover's Progress	2,472
The Island Princess	2,510
The Humorous Lieutenant	2,668
The Maid in the Mill	2,392

---

[65] The Lord Chamberlain's letter is quoted in E. K. Chambers, "Plays of the King's Men in 1641," in *Collections*, ed. W. W. Greg, The Malone Society (London: Oxford University Press, 1911), 364–69, 367.

[66] My count is based upon *Beaumont and Fletcher Canon*, gen. ed. Bowers.

The Prophetess	2,177
Bonduca	2,333
The Double Marriage	2,638
The Pilgrim	2,302
The Knight of Malta	2,717
The Woman's Prize	2,647
Love's Cure	2,302
The Honest Man's Fortune	2,687
The Queen of Corinth	2,433
A Wife for a Month	2,371
Valentinian	2,875
Love's Pilgrimage	2,640

The average length of these twenty-five plays is 2,491 lines. At 1,857 lines, *The Chances* is more than three hundred lines shorter than the next shortest play and seems to be a special case of some sort. The figures may thus be more representative if we calculate the average of the remaining twenty-four plays, which is 2,517 lines. The length of these twenty-four plays is quite evenly distributed between the longest, *Valentinian*, with 2,875 lines, and *Beggars' Bush*, the shortest, with 2,161 lines. Seventeen, more than two-thirds of these plays, have between 2,300 and 2,700 lines. Of the remaining seven, three have more than 2,300, four more than 2,700 lines. What is striking about these figures is that they are only insignificantly higher than those Alfred Hart identified as the average length of Elizabethan plays.

The plausibility of what I believe must have been the habitual radical abridgement of Shakespeare's "long" plays emerges even more clearly if we confine the statistics for a moment to the longest plays in both the Shakespeare and the Beaumont and Fletcher Folios. The average of the twelve longest Shakespeare plays of undoubted sole authorship is over 3,200 lines while that of the twelve longest "Beaumont and Fletcher" plays is approximately five hundred lines shorter. If "scenes and passages" were omitted in performance from at least some "Beaumont and Fletcher" plays, it seems difficult not to conclude that an additional five hundred lines or so had to be cut from Shakespeare's longest plays. The shortest of these, *Romeo and Juliet* and *1 Henry IV*, are not only longer than the longest in the "Beaumont and Fletcher" Folio, but they are also of a length that is very similar to Webster's *Duchess of Malfi* of which we know that its printed text contains substantially more than could be accommodated on stage.

The moment has come to return to Moseley's resonant prefatory comments and their implications for the nature and length of his texts. Moseley makes three statements that are difficult to reconcile with each other. On the one hand, he claims that the texts in his Folio, contrary to the ones that circulated in manuscript, reached him through those that had them from the authors and contain the full original text. Yet in a different passage, Moseley implies that some of the manuscripts came from a variety of other sources:

'Twere vain to mention the *Chargeablenesse* of this Worke; for those who own'd the *Manuscripts*, too well know their value to make a cheap estimate of any of these Pieces, and though another joyn'd with me in the *Purchase* and Printing, yet the *Care & Pains* was wholly mine, which I found to be more then you'l easily imagine, unless you knew into how many hands the Originalls were dispersed. They are all now happily met in this Book, having escaped these *Publike Troubles*, free and unmangled. (See note 61 above)

If we recall Moseley's earlier statement that "when private friends desir'd a Copy, they then (and justly too) transcribed what they *Acted*," it seems reasonable to assume that the "many hands" into which "the Originalls were dispersed" do not include those that received the private transcripts of the abridged performance texts. It may then be of interest to test the hypothesis that at least some of the remaining texts ended up in Moseley's Folio not because the King's Men were in a position to provide him with an authorial or a playhouse manuscript, but due to the fact that some of the private transcripts were recovered.

Four plays in the "Beaumont and Fletcher" Folio were added to the list in the Stationers' Register in September 1646: *The Mad Lover*, *The Lawes of Candy*, *The Women Pleased*, and *The Sea Voyage*. What evidence is there that they may have been set up from abridged private transcripts? As for the question of length, the average number of lines of these four plays is 2,127, nearly four hundred fewer than the average of the other twenty-five plays. In fact, if the exceptionally short *Chances* is excepted, none of the remaining twenty-four plays is shorter than *The Mad Lover*, *The Lawes of Candy*, or *The Sea Voyage*. We saw above that the length of most of the twenty-four plays is quite evenly distributed with upper limits at two hundred lines more or less than the average 2,500. Of the four plays that were entered later in the Stationers' Register, none falls within this range. This evidence therefore does not contradict the assumption that these plays may have been set up from some of the private transcripts Moseley refers to.

When it comes to *The Mad Lover*, we know that a private transcript did exist. Prefixed to Sir Aston Cokayne's *Small Poems of Divers Sorts* (1658), "The Authors Apology to the Reader" reads:

I have been demanded by some Persons of Quality and judgement, why in my copy of Verses before *M*r. *Fletchers* volume of Plaies, I chiefly reflect upon the *Mad Lover*, my noble friend and kinsman *M*r. *Charles Cotton*, sent me that single Play in a *M*anuscript, which I had divers years in my hands: therefore when I found the Players were prohibited to act, I writ those poor Verses with an intention to have had the *Mad Lover* printed single, and them to have waited on it; (which when the large Volume came forth) my Cosin *Cotton* commanded from me, and gave the Printers. (A 4ᵛ)

Cotton seems likely to be one of the "private friends" for whom private transcripts were prepared. Cockayne's is a resonant statement. It shows that some of the friends who received private transcripts felt free to have those texts published. Whether Cockayne's words should be taken to suggest that the manuscript he received and the one from which the Folio text was set up are identical is less clear. R. C. Bald suggested that they should.[67] Cockayne's "which … Cotton commanded from me, and gave the Printers" is admittedly ambiguous and does perhaps not exclude such a reading. It seems to me, however, that "which" refers more naturally to the verses. After all, the appearance of his verses on *The Mad Lover* in the folio edition is why he is telling the reader about this. On the other hand, *The Mad Lover* was among the four plays later added to the list of plays entered in the Stationers' Register, suggesting that the King's Men did not have to hand a manuscript of *The Mad Lover* when they were first planning the Folio. So, even if Bald is wrong, it does not seem unlikely that Cockayne, via Cotton and the King's Men, gave both the prefatory verses and the manuscript to the printer.

Twenty-five of the plays in the "Beaumont and Fletcher" Folio appear in the Stationers' Register in a list of September 4, 1646, and four were entered later the same year. The remaining five (*The False One, The Nice Valour, Wit at Several Weapons, The Fair Maid of the Inn*, and *Four Plays in One*) were not entered until June 29, 1660. It has been shown on bibliographical grounds that Moseley did not secure these manuscripts until a considerable part of the Folio had been printed.[68] Bald suggests that *The False One* and *The Nice Valour* are "private transcripts acquired from private owners who came forward with them,"[69] an argument that is consistent with the plays' relative brevity (2,268 and 1,726 lines). Of these five plays, however, only two can be linked to the King's Men on good grounds, and, while

[67] R. C. Bald, *Bibliographical Studies in the Beaumont & Fletcher Folio of 1647* (Oxford: Printed at the Oxford University Press for the Bibliographical Society, 1938 [for 1937]), 7.

[68] It appears that "the manuscripts of these pieces did not reach Moseley till after the sections had been allocated for they all appear at the end of their respective sections" (Greg, *Bibliography*, III.1017).

[69] Bald, *Beaumont & Fletcher Folio*, 110.

The False One is among them, *The Nice Valour* is not.[70] Nevertheless, Moseley's preface suggests and the belatedly entered plays corroborate that the relatively short "Beaumont and Fletcher" plays were further abridged on stage and in private transcripts.

Moseley's words imply that the purpose of the transcripts was to record an abridged acting text rather than "the perfect full Originalls." It has been wondered just how plausible this is. Greg believed that "Moseley is of course vaunting the superiority of his own wares: there seems no obvious reason why in making a transcript the players should have confined it to the actual stage version."[71] The extant material witnesses do not bear out Greg's skepticism, however.[72] A private transcript of *The Woman's Prize* is extant in the Folger Shakespeare Library (MS. J.b.3). The play was performed at court in November 1633. It may be, as Bowers conjectured, that the transcript was made in response to a request after that performance, though there is no hard evidence to confirm this.[73] If we compare the manuscript to the printed play in the Folio, we realize that the former, significantly, does omit "some *Scenes* and Passages." Two scenes (2.1, 4.1) disappear in their entirety, while ten passages of up to fourteen lines are similarly absent.[74] Some of the shorter omissions need not have originated in the playhouse, but the two omitted scenes are typical theatrical cuts. They contribute little if anything to the plot and are too innocuous for the censor to have struck them out.[75] All in all, more than two hundred lines present in the Folio seem to have been omitted in the manuscript owing to theatrical cuts. It is true that F also omits certain passages present in the manuscript, but these passages seem "all such as Herbert might very well have objected to."[76] A misnumbering in the Folio's act and scene division corroborates the likelihood that the private transcript does and the Folio does not give us the text as abridged

---

[70] For *The False One* and for *The Nice Valour*, see Bentley, *Jacobean and Caroline Stage*, 111.341, 111.381–84; for *Four Plays in One* and for *Wit at Several Weapons*, see Chambers, *Elizabethan Stage*, 111.231–32; for *The Fair Maid of the Inn*, see Joseph Quincy Adams, ed., *The Dramatic Records of Sir Henry Herbert, Master of the Revels, 1623–1673* (New Haven: Yale University Press, 1917), 31.

[71] Greg, "Prompt Copies," 148.

[72] As Paul Werstine has shown, the manuscripts Greg examined for his influential study of *Dramatic Documents from the Elizabethan Playhouses* covered only a portion of the extant manuscripts, especially of those not available in London libraries (Werstine, "Plays in Manuscript," 481–97, esp. 482–83). In particular, as Werstine notes, Greg did not examine the manuscripts in the Lambarde Collection (already in Henry Clay Folger's possession), as the Folger Shakespeare Library did not open until the year after Greg's *Dramatic Documents* had been published. If Greg had had access to more manuscripts, his conclusions, I believe, might well have been different.

[73] Bowers, gen. ed., *Beaumont and Fletcher Canon*, IV.6.

[74] See Bald, *Beaumont & Fletcher Folio*, 60.

[75] See Bowers, gen. ed. *Beaumont and Fletcher Canon*, IV.8.

[76] Bald, *Beaumont & Fletcher Folio*, 60.

for the stage. While act four in the Folio is headed "*Actus Quartus. Scæna prima*," there is no heading for the second scene, and the third is announced as "*Scæna Secunda.*" As 4.1 was cut in the private transcript, this confusion seems to be due to the fact that what should be 4.3 in the Folio was in fact the second scene of the fourth act that was actually performed.[77] Summing up his analysis, Bald concluded that the manuscript "gives the play as cut for acting before Herbert's time," which the Folio "gives a fuller version of the play, but observes the cuts that were made by Herbert in 1633."[78]

Like the private transcript of *The Woman's Prize*, that of *Beggars' Bush* (Folger MS. J.b.5) may have been commissioned after performance at court (recorded in 1636 and 1639). Stage directions such as "Table out" or "A table kans and stools set out" suggest that it was transcribed from the "playbook" (which earlier scholars anachronistically referred to as the "promptbook").[79] Five Folio passages of four to fourteen lines are absent from the manuscript and "probably represent theatrical cuts."[80] Considering *Beggars' Bush* is one of the shortest plays in the 1647 Folio, it is not greatly surprising that little was omitted.

Irregularities in the Folio also suggest that the manuscript from which it was set up had at one stage been shorter than the version surviving in print. Bertha, the kidnapped heiress of Brabant, makes the following lament:

> O I am miserably lost, thus falne
> Into my vncles hands from all my hopes,
> Can I not thinke away my selfe and dye?
> O I am miserably lost; thus fallen

---

[77] See Ibid., 61. On similar grounds, Bald (83) argued that two scenes (2.4 and 2.5) of *The Woman's Prize* that had suffered under Herbert's hands may have been completely omitted, resulting in the reprinting of 2.3 at the end of 2.5 and the heading *Scena tertia* before 2.6.

[78] Bald, *Beaumont & Fletcher Folio*, 60. Fredson Bowers concurred with Bald's judgment: "the Folger manuscript was copied from a prompt-book, cut for acting before Herbert's interference with the text" (*Beaumont and Fletcher Canon*, IV.5).

[79] See Bald, *Beaumont & Fletcher Folio*, 62. William B. Long ("Performing Texts: Shakespeare's Players and Editors," *TEXT: An Interdisciplinary Annual of Textual Studies*, 8 (1995), 381) has rightly insisted that the use of the Elizabethan term "playbook" is to be preferred to that of the "modern and teleological term 'prompt-book'" which textual scholars used for most of the twentieth century:

The issue is not a pedantic one of nomenclature. The two terms reflect radically different sets of assumptions about how playwrights tailored their manuscripts for acting companies and how the players used these manuscript plays. Thus these attitudes in turn radically condition how one regards early printed editions. "Promptbook" connotes an authoritarian document with heavy extra-authorial alterations and a managerial direction of players. "Playbook" connotes a co-operative venture in which the playwright and the players collaborate by contributing separate, complementary elements to create a play production.

See also Long's " 'A bed / for woodstock': A Warning for the Unwary," *Medieval & Renaissance Drama in England* 2 (1985): 91–118, esp. 93, and " 'Precious Few,' " 414–33, esp. 415.

[80] Bald, *Beaumont & Fletcher Folio*, 64.

> Into my Uncles hands, from all my hopes:
> No matter how, where thou be false or no,
> *Goswin*, whether thou love an other better;
> Or me alone; or where thou keep thy vow,
> And word, or that thou come, or stay: for I
> To thee from henceforth, must be ever absent,
> And thou to me: no more shall we come neere,
> To tell our selves, how bright each other eyes were,
> How soft our language, and how sweet our kisses,
> Whil'st we made one our food, th'other our feast,
> Not mix our soules by sight, or by letter
> Hereafter, but as small relation have,
> As two new gon to inhabiting a grave:
> Can I not thinke away my selfe and dye?   (Mm3ʳ)

What is remarkable, of course, is that the first three lines reappear in the course of the speech, the first two immediately after the initial three, the last at the very end. In other words, the Folio prints successively two versions of the same speech, a short and a long one. Significantly, the manuscript only contains the short three-line speech. John Dorenkamp, following Bald, has plausibly suggested that copy was a stage version to which the fuller, original passages had been added.[81] In any case, the long and the short versions of Bertha's speech must somehow have been present in the copy, and the compositor seems to have failed to notice that the long version would make the short superfluous.

Dorenkamp's theory is supported by Folio passages that break up metrically regular lines:

> WOOL[FORT]. Oh *Hubert*, these your wordes and reasons have
> As well drawne drops of blood from my griev'd hart,
> As these teares from mine eyes;
> Despise them not
> By all that's sacred, I am serious *Hubert*,
> You now have made me sensible, what furyes,
> Whips, hangmen, and tormentors a bad man
> Do's ever beare about him: let the good
> That you this day have done, be even numberd,
> The first of your best actions;
> Can you think,
> Where *Floriz* is or *Gerrard*, or your love,
> Or any else, or all that are proscrib'd?   (Kk2ᵛ)

---

[81] John Fletcher and Philip Massinger, *Beggars Bush*, ed. John H. Dorenkamp (The Hague and Paris: Mouton, 1967), 17; and Bald, *Beaumont & Fletcher Folio*, 81–82.

The manuscript omits the words from "Despise them not" to "The first of your actions" without which the passage still makes good sense. It seems again plausible to assume that when the Folio text was printed, passages that had been previously omitted were restored.

The private transcripts of *The Woman's Prize* and *Beggars' Bush* reveals, as Bald argued, "the extent to which Moseley's preface is to be relied upon."[82] They suggest that the King's Men did omit "some *Scenes* and *Passages*" in performance. They further confirm that, *pace* Greg, the company as a rule sold private transcripts not of the full authorial foul papers but of the abridged stage version "when private friends desir'd a Copy." In fact, the "Beaumont and Fletcher" plays which the King's Men performed on stage appear to have been of a length closer to that of the first,"bad," quarto of *Hamlet* (2,154 lines) than to that of the long Shakespearean text(s) we normally study.

Among the theatrical manuscripts that can teach us much about theatrical process are not only private transcripts but also the original manuscript playbooks the writers submitted and the companies altered, annotated, and at times abridged, in preparation for performance. The total number of extant English manuscript playbooks from the years between 1576 and 1642 is a mere eighteen. Given the unique value of these material witnesses, we would expect that they have long been studied in depth and that editions and other works of scholarship about the English Renaissance professional stage make regular use of the insights they provide. Surprisingly, the contrary is the case. Consequently, William Long has argued, "the investigation of the texts of Shakespeare and others has stagnated badly. Existing evidence has been ignored regularly; knowledge of working theater avoided studiously; and we are little closer to understanding what happened with English Renaissance drama texts than we were half a century ago."[83]

I intend to discuss these invaluable documents insofar as they have an impact upon my argument. Long has recently provided an extremely useful survey of the "precious few" extant manuscript playbooks, a survey that allows me to restrict my discussion to the question of length and abridgement.[84] To the eighteen manuscript playbooks Long discusses, I add Middleton's *Hengist, King of Kent; or The Mayor of Queensborough* of

---

[82] Ibid., 114.

[83] William B. Long, "Perspective on Provenance: The Context of Varying Speech-heads," in *Shakespeare's Speech-Headings: Speaking the Speech in Shakespeare's Plays*, ed. George Walton Williams (Newark: University of Delaware Press; London: Associated University Presses, 1997), 35.

[84] Long, " 'Precious Few,' " 414–33.

which two private transcripts survive which carefully preserve playbook features such as prompter's notes and deletion marks, giving us access to the same kind of information about abridgement as manuscript playbooks do.[85]

Before summarizing what conclusions can be drawn from a survey of the length and abridgement of the extant manuscript playbooks, I need to explain briefly how I arrived at my data. For the line count of the omitted passages, I have chiefly relied upon the plays' Malone Society Reprints whose meticulous description of the manuscript playbooks has been invaluable.[86] Despite the availability of the Malone Society Reprints, the reasons for which passages have been marked for omission or crossed out are often beyond recovery. Apart from censorship, passages may have been omitted in anticipation of the Master of the Revels' objections, by an author unsatisfied with a passage he had written, for casting arrangements, to get rid of artistically unsatisfactory material, or for the purpose of shortening the play. When a passage has been deleted and subsequently replaced,

---

[85] "A dramatic manuscript containing such clearly marked theatrical cuts and various actors' names in stage-directions would, under normal circumstances, be unhesitatingly pronounced a prompt-copy, but here, where the same features appear in the two manuscripts of the play, and where the manuscripts are in the hand of the same scribe, both can scarcely be prompt-copies, and it is probable that neither is ... The two manuscripts of *Hengist*, therefore, are probably private transcripts; but there is little doubt that the scribe's 'copy' was an annotated prompt-book" (Thomas Middleton, *Hengist, King of Kent; or The Mayor of Queenborough*, ed. R. C. Bald (New York: Charles Scribner's Sons, 1938), xxvii–xxix).

[86] Anthony Munday, *John a Kent and John a Cumber*, ed. Muriel St. Clare Byrne (London: Oxford University Press, 1923); Anthony Munday and others, *The Book of Sir Thomas More*, ed. W. W. Greg (London: Oxford University Press, 1911); *John of Bordeaux or The Second Part of Friar Bacon*, ed. William Lindsay Renwick (London: Oxford University Press, 1935 [for 1936]); *The First Part of the Reign of King Richard the Second or Thomas of Woodstock*, ed. Wilhelmina P. Frijlinck (London: Oxford University Press, 1929); *Edmond Ironside; or War Hath Made All Friends*, ed. Eleanore Boswell (London: Oxford University Press, 1928); *Charlemagne; or, The Distracted Emperor*, ed. John Henry Walter (London: Oxford University Press, 1937 [for 1938]); *The Second Maiden's Tragedy*, ed. W. W. Greg (London: Oxford University Press, 1909); John Fletcher and Philip Massinger, *Sir John van Olden Barnavelt*, ed. T. H. Howard-Hill (London: Oxford University Press, 1979 [for 1980]); *The Two Noble Ladies*, ed. Rebecca G. Rhoads (London: Oxford University Press, 1930); *The Welsh Embassador*, ed. H. Littledale (London: Oxford University Press, 1920); Philip Massinger, *The Parliament of Love*, ed. Kathleen Marguerite Lea (London: Oxford University Press, 1928 [for 1929]); John Clavell, *The Soddered Citizen*, ed. John Henry Pyle Pafford (London, 1935 [for 1936]); Philip Massinger, *Believe As You List*, ed. Charles J. Sisson (London: Oxford University Press, 1927); Walter Mountfort, *The Launching of the Mary*, ed. John Henry Walter (London: Oxford University Press, 1933); Henry Glapthorne, *The Lady Mother*, ed. Arthur Brown (London: Oxford University Press, 1958 [for 1959]); *The Wasp or Subject's Precedent*, ed. J. W. Lever (Oxford, 1974 [for 1976]). For Heywood's *Captives*, see *Thomas Heywood: Three Marriage Plays*, ed. Paul Merchant, The Revels Plays Companion Library (Manchester University Press, 1996). Merchant prints in an appendix the lines Heywood canceled. For Fletcher's *Honest Man's Fortune*, see Cyrus Hoy's edition in *Beaumont and Fletcher Canon*, gen. ed. Bowers, volume 10. For Thomas Middleton's *Hengist, King of Kent; or The Mayor of Queenborough*, see Bald's edition. It is a convention of the Malone Society Reprints to provide a through-line numbering that includes stage directions and act and scene headings. For the total line count, I have therefore subtracted the lines that do not contain dialogue.

the deletion clearly cannot be considered part of a theatrical abridgement and is thus not included in my count. When an omitted passage has not been replaced, however, I include it in my count of passages that shortened performances, independently of whether the reason for the omission can be established. My ambition is not to isolate those passages that were omitted in order to abridge a play – which is bound to be a fruitless endeavor. Rather, I attempt to arrive at the approximate number of lines that originally belonged to the dramatic dialogue but were marked for omission before the play reached the stage.

The evidence may be summed up as follows: of the nineteen extant manuscript playbooks, twelve are shorter while seven are longer than 2,500 lines. Of the twelve playtexts that are shorter than 2,500 lines, five contain cuts of considerable length, totaling up to *c.* 380 lines. Even the very short *Edmond Ironside* (1,960 lines) marks some two hundred lines for omission. The remaining seven relatively short manuscripts are virtually or entirely uncut: Massinger's *Believe As You List* (2,430 lines), the same author's *Parliament of Love* (2,300 lines), the anonymous *Welsh Ambassador* (2,280 lines) and *Two Noble Ladies* (2,120 lines), the famous *Sir Thomas More* by Munday et al. (2,390 lines), Fletcher and Massinger's *Barnavelt* (2,440 lines), and *The Second Maiden's Tragedy* (2,180 lines), attributed to Middleton in the forthcoming Oxford *Works*.[87] The tentative conclusion these facts invite is that while some relatively short plays *were* cut (for reasons which, presumably, had little to do with the plays' length), the majority of them *were not.*

This picture changes when we move to the seven remaining manuscript playbooks of more than 2,500 lines. They range from the anonymous *Charlemagne* and Glapthorne's *Lady Mother* (both *c.* 2,570 lines) via Fletcher's *Honest Man's Fortune*, Clavell's *Soddered Citizen*, and Middleton's *Hengist* (2,690, 2,720, and 2,830 lines) to the anonymous *Woodstock* and Mountfort's *Launching of the Mary* (both just over 2,900 lines). All of these were substantially cut, by a minimum of one hundred and by an average of nearly two hundred lines. It would be simplistic to argue that all of these cuts were made in order to reduce the plays' length. Nevertheless, these figures do suggest that length was one (though not the only) consideration when a playbook was (or was not) marked with theatrical cuts (see Figures 9 and 10).

---

[87] *The Parliament of Love* runs to 2,123 lines in Edwards and Gibson's Oxford edition of *The Plays and Poems of Philip Massinger*, 5 vols. (Oxford: Clarendon Press, 1976), II.109–76. The beginning of the first act is missing, however, and the foot of the pages has been damaged, causing more lines to disappear. It has been estimated that the original length was close to 2,300 lines (ibid., II.98–99).

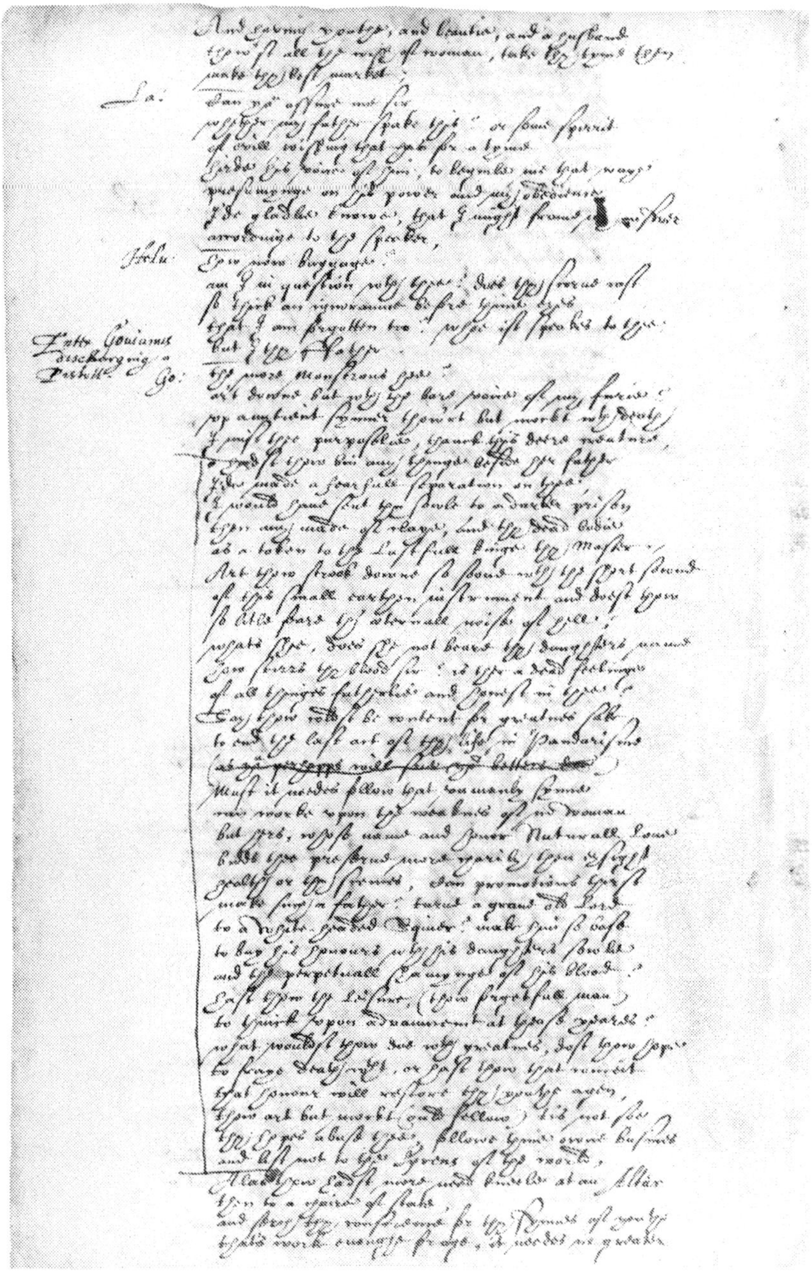

Figure 9. Folio 54a of *The Second Maiden's Tragedy, c.* 1612 (British Library MS Lansdowne 807), with passages marked for deletion.

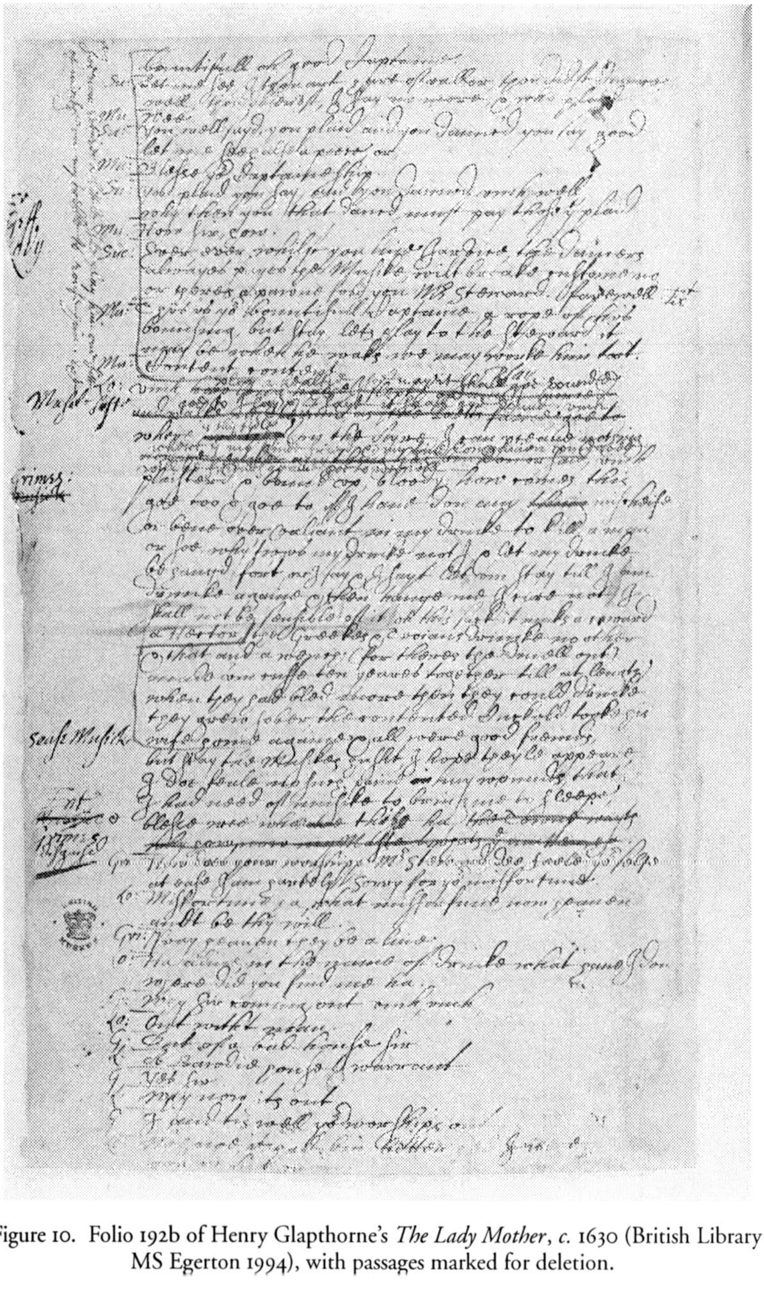

Figure 10. Folio 192b of Henry Glapthorne's *The Lady Mother*, c. 1630 (British Library MS Egerton 1994), with passages marked for deletion.

Two additional points need to be borne in mind: Firstly, even the longest of these plays is shorter than any of Shakespeare's "long" plays. Secondly, while manuscript playbooks mark passages that were omitted in performance, we can never be entirely sure that further passages would not have been deleted if, in rehearsal, the play was still deemed too long. At that stage, the most likely candidates for omission would have been central parts of speeches and soliloquies which leave the cues – and thus all but the speaker – unaffected. These omissions might well not have found their way into the extant manuscripts. A playbook, as William Long reminds us, was "not nearly so important a directional document as it was to become in later centuries."[88] Therefore, "it always must be remembered that the change that mattered was recorded in the player's part, which he would memorize without reference to the book. The playbook was a matter of record and of convenient reference, not of remembrance."[89]

The pattern according to which relatively long manuscripts were cut while relatively short manuscripts often were not also emerges from the smaller sample of extant plays performed by the King's Men. Of the relatively short *Barnavelt*, *Believe As You List*, and *Second Maiden's Tragedy*, only the last marks any passages for omission. The relatively long *Honest Man's Fortune*, *Soddered Citizen*, and *Launching of the Mary* are all marked with cuts, however, reducing their texts from *c.* 2,690, 2,720, and 2,910 lines to *c.* 2,500, 2,550, and 2,650 lines respectively.

It is with these figures in mind that we need to read Steven Urkowitz's argument that "Some short plays were cut severely, some long plays were not reduced at all."[90] The first half of this contention, as I have shown, is true, but the second half is not. Urkowitz is, in fact, only following Greg who, more than Urkowitz himself, may be to blame for the conclusion he arrives at. For Greg's example of a long, uncut "prompt-book" is *Believe As You List* which, according to Greg, "runs to over 3,000 lines."[91] It is difficult to know how Greg arrived at this figure. The play's Malone Society Reprint (MSR) runs to 2,894 lines.[92] If we add the prologue and the epilogue, the total amounts to 2,928 lines. This line count includes not only all the mutilated lines from a torn sheet (Folio 5), but also all stage directions and act headings. Moreover, substantial parts of the text read something like this:

[88] Long, " 'A bed / for woodstock,' " 114.   [89] Ibid., 106.
[90] Urkowitz, "Back to Basics," 268.   [91] Greg, *First Folio*, 146.
[92] Massinger, *Believe As You List*, ed. Sisson (note 86 above).

flaminivs: thow shalt orecome.
Theres noe contendinge with thee.
3 marchant: hitherto
the flamen hath the better
1 marchant. but I feare
Hee will not keepe it.
(MSR, lines 375–80)

These lines, it will be admitted, simply cannot be compared to most lines in Shakespearean playbooks. The text of *Believe As You List* in Philip Edwards and Colin Gibson's edition of *The Plays and Poems of Philip Massinger* (which also includes all mutilated lines) adds up to approximately 2,430 lines.[93] Greg's and, following him, Urkowitz's example of a "long" and uncut manuscript playbook is in fact a play of moderate length. It may then be concluded that the evidence yielded by manuscript playbooks corroborates the probability that Shakespeare's long dramatic texts must have been significantly shortened before they reached the stage.

To this survey of abridgement in manuscript playbooks, I need to add what evidence can be derived from the few marked-up printed play quartos that may have served as playbooks in the theater. A copy of the 1607 quarto edition of Edward Sharpham's *The Fleire*, a short text of little more than 2,000 lines, is abridged by more than a third, probably because it was prepared for a paired performance with another play.[94] A copy of *A Looking Glass for London and England* (*c.* 2,300 lines) in the University of Chicago Library cuts a number of relatively short passages.[95] The most interesting marked-up quarto is a copy of the 1620 edition of *The Two Merry Milkmaids*, "By *I. C.*," in the Folger Shakespeare Library.[96] Much of the first and nearly all of the last act are missing, but the remainder makes clear that whoever prepared the play for the stage realized that the long printed text needed to undergo substantial abridgement. Of the 2,402 lines present in the fragment, 438 are marked for abridgement. The entire play contains 3,434 lines of dialogue.[97] Owing to the missing portion,

[93] *Plays and Poems of Philip Massinger*, eds. Edwards and Gibson, III.303–90.
[94] See Clifford Leech, "The Plays of Edward Sharpham: Alterations Accomplished and Projected," *Review of English Studies*, 11 (1935), 69–74.
[95] See Charles Read Baskerville, "A Prompt Copy of *A Looking Glass for London and England*," *Modern Philology*, 30 (1932–33), 29–51.
[96] See Leslie Thomson, "A Quarto 'Marked for Performance': Evidence of What?," *Medieval and Renaissance Drama in England*, 8 (1996), 176–210.
[97] These figures are based upon my own count. Note that the figure quoted by Leslie Thompson ("about 3,600 lines," " 'Marked for Performance,' " 188) relies on G. Harold Metz's edition (New York and London: Garland, 1979) whose line count includes not only dialogue but also stage directions, act and scene headings, and even the title page and the list with "The Names of the Persons."

it is impossible to know the extent of the total abridgement. Yet if we assume that the extant fragment and the lost portions would have been abridged at the same proportion, the marked-up quarto would have reduced the text to approximately 2,800 lines.[98]

Some of Shakespeare's plays were among the first to be played once the Restoration had lifted the ban on public performances. We know, thanks to Pepys, that *Othello* was performed at the Cockpit in Drury Lane on October 11, 1660. *1 Henry IV* and *The Merry Wives of Windsor* were also acted before the end of the year.[99] Despite the fact that boy actors had been replaced by actresses, there is no reason to believe that other theatrical customs had radically changed after the eighteen-year ban on public performances.[100] After all, some playing seems to have continued in private venues.[101] Moreover, some of the actors, like John Lacy, or playwrights, like Killigrew, were active before and after the Interregnum.[102] Ambrose Beeland was among the musicians of the King's Men/Company as early as 1624 and as late as 1671.[103] Joseph Taylor, who replaced Burbage after his death in 1619, remained among the leading players and shareholders of the King's Men until the theatres were closed in 1642. He appears among the signatories of the dedication in the "Beaumont and Fletcher" Folio in 1647 and did not die until 1652, only nine years before Betterton played Hamlet for Davenant's Duke of York's. In his *Roscius Anglicanus, or an Historical Review of the Stage* (1708), John Downes, bookkeeper of the Duke of York's Company from 1662 to 1706, may well exaggerate the degree of continuity from Shakespeare's time to the Restoration: "*Hamlet* being Perform'd by *M*r. *Betterton*, Sir *William* [Davenant] (having seen *M*r. *Taylor*

---

[98] The address "The Printer to the Reader" also suggests that "*I. C.*" was not entirely without literary ambition. Despite the printer's conventional claim that the author did not seek print publication, the address ends with the promise that "hereafter [the author] hath promis'd you better Language" (a4ʳ). The address further claims that manuscript copies of the play "trauail'd abroad (euen to surbating)," suggesting that, like many "Beaumont and Fletcher" plays, *The Two Merry Milkmaids* had a first "literary" existence in manuscript before reaching print.

[99] See William Van Lennep, ed., *The London Stage 1660–1800: Part 1, 1660–1700* (Carbondale, Illinois: Southern Illinois University Press, 1965), 18–20.

[100] As Tiffany Stern puts it: "the Restoration theatre in many ways picked up from where the Renaissance theatre left off. The new theatre companies studied, rehearsed, and performed their plays in much the same manner" (*Rehearsal from Shakespeare to Sheridan* (Oxford: Clarendon Press, 2000), 122–23).

[101] See Dale B. J. Randall, *Winter Fruit: English Drama, 1642–1660* (Lexington, Kentucky: University of Kentucky Press, 1995), 47–49.

[102] For Lacy, see Bentley, *Jacobean and Caroline Stage*, 11.495–96. Killigrew wrote two plays for the commercial theater before 1642 (*The Parson's Wedding* and *The Prisoners*) and managed the King's Company until 1676.

[103] See Bentley, *Jacobean and Caroline Stage*, 11.362–63.

of the *Black-Fryars* Company Act it), who being Instructed by the Author *M*r *Shaksepeur* [*sic*]) taught Mr. *Betterton* in every particle of it."[104] Given that Taylor did not join the King's Men until after Burbage's death in 1619 when Shakespeare had been dead for three years, it seems unlikely that he had received instructions from the author of *Hamlet*. Nevertheless, it remains true that theatrical practice at the Restoration in many ways does not seem to have constituted a radical break from the pre-Civil War tradition that goes back to Shakespeare and the Lord Chamberlain's/King's Men.[105]

The most important bearer of acting traditions was no doubt William Davenant, Shakespeare's godson according to a seventeenth-century Oxford tradition which his biographer is not inclined to dismiss.[106] He arrived in London the year before the publication of Shakespeare's Folio. His earliest plays, *The Cruel Brother* (1626/27) and *Albovine* (publ. 1629), show him steeped in Shakespeare's plays.[107] Davenant was well acquainted with John Lowin, one of the King's Men's "Principal Actors" named in the First Folio. When Davenant came to direct Shakespeare's *Henry VIII* after the Restoration, he allegedly used Lowin's account of Shakespeare's direction of the play.[108]

As has been pointed out, Davenant's "importance as a champion of continuity can hardly be overestimated. When he came to direct Shakespeare plays and adaptations at his own theatre in Lincoln's Inn Field, he stood at the centre of the transmission of acting traditions going back to Elizabethan days."[109] It may then be of considerable interest that we have specific information about Davenant's Restoration abridgement of Shakespeare's *Hamlet*. The tragedy was among the few plays that were not "improved." As *Romeo and Juliet* and *King Lear* were shorn of their tragic endings and as *Antony and Cleopatra* became *All for Love*, *Hamlet* remained *Hamlet*, both in performance and in print. It was first performed at the Duke of York's Theatre on August 24, 1661, with Betterton in the title role.[110] According to Downes, "No succeeding Tragedy for several Years got more

---

[104] John Downes, *Roscius Anglicanus, or an Historical Review of the Stage* (London, 1708), 21.

[105] Hazelton Spencer, in "Seventeenth-Century Cuts in Hamlet's Soliloquies," *The Review of English Studies*, 35 (1933), 257–65, also argued for considerable continuity between Shakespeare's and Betterton's *Hamlet*.

[106] Mary Edmond, *Rare Sir William Davenant: Poet Laureate, Playwright, Civil War General, Restoration Theatre Manager*, Revels Plays Companion Library (Manchester University Press, 1987), 14. Note that Edmond also refers to Davenant as "the principal custodian of stage tradition" (141).

[107] Ibid., 27–43. John Davenant (1565–1622), William's father, in his London days, had already been "an admirer and lover of plays and play-makers, especially Shakespeare." After the Davenants moved from London to Oxford, he may have had an opportunity to see *Hamlet* there before 1603. See Anthony Wood (1632–95), *Athenae Oxonienses*, quoted in Edmond, *Rare Sir William Davenant*, 14.

[108] See ibid., 140–41.　[109] Ibid., 141.　[110] See Van Lennep, ed., *The London Stage*, 32.

Reputation, or Money to the Company."[111] Davenant's version survives in the players' quarto of 1676, which provided what no other earlier quarto had done before: the original authorial and the then current theatrical text.[112] According to the title page, the play was printed "as it is now acted at His Highness the Duke of York's Theatre." Between the title page and the beginning of the text, a note in large print, taking up an entire page, reads:

To the Reader.
This Play being too long to be conveniently Acted, such places as might be least prejudicial to the Plot or Sense, are left out upon the Stage: but that we may no way wrong the incomparable Author, are here inserted according to the Original Copy with this Mark " (A 2ʳ)

No fewer than seven editions appeared with this prefatory note, two dated 1676, one in 1683, one in 1695, and three dated 1703.[113] Peter Holland has commented that the above address "is a complex and resonant one. It marks one step in the opening of an explicit gap between text and performance in the representation of the text."[114] Holland rightly suggests that the note in the 1676 quarto points to a bibliographical and not to a theatrical milestone. While earlier publications had generally claimed to render a dramatic text either according to the original copy or as it has been performed, the present quarto is the first one that shows an awareness of the discrepancy between authorial and performance texts and attempts to record both (see Figure 11).

The omissions include nearly all references to Fortinbras before his final appearance (including Hamlet's "How all occasions do inform against me" soliloquy in 4.4); about half of 1.3 (Laertes's departure to Paris), including Polonius's advice to his son ("This above all – to thine own self be true"); the encounter between Polonius and Reynaldo in 2.1; about half of Hamlet's "O, what a rogue and peasant slave am I" soliloquy (2.2.551–607); and Hamlet's advice to the Players (3.2.1–45). Whereas the Folio text of *Hamlet* is less than two hundred lines shorter than Q2, the players' quarto of 1676 reveals the omission of almost 900 lines, reducing the play to approximately 2,800 lines. McManaway may have overstated his case when writing: "if Downes was not misinformed, the Restoration *Hamlet* is in essence the

---

[111] Downes, *Roscius Anglicanus*, 21.
[112] Like *Hamlet, Othello, Julius Caesar*, and *1 Henry IV* continued to be printed in Shakespeare's rather than adapted versions. See Henry B. Wheatley, "Post-Restoration Quartos of Shakespeare's Plays," *The Library*, 3rd series, 4 (1913), 237–69.
[113] The text of the first Restoration quarto is based upon the last pre-Civil War edition (1637) which ultimately goes back to Q2.
[114] Holland, "Measuring Performance," 50.

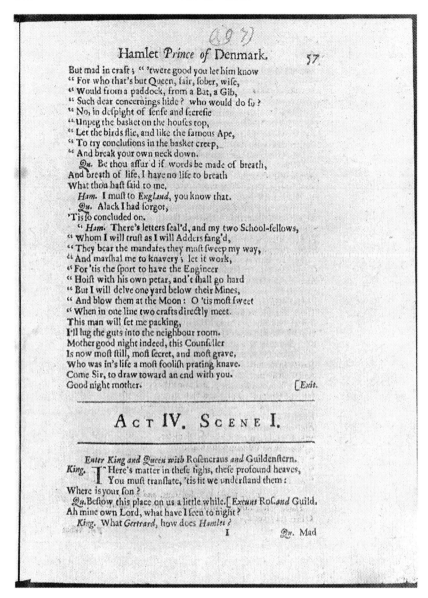

Figure 11. Page 57 of the 1676 quarto edition of *Hamlet*, with passages that
are "left out upon the Stage: but . . . are here inserted according to
the Original Copy with this Mark "."

Elizabethan *Hamlet*."[115] Nevertheless, we may safely assume that there was considerable continuity between the pre-Civil War and the Restoration stage, between Shakespeare and Davenant, and that by considerably abridging *Hamlet* in preparation for performance, Davenant was only doing what Shakespeare and his fellows had done long before him.[116]

The Restoration *Hamlet* is not an isolated case. *1 Henry IV* also escaped "improvement" and was published in 1700 "As it is Acted at the THEATRE in *Litttle[sic]-Lincolns-Inn-Fields* BY His Majesty's Servants. Revived, with Alterations." In fact, the "Alterations" are almost exclusively abridgements, made by Betterton and apparently observed in performance. A great number of short passages are cut throughout. The opening scene is shortened by about a quarter. In the second scene, Hal's "I know you all" soliloquy is reduced by more than twenty percent. In 2.4, Lady Percy's first speech loses more than twenty lines. The first scene in the third act (Hotspur, Mortimer, and their wives) ends about half way through. In the following scene, a lengthy passage has disappeared from the King's admonitions to his son (3.2.50–87). Act four, scene four, with the Archbishop of York and Sir Michael, is cut in its entirety. Perhaps most surprisingly, even the decisive battle scene (5.4) is deprived of its first part (5.4.1–57) in which Hal reveals himself to be a brave warrior, refuses to quit the battlefield despite his wounds and goes on to save his father's life. The last scene, finally, preserves less than half its original length. All in all, the players' quarto reduces the play to somewhere between 2,500 and 2,600 lines.

Some of the earliest extant Shakespearean manuscript playbooks reveal similar patterns of abridgement. A copy of Shakespeare's Third Folio (1664) that was annotated for performances at Dublin's Smock Alley Theatre in the 1670s and 1680s allows important insights into theatrical process related to Shakespeare's plays.[117] As G. Blakemore Evans has shown, "The usual first step in preparing a play for the stage seems to have been a rough preliminary cutting" which, in some cases, was later refined.[118] In

---

[115] James G. McManaway, "The Two Earliest Prompt Books of *Hamlet*," *The Papers of the Bibliographical Society of America*, 43 (1949), 289.

[116] For Davenant's abridgement of *Hamlet*, see also Mongi Radaddi, *Davenant's Adaptations of Shakespeare*, Studia Anglistica Upsaliensis, 36 (Uppsala: Almqvist & Wiksell International, 1979), 64–78.

[117] The volume was later taken apart by J. O. Halliwell-Phillipps, and the remnants are extant in various libraries. See R. C. Bald, "Shakespeare on the Stage in Restoration Dublin," *PMLA*, 56 (1941), 369–78; James G. McManaway, "Additional Prompt-Books of Shakespeare from the Smock Alley Theatre," *Modern Lanugage Review*, 45 (1950), 64–65; Gunnar Sorelius, "The Smock Alley Prompt-Books of *1* and *2 Henry IV*," *Shakespeare Quarterly*, 22 (1971), 111–27.

[118] G. Blakemore Evans, ed., *Shakespearean Prompt-Books of the Seventeeth Century*, 8 vols. (Charlottesville, VA: Bibliographical Society of the University of Virginia, 1960–1996), 1.21.

this process, all of Shakespeare's long plays were significantly abridged with the longest, *Hamlet* and *Othello*, conserving almost exactly 2,800 lines for performance with others being reduced to far less.[119] The extensive cuts in the *Othello* promptbooks, for instance, include much of the last scene of act four with Desdemona and Emilia, including the "Willow Song." As has been shown, the links between the Theatres Royal in Dublin and in London were close, and there is no reason to suppose that theatrical practices were radically different from those in pre-Civil War London.[120]

Another play of which a players' quarto survives is Webster's *Duchess of Malfi*. As shown above, the first edition of Webster's 3,000-line play (Q1623) announces that it is "with diverse things Printed, that the length of the Play would not beare in the Presentment." The fourth quarto was published in 1708 as "The Unfortunate Dutcheß of Malfy, or the Unnatural Brothers... Now Acted at the Queen's Theatre in the Hay-market, By Her Majesties Company of Comedians." A prefatory note announces that "Those lines which were omitted in the Acting, by reason of the Length of the Play, are marked with (")" (A1ᵛ). The number of lines thus marked is close to three hundred. What the prefatory note does not make clear is that many other passages are simply not printed. In fact, the two stages of abridgement to which the fourth quarto of *The Duchess of Malfi* bears witness reduces the "Poem" to a playtext of almost exactly 2,500 lines (see Figure 12).

If Shakespeare wrote plays that were substantially too long and reduced them himself to manageable length in preparation for the stage, he was not the only English seventeenth-century playwright to do so. Thomas Killigrew wrote eight plays from the 1630s to the 1650s that were published in a folio edition in 1663. Killigrew's own copy survives in the library of Worcester College, Oxford, and contains extensive deletions in his own hand. Some of his plays were written during the interregnum and may not have been originally intended for performance. It would therefore be

---

[119] Ibid., VIII.3.
[120] See McMannaway, "Additional Prompt-Books," 65. The few other marked-up seventeenth-century playbooks of Shakespeare's plays include an annotated First Folio *Winter's Tale* (2,925 lines in Hart's count) in the Biblioteca Universitaria, Padova, of which only the first two scenes have been cut. Of the approximately five hundred lines, about a hundred and twenty have been marked for omission (see Evans, ed., *Shakespearean Prompt-Books*, 11.25–26; and, for the dating of the playbook, G. Blakemore Evans, "New Evidence on the Provenance of the Padua Prompt-Books of Shakespeare's *Macbeth*, *Measure for Measure*, and *Winter's Tale*," *Studies in Bibliography*, 20 (1967), 239–42). An abridged transcript (1694/95) of the Folio *Romeo and Juliet* (2,989 lines) also reduces the play's length by several hundred lines. As the manuscript was clearly made for amateur staging for the English seminarians in Douai, however, it tells us little about the practices of professional players (see G. Blakemore Evans, "The Douai Manuscript – Six Shakespearean Transcripts (1694–95)," *Philological Quarterly*, 41 (1962), 158–72).

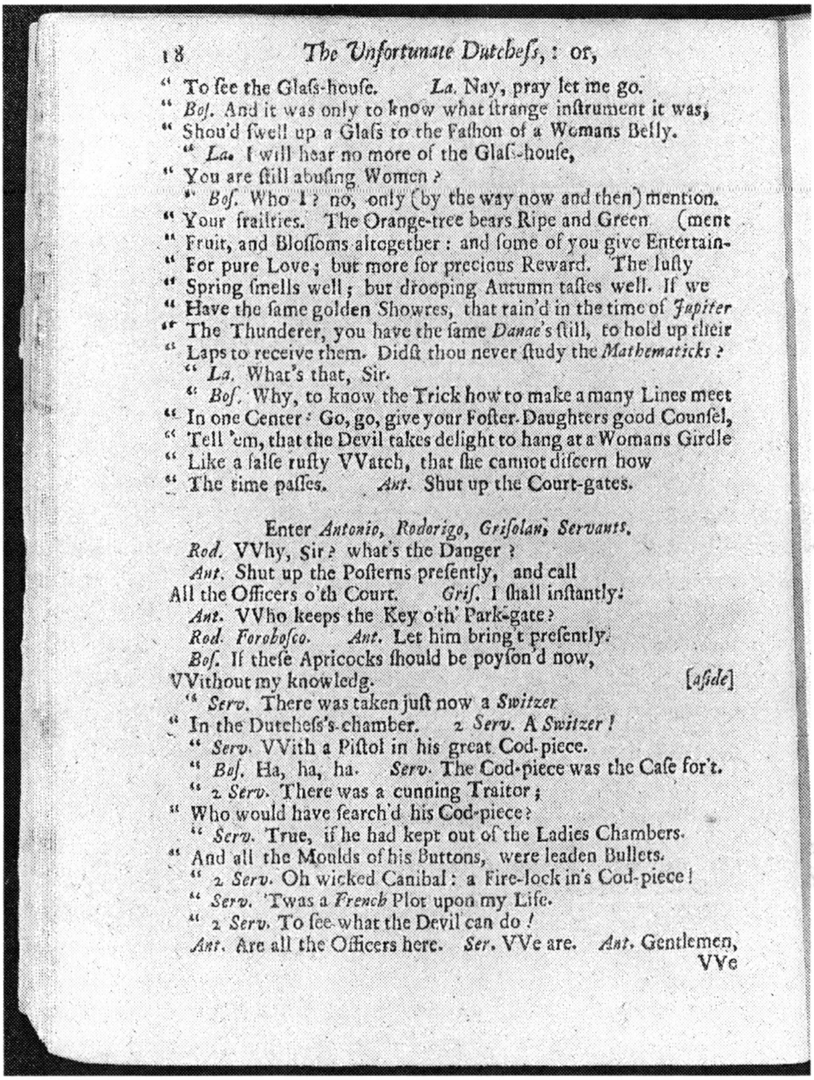

18   *The Unfortunate Dutchefs,* : or,

" To fee the Glafs-houfe.   *La.* Nay, pray let me go.
" *Bof.* And it was only to know what ftrange inftrument it was,
" Shou'd fwell up a Glafs to the Fafhon of a Womans Belly.
" *La.* I will hear no more of the Glafs-houfe,
" You are ftill abufing Women ?
" *Bof.* Who I ? no, only (by the way now and then) mention,
" Your frailties. The Orange-tree bears Ripe and Green   (ment
" Fruit, and Bloffoms altogether : and fome of you give Entertain-
" For pure Love ; but more for precious Reward. The lufty
" Spring fmells well ; but drooping Autumn taftes well. If we
" Have the fame golden Showres, that rain'd in the time of *Jupiter*
" The Thunderer, you have the fame *Danae's* ftill, to hold up their
" Laps to receive them. Didft thou never ftudy the *Mathematicks* ?
" *La.* What's that, Sir.
" *Bof.* Why, to know the Trick how to make a many Lines meet
" In one Center : Go, go, give your Fofter-Daughters good Counfel,
" Tell 'em, that the Devil takes delight to hang at a Womans Girdle
" Like a falfe rufty VVatch, that fhe cannot difcern how
" The time paffes.   *Ant.* Shut up the Court-gates.

       Enter *Antonio, Rodorigo, Grifolan, Servants.*
Rod. VVhy, Sir ? what's the Danger ?
Ant. Shut up the Pofterns prefently, and call
All the Officers o'th Court.   *Grif.* I fhall inftantly:
Ant. VVho keeps the Key o'th' Park-gate ?
Rod. Forobofco.   *Ant.* Let him bring't prefently:
Bof. If thefe Apricocks fhould be poyfon'd now,
VVithout my knowledg.   [*afide*]
" *Serv.* There was taken juft now a *Switzer*
" In the Dutchefs's-chamber.   2 *Serv.* A *Switzer* !
" *Serv.* VVith a Piftol in his great Cod-piece.
" *Bof.* Ha, ha, ha.   *Serv.* The Cod-piece was the Cafe for't.
" 2 *Serv.* There was a cunning Traitor ;
" Who would have fearch'd his Cod-piece ?
" *Serv.* True, if he had kept out of the Ladies Chambers.
" And all the Moulds of his Buttons, were leaden Bullets.
" 2 *Serv.* Oh wicked Canibal : a Fire-lock in's Cod-piece !
" *Serv.* 'Twas a *French* Plot upon my Life.
" 2 *Serv.* To fee what the Devil can do !
Ant. Are all the Officers here. *Ser.* VVe are. *Ant.* Gentlemen,
                                      VVe

Figure 12. Page 18 of the 1708 quarto edition of John Webster's *The Duchess of Malfi*,
1708, with "Those lines which were omitted in the Acting, by reason of the Length
of the Play, ... marked with (")"

of little significance to compare them to Shakespeare's plays. *The Parson's
Wedding*, however, was written for the stage in the late 1630s. By a rough
count, it is a couple of hundred lines longer even than *Hamlet*. When
Killigrew prepared it for the stage in early May 1664, he cut it down by

more than one third.[121] That Killigrew's deletions are aimed at reducing the play to a certain length and not (only) at tightening and improving its dramatic structure is borne out by a manuscript note he left for the copyist for the Theatre Royal at the top of the first page of the two-part play *Cicilia and Clorinda*: "pray write both theis partes of Cissillia and Clorinda intiere as thay ar in this booke in to parts for they are short anufe with out cutting."[122] In contrast, *The Parson's Wedding* clearly was not "short anufe" and thus required abridgement. Killigrew and, I believe, Shakespeare knowingly wrote plays that were too long for the purpose of the stage and applied the scissors themselves when it came to preparing them for performance.

Unless we want to argue for a radical break between performance practices before and after the Civil War – a break for which there would seem to be little evidence – the plays that were published after the Restoration provide additional evidence that Shakespeare's "long" plays were regularly performed in significantly abridged versions. The address "To the Reader" prefacing the 1676 quarto of *Hamlet* announces that the omitted passages are those that are "least prejudicial to the Plot or Sense." While it is clear that *Hamlet* without the prince's advice to the players and Polonius's advice to Laertes, or *1 Henry IV* with important cuts in the "I know you all" soliloquy or in King Henry IV's admonitions to his son still basically have the same "plot," it seems more difficult to agree today that the abridged plays would not have lost some of their "sense." In other words, *Hamlet* and *1 Henry IV* (as well as all other of Shakespeare's "long" plays), shorn of many hundreds of lines, of key passages that contain central constitutive elements of the plays' dramatic architecture, are, in many ways, simply different plays from the ones we know.

In this chapter, I have drawn upon a variety of sources to argue that about a dozen of Shakespeare's plays are too long to have been performed – or to have been intended to be performed – in their entirety. This is suggested by what we know about the length of theatrical performances in Shakespeare's time; by a comparison of the length of Shakespeare's plays to that of Ben Jonson's, on the one hand, and to that of Shakespeare's other contemporaries, on the other; by the title pages and other apparatus of a number of printed playbooks; by the "Beaumont and Fletcher" Folio

[121] William Van Lennep, "Thomas Killigrew Prepares His Plays for Production," in *Joseph Quincy Adams Memorial Studies*, eds. James G. McManaway, Giles E. Dawson, and Edwin E. Willoughby (Washington, DC: The Folger Shakespeare Library, 1948), 803–8. Pepys refers to the production of *The Parson's Wedding* in early October 1664 (see Bentley, *Jacobean and Caroline Stage*, IV.701–2).

[122] Van Lennep, "Killigrew," 805.

of 1647, in particular by Humphrey Moseley's address "The Stationer to the Readers;" by the length and abridgements of extant manuscript play-books; and by the gap between plays as they were first written and as they were performed that becomes visible in Restoration players' quartos and prompt-books. Even though there is no reason to suppose that theatrical companies conformed to a rigid playing time and that their plays were reduced to a standard length, there is considerable evidence suggesting that any playtext of a length exceeding approximately 2,800 lines would have been subject to abridgement. This evidence has far-reaching implications for the study of Shakespeare's texts. In the various critical debates over *The History* vs. *The Tragedy of King Lear*, Q2 vs. Folio *Hamlet*, and over what they tell us about how Shakespeare's tragedies were performed, what may have been lost from sight is that all of these texts may have less to do with the plays Elizabethan and Jacobean playgoers witnessed than we have commonly assumed (see chapter 7). In addition, while the "bad" quartos of Shakespeare's plays have in recent times been released from the scholarly and critical limbo to which they had long been confined, the proximity of their length to that of the theatrically abridged "Beaumont and Fletcher" plays may indicate that their importance has still not been fully recognized (see chapters 8 and 9).

Editorial policy and the length of Shakespeare's plays

In the previous chapter, I have brought together in some detail what evidence there is to suggest that Shakespeare's "long" plays were not performed in anything close to their entirety in the sixteenth and seventeenth centuries. There would have been no need to write these pages if it were not that some of the leading Shakespeare scholars have taken a view that is diametrically opposed, arguing that the full text of even Shakespeare's longest plays like *Hamlet* and *Antony and Cleopatra* was acted.[1] Much performance-oriented criticism has tacitly endorsed this view, thereby failing to address the question of the relationship between early modern performance and the printed playbooks. An investigation of *what* was performed seems to be a necessary precondition of any historically informed performance criticism.

The length of Shakespearean performances, the relationship between the early printed texts and what spectators would have witnessed at the Globe or at Blackfriars', and the frequency and extent of the practice of theatrical abridgement have far-reaching implications. The preceding chapters have developed one important implication of the assumption that Shakespeare wrote considerably more than his company would perform. It may be useful to recall David Bradley's objection that this assumption "implies that Shakespeare's originals were filled out with irrelevant and tawdry material which he must have composed in the sure expectation that it would be jettisoned in performance. Alas, poor Shakespeare!"[2] Not so poor, once we come around to the idea that Shakespeare conceived of his plays not only as plays for the stage but also as dramas for the page, to be read "by the wiser sort," as Harvey put it.[3]

What are some of the other implications for critics and editors of these "long" plays if we take the above evidence seriously? A few decades ago, their importance might have been relatively slight. Greg postulated: "The

---

[1] See Wells, Taylor, et al., *Textual Companion*, 276.   [2] Bradley, *Text to Performance*, 12.
[3] G. C. Moore Smith, ed., *Gabriel Harvey's Marginalia* (Stratford-upon-Avon: Shakespeare Head Press, 1913) 232.

aim of a critical edition should be to present the text, so far as the available evidence permits, in the form in which we may suppose that it would have stood in a fair copy, made by the author himself, of the work as he finally intended it." What followed from this was that "an editor should select as the basis of his own edition (as his copy-text, that is) the most 'authoritative' of the early prints, this being the one that on critical consideration appears likely to have departed least in wording, spelling, and punctuation from the author's manuscript."[4] At a time when the central aim of editing was still the best-possible recovery of a final authorial intention represented by a lost manuscript, the fact that this text would subsequently have been mutilated for the needs of the stage did not much alter the critics' and the editors' task. If today, however, critical attention has shifted to the plays as presented on stage, the implications of the practice of stage abridgement are considerable and need to be explored in full.

The edition which has most fully embraced the shift to performance-centered criticism is the Oxford *Complete Works* in which Stanley Wells and Gary Taylor claim to "have devoted [their] efforts to recovering and presenting texts of Shakespeare's play as they were acted in the London playhouses."[5] In *A Textual Companion*, the Oxford editors explain the rationale of their stage-centered editorial policy: "Shakespeare...devoted his life to the theatre, and dramatic texts are necessarily the most socialized of all literary forms. Where matters of verbal and theatrical substance are involved, we have therefore chosen, in our own edition, to prefer – where there is a choice – the text closer to the prompt-book of Shakespeare's company." In other words, their edition is designed first and foremost for "anyone who wishes to consider Shakespeare's works *as performed* in his lifetime."[6] This sounds attractive and in line with the recent shift toward performance criticism. In practice, however, it is fraught with problems.

Wells and Taylor grant that their policy sometimes "requires the omission from the body of the text of lines that Shakespeare certainly wrote." They go on to explain that "there is, of course, no suggestion that these lines are unworthy of their author; merely that, in some if not all performances, he and his company found that the play's overall structure and pace were better without them."[7] Wells and Taylor's preference for the "socialized text" has here resulted in a value judgment (the "socialized" text is better than the "private" text) that many might not share and with which even

---

[4] Greg, *Editorial Problem*, xii.
[5] Wells, "General Introduction," in Shakespeare, *Complete Works*, gen. eds. Wells and Taylor, xxxvii.
[6] Wells, Taylor, et al., *Textual Companion*, 15.
[7] Shakespeare, *Complete Works*, gen. eds. Wells and Taylor, xxxv.

Shakespeare might have disagreed. In particular, the Oxford editors fail to address the contingencies that may have impinged on what they call "the play's transition from a private to a socialized script."[8] Brian Vickers has incisively commented on this aspect of the Oxford editors' editorial policy: "omissions made on the grounds of length – to fit the 'two-hour traffic of the stage' – are made out of theatrical necessity, and do not necessarily improve a play's structure. They may obscure it, weaken significance, flatten out characterization."[9] It is true that artistic revision and theatrical abridgement do not necessarily exclude each other, and it is possible that Shakespeare approved of some cuts on artistic grounds. Other cuts, however, were clearly necessary because some of the original manuscripts were simply too long. Unsurprisingly, Wells faces the same problem when introducing *Hamlet*: "passages present in the 1604 quarto but absent from the Folio are printed as Additional Passages because we believe that, however fine they may be in themselves, Shakespeare decided that the play as a whole would be better without them."[10] This presumes that when Shakespeare and his fellows started preparing their new 3,800-line play for the stage, the only considerations that guided them were of an artistic nature. Vickers's objection is again to the point: "it was the practicalities of performance, not 'the play as a whole,' that caused these cuts; and at 3,535 lines the Folio is still far too long for performance, and would have had to 'lose' another 800 to 1,000 lines."[11] Having studied in detail the various extant texts of *A Game at Chess*, Howard-Hill points out that it is "possible to make a distinction between Middleton's final intention for drama, the work *A Game at Chess*, and his final intention for the theatre, realised on the stage in 1624."[12] Arguing that any theatrical cut in *Hamlet* improved, according to Shakespeare, "the play as a whole" without distinguishing between "drama" and "theater," Wells and Taylor exclude the possibility that something similar may have applied to Shakespeare, too.

Shortly after the publication of the Oxford *Complete Works*, Howard-Hill, in a different article, theorized what Wells and Taylor had practiced. Arguing that it is highly problematic to adapt to plays the principle for selection of copy-text promulgated by Greg, McKerrow, and Bowers,

[8] Wells, Taylor, et al., *Textual Companion*, 16.
[9] Brian Vickers, "Review of William Shakespeare, *The Complete Works* and *A Textual Companion*, ed. Stanley Wells and Gary Taylor (Oxford, 1986–7)," *The Review of English Studies*, 40 (1989), 404.
[10] Shakespeare, *Complete Works*, gen. eds. Wells and Taylor, 735.
[11] Vickers, "Review," 404. My position may be somewhat different from Vickers' since I believe, as pointed out above, that *some* cuts may have been motivated by artistic rather than by practical considerations.
[12] Howard-Hill, "Scribe or Reviser," 306.

Howard-Hill holds that "a playwright's intentions are represented best (if perhaps not completely) in a manuscript associated with the theatre."[13] Yet if we take Howard-Hill at his own words, the question that needs to be asked first is: intentions for what, theater or drama? Like many before him, Howard-Hill assumes that Shakespeare simply had no intentions for drama: "For modern playwrights like Stoppard and even some earlier ones (Jonson and Webster in some instances) it is possible to claim that the playwright's final intention is realized in print. For most early dramatists it was otherwise. No evidence at all suggests that Shakespeare...was ever involved in the publication of his plays."[14] If Shakespeare's indifference to the publication of his plays is more of a long-standing myth than a historical fact, then we cannot so easily dispose of Shakespeare's intentions for drama. In fact, there is every reason to suppose that those playtexts which are generally believed to go back to Shakespeare's "foul papers" (such as Q2 *Hamlet*) tell us considerably more about Shakespeare's intentions for drama than the allegedly "socialized texts" (such as F *Hamlet*) tell us about Shakespeare's intentions for the theater. For in many cases, it is simply impossible to know which parts of Shakespeare's overlong plays would not have been performed. Accordingly, the effort to present "texts of Shakespeare's plays as they were acted in the London playhouses" is, to a certain extent, doomed to failure. Greg's project of recovering a lost authorial manuscript has been subjected to harsh criticism in recent times. Compared to the Oxford editors' alleged recovery of performance, the leap of faith it requires from what exists (in the printed text) to what may have existed (in the manuscript) seems decidedly minor.

On some occasions, however, the corresponding short texts allow inferences about what would have been omitted in performance. Andrew Gurr has argued on good grounds, for instance, that the choruses in *Henry V* were omitted in London's theaters.[15] As we will see more fully below, it seems clear that various passages of *Hamlet* present in the second quarto or the Folio or both were cut in performances. There is no reason to suppose that the omission of these passages on stage did not have Shakespeare's approval. According to the logic expounded in *A Textual Companion*, these and all other passages present in Shakespeare's "long" plays that can be

[13] T. H. Howard-Hill, "Modern Textual Theories and the Editing of Plays," *The Library*, 6th series, 11 (1989), 112. See W. W. Greg, "The Rationale of Copy-Text," *Studies in Bibliography*, 3 (1950–51), 19–36, rpt. in Greg, *Collected Papers*, ed. J. C. Maxwell (Oxford: Clarendon Press, 1966), 374–91.
[14] Howard-Hill, "Modern Textual Theories," 104.
[15] Andrew Gurr, ed., *The First Quarto of King Henry V*, New Cambridge Shakespeare: The Early Quartos (Cambridge University Press, 2000), 9–12.

shown to have been omitted from performances would have to be absent from a modern edition. As will emerge more fully in the next chapter, an edition of *Hamlet* that tried to give the text "*as performed* in his lifetime" would have to be what Giorgio Melchiori calls "the really 'revised' text... hidden behind the unseemly report in the First Quarto."[16]

Eric Rasmussen has recently surveyed the evidence for "Theatrical Cutting."[17] Referring to the title pages of Jonson's *Every Man Out of His Humour* (1600) and *The Duchess of Malfi* (1623), to the note at the end of Richard Brome's *Antipodes* (1640) and to the prefatory material in the "Beaumont and Fletcher" Folio (1647), he rightly concludes that "scripts were often deemed to be too long and were cut in order to reduce overall playing time."[18] It seems problematic to argue, however, that Folio *Hamlet* and *King Lear* are examples of texts that have been reduced to manageable length. If *The Antipodes* and *The Duchess of Malfi*, at roughly 2,700 and 3,000 lines, were too long, how can we assume that Folio *King Lear* and *Hamlet*, at about 2,900 and 3,500 lines, were not?

This is not to deny that Folio *Hamlet* reflects *some* of the cuts needed to reduce the play to manageable length. What lends support to this possibility is that passages absent from the Folio text are not present in the short first quarto edition either. Two compositors' errors in Q2 lend further credibility to the theory that Shakespeare's manuscript was heavily cut before the play reached the stage. At the end of what corresponds to 4.1 in modern editions, the King speaks the following lines according to the Folio:

> Come *Gertrude*, wee'l call vp our wisest friends,
> To let them know both what we meane to do,
> And what's vntimely done. Oh come away,
> My soule is full of discord and dismay.   *Exeunt*.
>   (pp2ʳ)

The Folio omits several Q2 lines occurring between "vntimely done" and "Oh come away." Yet at the very place where the cut begins, Q2 appears to have lost a half line:

> Come *Gertrard*, wee'le call vp our wisest friends,
> And let them know both what we meane to doe
> And whats vntimely doone,
> Whose whisper ore the worlds dyameter,

[16] Giorgio Melchiori, "Acting Version," 209.

[17] Eric Rasmussen, "The Revision of Scripts," in *A New History of Early English Drama*, eds. Cox and Kastan, 441–60, esp. 442–47.

[18] Rasmussen, "Revision of Scripts," 443.

> As leuell as the Cannon to his blanck,
> Transports his poysned shot, may misse our Name,
> And hit the woundlesse ayre, ô come away,
> My soule is full of discord and dismay.   *Exeunt*.
>
> (κ1ʳ)

Most editors have followed Capell's suggestion in supplying the words "so haply slander" to fill the gap. Harold Jenkins has preferred "so envious slander."[19] Whichever solution we prefer, it seems clear that a half line has gone missing. Before exploring the reasons for this omission, I wish to quote another passage with a similar textual deficiency. In F1, the First Player recites twenty-nine lines of the Pyrrhus speech before he is interrupted by Polonius. I quote the first ten lines:

>   1. PLAYER. Anon he findes him,
>   Striking too short at Greekes. His anticke Sword,
>   Rebellious to his Arme, lyes where it falles
>   Repugnant to command: vnequall match,
>   *Pyrrhus* at *Priam* driues, in Rage strikes wide:
>   But with the whiffe and winde of his fell Sword,
>   Th'vnnerued Father fals. Then senselesse Illium,
>   Seeming to feele his blow, with flaming top
>   Stoopes to his Bace, and with a hideous crash
>   Takes Prisoner *Pyrrhus* eare.   (oo4ʳ)

Old Priam is too weak to resist savage Pyrrhus. Indeed, the wind which Pyrrhus' sword produces as he tries to strike him down is enough to make Priam fall. Before Pyrrhus can finish off Priam, Illium – which here stands for the citadel or the royal palace of Troy – collapses, and the noise so surprises Pyrrhus that he stops the fight for a moment. The speech continues for about another twenty lines. Q1 reproduces the first six lines with minor changes but contains none of the remaining twenty-three lines:

>   PLAY. Anon he findes him, striking too short at Greeks,
>   His antike sword rebellious to his Arme,
>   Lies where it falles, vnable to resist.
>   *Pyrrus* at *Pryam* driues, but all in rage,
>   Strikes wide, but with the whiffe and winde
>   Of his fell sword, th'unnerued father falles.   (e4ʳ)

In Q2, the speech has the same length as in the Folio, but at the exact position where the cut occurs in Q1, Q2 omits half a line ("Then senselesse Illium") without which the remaining sentence fails to make sense:

19 Harold Jenkins, ed., *Hamlet*, The Arden Shakespeare (London: Methuen, 1982), 336.

PLAY. Anon he findes him,
Striking too short at Greekes, his anticke sword
Rebellious to his arme, lies where it fals,
Repugnant to commaund; vnequall matcht,
Pirrhus at *Priam* driues, in rage strikes wide,
But with the whiffe and winde of his fell sword,
Th'vnnerued father fals:
Seeming to feele this blowe, with flaming top
Stoopes to his base; and with a hiddious crash
Takes prisoner *Pirrhus* eare,   (F3ᵛ)

The most plausible explanation for the loss of the two half lines is that
the compositor mistook a sign indicating the beginning of a theatrical
cut for a sign of deletion.[20] Considering many of the extant theatrical
manuscripts contain such signs, there is nothing surprising about the fact
that Shakespeare's manuscript of *Hamlet* appears to have been marked for
cutting. What is important about the present example is that, exceptionally,
a printing-house error combined with a missing passage in Q1 allows us to
infer the presence of a deletion mark where, normally, the printed text
erases all evidence of theatrical abridgement in the manuscript from which
it was set up. There is ample evidence suggesting that compositors had no
reason to respect theatrical cuts marked in the manuscript and that, as a
rule, they printed as much as possible: Q2 *Romeo and Juliet* and Q1 *Love's
Labour's Lost* show false and corrected starts, first and second drafts side
by side.[21] Similarly, a scene in the A-text of *Doctor Faustus* has a double
ending probably, as Eric Rasmussen has shown, because "the printer's copy
was a draft manuscript in which the first version of the passage had been
cancelled."[22] More examples could be given.[23] Clearly, there was no earthly
reason for a compositor not to print a passage that made sense and was
readable even though it had been marked with a deletion sign in the left
margin.

The missing half lines in Q2 *Hamlet* are therefore a reminder that no
printed text allows us to recover how much would have been marked for

---

[20] See ibid., 43.

[21] See Wells, Taylor, et al., *Textual Companion*, 296, 298, 301 (notes to *Romeo and Juliet*, 2.3.1, 3.3.40–3, and 5.3.108); and Woudhuysen, ed., *Love's Labour's Lost*, 339–41.

[22] Eric Rasmussen, *A Textual Companion to "Doctor Faustus,"* The Revels Plays Companion Library (Manchester University Press, 1993), 16.

[23] The point is argued most fully in Kristian Smidt's "Repetition, Revision, and Editorial Greed in Shakespeare's Play Texts," *Cahiers Elisabéthains*, 34 (1988), 25–37. See also Greg's *Two Elizabethan Stage Abridgements: "The Battle of Alcazar" & "Orlando Furioso"* (Oxford University Press, 1923): "Most manuscript plays of the period that have been prepared for the stage show cancelled passages that a printer might very likely have retained" (253, note 2).

omission in its copy-text and, consequently, would have been cut in performance. When it comes to the length of the text that would have been performed, we can never be sure that printed playbooks – whatever the manuscripts from which they had been set up – are not longer than the play that would have been performed. In this sense, there never need be, to allude to the title of Janette Dillon's fine article, a performance in a text.[24] What we can be confident about, on the other hand, is that all playbooks that significantly exceed an approximate length of 2,800 lines would have been abridged in performance.

While preparing their Arden3 edition of *Hamlet*, the editors Ann Thompson (one of Arden's general editors) and Neil Taylor have given us access to some of their work in progress.[25] Thompson and Taylor take G. R. Hibbard and Philip Edwards to task for arguing that the removal of Q2 passages in F speed up the action: "they seem to assume at times that Shakespeare in writing *Hamlet* was trying to produce a fast-moving action thriller with a no-nonsense hero who never repeats himself and never thinks or says anything that is not 'essential to the plot.' "[26] Reduced to the length of the Folio text, *Hamlet* is hardly a "fast-moving action thriller," however. If such it were, it would hardly be possible to omit many hundred lines as Q1 *Hamlet*, Q6 *Hamlet* (the players' quarto), or most modern productions do.

Like Vickers, Thompson and Taylor seem to prefer *Hamlet* Q2 to an abridged text. Yet, while Vickers recognizes that Shakespeare and his fellows could not accommodate Q2 or F to the stage, Thompson and Taylor – disregarding what Vickers calls "the practicalities of performance" – argue for "the theatrical effectiveness of the uncut Q2 text" in a way that seems problematic.[27] Having accused conflationist editors of producing a text they wish the author had written, Thompson and Taylor in fact argue for the theatrical effectiveness of a text they wish Shakespeare had designed for performance and mistakenly assume Shakespeare and his fellows performed.

It will be asked what kind of text Folio *Hamlet* represents if it does not constitute a stage abridgement. After all, if Q1 *Hamlet* is anything to go by, there is good evidence suggesting that the passages present in Q2 and absent from the Folio were omitted in performance. It seems likely that Folio *Hamlet* is a preliminary abridgement from which another 800 lines or so were omitted before the play reached the stage. What evidence is there

---

[24] See Dillon, "Performance," 74–86.

[25] Ann Thompson and Neil Taylor, " 'O That This Too Too XXXXX Text Would Melt': *Hamlet* and the Indecisions of Modern Editors and Publishers," *TEXT: An Interdisciplinary Annual of Textual Studies*, 10 (1997), 221–36.

[26] Ibid., 234–35.   [27] Ibid., 235; Vickers, "Review," 404.

for the existence of such preliminary abridgements? As is to be expected, not many material witnesses have survived, but there is one. A manuscript of *The Honest Man's Fortune* in the hand of Edward Knight, bookkeeper of the King's Men, bears a note by Sir Henry Herbert, Master of the Revels which reads: "This Play, being on olde one, and the Originall lost was reallowd by mee this 8. Febru. 1624 [new dating: 1625]."[28] The same play survives in the "Beaumont and Fletcher" Folio in a somewhat different text. Editing the play for the last volume of the Cambridge "Beaumont and Fletcher" edition in 1996, Cyrus Hoy has written:

> The relation of the two texts is very close. It would appear that both derive from the same manuscript: the foul papers of the three authors [Fletcher, Massinger, and Field] who wrote the play. What Herbert refers to as "the Originall" (meaning, presumably, the original licensed prompt-book) was said to be missing in 1625, and the authorial foul papers appear to have served as the copy from which Knight prepared the new one . . . They also appear to have served, twenty-two years later, as copy for the printed text in the 1647 Folio. The two most immediately apparent differences between the two texts – MS's omission of one scene (V.iii), and its altered version of the final scene (V.iv.246ff.) – do not call into question the basic identity of the sources from which each derives. F1 gives us the earlier pre-1625 version of the play; MS gives us a somewhat altered version prepared (presumably) for the 1625 revival, with the unnecessary V.iii cut in the interest of shortening a long play, and the rewritten V.iv.246ff. serving to replace the indelicacy of the original ending.[29]

The extant manuscript contains a number of "scribal signs (vertical bars) marking theatrical cuts made to tighten and quicken the pace of the stage action."[30] Following Hoy's analysis, we can thus distinguish between three different versions of *The Honest Man's Fortune*. Firstly, there is the original authorial manuscript ("foul papers") from which the Folio text was set up. Secondly, Knight's 1625 transcript of this authorial manuscript integrates a preliminary abridgement (5.3) and local revision (5.4). Thirdly, this preliminary abridgement is further reduced by theatrical cuts to something like standard playing time (*c.* 2,500 lines).[31] The history that led to these

---

[28] An entry in Herbert's office-book confirms this information: "For the king's company. An olde play called *the Honest Man's Fortune*, the originall being lost, was re-allowed by mee at Mr Taylor's intreaty, and on condition to give mee a booke, this 8 Februa. 1624."

[29] *Beaumont and Fletcher Canon*, gen. ed. Bowers, x.5.

[30] Ibid., x.6. See x.6–7 for a summary of these theatrical cuts.

[31] Note that, by omitting an entire scene present in the foul papers from the manuscript the company went on to submit to the Master of the Revels, the King's Men's bookkeeper effectively ruled out that his company would be allowed to perform that scene. Andrew Gurr's argument that the King's Men found it desirable to have "maximal texts" licensed is thus not corroborated by the extant texts of *The Honest Man's Fortune* (see "Maximal and Minimal Texts," 68–87).

three states bears interesting similarities, I believe, to the theatrical process accounting for Q2 (the "foul papers"), Folio (with some revision and cuts "in the interest of shortening a long play"), and Q1 *Hamlet*. The argument that the Folio text of Shakespeare's tragedy *Hamlet* presents a preliminary abridgement rather than an acting text thus finds support in the textual history of another play the King's Men performed. Whether they are based on Q2 (like Harold Jenkins's) or the Folio (like Wells and Taylor's), modern editions of *Hamlet* do not give us the play as it was performed in Shakespeare's time.

The textual history of *The Honest Man's Fortune* should be borne in mind when we consider some of Shakespeare's other plays of which two substantive, "good," texts have come down to us. The first quarto of *Othello*, for instance, is about 160 lines shorter than the Folio text. This corresponds to a difference in playing time of an estimated eight minutes. Arguing against Ernst Honigmann's suggestion that "eight minutes is too little a saving," Scott McMillin contends: "The manuscript that lies behind Q1 *Othello* seems to reflect the play as it was abridged for the theater sometime between its composition in the early 1600s and its entry in the *Stationers' Register* in 1621."[32] What remains absent from his discussion, however, is an awareness that at 3,055 lines Q1 *Othello* is still substantially too long to have been performed in its entirety. McMillin convincingly suggests that Q1 *Othello* was set up from a private transcript. As he points out, the stage directions seem more literary than usual. Furthermore, *A King and No King*, published by the same Walkley three years earlier, *was* set up from a private transcript.[33] At 3,049 lines, *A King and No King* is considerably longer than the longest of the thirty-four plays in the "Beaumont and Fletcher" Folio, making it unlikely that it was set up from a transcript of the play "as it was abridged for the theater." In other words, if Q1 *Othello* was set up from a private transcript, this transcript, like that underlying Q1 *A King and No King*, would seem to have reflected an only partly abridged, literary, rather than the fully abridged, theatrical, text. Honigmann's point that the omission of 160 lines is not enough to reduce *Othello* to manageable stage length and McMillin's reminder that Q1 *Othello* may go back to a scribal transcript can both be accommodated once we remember the evidence that can be

---

[32] E. A. J. Honigmann, *The Texts of "Othello" and Shakespearian Revision* (London and New York: Routledge, 1996), 13; Scott McMillin, "The *Othello* Quarto and the 'Foul-Paper' Hypothesis," *Shakespeare Quarterly*, 51 (2000), 82. See also McMillin's introduction to his edition of *The First Quarto of Othello* in the New Cambridge series (Cambridge University Press, 2001), 1–44.

[33] See ibid., 83.

derived from the extant texts of *The Honest Man's Fortune* and *Hamlet*: a manuscript that constitutes a first abridgement was still subject to being peppered with deletion marks which a compositor would have ignored.

Lack of awareness of "the practicalities of performance" also seems to have marred some of the revisionary work on the texts of *King Lear*. The history of textual scholarship on *King Lear* is well known: for most of the twentieth century, the accepted view was that the "real" *King Lear* had disappeared from the English stage soon after the Restoration and only returned in 1838 when William Charles Macready restored Shakespeare's play. More recently, we have become accustomed to the argument that the conflated *Lear* which editions up to the 1980s provided was not the "real" play after all. Rather, according to the new orthodoxy of the 1980s, there are two "real" *Lears*, original and revised, the former published in 1608 as *The History of King Lear*, the latter in 1623 as *The Tragedy of King Lear*. While the *History* contains some 300 lines absent from the Folio, the *Tragedy* has about 100 lines that are not in Q1, the absolute length of Q1 *Lear* being just under 3,100, that of the Folio 2,900 lines. The differences between Q and F are more than a matter of length, however. Albany speaks the play's crucially important last lines in the quarto, Edgar in the Folio. Passages alluding to the presence of the French army in England are absent from the Folio. What corresponds to 3.6 in most modern editions with Lear's important mock trial is only in the quarto. Edgar is a more, Kent a less prominent character in the Folio than in the quarto. According to this new orthodoxy, *The History* and *The Tragedy of King Lear* are in some ways simply different plays.

By including two texts of *King Lear*, the Oxford *Complete Works* became the first major edition to apply the two-text theory in editorial practice, a decision that has been followed up by two *Lears* in the New Cambridge Shakespeare.[34] The prolonged scholarly debate over the texts of *King Lear* has led to little agreement, however. At one extreme, scholars like Michael Warren and Gary Taylor believe that characters and themes have been intelligently reworked in a way that suggests Shakespeare as their only possible originator.[35] Similarly, Steven Urkowitz has argued that "the major variants in *King Lear* are the result of careful revision performed by a theater artist,

---

[34] Note that the Norton Shakespeare contains three texts of *King Lear*: *The History* of 1608, *The Tragedy* of 1623, and a conflated text.

[35] Michael Warren, "Quarto and Folio *King Lear* and the Interpretation of Albany and Edgar," in *Shakespeare: Pattern of Excelling Nature*, eds. David Bevington and Jay L. Halio (Newark: University of Delaware Press; London: Associated University Presses, 1978), 95–107, and Gary Taylor, "The War in *King Lear*," *Shakespeare Survey*, 33 (1980), 27–34. See also Michael Warren's *The Complete "King Lear," 1608–1623* (Berkeley and Los Angeles: University of California Press, 1989).

most probably by Shakespeare himself," and thinks that in order to account for the agency that turned Q into F, "all that is needed is Shakespeare."[36] Yet other scholars disagree. René Weis has argued: "The disintegrationist school, partly because it champions Shakespeare-the-reviser, has tended to play down the importance of censorship in theories about the genesis of the two texts." He concludes much more tentatively: "The most we can safely say about Q and F *Lear* is that they differ in several important ways, and that these do not necessarily form part of a systematic revision."[37] R. A. Foakes has usefully reminded us that "none of the differences between Q and F radically affects the plot of the play, or its general structure, and there is every reason to think that we have two versions of the same play, not two different plays."[38] Others, like Sidney Thomas, have attempted to refute the arguments for a two-text *King Lear*, while Richard Knowles believes that Folio *Lear* represents "local improvements, not significant revisions."[39] Roughly two decades after the heydays of the two-text *King Lear* and "Shakespeare-the-reviser" theories, Paul Werstine has come to the sobering conclusion that "the theory of authorial revision seems to have receded to the only position it can reasonably achieve – that of an unverifiable hypothesis."[40]

Independently of how much evidence there is for Shakespeare's revision of *King Lear*, Peter Blayney, Michael Warren, Steven Urkowitz, and Gary Taylor have made a strong case for the authority of the first quarto of *King Lear*, thereby disposing of earlier theories that had little to recommend themselves. The theory that the manuscript from which Q1 was set up goes back to a shorthand report had numerous supporters in the later part of the nineteenth and the earlier half of the twentieth centuries and has

---

[36] Steven Urkowitz, *Shakespeare's Revision of "King Lear"* (Princeton University Press, 1980), 16–17, 149.

[37] René Weis, *"King Lear": A Parallel Text Edition* (London and New York: Longman, 1993), 15, 34.

[38] Foakes, ed. *King Lear*, 118–19.

[39] Sidney Thomas, "Shakespeare's Supposed Revision of *King Lear*," *Shakespeare Quarterly*, 35 (1984), 506–11, and "The Integrity of *King Lear*," *Modern Language Review*, 90 (1995), 572–84; and Richard Knowles, "Revision Awry in Folio *Lear* 3.1," *Shakespeare Quarterly*, 46 (1995), 32–46, 45.

[40] Review of Honigmann's *Texts of "Othello" and Shakespearian Revision*, in *Shakespeare Quarterly*, 51 (2000), 241. Barbara Mowat has recently argued that work by William B. Long and Paul Werstine has effectively undermined the grounds on which the New Bibliography diagnosed the origins and nature of manuscripts underlying the printed texts ("The Reproduction of Shakespeare's Texts," in *The Cambridge Companion to Shakespeare*, eds. Margreta de Grazia and Stanley Wells (Cambridge University Press, 2001), 13–29). In the 1970s and early 1980s, the argument that there are two versions of *King Lear* and that Shakespeare's revision is responsible for the significant differences between Q and F revolutionized Shakespearean textual studies. Ironically, however, if Shakespearean textual studies are currently undergoing a paradigm shift, as Mowat argues, then the confidence with which the proponents of a two-text *Lear* claim to be able to determine the agency that is responsible for the difference between the two texts really belongs to the old paradigm.

recently had a comeback.[41] The length of Q1 *King Lear* strongly militates against the possibility, however, that the text goes back to a transcription of a performance. The same applies to the now discredited theory that Q1 was set up from a memorial reconstruction.[42]

What can account for the passages present in one but absent from the other text of *King Lear*? Assuming that Shakespeare revised *The History of King Lear* to produce *The Tragedy* in a conscious artistic effort, various scholars were led to argue that precisely such an effort went into the omission of passages absent from the Folio. For instance, in *Shakespeare's Revision of "King Lear,"* Urkowitz argued: "The cuts in *King Lear* ... reflect artistic revision rather than mechanical care about playing time." He believed that "plays were never cut because they were too long," a view that seems indefensible in view of such unambiguous statements as those made by Webster and Brome.[43] Roger Warren pursued the same line of argument, holding that the omission of the mock trial in 3.6 constitutes a theatrical improvement.[44]

The considerable merits of Urkowitz's revisionary work on the texts of *King Lear* are not in question here. What does need to be questioned, however, is the view that since the Folio text (purportedly revised by Shakespeare) omits passages present in the quarto, the omissions constitute a theatrical improvement. Generations of directors and theatergoers have found Lear's mock trial in 3.6 a powerful moment, and the argument that it was Shakespeare's special achievement to cut it seems misguided. The necessity for such an argument only exists as long as we disregard

---

[41] See Alexander Schmidt, *Zur Textkritik des "King Lear,"* (Königsberg, 1879); Greg, *Editorial Problem*, 88–101, Adele Davidson, "Shakespeare and Stenography Reconsidered," *Analytical & Enumerative Bibliography*, 6, n.s. (1992), 77–100, "'Some by Stenography'? Stationers, Shorthand, and the Early Shakespearean Quartos," *Papers of the Bibliographical Society of America*, 90 (1996), 417–49, and "'*King Lear* in an Age of Stenographical Reproduction' or 'Sitting Down to Copy *King Lear* Again,'" *Papers of the Bibliographical Society of America*, 92 (1998), 297–324.

[42] See George Ian Duthie, ed., *"King Lear": A Critical Edition* (Oxford: Blackwell, 1949), 19–116, esp. 75–116.

[43] Urkowitz, *Revision of "King Lear,"* 144–45.

[44] Roger Warren, "The Folio Omission of the Mock Trial: Motives and Consequences," in *The Division of the Kingdoms*, eds. Gary Taylor and Michael Warren (Oxford: Clarendon Press, 1983), 45–57. Assuming that Shakespeare was "so dissatisfied with [the mock trial] as to omit it entirely," (45) Warren, predictably, constructs arguments to support the excellence of Shakespeare's decision: Act four, scene six "expresses in a much more successful manner the 'mad' insights of the mock trial" (53). In other words, Shakespeare did not get it quite right in 3.6, so the scene is cut to give way to the other, "better" scene, 4.6, which allegedly deals with the identical topic. Also, Warren contends, the cut "strengthens the dramatic structure of the play" (49) and it occurs "when an audience is beginning to tire anyway" (47). Warren's arguments seem prompted (and marred) less by the theatrical merits of the mock trial scene than by his initial assumption that it was Shakespeare's dissatisfaction with the scene rather than "the practicalities of performance" that led to its omission.

the constraints within which a 3,100 line text was prepared for the stage. Whether we find the quarto, the Folio, or even a conflated text of *Lear* artistically and theatrically most successful will remain a matter of taste. Insofar as Shakespeare and his fellows were responsible for choosing "disposable" passages for omission (and what exactly lies behind the omission of any one passage present in the parallel text is not something that is easily assessed), we can take for granted that the abridgement was carried out by people who had enough experience to know what they were doing. Yet, to argue that the cuts in the Folio version "reflect artistic revision," and that the resulting text is theatrically "a great improvement on the Quarto text," fails to consider that abridgement of the text behind Q1 *Lear* would have been necessary independent of whether Shakespeare would have found it artistically desirable.

Taking "the practicalities of performance" seriously also allows us to shed light on the variant texts of *Richard III*. D. L. Patrick first suggested that the first quarto of *Richard III* was set up from a memorial reconstruction made by the company, a suggestion which, in the heydays of the "memorial reconstruction" theory, many scholars (though not Chambers) accepted.[45] Even before the theory of "memorial reconstruction" came under attack, Kristian Smidt argued in two studies that Q1 is a revision rather than a memorial reconstruction.[46] Kathleen O. Irace and Laurie E. Maguire have advanced other arguments that undermine the view that *Richard III* is a memorial reconstruction.[47]

Patrick's theory that Q1 *Richard III* was set up from a memorial reconstruction lingers on, however, most recently in Peter Davison's edition of the

---

[45] D. L. Patrick, *The Textual History of "Richard III"* (Stanford and London: Stanford University Press, 1936). For Chambers, see *William Shakespeare*, 1.299.

[46] Kristian Smidt, *Iniurious Imposters and "Richard III"* (Oslo: Norwegian Universities Press; New York: Humanities Press, 1964), and *Memorial Transmission and Quarto Copy in "Richard III": A Reassessment* (Oslo: Universitetsforlaget; New York: Humanities Press, 1970). See also Smidt's useful edition *The Tragedy of King Richard the Third: Parallel Texts of the First Quarto and the First Folio with Variants of the Early Quartos* (Oslo: Universitetsforlaget; New York: Humanities Press, 1969).

[47] Kathleen O. Irace, *Reforming the "Bad" Quartos: Performance and Provenance of Six Shakespearean First Editions* (Newark: University of Delaware Press; London: Associated University Presses, 1994), 17–18; and Laurie E. Maguire *Shakespearean Suspect Texts: The "Bad" Quartos and Their Context* (Cambridge University Press, 1996), 299–300. As the Oxford editors point out in *The Textual Companion*, "the example of *Lear* raises again the possibility, extensively debated by earlier editors, that Quarto *Richard III* might represent an authorial first draft, rather than a memorial reconstruction" (228). This possibility has been examined in some detail by Steven Urkowitz who offers a "model of *Richard III* as a work in progress, an early state in the Quarto, a later state in the Folio" ("Reconsidering the Relationship of Quarto and Folio Texts of *Richard III*," *English Literary Renaissance*, 16 (1986), 442–66, 466).

1597 quarto.[48] Like Patrick, Davison believes that the Lord Chamberlain's Men collectively put together the text while on provincial tour. It deserves pointing out how inherently implausible this scenario is. The Lord Chamberlain's Men, on tour in the provinces, lose their "prompt book" and sit down together in order to produce a generally very faithful substitute by means of a collective memorial reconstruction. Yet why, if the players knew their parts, would there have been a need for such a text? Once the actors' parts had been copied, there was little need for the manuscript with which the bookkeeper helped manage performances except for the timing of certain off-stage business such as the occasional "alarum" of which Q1 *Richard III* records only a single instance. No one, in such a situation, was in need of a word-for-word reconstruction of the full text. The use of the anachronistic term "promptbook," against which William Long rightly warns us, has effectively masked the fact that the narrative supporting the "memorial reconstruction" hypothesis relied on a modern rather than on a Renaissance use of the term "promptbook."[49]

Moreover, the most important, indeed the only essential, part of a manuscript playbook was the Master of the Revels's signature licensing the play. All local authorities had been made aware that, "No play is to bee played, but such as is allowed by the sayd Edmond [Tilney], & his hand at the latter end of the saide booke they doe play."[50] As Andrew Gurr points out, if a company performed a play of which they did not have a licensed playbook, "they could suffer whatever punishment the authorities chose to apply, from imprisonment in the local jail to loss of their patent to play."[51] In fact, the only part of a playbook which a touring company absolutely needed in order to perform the play is precisely the one no memorial reconstruction could have recovered.

Apart from the above arguments and those advanced by Maguire, Irace, and Urkowitz, the length of Q1 *Richard III* powerfully militates against the possibility that it was performed (and could thus be memorially reconstructed) in its entirety. With 3,570 lines, *Richard III* is the longest play in the Folio, slightly longer even than Folio *Hamlet* (3,537 lines). Q1 *Richard III*, in comparison, is just under 3,400 lines long and omits more than two hundred lines present in, while containing some thirty lines absent from, the

[48] Peter Davison, ed., *The First Quarto of Richard III*, New Cambridge Shakespeare: The Early Quartos (Cambridge University Press, 1996).

[49] See Long, "Performing Texts," 381.

[50] I quote from J. T. Murray, *English Dramatic Companies, 1558–1642*, 2 vols. (London: Constable, 1910), II.320. See also Gurr, "Maximal and Minimal Texts," 74–75.

[51] Ibid., 75.

Folio. The implications of what we know about the length of Elizabethan performances and playtexts thus adds another argument to those serving to discredit the traditional view of Q1 *Richard III* as a memorial reconstruction.

The existence of more than one substantive text of a Renaissance play can have a variety of origins, among them the hazards of textual transition. Where design accounts for at least part of the differences, it is generally interpreted as having one of two origins: the author or the theater. Ben Jonson, revising *Every Man in His Humour* before the publication of his *Workes*, producing a revised text that differs in significant ways from the original, is an instance of the former. If the original, theatrical text of Barnabe Barnes's *The Devil's Charter* – "plaide before the Kings Maiestie... and augmented since by the Author, for the more pleasure and profit of the reader," according to the title page – were extant, Barnes would have to be counted in the same category. The existence of multiple texts of Shakespeare plays, however, is usually accounted for by the theater. I have argued in this chapter that this view may be at least partly mistaken. If, as an increasing number of scholars believe, Shakespeare reworked his plays, adding lines and passages, changing speech prefixes, rephrasing sentences, substituting one word for another in seemingly innocuous contexts, this may tell us more about Shakespeare the self-conscious dramatist and less about Shakespeare the Lord Chamberlain's and King's Men's playwright than is often supposed. As John Kerrigan has rightly pointed out: "the *details* of revision change our idea of Shakespeare. He becomes a self-considering artist," a "poet willing to engage with his own work critically, as reader and rethinker."[52]

Having dwelt on the implications of what we know about the length of dramatic performances for Shakespeare's "long" plays, I will conclude this chapter with a few observations about a play that is particularly short. At 2,084 lines, *Macbeth* is among Shakespeare's shortest plays, longer only than *The Tempest* and *The Comedy of Errors*. Scholars have long pointed out that *Macbeth*'s brevity seems to be a matter of stage abridgement.[53]

---

[52] See John Kerrigan, "Shakespeare as Reviser," in *English Drama to 1710*, ed. Christopher Ricks (New York: Peter Bedrick Books, 1987), 260–61. See also Gary Taylor, "Revising Shakespeare," *TEXT: An Interdisciplinary Annual of Textual Studies*, 3 (1987), 285–304; Stanley Wells, "Revision in Shakespeare's Plays," in *Editing and Editors: A Retrospect*, ed. Richard Landon (New York: AMS Press, 1988), 67–97; Grace Ioppolo, *Revising Shakespeare* (Cambridge, Mass.: Harvard University Press, 1991); and John Jones, *Shakespeare at Work* (Oxford and New York: Oxford University Press, 1995).

[53] The only substantive text of *Macbeth* contains a number of stage directions that seem to signal the bookkeeper's intervention: "Drum within," "Knocking within," "Musicke and a Song. Blacke

Chambers held: "The text is unsatisfactory, not so much on account of verbal corruption, as of a rehandling to which it bears evidence. This seems to have been most obviously a matter of abridgement."[54] Greg found "there is clear evidence of cutting at some points in short abrupt lines accompanied by textual obscurities," and the editors of the Oxford Shakespeare similarly concluded *Macbeth* "suffered from posthumous theatrical adaptation."[55] Ivor Brown realized how far-reaching the implications of the text of *Macbeth* are. Heminge and Condell, Brown writes:

> claimed to preserve Shakespeare's plays "absolute in their numbers, as he conceived them." But for one of the greatest tragedies, *Macbeth*, they lacked Shakespeare's original manuscript and had to print the acting version. This contained only 2,084 lines, which must be compared with the 3,750 of the Second Quarto of *Hamlet*. If the full text of *Macbeth* had been up to this size, as is probable since the other great tragedies all approached that length, more than a third had been cut.[56]

The idea that "more than a third" may have been cut from the original *Macbeth* is no doubt difficult to accept for those who believe that the play's concision is one of its intrinsic features. Yet, if we discount the possibly un-finished *Timon of Athens*, Shakespeare's other seventeenth-century tragedies have an average length of 3,274 lines and would have to be abridged by more than a third to be reduced to the length of *Macbeth*. It is possible to argue, of course, that *Macbeth* simply *is* a short play. Apart from disregarding the internal evidence which scholars have adduced, this view is also prob-lematic because the coincidence of brevity and theatrical origins confirms what we know about the theatrical conventions of the time. While the long texts of Shakespeare's tragedies preserve "the poem," the only extant text of *Macbeth* conserves what Webster called "the play." As Webster pointed out, the poem contains much "that the length of the Play would not beare in the Presentment." Nicholas Brooke, the editor of *Macbeth* in the Oxford Shakespeare series, has come to the conclusion that "If the 'bad quarto'

Spirits, &c." One note is particularly likely to have been added by him. The Folio reads:

> Macd[uff].... Malcolme, Banquo, ...
> As from your Graues rise vp, and walke like Sprights,
> To countenance this horror. Ring the Bell.
> *Bell rings.*   *Enter Lady.*   (TLN 833–36)

The bookkeeper's additional note "Ring the Bell" seems to have mistakenly found its way into the text. A similar instance occurs towards the end of act three scene five where "*Musicke, and a Song*" is followed, two lines later, by "*Sing within. Come away, come away, &c.*" (TLN 1464, 1467). Presumably, an authorial stage direction was printed along with the bookkeeper's additional note.

[54] Chambers, *William Shakespeare*, 1.471.
[55] Greg, *Editorial Problem*, 147; Wells, Taylor, et al., *Textual Companion*, 15.
[56] Ivor Brown, *Shakespeare and the Actors* (London: Bodley Head, 1970), 63–64.

of *Hamlet*...were fleshed out with more perfectly remembered words it would only be slightly longer than *Macbeth* and few would notice the omissions. I take *Macbeth*'s brevity to be entirely a matter of its derivation from performance."[57] In other words, the great economy of *Macbeth* which generations of commentators have praised appears to be not so much a feature of the play as of the text that has come down to us. By extension, all stage versions of Shakespeare's seventeenth-century tragedies (the "plays") rather than only that of *Macbeth* must have been characterized by greater economy and concision than the "True Originall Copies" (the "poems"). The communal, theatrical versions prepared by the company and performed on stage and the authorial, dramatic versions written (and occasionally revised) by William Shakespeare in the expectation of a readership must thus have been significantly different texts. This difference will be at the center of the two remaining chapters.

[57] Nicholas Brooke, ed., *The Tragedy of Macbeth*, The Oxford Shakespeare (Oxford University Press, 1990), 56.

CHAPTER 8

"Bad" quartos and their origins: Romeo and Juliet, Henry V, *and* Hamlet

I have argued in the preceding chapters that many of Shakespeare's plays existed in two significantly different forms in the late sixteenth and in the seventeenth centuries. On the one hand, Shakespeare produced "authorial manuscripts," instances of what John Webster called the "poem" and what some title pages refer to as "the true original copy." On the other hand, there were manuscripts that had undergone the company's preparation for actual performance, what Webster calls "the play," or, in other words, the text "as it has been sundry times performed." Whereas texts in the former group were of a length which the actors found impossible to reconcile with the requirements of performance, the latter had been reduced to what was compatible with the "two hours' traffic of our stage." Contrary to the theatrical scripts, the *raison d'être* of the long "poems," I have argued, was basically literary.

There is a group of Shakespeare plays, then, which is of particular importance for this study owing to the fact that they survive in "short" and "long" versions. They belong to, although they are not identical with, the group of plays of which a so-called "bad" quarto has survived. *Pericles* shares some of the characteristics of the other "bad" quartos, but the play's textual situation is different insofar as no corresponding "good" text has survived. For reasons that are difficult to recover today, it failed to be included in the collection.[1] Even though the First Folio does include *The Taming of the Shrew*, the differences between it and the earlier *Taming of*

---

[1] It is not often noted how surprising the non-inclusion of *Pericles* in the First Folio is. Scholars have never doubted that at least substantial parts of it are by Shakespeare. The play was published as Shakespeare's in 1609, reprinted the same year, and again in 1611 and 1619, always with Shakespeare's name on the title page. In the fifteen years prior to the publication of the First Folio, *Pericles* was, in fact, printed more often than any other of Shakespeare's plays. Not included in the First Folio and only extant in a problematic text, *Pericles* may seem today like less than a fully canonical Shakespeare play. In the years prior to 1623, however, it was both immensely popular and clearly thought of as Shakespearean. So why was it not included in the First Folio? If we believe that it was not included because Shakespeare wrote it in co-authorship, we are faced with the question of why other plays that are not his unaided work (such as *Henry VIII* and, probably, *Titus Andronicus* and *1 Henry VI*) were

a Shrew (QI 1594) are neither so much a matter of length nor, in the first place, a matter of the textual quality. Particularly in the subplot, *A Shrew*, whether by Shakespeare or not, is simply a different play.[2] The Folio text of *Merry Wives* is only 2,527 lines long and the brevity of the "bad" quarto (*c.* 1,600 lines) has been convincingly argued to be a matter of faulty report rather than prior abridgement.[3] *1 Contention* and *Richard Duke of York* in some ways yield evidence similar to that of the "bad" quartos of *Romeo and Juliet*, *Henry V*, and *Hamlet*, but the extent of Shakespeare's authorship of 2 and *3 Henry VI* is still a matter of debate. Meres's *Palladis Tamia* of 1598 refers to most plays Shakespeare is known to have written by that time, but not to the *Henry VI* plays. Stylistic features have further contributed to casting doubt upon Shakespeare's undivided authorship. Wells and Taylor hold that "the question of the authorship of the bulk of *Contention* should be regarded as open," and that "pending further investigation Shakespeare's responsibility for every scene of [*Richard Duke of York*] should be regarded as uncertain."[4] Ronald Knowles, in a recent Arden edition of *2 Henry VI*, similarly believes "that the question of mixed authorship remains open."[5] It would seem unwise to make claims about "Shakespeare's" texts and plays if we cannot be sure that they are straightforwardly his.

included. If we argue that it was not printed because no "good" text was available, it may be objected that the play was popular and kept being performed by the King's Men – for instance at court in 1619. If the company had a text that was good enough to perform the play at court, why would they not have had access to a text they deemed of sufficient quality for inclusion in the First Folio? If we hold that the text was not included because the publishers of the First Folio failed to come to an agreement with the stationer who owned the rights to *Pericles*, the problem is that this stationer was Thomas Pavier who also owned *Henry V* and 2 and *3 Henry VI*. If Pavier agreed to the publication of these plays, why would he have been opposed to the publication of *Pericles*? The non-inclusion of *Pericles* in the First Folio is a bibliographical fact that cannot be easily explained.

[2] Stephen Roy Miller, the most careful student of *A Shrew* in recent years, has shown the weaknesses of Peter Alexander's argument according to which *A Shrew* is a memorial reconstruction of *The Shrew*. Brian Morris, editor for the Arden2 (1981) and Ann Thompson for the New Cambridge (1984) still largely endorsed Alexander's position. After a detailed investigation, Miller comes to the conclusion that *A Shrew* is likely to be "an adaptation of *The Shrew*" (*The Taming of a Shrew: The 1594 Quarto*, The New Cambridge Shakespeare: The Early Shakespeare (Cambridge University Press, 1998), 9). See also Miller's "*The Taming of a Shrew* and the Theories; or, 'Though this be badness, yet there is method in't,' " in *Textual Formation and Reformation*, eds. Laurie E. Maguire and Thomas L. Berger (Newark: University of Delaware Press; London: Associated University Presses, 1998), 251–63; and Leah Marcus, "The Editor as Tamer," in *Unediting the Renaissance: Shakespeare, Marlowe, Milton* (London and New York: Routledge, 1996), 101–31. Note that Maguire argues that *A Shrew* is "Part M[emorial] R[econstruction] (most notably in taming plot)" (*Suspect Texts*, 310).

[3] See, for example, Chambers, *William Shakespeare*, 1.430–31; Greg, *First Folio*, 334–37.

[4] Wells, Taylor, et al., *Textual Companion*, 112.

[5] Ronald Knowles, ed., *King Henry VI Part 2*, The Arden Shakespeare (Walton-on-Thames, Surrey: Thomas Nelson, 1999), 118. See also Thomas Merriam, "Tamburlaine Stalks in *Henry VI*," *Computers and the Humanities*, 30 (1996), 267–80.

In this and the next chapter, I will therefore concentrate on *Romeo and Juliet*, *Henry V*, and *Hamlet*, three plays that Shakespeare wrote for the Lord Chamberlain's Men in the space of five years or so at the very end of the sixteenth century. The variant substantive texts of the early editions are key witnesses for my argument, giving us access, I believe, to the difference between the writing practice of Shakespeare the dramatist, on the one hand, and the performance practice of Shakespeare and his fellows, on the other. With about 3,000, 3,200, and 3,600 lines respectively, the "good" texts of *Romeo and Juliet*, *Henry V*, and *Hamlet* must have been substantially abridged. The first quartos of *Romeo and Juliet* (2,215 lines), *Henry V* (1,623 lines), and *Hamlet* (2,154 lines) allow us to guess behind their partly problematic texts such abridgements.[6] These three plays thus allow us to assess with relatively good (though never fully transparent) textual evidence the theatrical implications of what Stephen Orgel has called "the disparity between the performing time and the length of the surviving texts."[7]

Having affirmed that the "bad" quartos are in some ways the best witnesses we have of what would actually have been performed on London's stages, I hasten to add what claims I believe *cannot* be made about their authority. I do not argue – as Graham Holderness and Brian Loughrey do – that the first quartos of *Hamlet*, *Henry V*, and *Romeo and Juliet* are stage-worthy texts in their own right.[8] Or, rather, I believe that, if productions of these texts make for exciting theater, this is largely despite – and not because of – what is characteristic about their verbal texture. *Hamlet* Q1, for instance, *is* a bad text insofar as it contains badly versified passages, misplaced lines, and expressions distorted by imperfect textual transmission. While I believe that the first quartos of *Romeo and Juliet*, *Henry V*, and *Hamlet* are of extraordinary *scholarly* interest (as they are the closest we can get to what Shakespeare and his fellows performed), the linguistic texture they are made of seems to be of minor interest for the purposes of modern performance.

---

[6] For the length of the "bad" quartos, see Hart, *Stolne and Surreptitious Copies*, 18.

[7] Orgel, "Authentic Shakespeare," 25.

[8] Graham Holderness and Bryan Loughrey, eds., *The Tragicall Historie of Hamlet Prince of Denmarke*, Shakespearean Originals: First Editions (Hemel Hempstead: Harvester Wheatsheaf, 1992), 23–27. Holderness and Loughrey's endeavor to reproduce the characteristics of the early printed text in an affordable edition is a worthy project. That attempt is realized with more success, however, in a facsimile edition added to a fully annotated edition of the long text as in T. W. Craig's recent Arden edition (*King Henry V* (London and New York: Routledge, 1995), 374–99) Holderness and Loughrey's argument that their edition recovers both an early textual witness and a play that is stage-worthy in its own right seems to me a flawed attempt at having it both ways.

More generally, the value of the "bad" quartos as witnesses of stage practice is further relativized because the relationship of performances to the actual material witnesses that have come down to us can never be more than well-informed conjecture. It would thus be simplistic to affirm without further qualifications that the "bad" quartos of *Romeo and Juliet*, *Henry V*, and *Hamlet* reflect the plays as they were performed in Shakespeare's time. By its very nature, the theater is a very unstable medium and changes between performances at the Globe and Blackfriars, between one year and the next, even between one evening and the next are possible. Writing about *Romeo and Juliet*, Jonathan Goldberg has correctly argued: "what stands behind Q2 is a manuscript that offers an anthology of possible performances of the play, one of which is captured by Q1."[9] This point, I believe, also applies to *Henry V* and *Hamlet*. Yet these cautions borne in mind, an investigation of the relationship between the extant texts and what was, and what was not, performed on the Elizabethan stage is not only possible and desirable but indeed necessary if we wish to know more about the relationship between what Shakespeare wrote and what his company performed.[10] As Stephen Orgel put it, there is "very little evidence that will reveal to us the nature of a performing text in Shakespeare's theater; but there is a little. There are the 'bad' quartos, whose evidence, in this respect, is not bad, but excellent."[11] This chapter takes seriously the "bad" quartos in order to come to a better understanding of both what Shakespeare and his fellows performed and what separates these performances from the long, "good" texts that have come down to us.

The claims I am making for the importance of the "bad" quartos largely contradict the dominant critical views during the last century. As the unfortunate epithet with which Pollard chose to characterize the quartos implies, what was long considered their most important feature is their textual quality, a quality that largely disqualified them from scholarly and critical

[9] Jonathan Goldberg, " 'What? in a Names that which we call a Rose': The Desired Texts of *Romeo and Juliet*," in *Crisis in Editing: Texts of the English Renaissance*, ed. Randall McLeod (New York: AMS Press, 1994), 186.

[10] I thus readily grant that the authority of any text that somehow derives from performance is limited by the fact that it *may* reflect no more than one stage run among many. Nevertheless, it is also necessary to point out what happened on the one occasion when a manuscript allows us insights into the relationship of one stage run to another. As William Long has shown, the manuscript of *Thomas of Woodstock* shows that the play was revived early in James's reign, about a decade after its original production. Long points out that "it is significant to note that the players have found nothing either unusable or in need of change. The customs of staging and of marking playbooks have continued unaltered. New notations facilitate smooth presentation but offer no divergences" (Long, " 'A Bed / for Woodstock,' " 110). While texts may have been altered between two stage runs, theatrical convenience makes it likely that they often were not.

[11] Orgel, "Acting Scripts," 253.

investigation. Only relatively recently have scholars become more willing to pay attention to the "bad" texts and their bearing on our investigations of English Renaissance stage practice. Most remarkably, perhaps, Andrew Gurr has recently argued that the first quarto of *Henry V* is "a version closely based on the Shakespeare company's own performance script of the play, a text made for or from its first performances in 1599."[12] As we have seen above, the prevalent view still takes for granted, however, that substantially uncut texts were performed in the London theaters and that, consequently, the "bad" quartos tell us little about stage practice on Shakespeare's stage.

In this chapter, I will try to establish the grounds on which I consider Q1 *Romeo and Juliet*, *Henry V*, and *Hamlet* to be texts that yield important information about what Shakespeare's company performed in London. An approach that takes seriously what we know about stage abridgements and the length of performances can make a contribution, I believe, to the study of Shakespeare's "bad" quartos. Even though the "bad" quartos have been hotly debated, scholars have generally failed to question that a text of well over three thousand lines could have been performed. For instance, Kathleen Irace has recently argued that the first quarto of *Hamlet* is a memorial reconstruction undertaken by an actor who had taken part in performances of the long Folio text.[13] My argument in the preceding chapters implies that such a scenario is unfeasible, a contention I intend to corroborate in this chapter.

In the subsequent chapter, I will try to uncover some of the ways in which the long and short plays are essentially different. On the one hand, the short quartos behind which we can guess actual performances reveal textual features that seem specifically for and of the stage. On the other hand, the difference between short and long quartos also reveals the specificity of the long texts. This specificity allows us access to what Shakespeare, the emerging dramatic author, must have written with an awareness that much of it would not survive the text's preparation for the stage but that he and his company made available to a readership.

The genesis of the traditional view of the "bad" quartos is important for an understanding of recent discontents with this view. It may then prove helpful to trace its basic outline. If we want to understand the scholarly reception of the "bad" quartos in the twentieth century, we will do well to start by considering two publications that appeared at the end of its

---

[12] Gurr, ed., *The First Quarto of King Henry V*, ix.
[13] See Irace, *Reforming the "Bad" Quartos*, 122–24.

first decade. In *Shakespeare Folios and Quartos*, Alfred W. Pollard invented the textual category labeled "bad" quartos.[14] This invention followed from his revisionary reading of Heminge and Condell's address: "To the Great Variety of Readers." While earlier commentators had believed that their reference to "diuerse stolne, and surreptitious copies," with which the readers had previously been "abus'd," was to the quarto editions in general, Pollard insisted that only the "bad" quartos were meant.[15] Since several "good" quartos had been used as copy when the Folio was printed, Heminge and Condell, Pollard argued, could hardly have claimed to have "cur'd" all the "surreptitious" and "maimed" quartos. The texts he identified as "bad" quartos were Q1 *Romeo and Juliet* (1597), Q1 *Henry V* (1600), Q1 *The Merry Wives of Windsor* (1602), Q1 *Hamlet* (1603), and Q1 *Pericles* (1609).[16]

Even though the "bad" quartos, "differing widely and for the worse from those of the First Folio," are credited with textual "badness," Pollard spent in fact more pages dwelling on the moral badness of the people involved in the book trade which he held responsible for the "bad" quartos' genesis. Dishonest "pirates" had procured the manuscripts "by sending reporters to performances of the play" who passed them on to be "surreptitiously published" by people "troubled with no scruples as to honesty."[17]

In the preface to *Shakespeare Folios and Quartos*, Pollard acknowledges: "Mr Greg and I have been fellow-hunters, communicating our results to each other at every stage, so that our respective responsibilities for them have become hopelessly entangled."[18] It is then significant that Greg published another milestone in Shakespearean textual scholarship only one year later. In his edition of the "bad" quarto of *The Merry Wives of Windsor* (1602), he revised and refined that part of the narrative to which Pollard had paid little attention: the agency behind the manuscript copy of the "bad" quarto that allows us to account for the text's relationship to the "good" Folio text. Noting "the very unusual accuracy with which the part of mine Host is

---

[14] Alfred W. Pollard, *Shakespeare Folios and Quartos: A Study in the Bibliography of Shakespeare's Plays 1594–1685* (London: Methuen, 1909). See, in particular, the chapter on "The Good and the Bad Quartos" (64–80).

[15] Malone wrote about the quartos: "undoubtedly they were all surreptitious, that is stolen from the playhouse, and printed without the consent of the author or the proprietors" (quoted without reference in Henrietta C. Bartlett and Alfred W. Pollard, *A Census of Shakespeare's Plays in Quarto* (New Haven: Yale University Press, 1916), xiv). See also Appendix B.

[16] Pollard excluded *1 Contention* and *Richard Duke of York* on the grounds that they were "very doubtfully by Shakespeare" (*Shakespeare Folios and Quartos*, 101).

[17] Ibid., 65–69. For the fullest refutation of Pollard's argument that the "good" and authorized texts were entered in the Stationers' Register whereas the "bad" and surreptitious were not, see Kirschbaum, *Shakespeare and the Stationers*, 87–153.

[18] Pollard, *Shakespeare Folios and Quartos*, vi.

reported" and "the comparative excellence of the reporting of those scenes in which the Host is on the stage," Greg concluded that "the pirate who procured the copy...was none other than the actor of the Host's part."[19] Even though Greg cannot be credited with having invented the concept, he seems to have provided both the label and the first detailed investigation of what has since been known as "memorial reconstruction."[20]

The twin theories of "bad" quartos and "memorial reconstruction" thus having been put forward in the space of two years by two of the leading scholars of their time, much of the scholarship in the following decades went into consolidating Pollard and Greg's publications of 1909 and 1910. In *Shakespeare's Fight with the Pirates*, Pollard elaborated the "bad" quarto theory as well as the rhetoric he had used to deploy it.[21] Attention soon turned from piratical publishers to thievish players, however, as scholars started applying Greg's findings to other plays. As early as 1915, H. D. Gray suggested that Q1 *Hamlet* is also a memorial reconstruction, undertaken by the actor who played the role of Marcellus.[22] In 1919, Pollard himself, in co-authorship with J. Dover Wilson, agreed that the "bad" quartos may have been more easily produced by actors who had performed in the plays than by reporters whom stationers had sent to the playhouse.[23] In *Shakespeare's First Folio*, R. Crompton Rhodes similarly argued against Pollard's "arranged piracy at the instigation of a London Stationer." He suggested instead that the "bad" quartos were "printed from the prompt-books of strolling players" who reconstructed, partly or wholly by memory, London performances in which they had previously participated.[24] Once "memorial reconstruction" had been applied not only to Q1 *Merry Wives* but to all of Pollard's Shakespearean "bad" quartos, the time was ripe for the theory to spread beyond the bounds of the Shakespeare canon. Comparing the quarto edition of *Orlando Furioso* with Edward Alleyn's extant part

---

[19] W. W. Greg, ed., *Shakespeare's "Merry Wives of Windsor," 1602* (Oxford: Clarendon Press, 1910), xxxvii, xxxviii, xl.

[20] Ibid., xxvii. The German scholar Tycho Mommsen used the concept of memorial reconstruction to explain the origins of the first quartos of *Hamlet* and *Romeo and Juliet* more than half a century before Greg. See Mommsen, "*Hamlet*, 1603; and *Romeo and Juliet*, 1597," *The Athenaeum*, 29 (1857), 182.

[21] Alfred Pollard, *Shakespeare's Fight with the Pirates and the Problems of the Transmission of His Text* (London: A. Moring, 1917). To do justice to Pollard, he later recanted, realizing that he had been "hypnotized by the old idea of the wicked publisher." See his "Introduction" to Peter Alexander, *Shakespeare's "Henry VI" and "Richard III"* (Cambridge University Press, 1929), 4.

[22] Gray, "The First Quarto of *Hamlet*," *Modern Language Review*, 10 (1915), 171–80.

[23] Pollard and Wilson, "The 'Stolne and Surreptitious' Shakespearian Texts," *The Times Literary Supplement*, January 9, 1918, 18; January 16, 1919, 30; March 13, 1919, 134; August 7, 1919, 420; August 14, 1919, 434.

[24] R. Crompton Rhodes, *Shakespeare's First Folio* (Oxford: Blackwell, 1923), 72–83, esp. 82–83.

of the title character, Greg concluded in 1923 that the quarto is "a version severely abridged... for performance by a reduced cast" and that the text "is based almost throughout on reconstruction from memory."[25] A few years later, Peter Alexander was responsible for adding three more Shakespeare plays to the list of contenders, arguing that Q1 *The Taming of a Shrew* (1594) is a memorially reconstructed "bad" quarto of *The Taming of the Shrew*, and that *The First Part of the Contention* and *Richard Duke of York* are "bad versions of 2 and 3 Henry VI."[26] While the earliest quartos of *Richard III* and *King Lear* were recognized to be textually superior to the "bad" quartos, they, too, came in due time to be diagnosed as "memorial reconstructions," as did the only extant text of *Pericles*.[27] By 1930, E. K. Chambers fixed the canon of Shakespeare's "bad" quartos by endorsing the cases advanced for *1 Contention*, *Richard Duke of York*, *Romeo and Juliet*, *Henry V*, *The Merry Wives of Windsor*, and *Hamlet*, while rejecting *The Taming of a Shrew*.[28]

Following Greg and Alexander's authoritative work on *Merry Wives* and the *Henry VI* plays, it was left to other scholars to argue the full case for *Romeo and Juliet*, *Henry V*, and *Hamlet* that did much to silence what dissenting voices there remained. H. R. Hoppe, in *The Bad Quarto of "Romeo and Juliet*," proposed "to demonstrate that Q1 of *Romeo and Juliet* is a memorial reconstruction of a version that Q2 represents in substantially correct form."[29] In a book-length study of *The "Bad" Quarto of Hamlet*, George Ian Duthie argued that the first quarto of *Hamlet* "is a memorial reconstruction, made for provincial performance by an actor who had taken the part of Marcellus and perhaps another part or parts in the full play."[30] In a later study, he went on to argue that the first quarto of *Henry V* contains "certain textual features" that "indicate strongly the theory of imperfect memorial transmission of Q."[31] The same scholar laid to rest the ghost that had occasionally troubled supporters of memorial reconstruction by providing another explanation for the derivative nature of the "bad" quartos: while H. T. Price, in *The Text of "Henry V"* (1920), could still

[25] Greg, *Stage Abridgements*, 133–34.

[26] Peter Alexander, "*The Taming of a Shrew*," *The Times Literary Supplement*, September 16, 1926, 614, and Alexander, "*Henry VI*" and "*Richard III*," 35.

[27] See Patrick, *Textual History of "Richard III"*; Duthie, ed., *Shakespeare's "King Lear": A Critical Edition* (Oxford: Blackwell, 1949); and Philip Edwards, "An Approach to the Problem of *Pericles*," *Shakespeare Survey*, 5 (1952), 25–49.

[28] Chambers, *William Shakespeare*, 1.281–85, 324–28, 341–45, 391–94, 415–22, 429–34.

[29] H. R. Hoppe, *The Bad Quarto of "Romeo and Juliet"* (Ithaca: Cornell University Press, 1948), 58.

[30] George Ian Duthie, *The "Bad" Quarto of Hamlet* (Cambridge University Press, 1941), 273.

[31] George Ian Duthie, "The Quarto of Shakespeare's *Henry V*," in *Papers Mainly Shakespearian*, ed. Duthie (Edinburgh: Published for the University of Aberdeen by Oliver and Boyd, 1964), 113.

argue that "the Quarto is the work of a shorthand note-taker," Duthie's *Elizabethan Shorthand* largely silenced any such claims.[32]

After Chambers's authoritative study of *William Shakespeare* in 1930, the "bad" quarto and "memorial reconstruction" theories remained largely unchallenged in their broad outlines for roughly half a century. Summing up in a few sentences a critical territory on which much ink and scholarly ingenuity was spent inevitably results in simplifications. It is certainly true that there was considerable argument as to what exactly was memorially reconstructed, by whom, and to what purpose. A reference work such as F. E. Halliday's *Shakespeare Companion* can give a good impression, however, of how entrenched the orthodoxy had become. The six Shakespearean "bad" quartos, Halliday wrote, "were reconstructed from memory by one or more actors who had played minor parts in a London production, and tried to reproduce the play for a provincial performance. This theory is generally accepted."[33] Period. With the orthodoxy thus in place, "memorial reconstruction" became an explanation with which scholars tried to account for textual features of a growing number of early modern playtexts, a number that, by the 1990s, reached a total of more than forty.[34]

The most important implication of Greg's "memorial reconstruction" theory is that the text so diagnosed is recognized as derivative rather than original, a *re*-construction rather than an early draft. Previously, the dominant view of the "bad" quartos had been that they were Shakespeare's early drafts. So even though printed first, the "bad" quarto was basically written after and was dependent on the later "good" text(s). At a time when the

---

[32] H. T. Price, *The Text of "Henry V"* (Newcastle-under-Lyme: Mandley & Unett, 1920), 20; George Ian Duthie, *Elizabethan Shorthand and the First Quarto of "King Lear"* (Oxford: Blackwell, 1949). (On the subject of stenography and English Renaissance plays, see also G. N. Giordano-Orsini, "Thomas Heywood's Play on 'The Troubles of Queen Elizabeth,'" *The Library*, 4th series, 14 (1933–34), 313–38; W. Matthews, "Shorthand and the Bad Shakespeare Quartos," *Modern Language Review*, 27 (1932), 243–62, and 28 (1933), 81–83; W. Matthews, "Shakespeare and the Reporters," *The Library*, 4th series, 15 (1934–35), 481–98; and I. A. Shapiro, "Stenography and 'Bad Quartos,'" *The Times Literary Supplement*, May 13, 1960, 305.) Consequently, Steven Urkowitz, in 1980, could assert that "it has been conclusively proven and universally accepted that no technique of stenography known in England in 1608 was capable of transcribing anything as difficult as a play" (*Revision of "King Lear,"* 7). As mentioned above, Adele Davidson has since returned to the question, however, and has cautiously concluded that "some person may have copied Q *Pericles* and/or Q *Lear* using (at least a few) techniques of short-writing, and thus may have influenced the printer's copy for these plays" ("Shakespeare and Stenography Reconsidered," 94).

[33] F. E. Halliday, *A Shakespeare Companion, 1564–1964* (Harmondsworth, Middlesex: Penguin Books, 1964), 49. In the entry on "reported texts," Halliday writes that these plays "are generally admitted to have been reconstructed from memory for provincial performance by actors who had taken part in the plays in London. The prompt-book thus put together was sometimes sold to a stationer for publication. This, briefly, is the probable history of the six 'bad' Quartos of Shakespeare's plays" (408).

[34] Maguire, *Suspect Texts*, 227–322.

central aim of editing was the best-possible recovery of a final authorial intention represented by a definitive text to be analyzed by the critics, the text's derivative nature alone militated strongly against taking the "bad" quartos seriously.

Taking for granted that substantially uncut texts were performed in the London theaters, scholars from Greg to Harold Jenkins argued that the "bad" quartos are versions "acted by a company touring in the country."[35] This topologic marginalization went hand in hand with a more general critical and editorial marginalization of the "bad" quartos. Once their badness had been identified, they could be discarded from consideration altogether. Again, it is Greg who had set the tone in his edition of *The Merry Wives of Windsor*, writing: "The playhouse thief reveals himself in every scene, corrupting, mutilating, rewriting," and "there is everywhere gross corruption, constant mutilation, meaningless inversion and clumsy transposition," a judgment Chambers took over in word and many others in spirit.[36]

Since it has long been generally recognized that the "bad" quartos record features that derive from performance, the importance of those features has been increasingly acknowledged even by those who have kept marginalizing the texts as a whole. The following comment on *Hamlet* by one of the leading Shakespeare critics is typical of the status the "bad" quartos still widely enjoy: "Q1 is a classic bad quarto, based on actors' memorial reconstruction. It is useful in certain respects because it derives from the theatre. From it we know, for instance, that in at least one early production the mad Ophelia entered 'playing on a lute, and her hair down, singing.' But since it does not derive from Shakespeare's script, I shall set Q1 aside."[37]

The theory of memorial reconstruction first came under attack from an offshoot of the scholarship that reconsidered the possibility of Shakespeare having revised his own plays. This theory, we remember, had had many adherents in the nineteenth century. It was revived in the 1960s by Ernst Honigmann who investigated "the possibilities of authorial 'second thoughts' *before* its delivery to the actors," resulting in "two copies of a play, each in the author's hand, disagreeing in both substantive and indifferent readings."[38] In the 1970s and 1980s, the authorial revision debate centered around *King Lear* which many scholars came to recognize as extant

---

[35] Greg, *First Folio*, 300.
[36] Greg, ed., *Merry Wives*, xxvi–xxvii. For Chambers, see *William Shakespeare*, 1.429.
[37] Jonathan Bate, "Shakespeare's Tragedies As Working Scripts," *Critical Survey*, 3 (1991), 122.
[38] Honigmann, *Stability*, 2.

in two substantially different authorial versions.[39] As Greg's argument for memorial reconstruction had created a search for evermore memorially reconstructed plays, so the theory of an authorially revised *Lear* triggered a reconsideration of Shakespeare's possible revision of several other plays.

As part of this reconsideration, the possibility that the "bad" quartos in fact represent first versions which authorial revision turned into the longer and better known plays was again examined.[40] As recent scholarship makes clear, however, powerful arguments militate against this scenario. The derivative nature of most of the "bad" quartos is strongly suggested by passages whose sense only becomes entirely clear after a comparison with the "good" text.[41] More generally, whosoever advocates that a text like Q1 *Hamlet* is an early authorial version must face the objection that it often consists of a linguistic texture that is difficult to reconcile with Shakespeare's language elsewhere. As Sidney Thomas has pointed out:

> To accept feeble or incoherent verse as truly Shakespearean is to reveal a basic incomprehension of Shakespeare's achievement as a poetic dramatist. It is in the attempt to bypass or equivocate away the gross corruptions of language in Q1 that the theory of Shakespearean revision, even enlargement, of *Hamlet*, falls apart.[42]

---

[39] See Michael Warren, "Albany and Edgar," 95–107; Urkowitz, *Revision of King Lear*; Gary Taylor and Michael Warren, eds., *The Division of the Kingdoms* (Oxford: Clarendon Press, 1983). Note, though, that Paul Werstine ("Folio Editors, Folio Compositors, and the Folio Text of *King Lear*," in *The Division of the Kingdoms*, eds. Taylor and Warren, 247–312) argued against authorial revision, a position he has reiterated in "The Textual Mystery of *Hamlet*," *Shakespeare Quarterly*, 39 (1988), 2n.

[40] Steven Urkowitz has been a particularly influential advocate of Shakespeare's revision of the "bad" quartos. See his " 'Well-sayd olde Mole': Burying Three *Hamlets* in Modern Editions," in *Shakespeare Study Today*, ed. Georgianna Ziegler (New York: AMS Press, 1986), 37–70; " 'If I Mistake in Those Foundations Which I Build Upon': Peter Alexander's Textual Analysis of *Henry VI Parts 2 and 3*," *English Literary Renaissance*, 18 (1988), 230–56; "Good News about 'Bad' Quartos," in *"Bad" Shakespeare: Revaluations of the Shakespeare Canon*, ed. Maurice Charney (Rutherford, N.J.: Fairleigh Dickinson University Press; London and Toronto: Associated University Presses, 1988), 189–206; "Back to Basics," 257–91. That Q1 *Hamlet* is an authorial first draft has also been argued by Y. S. Bains, "The Incidence of Corrupt Passages in the First Quarto of Shakespeare's *Hamlet*," *Notes & Queries*, 40 (1993), 186–92; and Eric Sams, "Taboo or Not Taboo? The Text, Dating and Authorship of *Hamlet*, 1589–1623," *Hamlet Studies*, 10 (1988), 12–46. Among the other advocates of the "bad" quartos is Randall McLeod (alias Random Cloud) who has analyzed the impact of "terminology that has such overt and prejudicial connotations" upon the scholarly treatment the "bad" quartos have received ("The Marriage of Good and Bad Quartos," *Shakespeare Quarterly*, 33 (1982), 421–31, 421).

[41] Chapter 5 (95–114) on "Revision" in Irace's *Reforming the "Bad" Quartos* develops a number of obstacles to belief in the theory that the "bad" quartos were Shakespearean first versions. She concludes that "for the six short quartos, differences between the short and the longer versions point to other agents than Shakespeare's revising hand" (114). See also Robert E. Burkhart, *Shakespeare's Bad Quartos* (The Hague: Mouton, 1975), and, among earlier scholars, Alfred Hart, *Stolne and Surreptitious Copies*, 170–221.

[42] Sidney Thomas, "*Hamlet* Q1: First Version of Bad Quarto?," in *The "Hamlet" First Published*, ed. Clayton, 251.

All in all, the view of authorial revision as the principal alternative to memorial reconstruction has not been the decisive factor in the investigation of the multiple origins the "bad" quartos can have.[43]

More convincing challenges to the theory of memorial reconstruction have arisen from other quarters since the 1990s. Some of these challenges have subjected to close scrutiny the arguments that supported New Bibliographical orthodoxy. Paul Werstine and Laurie Maguire have shown to what extent the spread of "memorial reconstruction" has depended upon scholarly narratives that took on a life of their own in the course of the twentieth century, narratives that at times had no more than a tenuous relationship to what bibliographical methods allow to ascertain. After an investigation of the grounds upon which *Romeo and Juliet*, *Henry V*, and *Hamlet* (among others) have been diagnosed as memorial reconstructions, Werstine has argued that "twentieth-century Shakespeare textual criticism has not been able to maintain the memorial-reconstruction hypothesis on the basis of qualitative evidence."[44]

Similarly, Laurie Maguire's study of *Shakespearean Suspect Texts* attempts to show to what extent scholars have been content to have recourse to the label "memorial reconstruction" when no other easy explanation was found. Having drawn on a variety of sources to investigate "the textual effects of memory," Maguire goes on to examine both suspect and non-suspect dramatic texts for features that have often been taken as symptomatic of memorial reconstruction such as repetition, insertion, transposition, plot inconsistencies, aural errors, and reduced casting.[45] Few of these, she concludes, have much value in determining whether or not a dramatic text is the result of a memorial reconstruction. After subjecting to scrutiny all the forty-one plays (or parts of plays) that had been diagnosed as memorial reconstructions, Maguire believes that more than three-quarters of these plays are not, and only a handful of plays are likely to be, memorial reconstructions. Of the plays I am concerned with in this chapter, Maguire holds that Q1 *Hamlet* may or may not have been memorially reconstructed but is confident that Q1 *Romeo and Juliet* and *Henry V* have not.[46]

---

[43] It seems to me possible, however, that authorial revision provides at least a partial explanation for what turned the texts behind *1 Contention* and *Richard Duke of York* into *2* and *3 Henry VI*. See, for instance, Roger Warren, "The Quarto and Folio Texts of *2 Henry VI*: A Reconsideration," *The Review of English Studies*, 51 (2000), 193–207.

[44] Paul Werstine, "A Century of 'Bad' Shakespeare Quartos," *Shakespeare Quarterly*, 50 (1999), 327.

[45] Maguire, *Suspect Texts*, 95–148, 151–225.

[46] Ibid., 324–25. Note, however, that *The Merry Wives of Windsor* may well be a memorial reconstruction (Maguire, *Suspect Texts*, 285–86).

To these doubts about memorial reconstruction as an explanation for the genesis of Shakespeare's "bad" quartos, Peter Blayney and Scott McMillin have added plausible suggestions about the origins of these texts that do not rely on the traditional narratives. McMillin has considered the possibility that "English Renaissance play-books may have been produced after rehearsal, for both 'good' and 'bad' quartos, with actors slowly running through their lines for a scribe."[47] In such a scenario, the difference between "good" and "bad" becomes a matter of how closely the lines dictated by the actors corresponded to the authorial manuscript. The correspondence may be close because lines were dictated from an authorial manuscript or faithfully transcribed actors' parts. Alternatively, it may be less close because various other agents intervened.

Quoting Moseley's statement in the prefatory material to the 1647 "Beaumont and Fletcher" Folio that, "When these *Comedies* and *Tragedies* were presented on the Stage, the *Actours* omitted some Scenes and Passages (with the *Author's* consent) as occasion led them; and when private friends desir'd a Copy, they then (and justly too) transcribed what they *Acted*,"[48] Blayney has advanced a similar suggestion:

As I understand the passage, Moseley is expecting someone to object (because "everyone knows") that plays were usually and markedly abridged for performance, and that when actors made copies for their friends they wrote down what had been spoken onstage. No texts of that inferior kind, he boasts, will be found in *his* book. What he seems to be referring to, then, – texts of a kind so familiar that someone is bound to bring them up unless he forestalls the objection – are performance texts written down by actors who took part in them. The quality of such texts would vary greatly (both from each other and from scene to scene within a single text), depending on the infinitely variable circumstances of their origins...What Moseley has been trying to tell us since 1647 is, I believe, the commonplace and innocent origin of the kind of text that Pollard called Bad Quarto – but we have been too busy chasing imaginary pirates to listen.[49]

We have seen in chapter 6 that several private transcripts from which "some Scenes and Passages" had been omitted – such as the surviving manuscripts of *Beggars' Bush* and *The Woman's Prize* – reflect quite faithfully the texts that were later printed (with the exception of the missing lines). Yet other manuscripts, including the ones from which some of the "bad" quartos were set up, may well have borne a different relationship to the authorial manuscripts. Moseley's words and the number of extant private transcripts

---

[47] At a seminar on "The Language of the So Called 'Bad' Quartos" held at the 1996 International Shakespeare Conference, as reported by Jill L. Levenson, ed. *Romeo and Juliet*, The Oxford Shakespeare (Oxford University Press, 2000), 125.

[48] Greg, *Bibliography*, III.1233.   [49] Blayney, "Publication of Playbooks," 393–94.

of "Beaumont and Fletcher" plays suggest that private transcripts had become widespread by the 1640s. The absence of such material witnesses from Shakespeare's time suggests that they were less common and probably more improvised in the late sixteenth and early seventeenth centuries.

Blayney and McMillin's theories take us beyond what Werstine has called the "twentieth-century critical absorption with arresting a particular actor and charging him with producing a 'bad' quarto."[50] In this, they usefully revise New Bibliographical orthodoxy in which one narrative – actor(s) performing in the play memorially reconstructs the text for/of performances in the provinces – accounted for most if not all the suspect texts. Considering the wide range of linguistic and dramatic textures among the Shakespearean "bad" quartos – from the "jerky and pedestrian" *Merry Wives* to the "grammatically intact, smooth, and well developed" *Henry V* – any single narrative that claims to explain the origins of the entire group of plays traditionally labeled "the bad" quartos is likely to be wrong.[51] The formerly established view that all Shakespearean "bad" quartos are memorial reconstructions is, in fact, equally as doubtful as the claim, at the other end of the scale, that they are all early drafts.

What, then, are the advantages Blayney and McMillin's suggestions have over the traditional explanation? Firstly, they do not depend upon what I will argue to be an implausible link between our three "bad" quartos and the provinces. Secondly, they do not rely upon a single or a small number of reporters (e.g. "Marcellus") responsible for the entire text with all the other actors apparently unwilling or unable to contribute toward it. Consequently, their suggestions do not depend upon the prodigious memory of actors allegedly able to reproduce more or less verbatim long speeches they did not directly witness on stage (more of which below). Allowing for the "infinitely variable circumstances of their origins," they do not rule out the possibility that the actors had recourse to their "parts." When investigating the genesis of Q1 *Henry V*, Chambers considered the possibility that in the case of the actors playing Exeter, Gower, and the Governor of Harfleur (traditional contenders for the role of "memorial reporters") "the 'part'...may have been available."[52] Plausible as such a scenario is in the case of *Henry V* or some other of the "bad" quartos, it does not seem to have been given its due by later scholars. It is clearly among

[50] Werstine, "Narratives," 80.   [51] Maguire, *Suspect Texts*, 257, 285.

[52] Chambers, *William Shakespeare*, 1.391. Chambers was partly following H. T. Price, who not only suggested that the parts of Gower and the Governor of Harfleur had been supplied, but also made the intriguing point that the Governor's lines – prefixed by "*Gouer.*" in both the quarto and the Folio texts – may have been inadvertently included by a scribe in Gower's part (Price, *Text of "Henry V,"* 19).

the "infinitely variable circumstances," however, allowed for by Blayney and McMillin.

The "bad" quartos have been linked to the provinces in one of two ways, depending on whether the texts are believed to be records *of* or *for* provincial performances. The former contention need not detain us long. As has been pertinently asked: "Are we, then, to believe that all reporters knew only provincial versions?"[53] The latter position has proved longer-lived and has been advocated by Gary Taylor, Stanley Wells, Robert Burkhart, Michael J. B. Allen, and Kenneth Muir among others.[54] The grounds on which the "bad" quartos get confined to the provinces are questionable, however. Writing about Q1 *Henry V*, Gary Taylor finds it "difficult to imagine why such an abridgement would have been performed anywhere but in the provinces, especially as certain alterations presume a less sophisticated audience."[55] Yet the denigration of provincial audiences – a denigration with a long history – seems to be based on prejudice rather than on firm evidence. These allegedly unsophisticated provincial audiences were in fact often the same, as Maguire reminds us, as those who, not long ago, had performed and watched extremely long and theologically complex mystery cycles.[56] Her reminder that audiences in provincial towns "may have been relatively sophisticated" is pertinent, and we can be sure that noble households such as Pembroke's at Wilton were even more so.[57]

Another argument with which the "bad" quartos have been confined to the provinces is that they are designed for a reduced cast. Robert Burkhart, for instance, argued that "the bad quartos are the result of deliberate abridgments, made by a member of the acting company, for the purpose of permitting a play to be performed in the provinces by a smaller-than-normal company."[58] Yet such a hypothesis raises several questions: if the sole purpose of the reworking had been to make possible performance by a reduced cast, then why would the whole text have been reworked? Why would the number of actors have been reduced, in one scene from seventeen to thirteen, if a minimum of eighteen are required in another scene?[59] And why would speeches have been abridged for performance by a reduced cast in

---

[53] Burkhart, *Shakespeare's Bad Quartos*, 21.

[54] "It may well be that all the bad quartos were abridgments for touring purposes" (Allen and Muir, eds., *Shakespeare's Plays in Quarto*, xiv). Q1 *Henry V* is called a "memorial reconstruction for provincial tour" in Wells, Taylor, et al., *Textual Companion*, 375; see also page 28.

[55] Stanley Wells, *Modernizing Shakespeare's Spelling*, with Gary Taylor, *Three Studies in the Text of "Henry"* (Oxford: Clarendon Press, 1979), 110.

[56] See Maguire, *Suspect Texts*, 6.   [57] Ibid.

[58] Burkhart, *Shakespeare's Bad Quartos*, 23.

[59] The figures are taken from Burkhart's chart with the number of "Required Actors" in *The First Part of the Contention* (the "bad" quarto of *2 Henry VI*). See *Shakespeare's Bad Quartos*, 33–34.

the provinces but not in London? In the case of *Hamlet*, Scott McMillin has disposed of this argument by showing that the "bad" quarto takes in fact more, not fewer, actors to perform than the "good," second quarto.[60]

In *Three Studies in the Text of "Henry V,"* Taylor similarly argued that "The 1600 Quarto of *Henry V* is a corrupt, memorially reconstructed text of...a deliberate adaptation of the play designed for a cast of eleven."[61] Taylor worked out an extremely detailed casting pattern, based on the two assumptions that any character is played by the same actor thoughout the performance and that an actor doubling in two parts must be allowed sufficient time to change costume.[62] It has rightly been pointed out, however, that the latter assumption may be flawed, and, more seriously, that Taylor breaks both of his rules when they do not fit his argument.[63] Taylor's evidence seems strained.

Kathleen Irace has argued on different grounds that the manuscript underlying the first quarto of *Henry V* is a memorial reconstruction and was designed "as a promptbook for use in performances outside London."[64] She holds that the version the reporters knew was not an abridgement but a script linked directly to the Folio.[65] In her analysis of Q1 *Hamlet*, she arrives at the same conclusion. Her case against abridgement chiefly depends upon the fact that the proportion of the reporters' Folio lines in the quarto texts is significantly higher than what the relative length of the "bad" quartos compared to the Folio texts leads one to suppose. With regards to *Henry V*, she writes that:

Exeter's part in Q retains some 84% of his Folio lines with considerable accuracy, as noted above, while all 13 of Scrope's Folio lines and all seven of the Governor's reappear with equal accuracy. The Quarto, with 1629 spoken lines, includes only 50% as many lines as does the Folio (3253 lines). If the reporters had known only an abridgment, their lines presumably would have been cut in such an abridgment in roughly the same proportion as the rest of the play. (Irace, "Reconstruction and Adaptation," 233)

Concerning *Hamlet*, Irace similarly comments that "the proportion of lines in Marcellus's role suggests that Q1 *Hamlet* also stemmed directly from a version linked to the Folio: Q1 *Hamlet* is less than 60 percent as long as F,

[60] Scott McMillin, "Casting the *Hamlet* Quartos: The Limit of Eleven," in *The "Hamlet" First Published*, ed. Clayton, 179–94.

[61] Taylor, *Text of "Henry V,"* 72.   [62] Ibid., 72–73.

[63] See Paul Werstine's review of Taylor's study in *Shakespeare Studies*, 16 (1983), 382–91. Werstine refers to Bevington (*"Mankind" to Marlowe*, 97–98) for evidence of actors leaving the stage at the end of a scene and reentering as a different character at the beginning of the next scene.

[64] Irace, "Reconstruction and Adaptation in Q *Henry V,*" *Studies in Bibliography*, 44 (1991), 249.

[65] See ibid., 228–53.

yet Marcellus's role in Q1 retains 92 percent of its length in F – with more than 90 percent of these lines closely corresponding in the two versions."[66]

Even if we assume for the moment that memory is the primary agent behind these two "bad" quartos, Irace's conclusions do not seem warranted by her data. Not only much of Marcellus's part but, more generally, much of the scenes in which he appears survive in the first quarto. These scenes contain the play's exposition – in which a lot of information is communicated in little time – and the Ghost's appearances. In other words, the material in which Marcellus appears is either essential for the audience's understanding of the plot or eminently stage-worthy. Understandably, when the play was prepared for the stage, comparatively little seems to have been deleted.

When it comes to *Henry V*, Irace suggests that there were three reporters, "the actor playing Exeter, along with the actors playing Pistol and Gower, doubling Nym, Scrope and possibly the Governor and York."[67] According to her own count, the total number of Folio lines spoken by these characters is 403 (412 with the Governor and York), the number of quarto lines 322 (331).[68] The cut material among the alleged reporters thus amounts to a total of eighty-one lines, or 19.7 (20.1 with the Governor and York) percent. If we subtract the same percentage of lines from the Folio text (3,166 in Hart's count), we are left with 2,530 (2,542) lines. If, perhaps more accurately, we consider that the Chorus (223 lines) was cut in its entirety and thus subtract 20.1 (19.7) percent from the remaining Folio text (i.e. 2,943 lines), we are left with 2,351 (with "the Governor" and "York": 2,363) lines. Far from suggesting that "the reporters attempted to reconstruct a version similar to the Folio," Irace's own figures indicate that the text the reporters would have tried to recover had approximately 2,400 or 2,500 lines. These figures correspond surprisingly well to those Chambers arrived at in 1930: "the omissions of Q point to a performance for which much of the F text had been 'cut' . . . Cutting may be estimated to have reduced the 3381 lines of the play by about 1000, making a performance in two instead of three hours possible."[69]

Taking seriously Irace's belief that an abridgement of *Henry V* would normally be of a length that is shorter than the Folio text by about the same proportion as the most faithfully reported lines therefore does not necessarily lead to the conclusion she advances. It is true, however, that at 1,623 lines, the first quarto of *Henry V is* very short. The play's brevity even raises the question of whether it is, in any straightforward way, an authoritative

[66] Irace, *Reforming the "Bad" Quartos*, 123.   [67] Irace, "Reconstruction and Adaptation," 233.
[68] Ibid., 250–51.   [69] Chambers, *William Shakespeare*, 1.391–92.

text "closely based on the Shakespeare company's own performance script of the play," as Gurr suggests. It may well be more accurate to argue that the authoritative performance script is what the first quarto imperfectly recovers.[70] This would make sense of a number of textual features for which Gurr's theory does not fully account. In 1.2, for instance, Q1 *Henry V* omits eight Folio lines before continuing with "Daughter to *Charles*, the foresaid Duke of *Lorain*" (A2ʳ). As the Duke of Lorain is mentioned in the Folio lines which Q1 omits but in no other preceding quarto line, Q1's "foresaid" only makes sense if we assume that the preceding passage has been omitted accidentally. It may well be that when the manuscript underlying Q1 was put together, the stage abridgement Shakespeare and his fellows performed was further shortened.

Confining the "bad" quartos to the provinces, the above arguments seem ultimately problematic. More generally, it seems worthwhile pointing out how uneconomic the hypothesis is that dramatic scripts were routinely modified and abridged when actors went on tour. Research carried out as part of the Canadian REED (Records of Early English Drama) project has unearthed the extent to which touring was an integral part of otherwise London-based companies.[71] Actors, performing six different plays within a week and up to fifteen per month with little time for rehearsal had surely other things to worry about than to try to keep two versions of a role apart.[72] Anyone who has performed on stage must be aware of the difficulty of changing a part one has assimilated. To do so routinely with the number of parts an Elizabethan player had to know would have been an impossible strain on even well-trained memories. It would no doubt have constituted an important source of misrememberings and confusions on stage every time the players were required to switch (as they regularly would have been) from provincial to London versions. This is not to argue for theatrical texts as more fixed entities than they undoubtedly were. There is sufficient evidence suggesting that plays were revived, abridged, adapted, revised, and provided with additions or topical insertions. Yet, to acknowledge that many playtexts underwent manifold changes in the course of their theatrical history is not the same as to argue that players who were burdened with a great many different parts at any one time would have chosen for no obvious reason to assimilate alternative, abridged parts, too. Adaptation

---

[70] See also my review of Gurr's edition in *Cahiers Elisabéthains*, 59 (2001), 141–44.

[71] See also Siobhan Keenan's recent *Travelling Players in Shakespeare's England* (London and New York: Palgrave, 2002).

[72] According to Henslowe's diary, the Lord Strange's Men performed fifteen different plays in March 1592 and the same number in the following month. See Carson, *Companion to Henslowe's Diary*, 85.

for touring in the provinces is an uneconomic scholarly hypothesis about what would have been an uneconomic theatrical practice.

The scenarios imagined by Blayney and McMillin have the additional advantage of not depending upon incredible feats of memorization on the part of the reporters. Laurie Maguire has usefully raised what should really be a preliminary question to any study of a text supposed to be a memorial reconstruction: "what standards of memorial/textual accuracy did Shakespeare expect of his actors on the Elizabethan stage?" She writes that "a transitory culture, with 'secondary' or 'residual' orality, such as that of the Elizabethans, might conceivably aim for memorisation, but be satisfied with remembering. Authors, in other words, might be content to have actors and printers make free with their lines within certain limits."[73] We may be confident that the Elizabethans did not value textual fidelity the way we do in our firmly print-based culture today. In relation to Q1 *Henry V*, the question this raises is whether much of the "remembering" is not simply too good to be just that. Here, for example, is the beginning of Pistol's night-time encounter with the disguised King (4.1 in modern editions) as recorded in the first quarto:

> PIST. Ke ve la?
> KING. A friend.
> PIST. Discus vnto me, art thou Gentleman?
>   Or art thou common, base, and popeler?
> KING. No sir, I am a Gentleman of a Company.
> PIST. Trailes thou the puissant pike?
> KING. Euen so sir. What are you?
> PIST. As good a gentleman as the Emperour.
> KING. O then thou art better then the King?
> PIST. The kings a bago, and a hart of gold.
> PIST. A lad of life, an impe of fame:
>   Of parents good, of fist most valiant:
>   I kis his durtie shoe: and from my hart strings
>   I loue the louely bully. What is thy name?
> KING. *Harry* le Roy.   (D3ᵛ)

The Folio edition of 1623 prints the same passage with very few alterations:

PIST. *Che vous la?*
KING. A friend.
PIST. Discusse vnto me, art thou Officer, or art thou base, common, and popular?

73 Maguire, *Suspect Texts*, 146–48.

KING. I am a Gentleman of a Company.
PIST. Trayl'st thou the puissant Pyke?
KING. Euen so: what are you?
PIST. As good a Gentleman as the Emperor.
KING. Then you are a better then the King.
PIST. The King's a Bawcock, and a Heart of Gold, a Lad of Life, an Impe of
  Fame, of Parents good, of Fist most valiant: I kisse his durtie shooe, and from
  heart-string I loue the louely Bully. What is thy Name?
KING. *Harry le Roy.* (i2ʳ)

None of the traditional reporters advocated by Chambers, Duthie, and
Taylor is on stage during this sequence.[74] In the Folio edition, Pistol asks
the King if he is an "Officer" rather than a "Gentleman" and uses "thou"
instead of the more formal "you," while the quarto adds a few relatively
unimportant words ("No sir," "O," "my"). Apart from this, both texts
render, or recognizably try to render, exactly the same words. This seems
simply too accurate to reflect what players who worried little about precise textual accuracy would have remembered without themselves having
spoken (or even witnessed) the words on stage.

  As long ago as 1910, Greg pointed out that in Shakespeare's time, "there
were no consecutive runs to fix the dialogue in the minds of the actors,"
and that it is therefore "a legitimate surmise that the [actors] were far from
perfect in their parts." Greg imagined that instead actors "were quick at
substituting a passable makeshift if the actual words of the author eluded
their memory."[75] Leah Marcus has refined this idea, reminding us that
"Medieval literature culture had recognized two forms of memory: *memoria
ad res* and *memoria ad verba*, with a memory for the gist of a speech or written
passage frequently valued more highly than word-for-word memory."[76] Far
from being a "makeshift" solution, remembering the essence rather than
memorizing verbatim may have been an acceptable and economic solution
for actors who performed many parts in many plays with little time to
rehearse.[77] Such a form of memory would provide a plausible explanation
for some of the differences between "bad" and "good" texts. Here, for

---

[74] See Chambers, *William Shakespeare*, 1.391, Duthie, "Quarto of Shakespeare's *Henry V*," 106–30,
  and Taylor, *Text of "Henry V,"* 129–42.
[75] Greg, ed., *Merry Wives*, xl–xli.   [76] Marcus, *Unediting the Renaissance*, 160.
[77] For instance, it has been shown that for Thomas Dekker and Michael Drayton's *Civil Wars: Part
  One*, the only time the actors may have spent on learning their parts and rehearsing the play would
  have been the mornings between October 22 and November 4, 1598. See Peter Thomson, "Rogues
  and Rhetoricians: Acting Styles in Early English Drama," in *A New History of Early English Drama*,
  eds. Cox and Kastan, 324. For a comprehensive survey of the evidence and the conclusion that there
  was very little group rehearsal in Shakespeare's time, see Tiffany Stern, *Rehearsal from Shakespeare
  to Sheridan* (Oxford and New York: Clarendon Press, 2000).

instance, are the two versions of a speech by the nurse in *Romeo and Juliet* (4.5 in modern editions):

NUR: ...What lambe, what Lady birde? fast I warrant. What I*uliet* [*sic*]? Well, let the County take you in your bed, yee sleepe for a weeke now, but the next night, the Countie *Paris* hath set vp his rest that you shal rest but little. What lambe I say, fast still: what Lady, Loue, what bride, what I*uliet* [*sic*]? Gods me how sound she sleeps? Nay then I see I must wake you indeed. Whats heere, laide on your bed, drest in your cloathes and down, ah me, alack the day, some Aqua vitæ hoe. (Q1, 11ᵛ)

> NUR. Mistris, what mistris, *Iuliet*, fast I warrant her she,
> Why Lambe, why Lady, fie you sluggabed,
> Why Loue I say, Madam, sweete heart, why Bride:
> What not a word, you take your penniworths now,
> Sleepe for a weeke, for the next night I warrant
> The Countie *Paris* hath set vp his rest,
> That you shall rest but little, God forgiue me.
> Marrie and Amen: how sound is she a sleepe:
> I needs must wake her: Madam, Madam, Madam,
> I, let the Countie take you in your bed,
> Heele fright you vp yfaith, will it not be?
> What drest, and in your clothes, and downe again?
> I must needs wake you, Lady, Lady, Lady,
> Alas, alas, helpe, helpe, my Ladyes dead.
> Oh weraday that euer I was borne,
> Some Aqua-vitæ ho, my Lord my Lady.   (Q2, K2ʳ)

Q2's speech is set in verse while Q1 has prose. Whereas the nurse speaks 137 words in Q2, she only has ninety-six in Q1. Contrary to many other passages in the play, no single passage in Q2 is totally absent from Q1. Yet, even though most of Q2's verses partly survive in Q1, the latter text does not adhere to Q2's order. Q1's initial "lambe" does not occur in Q2 until line two. "[L]et the County take you in your bed" comes early on in Q1, but has its Q2 equivalent as late as line ten. "What lambe I say, fast still," which comes half-way through Q1's speech, takes up, transforms and repeats material from lines one and two in Q2. The nurse's determination to wake up Juliet and her discovery, on drawing the curtains, that Juliet is fully dressed, are present in both texts, but the order is reversed. And so on.

It is difficult to imagine either Shakespeare – revising his manuscript, possibly while undertaking the stage abridgement of his overlong original manuscript – or anyone else turning the Q2 passage into that in Q1. Abridgement does not seem to account for the difference. Why, otherwise, would Q1 repeat matter ("fast I warrant," "fast still") which Q2 only has once? Nor does Q1 in any way seem more stage-worthy. For instance, Q2's "Lady, Lady, Lady," a potentially powerful theatrical moment in which the nurse realizes that Juliet is not asleep, is precisely absent from Q1. Nor does a comparison of the two texts make clear what would have motivated the rearrangement of verbal material that seems in perfectly reasonable order. The changes thus do not seem to be of the kind Honigmann described when imagining Shakespeare as "an author so unconceited with himself and so fluent that little verbal changes, not necessarily always for the better, ran quite freely from his pen when the process of copying refired his mind."[78] If we imagine Shakespeare or someone else turning the nurse's speech in Q2 into that in Q1, considerable effort would have gone into what is in no conceivable way a worthwhile improvement.

If we recall McMillin and Blayney's scenario of "actors slowly running through their lines for a scribe" or of actors making copies for their friends, it is easy to imagine that the actor playing the nurse simply dictated a version of what he had spoken on stage. He might have done so either because he did not have his part ready to hand or because he did not think it worthwhile or necessary to consult it. Others, whose parts are better remembered, may either have remembered their lines in greater detail or may have had recourse to their parts. What the nurse's speech seems to suggest is that the actor never tried to memorize the speech in a way we know from modern practices. In the standard narrative governing the theory of memorial reconstruction, it was assumed that actors remembered their own parts with great accuracy and that a marked difference in a character's lines between "good" and "bad" text is evidence of other actors trying to recall his lines. While this may have happened at times, it is equally possible that the actors' attitudes toward textual fidelity was such that considerable variation from the corresponding "good" text need not imply a failing memory. As Laurie Maguire has put it, "in seeking evidence of faulty memory in a suspect text we should perhaps view it not as memorial error but as memorial variation."[79] "Bad" quarto language that does not match its counterpart in the "good" text may thus often reflect a version of what the players spoke on stage.

This possibility finds support in contemporary complaints about actors departing from their text of which Hamlet's well-known admonition to the players is by no means the only example. In Richard Brome's *The Antipodes* (1638, publ. 1640), a player is accused of "Tak[ing] licence to your selfe, to adde unto / Your parts, your owne free fancy; and sometimes / To

---

[78] Honigmann, *Stability*, 3.   [79] Maguire, *Suspect Texts*, 148.

alter, or diminish what the writer / With care and skill compos'd" (D3ᵛ).⁸⁰
According to a prefatory note to Thomas Hughes's *The Misfortunes of
Arthur* (1587), the text is printed "as it was presented, excepting certaine
wordes, and lines, where some of the Actors either helped their memories
by brief omission: or fitted their acting by some alteration" (•4ᵛ). Thomas
Nabbes's preface to *The Bride* (1640) implies that the players discarded some
of his words and added some of theirs.⁸¹ Thomas Dekker's preface to *The
Whore of Babylon*, finally, laments that the play's language is "made lame
by the [players'] bad handling" (A2ᵛ). These references lend plausibility
to the suggestion that some of the differences between "good" and "bad"
quartos may be accounted for by how players performed their own parts
rather than by what the memorial reporters remembered of their fellows'
parts.

As the traditional memorial actor-reporters fail to account for much
textual data, we will do well to broaden our view of what may have gone
into the making of the "bad" quartos. Complicating our beliefs about the
actors' attitude toward (or understanding of) textual fidelity may be one
way of doing so. Another way is to remember that considerable differences
between two manuscripts may result from the scribes' attitude toward textual accuracy. Like the actors', this attitude is likely to have been relatively
lax. There is one scribe, Ralph Crane, about whom quite a bit is known.
He was employed as a copyist by the King's Men, though probably not before Shakespeare's death.⁸² The various extant manuscripts of Middleton's
A Game at Chess allow the conclusion that "Crane substituted synonyms
and changed words of small significance in making two transcripts from
the same copy." Philip Oxley has concluded that "a major characteristic of
Crane as a copyist is his tendency to make small changes," and that he was
"more concerned to present an attractive copy than one entirely faithful
to his original."⁸³ It may well be that Crane's attitude was not exceptional
among scribes who produced manuscript copies of plays. Dealing with
the close correspondence between the parts of Marcellus, Lucianus, and
the Prologue in Q1 and Folio *Hamlet*, Kathleen Irace wrote that "minor

---

⁸⁰ For this and the following examples, I am indebted to Richard Levin's article, "Performance-Critics
vs Close Readers in the Study of English Renaissance Drama," *Modern Language Review*, 81 (1986),
545–59, esp. 553.
⁸¹ According to the preface, the text is: "is here drest according to mine owne desire and intention;
without ought taken from her that my selfe thought ornament; nor supplyed with any thing which
I valued but as rags" (A3ʳ⁻ᵛ).
⁸² See T. H. Howard-Hill, *Ralph Crane and Some Shakespeare First Folio Comedies* (Charlottesville:
University Press of Virginia, 1972).
⁸³ *A Critical Edition of John Fletcher's "The Humorous Lieutenant,"* ed. Philip Oxley, The Renaissance
Imagination, 24 (New York: Garland, 1987), 13.

discrepancies...suggest that the lines were recalled rather than copied."[84] Such a view does not seem to take full account of scribal practices in the early seventeenth century.

As many Elizabethan actors may well have been far from word-perfect, it is difficult to adhere to the argument – implied by the advocates of memorial reconstruction – that the reporters remembered with great accuracy sequences during which they were not even on stage. This difficulty is compounded by the fact that even passages during which one of the alleged reporters is on stage correspond less closely to the Folio than, for instance, the above-quoted encounter between Pistol and the King. Here, for instance, is the Folio version of what is the beginning of 4.7 in modern editions:

FLU. Kill the poyes and the luggage, 'Tis expressely against the Law of Armes, tis as arrant a peece of knauery marke you now, as can bee offert in your Conscience now, is it not?

GOW. Tis certaine, there's not a boy left aliue, and the Cowardly Rascalls that ranne from the battaile ha' done this slaughter: besides they haue burned and carried away all that was in the Kings Tent, wherefore the King most worthily hath caus'd euery soldiour to cut his prisoners throat. O 'tis a gallant King. (i4ᵛ)

The first quarto renders this dialogue as follows:

> FLEW. Godes plud kil the boyes and lugyge,
> Tis the arrants peece of knauery as can be desired,
> In the worell now, in your conscience now.
> GOUR. Tis certaine, there is not a Boy left aliue,
> And the cowerdly rascals that ran from the battell,
> Themselues haue done this slaughter:
> Beside, they haue carried away and burnt,
> All that was in the kings Tent:
> Whervpon the king caused euery prisoners
> Throat to be cut. O he is a worthy king.   (E4ᵛ)

As the most cursory reading makes clear, the differences are far more numerous and important than in the Pistol/King encounter quoted above. This has not kept Gary Taylor from concluding his investigation of Q1 *Henry V* as follows: "That both Gower and Exeter were involved in the reconstruction seems clear; that no one else was involved seems equally clear."[85] Since this implies that the reporters sometimes remembered less

---

[84] Irace, *Reforming the "Bad" Quartos*, 119.
[85] Taylor, *Text of "Henry V,"* 135. On the following page, Taylor adds that: "It seems reasonably clear then that Gower doubled Cambridge" (Ibid., 136). As Kathleen Irace has shown that "Cambridge"

accurately their own lines than those they neither spoke themselves nor witnessed on stage, the accuracy of Taylor's conclusion seems all but clear.

The scholars' inability to agree on the identity of the memorial reporters also militates against memorial reconstruction. The reconstructors of *Henry V*, for instance, have variously been identified as Exeter and Gower, one of them doubling as the Governor of Harfleur (Duthie), Exeter and/or Fluellen and/or Pistol (Hart), Exeter (possibly doubling as the Governor of Harfleur) and Gower (doubling as Cambridge, as a mute French lord in 2.4, and either as one of Henry's "Attendants" or as the Bishop of Ely in 1.2) (Taylor), or Exeter, Pistol and Gower, doubling Nym, Scrope, and possibly the Governor and York (Irace).[86] Paul Werstine has rightly pointed out that "Such disagreement is crippling to the success of any demonstration that Q is a memorial reconstruction by actors."[87]

Given the various discontents with the traditional memorial-reconstruction-for-provinces narrative, it is understandable and salutary that several scholars have recently come to different conclusions regarding the origins of the first quartos of *Romeo and Juliet*, *Henry V*, and *Hamlet*. Far from believing that a version related to the first quarto of *Hamlet* could not possibly have been performed in London, Alan Dessen has considered the possibility that Q1 *Hamlet* is "a reasonably faithful rendition of a *Hamlet* performed by Shakespeare's company."[88] Giorgio Melchiori has argued that behind the "very seriously debased" Q1 *Hamlet*, there is "an authorially revised version for the public stage."[89] Similarly, rejecting the traditional argument for the origins of the first quarto of *Henry V*, Andrew Gurr has come to the conclusion that:

It was put together for performance in London and elsewhere in late 1599 or early 1600 by several members of the company. It was undoubtedly an authoritative players' text. At least two, possibly more, of the company's players who had speaking parts shared the work. Most of the manuscript was recorded by dictation, chiefly

---

would have reported with greater accuracy the lines he witnesses than the ones he spoke, this suggestion can be laid to rest ("Reconstruction and Adaptation," 232).

[86] See Duthie, "Quarto of Shakespeare's *Henry V*," 117; Hart, *Stolne and Surreptitious Copies*, 347; Taylor, *Text of "Henry V*," 135–36; Irace, "Reconstruction and Adaptation," 233.

[87] Werstine, " 'Bad' Shakespeare Quartos," 324.

[88] Alan C. Dessen, "Weighing the Options in *Hamlet* Q1," in *The "Hamlet" First Published*, ed. Clayton, 76.

[89] Melchiori, "Acting Version," 208. That Q1 *Hamlet* reflects a stage version is corroborated by the fact that the German adaptation *Der bestrafte Brudermord* (*Fratricide Punished*), which traveling English players performed on the Continent, agrees with the short quarto in having the nunnery-scene come earlier than in the long texts, in naming Polonius Corambis, as well as in a number of specific details (see Bullough, *Sources of Shakespeare*, VII.21–22).

from the rough playscript, helped in places by the players' memories of their parts. On occasions there may also have been some resort to an authorial manuscript, either the one later used to set the Folio text, or one close to it, possibly a "maximal" copy of the author's papers.[90]

When it comes to *Romeo and Juliet*, David Farley-Hills and Jay Halio have also advanced convincing arguments to supersede the traditional label "memorial reconstruction." Farley-Hills believes that Q1 *Romeo and Juliet* was set up from a "shortened version of Shakespeare's original prepared by a redactor," and that "the copy for both the redactor of Q1 and the compositor of Q2 was the author's 'foul papers.' "[91] Halio suggests a similar scenario. Shakespeare, he writes:

first wrote out a full draft of his play, revising some parts as he went along. Since the draft was too long for a performance lasting two hours or so, a shorter draft was made, with further revisions as and when they were felt necessary or desirable, including numerous tinkerings with what had already been written and found generally acceptable. This became the acting version of the play, from which the promptbook was prepared. This revised, second draft was then printed in 1597 in the first quarto.[92]

I do not find it possible to adhere to all parts of these arguments. For example, Halio's revising Shakespeare does not account, it seems to me, for the manifold changes introduced into Q1 as exemplified by the nurse's speech quoted above.[93] Nevertheless, what the articles and editions I quote from above have in common is that they go some way toward demonstrating that the first quartos of *Romeo and Juliet*, *Henry V*, and *Hamlet* are related to what Shakespeare and his fellows performed in London. As this chapter has shown, various complicated explanations were advanced in the twentieth century to account for the first quartos of *Romeo and Juliet*, *Henry V*, and *Hamlet*. The arguments generally implied that these texts were unauthorized, put together by a small number of individuals, who had recourse to nothing but their memories so as to create a text that is different from the one that is usually performed. Only recently have these uneconomic

---

[90] Gurr, ed., *The First Quarto of King Henry V*, 9.

[91] David Farley-Hills, "The 'Bad' Quarto of *Romeo and Juliet*," *Shakespeare Survey*, 49 (1996), 27, 33.

[92] Jay L. Halio, "Handy-Dandy: Q1/Q2 *Romeo and Juliet*," in *Shakespeare's "Romeo and Juliet": Texts, Contexts, and Interpretations*, ed. Halio (Newark: University of Delaware Press; London: Associated University Presses, 1995), 137.

[93] The two versions of the nurse's speech may be compared to other passages, for instance, to the beginning of 4.4. Again, the speeches in the two quartos are of similar length, but much of the linguistic material and the order in which it is presented are different. Is it plausible to imagine that a revising Shakespeare spent his energy on turning the passage in the second quarto into that in the first?

hypotheses started to be dislodged by more economic arguments. This is not to claim that a master key to the "bad" quartos has been found that explains how exactly they came into being. On the contrary. There is little hope, I believe, of recovering what specific effect various agencies had upon the differences between the "bad" and the "good" texts. Recent work on the "bad" quartos by scholars such as Blayney, Maguire, Gurr, Halio, and Melchiori makes it seem reasonable to suppose, however, that the first quarto of *Romeo and Juliet*, *Henry V*, and *Hamlet* are products of a more authorized and communal undertaking than has often been assumed. The evidence suggests that while it should not be excluded that faulty memory may account for some of the differences between the "good" and the "bad" quartos, it accounts by no means for all, probably not even for most, of them. The manuscripts from which the "bad" quartos were set up do not seem to have been the result of attempts to create a theatrical text that radically departs from what was performed in London – a kind of text for which there is no good evidence. Rather, they are likely to have been set up from manuscripts that were put together according to what Moseley suggests became a common practice among the King's Men. Accordingly, their purpose is likely to have been literary rather than theatrical. Another conclusion to be drawn from this chapter is that narratives about "bad" quartos and the belief that Shakespeare's "long" plays were performed in their entirety have always been intimately bound up with each other. As long as it was taken for granted that Shakespeare thought of his plays exclusively as scripts for the theater, it was naturally assumed that even the longest of Shakespeare's plays was intended for performance. And as long as the question of the performability of Shakespeare's long texts was not raised, the fact that the "bad" quartos are substantially shorter than the "good" editions was generally taken as evidence that they could only be an abridgement for or a record of provincial performances. Gary Taylor's belief, in the introduction to *A Textual Companion*, that "the full text" of plays such as *Antony and Cleopatra* and the Folio *Hamlet* were performed is therefore clearly not unrelated to his contention, in *Three Studies in the Texts of "Henry V,"* that the first quarto of *Henry V* could not have been performed anywhere but in the provinces. Farley-Hills's work on *Romeo and Juliet* offers a similar example. Even though rejecting "memorial reconstruction" as the explanation for the origin of Q1 *Romeo and Juliet*, he still clings to the theory that the text was written for performance in the provinces: "There is general agreement that the version of *Romeo and Juliet* represented by Q1 is a version intended for the stage. As a shorter version of the text it was presumably intended for performance by a touring troupe in the provinces."[94] The mere fact that Q1 is "a shorter version" appears to prompt the explanation that the text was only performed in the provinces.

Conversely, the growing skepticism about "memorial reconstruction" which confined the "bad" quartos to the provinces has gone hand in hand with an increasing awareness that the length of many of Shakespeare's plays and what we know about the length of performances are not easily compatible. Believing that Moseley's preface refers to the practice from which the "bad" quartos originated, Peter Blayney understands Moseley as implying that " 'everyone knows'... that plays were usually and markedly abridged for performance."[95] According to Gurr, the texts of *Henry V* "suggest that Shakespeare and his company were in the habit of trimming and redrafting his scripts for use on the stage quite drastically. They shortened long speeches and cut redundant characters in order to streamline the text into something that could easily be put on as a two-hour performance."[96] Likewise, Halio, as shown above, argues that Shakespeare's original draft of *Romeo and Juliet* was "too long for a performance lasting two hours or so," and that, consequently, "a shorter draft was made." Since it has come to be recognized that "memorial reconstruction" does not provide a sufficient explanation for the complex textual situation of the "bad" quartos I have dealt with in this chapter, scholars appear to have started taking more seriously the "two hours' traffic of our stage."

There are good reasons to believe, then, that the first quartos of *Romeo and Juliet*, *Henry V*, and *Hamlet* reflect, or at least dimly reflect, what Shakespeare and his fellows performed in London and elsewhere. This entails a conclusion I also arrived at in chapter 5 when coming from a different angle: the "long" extant texts of these and other Shakespeare plays do not appear to have been meant for performance before undergoing abridgement and adaptation for the stage. The gap left between the long and the short, the literary and the theatrical texts of *Romeo and Juliet*, *Henry V*, and *Hamlet* allows insights into this process of abridgement and adaptation. Analyzing this process can reveal some of the specifically *theatrical* characteristics of the short and some of the specifically *literary* characteristics of the long texts. This analysis will be at the center of the last chapter of this study.

---

[94] Farley-Hills, " 'Bad' Quarto," 28.   [95] Blayney, "Publication of Playbooks," 394.
[96] Gurr, ed., *The First Quarto of King Henry V*, ix.

CHAPTER 9

Theatricality, literariness and the texts of
Romeo and Juliet, Henry V, *and* Hamlet

From its very beginnings, drama has existed on the intersection of theatricality and literariness or, to put it in the words of Walter J. Ong's now classic study, of orality and literacy.[1] As early as Greek antiquity, at a time when other verbal genres were still largely governed by oral delivery, drama was the one verbal genre whose inception was controlled by writing. Even though initiated by writing, drama was and still is orally performed, while originally oral genres such as epic and lyric poetry have long assumed a primarily textual existence. The drama of Shakespeare's age is situated on the trajectory from earlier pre-print culture to later, firmly print-based times. Few plays record this transitory status more distinctly than those – like *Romeo and Juliet*, *Henry V*, and *Hamlet* – that are extant in short and long, theatrical and literary versions. Even though printed within a few years of each other, the variant texts of these three plays record different stages on the trajectory from a predominantly oral to a heavily literate culture. The short, theatrical texts, I have argued, record in admittedly problematic fashion the plays as they were orally delivered on stage to spectators (better: audiences) that were in part illiterate but still endowed with considerable oral/aural faculties. The long, literary texts, I believe, correspond to what an emergent dramatic author wrote for readers in an attempt to raise the literary respectability of playtexts. With Robert Weimann, I thus "situate Shakespeare's text in the environment of a culture in which the new learning and writing had not fully supplanted the vitality in the oral communication of the unlettered," and hold that "the Elizabethan theatre participated in a residually oral culture that affected certain variant playtexts."[2] In this last

---

[1] See Walter J. Ong, *Orality and Literacy: The Technologizing of the Word* (London and New York: Methuen, 1982).

[2] Weimann, *Author's Pen and Actor's Voice*, 7, 43. Note that, in the case of *Hamlet* Q1, Weimann argues for the text's "greater proximity to all sorts and conditions of performance," but endorses Irace's argument that Q1 *Hamlet* "was adapted and reconstructed by traveling members of Shakespeare's

chapter, I cannot do more than indicate some of the ways in which these variant playtexts record what Leah Marcus has called the "competing forms of communication" in which they existed.[3] In order to tease out respective specificities of these competing forms, I will read the texts side by side, trying to observe in the gap that separates them how the plays' rival modes of existence have shaped the variant forms in which they survive.

The slightly differing passages of King Henry's discovery of the killed boys at the battle of Agincourt provides an opportunity to illustrate this procedure. In the text we know, the passage, quoted from the First Folio, reads as follows:

> KING. I was not angry since I came to France,
>   Vntill this instant. Take a Trumpet Herald,
>   Ride thou vnto the Horsemen on yond hill:
>   If they will fight with vs, bid them come downe,
>   Or voyde the field: they do offend our sight.
>   If they'l do neither, we will come to them,
>   And make them sker away, as swift as stones
>   Enforced from the old Assyrian slings:
>   Besides, wee'l cut the throats of those we haue,
>   And not a man of them that we shall take
>   Shall taste our mercy. Go and tell them so.
>
> *Enter Mountioy.*
>
> EXETER. Here comes the Herald of the French, my Liege.
> GLOUCESTER. His eyes are humbler than they vs'd to be.
> KING. How not, what meanes this Herald? Knowst thou not,
>   That I have fin'd these bones of mine for ransome?   (15ʳ)

The corresponding lines in the first quarto are similar but with significant exceptions:

> KING. I was not angry since *I* came into *France*,
>   Vntill this houre.
>   Take a trumpet Herauld,
>   And ride vnto the horsmen on yon hill:
>   If they will fight with vs bid them come downe,
>   Or leaue the field, they do offend our sight:

own company" (ibid., 27). Weimann's study provides a dense analysis of the ways in which "the conjuncture of 'pen' and 'voice' was crucial to the workings of the popular Renaissance theater in early modern England" (ibid., 54).

[3] Marcus, *Unediting the Renaissance*, 176.

Will they do neither, we will come to them,
And make them skyr away, as fast
As stones enforst from the old Assirian slings.
Besides, weele cut the throats of those we haue,
And not one aliue shall taste our mercy.

Enter the Herauld.

Gods will what meanes this? knowst thou not
That we have fined these bones of ours for ransome?

(FI[r])

Henry's lines show occasional substitution and condensation of words,
but are essentially the same. The lines spoken by Exeter and Gloucester,
however, have completely disappeared. Exeter, it may be well to recall, has
traditionally been counted among the "reporters" by advocates of memorial
reconstruction. His Q1 lines, in other words, are generally close to their Folio
equivalents. It therefore seems unlikely that the omission is accidental.

If we understand the Folio text and the script behind Q1 as designed for
two different media, what seems significant about the two missing lines

> EXETER. Here comes the Herald of the French, my Liege.
> GLOUCESTER. His eyes are humbler than they vs'd to be.

is that they can be *acted* and therefore do not need to be *spoken*. In performance, the words would unnecessarily reiterate what the actor conveys
through body language. For readers to be aware of Mountjoy's appearance –
contrasting sharply with his proud demeanor prior to the battle – they need
to be told so either in dramatic dialogue or in a stage direction. The latter
possibility is one Shakespeare used sparingly and not, generally, when the
contents of a stage direction can be conveyed in dialogue. The two lines
present in the readerly but absent from the theatrical text are thus crucial
for what Harry Berger calls "imaginary audition." They allow a reader to
imagine a point of stage business that could otherwise only be conveyed in
performance. The same applies to stage directions in the second quarto of
Hamlet, which is generally presumed to have been set up from an authorial
manuscript. For instance, Q1 and Q2 have Bernardo say that the Ghost
disappeared when the cock crew, but only Q2 provides a stage direction
that allows the readers to be aware of the crowing at the moment it occurs
(B3[r]). A few lines earlier, a Q2 stage direction makes clear that the Ghost,
facing Horatio, poignantly "spreads his armes" (B3[r]). Repeatedly, Q2 makes
available to readers what a spectator of the play behind Q1 is aware of but
what a reader of Q1 is not.

Passages from the variant texts of *Romeo and Juliet* similarly bespeak the different media for which they were designed. Having received orders from her father to marry Paris on "Thursday next," Juliet, in the second quarto says:

> Good Father, I beseech you on my knees,
> Heare me with patience, but to speake a word.
>
> (11ʳ)

In the first quarto, her speech is shorter but followed by a stage direction:

> Good father, heare me speake?
>
> *She kneeles downe.*
>
> (H1ʳ)

An audience that can see Juliet kneel does not need to be told that she is kneeling. Accordingly, Q1 avoids tautology by confining the information about Juliet's kneeling to a stage direction. A reader of Q2, however, only knows that Juliet kneels down because she says so.[4]

When Friar Laurence discovers the dead Romeo in the tomb, Q1 similarly has a stage direction where Q2 has dialogue. The longer text reads:

> FRIER [LAURENCE]. Go with me to the Vault.
> MAN [BALTHASAR]. I dare not sir.
> My master knowes not but I am gone hence,
> And fearfully did menace me with death
> If I did stay to look on his entents.
> FRIER [LAURENCE]. Stay, then, Ile go alone, feare comes vpon me.
> O much I fear some ill unthriftie thing.
> MAN [BALTHASAR]. As I did sleep vnder this yong tree heere,
> I dreampt my maister and another fought,
> And that my maister slew him.
> FRIER [LAURENCE]. *Romeo.*
> Alack, alack, what blood is this which staines
> The stony entrance of this Sepulchre? (L3ᵛ)

The corresponding passage in Q1 shows significant omissions:

> FR[IAR LAURENCE]: Goe with me thether.
> MAN: I dare not sir, he knowes not I am heere:
> On paine of death he chargde me to be gone,
> And not for to disturbe him in his enterprize.

---

[4] For Henry Chettle's possible role of "annotator" of Q1 *Romeo and Juliet*, affecting in particular the text's stage directions, see John Jowett's article "Henry Chettle and the first Quarto of *Romeo and Juliet*," *Publications of the Bibliographical Society of America*, 92 (1998), 53–74.

FR[IAR LAURENCE]: Then must I goe. My minde presageth ill.

Fryer stoops and lookes on the blood and weapons.

What bloud is this that staines the entrance
Of this marble stony monument?   (K2^r)

The moment between Friar Laurence's resolution to descend into the vaults
and his discovery of Romeo is clearly one of suspense, but the suspense is
achieved differently on stage and on page. In the performance we guess
behind Q1, suspense builds up through stage action as Friar Laurence approaches, stoops, looks, and realizes. The theatrical means with which
suspense is achieved are thus precisely non-verbal. The printed word, on
the other hand, progresses ineluctably from one sentence to the next,
making it impossible to create suspense through the temporary suspen-
sion of words. Consequently, it is created by the insertion of Balthazar's
three-line speech. On stage, suspense is achieved by, quite literally, sus-
pending words. On page, non-verbal suspense is replaced by a verbal
bracket that, appropriately, builds up toward the horror of Friar Laurence's
discovery.

In his recent edition of the first quarto of *Henry V*, Andrew Gurr has
shown that there are reasons to believe that the omission of the Chorus
along with other features of Q1 correspond to what Shakespeare and
his fellows performed at the Globe and elsewhere: "the Folio text, with
its famous Choruses and speeches such as Henry's exhortation to his troops
before Harfleur, was unlikely to have been heard at the Globe at any time
before 1623, and probably not until the play was revived with the aid of
the Folio-based editions of the eighteenth century."[5] If the Chorus was not
performed in front of audiences but only printed for the benefit of readers
(and may have been written by Shakespeare with an awareness that it may
be omitted in performance), its famous exhortation to "piece out our imperfections with your thoughts" needs to be reread with an awareness of the
medium in which it existed. The Chorus addresses spectators, but perhaps
less those physically present at the Globe than the spectators of the mind
who are imaginatively creating a playhouse performance through "imaginary audition." In other words, it seems that Shakespeare's dramatic writings
cater for the "imaginary audition" Berger advocates as an analytical tool that
does justice to both the theatricality and the literariness of Shakespeare's
plays. As we have seen above, a comparison of the variant theatrical and literary texts suggests that Shakespeare seems aware of and willing to provide

[5] Gurr, ed., *The First Quarto of King Henry V*, ix.

for what imperfections a dramatic text contains for a reader as opposed to a spectator. Gloucester's "His eyes are humbler" makes perfect sense on the page, allowing a reader to imagine the action that would have been performed on stage. Gloucester's words seem superfluous on stage, however, and, accordingly, are omitted in the theatrical text. The Chorus may thus be understood as the expression of a concern that was close to Shakespeare when he worked on his dramatic texts. Writing longer plays for readers than his company needed for the theatre, Shakespeare encourages and enables his readers to use their "imaginary forces" to construct in their mind's eye the "wooden O" that is made to "hold / The vasty fields of France" or in which Juliet kneels down. It is often assumed that Shakespeare's plays make for good reading despite the fact they were designed for performance. I am suggesting that they work well on the page because they are in certain ways designed for readers.

I have argued above that some passages present in the long, literary texts are omitted or abridged in the short, theatrical texts because they are chiefly of value for readers and not for spectators. I am not suggesting that the short texts eliminate in a systematic way every line for which stage action can provide a substitute. The contingencies of the media for which the manuscripts behind the short and the long editions were designed are one source, however, of differences between the variant texts.

Stage abridgement, resulting in the omission of various passages of considerable length present in the long texts, accounts for a much greater share of the textual differences between the short and the long texts. It is true that, on some occasions, it is not easy to delimit the absence or presence of Q2 or Folio material in the shorter text. Several lines can blend into one, passages are transposed and many words are considerably transformed. Yet on other occasions, the relationship is more clear-cut. A considerable number of passages present in the long texts leave no trace in the short texts, even though the preceding and following lines correspond closely to their counterparts in Q1. Among the deliberate cuts in Q1 *Hamlet* reflecting stage abridgement are the first twenty-six lines of Claudius's opening speech of the second scene (1.2.1–26), all but the first lines of the Pyrrhus speech (2.2.476–500), Hamlet's "mirror up to nature" speech (3.2.16–35) and all but the first two and the last four lines of the Player King's long speech (3.2.181–204). Omissions in Q1 *Henry V* include the Chorus, thirty-eight lines in Henry's long address to the traitors (2.2.105–42), the King's "Once more unto the breach" speech (3.1) and a thirty-one line passage in his speech before the gates of Harfleur (3.3.94–124). Among the passages present

in the second but entirely absent from the first quarto of *Romeo and Juliet*
are the sonnet spoken by the Chorus between the first and the second acts
(2.0.1–14), all but the first six lines of Juliet's soliloquy at the beginning of
Act two, scene five, all but four lines of her soliloquy at the beginning of act
three, scene two, and all of Lady Capulet's rhymed speech comparing Paris
with a "precious book" that "only lacks a cover" (1.3.81–96). These passages
share certain characteristics. They are not necessary for the understanding
of the plot. Most of them are not particularly stage-worthy. They are good
reading material, appealing to a fairly educated readership. In short, they
are "stuff to please the wiser sort," as Harvey put it.

The literariness of Shakespeare's long dramatic texts emerges quite clearly
from some of the passages that entirely disappear from the short, theatrical
texts. Commenting on the desolate state France is in, Burgundy speaks:

> Her vine, the merry cheerer of the heart,
> Unprunèd dies; her hedges even-plashed,
> Like prisoners wildly overgrown with hair
> Put forth disordered twigs; her fallow leas
> The darnel, hemlock, and rank fumitory
> Doth root upon, while that the coulter rusts
> That should deracinate such savagery.
> The even mead – that erst brought sweetly forth
> The freckled cowslip, burnet, and green clover –
> Wanting the scythe, all uncorrected, rank,
> Conceives by idleness, and nothing teems
> But hateful docks, rough thistles, kecksies, burs,
> Losing both beauty and utility.   (5.2.41–53)

And so on. It is hardly surprising that Q1 omits all but four of the
forty-five lines of this speech. Whatever the reason for which Shakespeare
wrote this speech, it seems hardly to have been intended for recital on
stage. The lengthy natural-history simile with which Montague describes
Romeo's melancholy state is another *tour de force* which the theatrical text
omits:

> But he, his own affections' counsellor,
> Is to himself – I will not say how true,
> But to himself so secret and so close,
> So far from sounding and discovery,
> As is the bud bit with an envious worm
> Ere he can spread his sweet leaves to the air
> Or dedicate his beauty to the sun.
>   (1.1.144–50)

Romeo's description of Rosaline deploys the kind of rhetoric that figures prominently in Elizabethan sonnet cycles:

> BENVOLIO. Then she hath sworn that she will still live chaste?
> ROMEO. She hath, and in that sparing makes huge waste;
> For beauty starved with her severity
> Cuts beauty off from all posterity.
> She is too fair, too wise, wisely too fair,
> To merit bliss by making me despair.
> She hath forsworn to love, and in that vow
> Do I live dead, that live to tell it now.   (1.1.214–21)

The scene continues in the same vein for another fourteen lines. The entire passage is absent from Q1. Friar Laurence's twenty-two lines speech, in which he explains to Juliet the working of the potion, contains a self-contained five-line purple patch that leaves no trace in Q1:

> FRIAR LAURENCE. The roses in thy lips and cheeks shall fade
> To wanny ashes, thy eyes' windows fall
> Like death when he shuts up the day of life.
> Each part, deprived of supple government,
> Shall, stiff and stark and cold, appear like death.
>
>   (4.1.99–103)

The point to be made about the omission of poetic passages in the stage versions is not that a theatre audience would have been unable to appreciate them. People able to absorb long and complex sermons must have had aural faculties that allowed them to cope with intricate poetic language. Yet, faced with a manuscript that was too long by many hundreds of lines, the players obviously had to omit those passages that would do least damage to the play's coherence. It may be well to recall the address "To the Reader" in Davenant's mildly adapted version of *Hamlet* which points out: "This Play being too long to be conveniently Acted, such places as might be least prejudicial to the Plot or Sense, are left out upon the Stage" (A2^r). "Poetic" or "literary" passages present in the long but absent from the short editions are thus of interest not because they constitute material Shakespeare's company considered unsuitable for performance (they do not), but because they give us access to dramatic material Shakespeare wrote with an awareness that much of it would not survive the play's preparations for the stage.

It may seem surprising that Shakespeare wrote purple patches into his dramatic texts in the knowledge that they might well be omitted on stage. Such a practice may seem less surprising, however, once we realize that these passages would have been particularly appreciated by readers. Shortly after *Romeo and Juliet* appeared in print, *Belvedere* and *England's Parnassus* gathered "The choysest Flowers of our Moderne Poets" with excerpts from poetry and plays, including *Romeo and Juliet*. Similar anthologies existed in manuscript, of which Edward Pudsey's Commonplace Book (*c.* 1600–1615) provides perhaps the best extant example. It includes passages from *Romeo and Juliet*, *Richard II*, *Richard III*, *Hamlet*, *The Merchant of Venice*, *Much Ado about Nothing*, *Titus Andronicus*, and from Jonson's *Every Man out of His Humour*.[6] The predilection of contemporary readers of dramatic texts for poetic highlights, passages that can be excerpted and anthologized, is further illustrated by an extant copy of the second quarto of *Romeo and Juliet* that was once in the possession of William Drummond, laird of Hawthornden and was read by him in 1606.[7] The passages Drummond marked by overscoring them are literary conceits rather than theatrical highlights, poetically ingenious rather than dramatically effective. In the opening scene, for instance, Drummond overscores Montague's metaphor for dawn:

> as the alcheering Sunne,
> Should in the farthest East begin to draw,
> The shadie curtaines from *Auroras* bed
>
> (B1ʳ)

In the play's last scene, Romeo's Petrarchan description of Juliet's face caught Drummond's fancy:

> bewties ensigne yet
> Is crymson in thy lips and in thy cheeks,
> And deaths pale flag is not aduanced there.
>
> (L3ʳ)

Both passages are not unlike the kind of "flowers" gathered in contemporary anthologies. Significantly, they are both absent from the short, theatrical Q1.[8]

---

[6] Pudsey's notebooks are now divided between the Bodleian Library (MS Eng. Poet. D. 3) and the Shakespeare Birthplace Trust Record Office in Stratford-upon-Avon (MS ER 82). See Richard Savage, *Shakespearean Extracts from "Edward Pudsey's Booke,"* Stratford-upon-Avon Note Books, no. 1 (Stratford-on-Avon and London, 1888), and Juliet Mary Gowan, "An Edition of Edward Pudsey's Commonplace Book (*c.* 1600–1615) from the Manuscript in the Bodleian Library" (unpubl. M.Phil. thesis, University of London, 1967).

[7] The copy, which bears his autograph name on the title page, is now in the Edinburgh University Library. See W. W. Greg's facsimile edition in the Shakespeare Quarto Facsimile series (Oxford: Clarendon Press, 1949).

[8] Other passages which Drummond overscored include Mercutio's "frozen bosome of the North" and "dewe dropping South" (C2ᵛ), Capulet's "When well appareld Aprill on the heele, / Of limping winter treads" (B2ᵛ), Benvolio's "forth the golden window of the East" (A4ᵛ), and Romeo's "then

An authorially revised four-line passage which happens to survive in the second quarto of *Romeo and Juliet* does nothing to refute the argument that Shakespeare took particular care in composing certain literary conceits. The four lines occur at the end of what is act two, scene two in modern editions, and are immediately repeated at the beginning of the following scene:

> The grey eyde morne smiles on the frowning night,
> Checkring the Easterne Clouds with streaks of light,
> And darknesse fleckted like a drunkard reeles,
> From forth daies pathway, made by *Tytans* wheeles.
> Hence will I to my ghostly Friers close cell,
> His helpe to craue, and my deare hap to tell.
>
> *Exit.*
> *Enter Frier alone with a basket.*
>
> FRI. The grey-eyed morne smiles on the frowning night,
> Checking the Easterne clowdes with streaks of light:
> And fleckeld darknesse like a drunkard reeles,
> From forth daies path, and *Titans* burning wheeles:
>
> (D4ᵛ)

Even though Heminge and Condell assured us that Shakespeare "never blotted line," this passage shows us Shakespeare at work, having second thoughts about where the four lines should go and by whom they should be spoken.[9] The differences between the first and second version show just the kind of authorial "tinkerings" which the variant texts of a play like *Troilus and Cressida* suggest. The change in word order ("darknesse fleckted" / "fleckeld darknesse") is a fairly common difference between Q1 and Q2. For instance, where the text of 1597 has "In hearbes plants, stones..." (D3ᵛ), that of 1599 has "In Plants, hearbes, stones..." (D4ᵛ). It is instructive to see what kind of passage Shakespeare had second thoughts about: a purple patch, as it were, that can be cut and pasted, patched in different scenes and attributed to different characters.[10] It may be significant that a similar passage ("as the all-cheering sun, / Should in the farthest east begin to draw / The shady curtains from Aurora's bed" (1.1.131–33)) is among the lines

---

turne teares to fier" (B3ᵛ) and "Shall I beleeue that vnsubstantiall death is amorous, / And that the leane abhorred monster keepes / Thee here in darke to be his parramour?" (L3ʳ).

[9] See Jones's *Shakespeare at Work* for a full analysis of this aspect of Shakespeare's texts.

[10] It may be worthwhile in this context giving an example of an elaborate speech that was *not* significantly cut: Mercutio's Queen Mab speech is of considerable length (1.4.55–94) and, in terms of plot, not strictly necessary. Mercutio's style and verbosity, however, are constitutive of his character rather than accidental. Contrary to "The grey eyde morne" passage, it clearly cannot be cut and pasted, and attributed to another character.

Drummond overscored. The poetic conceits Shakespeare took pains to
work into his plays do not seem to have been lost on his readers.

A comparison of isolated passages in the variant short and long texts of
Romeo and Juliet, *Henry V*, and *Hamlet* is one way of assessing the difference between what I think are basically theatrical and literary versions of
Shakespeare's plays. Comparing the short and long texts in their entirety is
another approach to assess the same difference. The first quarto of *Henry V*,
for instance, is a substantially different text from the one we usually read
and study. It is little more than half the length of its better-known counterpart and lacks some of the play's most famous passages including those by
the Chorus and Henry's "Once more unto the breach" speech. Act three
with the siege of Harfleur is thoroughly transformed and simplified. The
order of two scenes (4.4 and 4.5) is inverted. Several characters are omitted,
including the Bishop of Ely, Westmorland, Bedford, the French Queen,
Macmorris, and Jamy. A number of speeches are reassigned, in particular
those given to the Dauphin in Acts three and four in the long text which
are assigned to the Duke of Bourbon in the first quarto.[11] In many ways,
Q1 *Henry V* is as different from the Folio play as Q1 *Hamlet* is from the
tragedy we normally study.

What seems particularly significant about these differences is that the two
texts reveal important ideological differences. As some of the best criticism
on *Henry V* in the course of the twentieth century has made clear, the
Folio play has a deeply problematic view of its warrior-king hero and of
his military expedition into France. It is true that the play's traditional
patriotic interpretation has also had its adherents, most memorably in
Laurence Olivier's film of 1944, dedicated to the British soldiers at war.
A good many critics have contributed to complicating our response to the
play, however, pointing, for instance, to Henry's merciless command to kill
the French prisoners, to the discrepancy between what the Chorus *says* and
what the play *shows* about Henry, and to the Chorus's insistence that Henry
only brought temporary glory and was followed by a King who "made his

---

[11] It should be noted that very similar changes to those that appear to have affected *Henry V* are
observable in the extant manuscript of Fletcher and Massinger's *Sir John Van Olden Barnavelt*,
performed by the King's Men's in 1619. As with the disappearance of the Bishop of Ely in Shakespeare's
play, two clergymen, of which the second is not really necessary, is reduced to one (1.1). As with
Q's substitution of the Duke of Bourbon for the Dauphin at Agincourt, *Barnavelt* reallocates the
speeches of one conspirator, Vandermitten, to another, Grotius. As Taylor has shown that the change
from the Dauphin to Bourbon corresponds to the situation in the source material, Bowers has shown
that the introduction of the clergyman Horgerbeets (replacing Taurinus and Utenbogart) "could
have been managed only by the author drawing another name from the pamphlets" (Bowers, gen.
ed., *Beaumont and Fletcher Canon*, VIII.492).

England bleed" (Epilogue, l. 12). Henry's motives, in particular, have been subjected to criticism, with an increasing number of critics believing, as Stephen Greenblatt puts it, that "the play deftly registers every nuance of royal hypocrisy, ruthlessness, and bad faith."[12] Others have emphasized the play's ideological ambivalence, arguing that "*Henry V* can be either the story of an ideal king leading a unified nation to a glorious victory, or the story of a crafty and unscrupulous politician embarking on a cynical war of aggression in spite of its human costs," or that "Shakespeare created a work whose ultimate power is precisely the fact that it points in two opposite directions."[13]

In contrast, q1 *Henry V* is ideologically straightforward, displaying jingoistic patriotism where the multiple voices of the Folio play complicate and, at times, undermine each other. Among what have traditionally been considered the crucial issues of *Henry V* are the Chorus and the question of its reliability; the character of the King, especially his harsh treatment of former friends (Falstaff, Bardolph, the traitors) and of the prisoners as well as his night-time argument with Williams; the justification of the war advanced by the bishops; and the portrayal of the French antagonists.[14] Every one of these is dramatized very differently in the quarto and the Folio texts. Taylor provides a succinct summary. The first quarto of *Henry V*, he writes,

omits, from the play as we know it, the opening scene (with its revelation of mixed ecclesiastical motives for supporting Henry's claim to France), lines 115–35 of 1.2 (which culminate in the Archbishop's offer of church financing for the war), all reference in 2.1 to Henry's personal responsibility for Falstaff's condition, Cambridge's hint of motives other than simple bribery for the conspiracy against Henry (2.2.154–9), the bloodthirsty MacMorris and most of Henry's savage ultimatum in 3.3, all of Burgundy's description of the devastation Henry has wreaked on France (5.2.38–62). Whoever was responsible for them, the effect of the differences between this text and the one printed in all modern editions is to remove almost every difficulty in the way of an unambiguously patriotic interpretation of Henry and his war – that is, every departure from the kind of play which theatrical convention and the national mood would have led audiences of 1599 to expect.[15]

---

[12] Stephen Greenblatt, *Shakespearean Negotiations: The Circulation of Social Energy in Renaissance England* (Oxford: Clarendon Press, 1988), 56. For an earlier hostile response to Henry, see Harold Goddard's *The Meaning of Shakespeare*, 2 vols. (University of Chicago Press, 1951).

[13] James N. Loehlin, *Henry V*, Shakespeare in Performance (Manchester University Press, 1996), 9; and Norman Rabkin, "Either/Or: Responding to *Henry V*," in *Shakespeare and the Problem of Meaning* (University of Chicago Press, 1981), 33–34. See also Antony Hammond's argument according to which two contradictory versions of Henry are encoded in the text which cannot, however, coexist on the stage ("Prologue and Plural Text in *Henry V*," in *"Fanned and Winnowed Opinions": Shakespearean Essays Presented to Harold Jenkins*, eds. John W. Mahon and Thomas A. Pendleton (London and New York: Methuen, 1987), 133–50, esp. 144).

[14] Loehlin, *Henry V*, 9.   [15] Taylor, ed. *Henry V*, 12.

Clearly, the readerly text, designed for a reception in which the intellect is much involved, puts up greater resistence to the reader's mind than the short, theatrical text. Contrary to solitary reading, the communal experience of playgoing – especially in a theater in which Henry's speeches to his army would have been spoken to the audience – addressed first and foremost the spectators' emotions and senses rather than their intellect. A performance of the short play therefore activated more easily the audiences' patriotic prejudices than the long, literary drama would have.

An important result of the above omissions is that Q1 *Henry V* is also structurally a very different play from its Folio counterpart. In particular, the Folio, but not the quarto, text seems to employ several scenic juxtapositions that require from the reader a mental readjustment. The over-enthusiastic Chorus is repeatedly followed by the dramatization of a more sober reality, as when the fourth Chorus promises a sovereign Henry, in control of his troops and at peace with himself, while the following scenes show him to be a torn figure who meets resistence if not animosity from his own soldiers. The disappearance of the Chorus to a considerable extent disambiguates the protagonist of the Folio text.[16]

Another juxtaposition that complicates our response to the king has references to what Greenblatt calls "Hal's symbolic killing of Falstaff" – "The King hath run bad humours on the knight . . . His heart is fracted and corroborate" (2.1.116–19) – immediately followed by the uncovering of the traitors' plot against the King.[17] The order in which Shakespeare organizes his dramatic material is potentially damning for Henry as memories of his betrayal of Falstaff cannot but linger on when Henry accuses Scroop of having betrayed him: "thou cruel, / Ingrateful, savage, and inhuman creature [that] knew'st the very bottom of my soul" (2.2.91–4) are Henry's words to Scroop, but they follow shortly after we have been reminded that they could equally apply to Henry's ingratitude to Falstaff. Q1 not only omits the passages that incriminate Henry for the death of Falstaff

---

[16] Annabel Patterson has advanced a different reason for the Chorus's disappearance. She believes that print publication of the ambiguous fifth Chorus with its reference to the Earl of Essex – whose rebellion in the year following the publication of Q1 *Henry V* led to his execution – was deemed too dangerous and "brought down with it . . . the rest of the simpler patriotism of the Quarto text as a whole" (Annabel Patterson, *Shakespeare and the Popular Voice* (Oxford: Blackwell, 1989), 87). There is little to support such a view. The one local reference to Essex could easily have been omitted without repercussions on the entire rest of the play. For earlier views of the Chorus, see Warren D. Smith, "The *Henry V* Choruses in the First Folio," *Journal of English and Germanic Philology*, 53 (1954), 38–57; R. A. Law, "The Choruses in *Henry the Fifth*," *University of Texas Studies in English*, 35 (1956), 11–21.

[17] Greenblatt, *Shakespearean Negotiations*, 58.

but simultaneously restructures the events so as to dispose of an implicit equation of Henry with traitors to the English cause.

As pointed out above, the short theatrical text inverts the order of two scenes, 4.4 and 4.5, in the Folio. Gurr has argued that the switch occurred "possibly for casting reasons."[18] It seems just as likely, however, to be another instance of a juxtaposition that was thought inappropriate when the more straightforwardly patriotic acting version behind Q1 was prepared. In the long text, Henry's exhortation to his soldiers – "We few, we happy few, we band of brothers" – is immediately followed by the farcical scene with Pistol, his French prisoner, and a boy who functions as interpreter. The heroism, courage, and nobility that was to inform the conduct of the English according to Henry is immediately contradicted and deflated by the mercenary considerations which alone prompt Pistol to spare, at least temporarily, his prisoner's life. In the quarto text, however, Henry's exhortations are followed by a scene showing the French in discomfiture – "all is gone, all is lost" (E3^r) – the warrior king's bravery thus being revealed to be the cause of what the following scene shows to be its effect.

Commenting on an earlier play on Henry V, Thomas Nashe wrote: "what a glorious thing it is to have Henry the Fifth represented on the stage, leading the French king prisoner, and forcing both him and the Dolphin to swear fealty."[19] Though Shakespeare's original manuscript may have presented a more problematic and less glorious "thing," the Lord Chamberlain's Men, and Shakespeare among them, seem to have decided that it would be shrewd business to present the audience with the patriotic figure they craved at a time when Anglo-French relations remained profoundly problematic. The quartos's omission of Henry's "upon the king" soliloquy (4.1.227–81) does nothing to contradict such a view. Henry's pessimistic view of kingship ("what have kings that privates have not too, / Save ceremony") does not seem to have been deemed in keeping with a play from which the audience expected a glorification of kingship. The "carefully planned adaptation, designed to make a viable two-hour script for acting" which Gurr has detected somwhere "close behind the manuscript copied for the press in 1600 and printed as Q1," seems designed to work as a theatrical event that draws upon and activates collective English memories and passions.[20] It does relatively little, however, to provide much food for thought for someone who takes up the advice of Shakespeare's friends and fellow actors to "Reade him, therefore; and againe, and againe."[21]

[18] Gurr, ed., *The First Quarto of King Henry V*, 106.
[19] Nashe, *Works*, ed. McKerrow, 1.213.   [20] Gurr, ed., *The First Quarto of King Henry V*, 9.
[21] Heminge and Condell, "To the Great Variety of Readers," A3^r.

A similar insight emerges from an assessment of the variant texts of *Hamlet*.
Giorgio Melchiori has argued that "behind Q2 there is a play for the closet,
not for the stage," and that Shakespeare conceived the play "as a new form
of literary work that would take its place among the poetic achievements
extolled by the wiser sort."[22] I do not believe, as Melchiori does, that
Hamlet is an isolated case, but I do agree with his insistence on the play's
literariness as well as with his assessment of the relationship between the
long and the short texts of *Hamlet*. Like Melchiori, I believe that "the First
Quarto reflects faithfully at least one – but a very important – aspect of the
Tragedy of Hamlet: it reflects the new structure of the play carefully devised
at an early stage in view of its presentation in the public theater."[23]

The play's first six scenes all have their direct equivalent in Q1. Yet from
what corresponds to act two, scene two in modern editions, the differences
between Q1 and the long texts become more than a matter of deletions,
with Q1 restructuring the action dramatized in the long texts. In Q2 and the
Folio, Polonius and the King agree on the need to investigate the reasons
for Hamlet's melancholy disposition and Polonius suggests to set up an encounter with the Prince and Ophelia on which they would eavesdrop. The
so-called "Fishmonger" episode with Hamlet and Polonius ensues, followed
by Hamlet's encounter with Rosencrantz and Guildenstern. Next, the players are announced, they arrive, and, after the Pyrrhus speech, Hamlet asks
them to prepare a play, "The Mousetrap," for the following day. The second
act closes with Hamlet's soliloquy and his determination that "the play's
the thing / Wherein I'll catch the conscience of the king." In the following
scene which takes place the next day, the King and Polonius finally carry
out the eavesdropping plan. They set up Ophelia's encounter with Hamlet
and hide before he enters. After the "To be or not to be" soliloquy follows
the nunnery sequence which leaves the spying King and Polonius even
more anxious than before. The next scene begins with Hamlet's advice
to the players and procedes with the performance of the Mousetrap that
Hamlet had ordered the day before.[24]

---

[22] Melchiori, "The Acting Version and the Wiser Sort," 200, 196.   [23] Ibid., 207.

[24] There is nothing to suggest that such restructurings were at all common. It should be noted, however,
that one of the eighteen extant manuscript playbooks does give evidence of such rearrangement. As
the editor of Glapthorne's *Lady Mother* has pointed out, the manuscript shows that it was "decided
to play the long serious scene between Sir Geffrey and Lady Marlove, Bonvill and Belisea (854–1056)
before the awakening of Lovell and his scene with Grimes (735–853)" (Henry Glapthorne, *The Lady
Mother*, ed. Arthur Brown [London: Oxford University Press, 1958], x). Accordingly, the person
who was involved in preparing the play for the stage deleted the original warning for Sir Geffrey
and Lady Marlove at lines 845–46 and added a new warning (1048–49) at the end of what is, in the
manuscript, the later scene of Lovell's awakening.

Melchiori and Irace have shown that the effect of the structural rearrangement is to speed up the action.[25] While this is so, it seems equally significant that the structural changes fundamentally affect our understanding of the causal relationship between various parts of the play's action. My analysis of *Henry V* has shown how the long text – contrary to the short – contains juxtapositions (such as reminiscences of Henry's betrayal of Falstaff followed by Scroop's betrayal of Henry) that defy expectations and therefore require explanations, suggesting that the causal relationships in the play are dense and complex rather than self-explanatory. The same applies to *Hamlet*. For the order in which the long texts dramatize events seems in some ways rather odd. Polonius suggests spying on Hamlet with the help of Ophelia, but rather than putting this plan into practice, Polonius and the King wait until the next day. The succession of Hamlet's moods is perhaps even more surprising. After the arrival of the actors, he forges a plan: "I'll have these players / Play something like the murder of my father / Before mine uncle. I'll observe his looks, / I'll tent him to the quick. If a but blench, / I know my course" (2.2.596–600). At the end of the second act, Hamlet, surely, is finally ready to take action. Yet, when he re-enters some fifty lines later, he muses on suicide and seems to have forgotten about his project.

The restructuring of Q1 makes these problems disappear by moving the "To be or not to be" soliloquy and the "nunnery" sequence from what we know as act three, scene one to act two, scene two. The sequence therefore follows just after the King and Corambis (as Polonius is called in Q1) have forged the eavesdropping plan. With this sequence of events, cause and effect are more easily understandable: the eavesdropping plan is formed and then immediately carried out rather than postponed to the next day. Hamlet's melancholy state when he enters for the "To be or not to be" soliloquy corresponds well to what we have last heard of him in Ophelia's report to her father. He is cheered up by the arrival of Rossencraft and Gilderstone (Q1's spelling for Rosencrantz and Guildenstern) and the players. When he has the idea to test the King by means of the Mousetrap, this is again carried out the very same day rather than postponed to the next. In the resulting sequence, the represented time is thus reduced from two days to one. The emphasis is on the swiftly moving action, on plans formed and carried out, rather than on Hamlet's delay owing to his melancholy disposition and his lack of determination.

[25] Melchiori, "The Acting Version and the Wiser Sort," 207; Kathleen O. Irace, ed., *The First Quarto of Hamlet*, The New Cambridge Shakespeare: The Early Quartos (Cambridge University Press, 1998), 11.

I am not suggesting that the order of events in Q1 makes sense whereas that in the two long texts does not. Rather, the difference shows where the short version for the stage and the long version for the page fundamentally differ. If a character passes within a few lines from enthusiasm to dejection, this challenges expectations and requires explanation. The long texts thus invite us to inquire into a character who conveys a strong sense of interiority and psychological complexity. In Q1, in contrast, the Prince's character is more easily understandable and therefore can recede behind the intrigue and action which the stage play is most interested in.

In order to establish how the latter part of the play is also consciously and intelligently reworked to make it fit for the stage, it is necessary to investigate the play's structural design. The closet scene (3.4) occupies a central position within the play's architecture. Hamlet's pursuit of revenge for the murder of his father has still come to nothing. Having been given the opportunity to kill Claudius in the preceding prayer scene, he has refrained from the deed. In the closet scene, he is finally resolute and stabs the man hidden behind the arras, believing him to be Claudius. Yet, by killing Ophelia's and Laertes's father rather than the King, he becomes the object of revenge at the very moment he believes he is its subject. In a ferociously ironic reversal he not only fails to kill the murderer of his father but simultaneously becomes the murderer of another father. This pivotal moment structurally divides the play into two halves, the first showing Hamlet as the subject, the second as the object of revenge.

Carefully planned as this two-part structure is, it nevertheless threatens to result in an imbalance. The first half is filled with action and suspense from the moment the Ghost appears to the play within the play. Once Hamlet has killed Polonius, however, the play draws ineluctably toward the final confrontation between Laertes and Hamlet. Laertes is soon returned from Paris and hot for action; no delay is to be expected from him. So Shakespeare needs two devices to postpone the final confrontation: Ophelia's madness and death, and Hamlet's sea-voyage to England. Ophelia's decline is highly stage effective and must have been appreciated by Elizabethan audiences that never seem to have grown tired of scenes of madness. Hamlet's sea-voyage, on the other hand, is given what may well seem too much attention considering its basic lack of dramatic interest.

In the long texts, the King's plan to get rid of Hamlet by sending him to England is already announced as early as act three, scene one (3.1.167–79) and then somewhat lengthily introduced in an encounter between the King and Rosencrantz and Guildenstern (4.3). Often cut in modern productions, these passages leave no trace in Q1. The dramatization of Hamlet's return is, from the point of view of the stage, equally heavy-handed. After the lethal stabbing of Polonius has shown Hamlet's determination, Claudius is eager to get rid of the Prince and has him sail to England, accompanied by Rosencrantz and Guildenstern. At night, Hamlet finds out that the sealed message which his companions are to carry to the King of England contain an order to have him executed. Hamlet forges a new order commanding the death of Rosencrantz and Guildenstern and exchanges the two commissions. Later on pirates attack them and take Hamlet prisoner while his companions sail on to their destruction in England. The pirates treat him kindly and free him in exchange for certain services, after which Hamlet returns to Denmark.

All these intricate events take place offstage between act four, scene four, when Hamlet is leaving Denmark, and the beginning of act five when we see him back in his country. They are not directly dramatized but narrated in several installments: act four, scene six has a sailor deliver Hamlet's letter to Horatio who learns from it part of the story. The following scene opens with the King and Laertes still unaware of Hamlet's escape until another letter arrives from the Prince. At the beginning of act five, scene two, finally, another sequence has Hamlet tell Horatio those events which he did not communicate in the letter. These various passages, which are all narrative rather than dramatic, considerably slow down the pace of the action.

This fact seems to have been taken into account when the play was prepared for the stage.[26] After Ophelia's second madness scene (act four, scene five in modern editions), Q1 inserts the only scene that has no equivalent in the long texts. It has been believed that the reporter or reporters who undertook the memorial reconstruction failed to remember substantial parts of the original play and consequently had to invent a new scene.[27] It is more likely, however, that the scene is part of a conscious reworking designed to shorten and speed up the play in preparation for the stage. In order to substantiate these claims, I need to quote the scene in its entirety:

---

[26] Whoever turned *Hamlet* into *Der Bestrafte Brudermord* (*Fratricide Punished*) – which was performed on the Continent by English comedians – appears to have been similarly dissatisfied by the longwinded, narrative handling of Hamlet's journey to England. In this version, the "two ruffians" (Rosencrantz and Guildenstern) are ordered to kill Hamlet as soon as they reach England. Act four, scene one dramatizes their attempt to carry out this order which results in a farcical failure when Hamlet "falls down forward between the two servants, who shoot each other." I quote from H. Howard Furness's translation in Bullough's *Sources of Shakespeare* VII.150.

[27] See, for instance, Duthie, *"Bad" Quarto of Hamlet*, 86–93.

Enter Horatio and the Queene.

HOR[ATIO]. Madame, your sonne is safe arriv'de in *Denmarke.*
  This letter I euen now receiv'd of him,
  Whereas he writes how he escap't the danger,
  And subtle treason that the king had plotted,
  Being crossed by the contention of the windes,
  He found the Packet sent to the king of *England*,
  Wherein he saw himselfe betray'd to death,
  As at his next conuersion with your grace,
  He will relate the circumstance at full.
QUEENE Then I perceiue there's treason in his lookes
  That seem'd to sugar o're his villainie:
  But I will soothe and please him for a time,
  For murderous mindes are always jealous.
  But know not you *Horatio* where he is?
HOR[ATIO] Yes Madame, and he hath appoynted me
  To meete him on the east side of the Cittie
  To morrow morning.
QUEENE O faile not, good *Horatio*, and withall, commend me
  A mothers care to him, bid him a while
  Be wary of his presence, lest that he
  Faile in that he goes about.
HOR[ATIO]. Madam, neuer make doubt of that:
  I thinke by this the news be come to court:
  He is arriv'de, obserue the king, and you shall
  Quickly finde, *Hamlet* being here,
  Things fell not to his minde.
QUEENE But what became of *Gilderstone* and *Rossencraft?*
HOR[ATIO]. He being set ashore, they went for *England.*
  And in the Packet there writ down that doome
  To be perform'd on them poynted for him:
  And by great chance he had his fathers Seale,
  So all was done without discouerie.
QUEENE Thankes be to heauen for blessing of the prince,
  Horatio, once again I take my leaue
  With thowsand mothers blessings to my sonne.
HORAT[IO]. Madam adue.   (H2ᵛ–H3ʳ)

In little more than thirty lines, the scene sums up all the necessary information that the long texts spread out over different passages. All of these
narrative passages, accordingly, have been omitted from the short text. This
fusion of several sequences into one short scene considerably condenses
the action where Q2 and F slows it down, thereby allowing for a swift,
action-packed and exciting finale. The considerable difference in pace

between Q1 and Q2/F *Hamlet* raises the intriguing possibility that the time-honored belief that procrastination and delay are central to the play has much to do with the text readers have studied but little with the play Elizabethan theatre-goers would have witnessed.[28]

Besides this dramatic restructuring, the new scene in Q1 also allows us to glimpse a Queen who is substantially different from her counterpart in Q2 and the Folio. In the play we know, she is a highly complex figure whose motives and allegiances are far from clear. In Q1, on the other hand, her allegiance to Horatio and Hamlet is unambiguous. She says about her second husband:

> Then I perceiue there's treason in his lookes
> That seem'd to sugar o're his villainie:
> But I will soothe and please him for a time,
> For murderous mindes are always jealous.

This is consistent with the Closet Scene in Q1 where she explicitly asserts that she ignored how her first husband died: "as I haue a soule, I sweare by heauen, / I neuer knew of this most horride murder" (G3ʳ). Later on in Q1's Closet Scene, she promises Hamlet that "I will conceale, consent, and doe my best, / What stratagem soe're thou shalt deuise" (G3ᵛ).[29] This explicit and wholehearted allegiance to her son is again unparallelled in the long texts where her degree of complicity with Claudius is far from clear and has been the subject of critical speculation.[30]

---

[28] The swift pace called for by the short theatrical texts can also be inferred from 2.6 in *Romeo and Juliet*, the one scene that is made up of substantially different material from its counterpart in the second quarto. In Q1, the emphasis is on haste throughout the scene: "Without more words I will doo all I may," the Friar assures Romeo even before Juliet's arrival. As soon as Romeo has optimistically announced that "come she will," Juliet enters, and does so "somewhat fast," as the stage direction puts it. In the scenes closing lines, all three characters seem equally bent on speeding up the action:

> FR[IAR]: Come wantons, come, the stealing houres do passe [. . .]
> ROM[EO]: Lead holy Father, all delay seemes long.
> IUL[IET]: Make hast, make hast, this lingring doth vs wrong.
>
> (E4ᵛ)

In Q2, in contrast, none of the quoted lines have an equivalent. Instead of hastening to their marriage, Romeo and Juliet express their love in lyrical conceits. Similarly, after bidding farewell to Romeo, Juliet has a speech in which she addresses Fortune in Q2, which is replaced in Q1 by the nurse entering "hastely" to warn Juliet of her mother's arrival (G3ᵛ).

[29] Matters are further complicated by the fact that the Queen's lines echo Bel-imperia in *The Spanish Tragedy* (4.1.46–48).

[30] C. H. Herford, for instance, wrote of "the veil which in Q2 is studiously made to conceal the precise measure of her complicity in the murder," a suggestion later critics elaborated (*The First Quarto Edition of "Hamlet," 1603* (London, 1880)). For the Q1 Queen, see also Urkowitz, " 'Well-sayd olde Mole,' " 46–49; and Dorothea Kehler, "The First Quarto of *Hamlet*: Reforming Widow Gertred," *Shakespeare Quarterly*, 46 (1995), 398–413.

It is a feature not just of Q1's Queen but of the short text as a whole that characterization is less multi-layered and complex than it is in the long texts. Q1's Leartes (Laertes), for instance, is a straightforward revenger out for retribution for his father'd death, but he does not become a public danger by leading a rebellion. Similarly, Q1's King is more of a straightforward villain than his counterpart in the long texts.

This also applies to the play's hero as the restructurating of acts two and three discussed above has already suggested. Q1's graveyard scene, in particular, presents us with a different Hamlet from the one we are used to. The Prince who has returned from the sea-voyage is traditionally seen as a matured man, wiser and more measured, less flippant and histrionic than earlier on, calmly accepting of providence rather than madly defiant. At the funeral of Ophelia, Hamlet is accordingly on the defensive in the confrontation with Laertes: "take thy fingers from my throat" (5.1.257) and "[a]way thy hand" (5.1.264) Hamlet begs his opponent. Yet a stage direction in Q1 is not easy to reconcile with this view of the Prince. After Ophelia's brother has jumped into her grave, Hamlet "leapes in after Leartes" (as Laertes is called in Q1), thus attacking rather than being attacked by Ophelia's brother. Clearly, this is not the matured prince in control of his emotions which the above interpretation of his character presupposes. Hamlet's gesture has understandably disturbed critics and editors of the play. Philip Edwards, for instance, was convinced that "Shakespeare cannot have intended Hamlet to leap into the grave and so become the attacker," and consequently excludes the stage direction from his edition.[31] Yet a near-contemporary document that happens to survive proves Edwards wrong. An elegy of 1619 written on the death of Richard Burbage, the leading actor of Shakespeare's company, mentions that the deceased had played, among other parts, that of "young Hamlett."[32] Evoking what he remembers most vividly from Burbage's performance of the part, the anonymous elegist writes: "Oft haue I seene him leap into the graue."[33] Richard Burbage's Hamlet at the Globe of which we find a reflection in the Hamlet of Q1 seems to have been a

---

[31] Philip Edwards, ed., *Hamlet, Prince of Denmark*, New Cambridge Shakespeare (Cambridge University Press, 1985), 223.

[32] The adjective with which Hamlet is here qualified is of some interest. In the long texts, the Prince's age represents a well-known problem. Early on in the play, he is referred to as "young Hamlet" and is said to have returned from Wittenberg where he is a student. Yet, in the last act, the Gravedigger suggests that he is thirty years old. In Q1, the latter indication has disappeared and nothing contradicts the impression of Hamlet's youthful age. Yorick's skull "hath bin here this dozen yeare" (line 1987) – not twenty-three as in the long texts – and the Prince is again referred to as "yong" (line 1989). The elegy on Burbage thus seems to corroborate what Q1 – but not Q2 and F – suggest about Hamlet's age.

[33] The passage is quoted in Chambers, *Elizabethan Stage*, 11.309.

rather different character from the one modern critics and editors imagine him to have been.[34]

The above analyses of *Hamlet* and *Henry V* have shown that the short, theatrical texts repeatedly flatten out the complex, "life-like" characters of the long, literary texts, turning ambiguous figures, whose "motivations" can and have been subjected to extensive analysis, into "mere types," the villainous king, the loyal mother Gertrude, or, in *Henry V*, the successful warrior king. This difference in characterization is best understood not in qualitative terms, equating "life-like" with "good" and "types" with "bad." Rather, it seems useful to understand the difference in characterization between the long and short texts of Shakespeare's plays as resulting from the respective media for which they were designed. As Ong has put it:

> The modern reader has typically understood effective "characterization" in narrative or drama as the production of the "round" character, to use E. M. Forster's term . . . the character that "has the incalculability of life about it." Opposed to the "round" character is the "flat" character, the type of character that never surprises the reader but, rather, delights by fulfilling expectations copiously. We know now that the type "heavy" (or "flat") character derives originally from primary oral narrative, which can provide characters of no other kind.[35]

This account has the advantage of describing the effect ("fulfilling expectations copiously") of so-called "flat" characterization rather than judging it solely by the standards of a modern, print-based culture. As this kind of characterization needs to be viewed in the context of the cultures of orality out of which it grows, "round" characterization is profitably understood as part of the advent of increasing literacy:

> As discourse moves from primary orality to greater and greater chirographic and typographic control, the flat, "heavy" or type character yields to characters that grow more and more "round," that is, that perform in ways at first blush unpredictable but ultimately consistent in terms of the complex character structure and complex motivation with which the round character is endowed . . . In the private worlds [writing and reading] generate, the feeling for the "round" human character is born – deeply interiorized in motivation, powered mysteriously, but consistently, from within. First emerging in chirographically controlled ancient Greek drama,

---

[34] Even though I am less certain than Janis Lull that Q1 *Hamlet* is a memorial reconstruction, her argument that Q1 "reinterprets the play, making it affirm the very warrior values that the F version calls into question" seems to me pertinent. See Lull, "Forgetting *Hamlet*: The First Quarto and the Folio," in *The "Hamlet" First Published*, ed. Clayton, 137–50, 149.

[35] Ong, *Orality and Literacy*, 151.

the "round" character is further developed in Shakespeare's age after the coming of print, and comes to its peak with the novel, when, after the advent of the Age of Romanticism, print is more fully interiorized.[36]

Ong's analysis of the relationship of characterization and orality and literacy provides an enabling context for an examination of the variant texts of *Hamlet* and *Henry V*. It seems significant that the protagonists of the long texts are the complex, at first unpredictable and deeply interiorized characters Ong associates with the private world of reading while the protagonists of the short texts are considerably more typified. For audiences familiar with Kyd's *Spanish Tragedy* and his lost "Hamlet", or with the heroic warrior king Nashe recalls having seen on stage, the title characters of the short, but not of the long, texts would have "fulfill[ed] expectations copiously."

The respective kinds of characters orality and literacy tend to produce can also account for differences in the speech prefixes between the long and short texts. Mountjoy in *Henry V* is simply the "Herauld" in Q1, and Williams, who questions the King so eloquently about his responsibilites, is the "2. Souldier." Speech prefixes in Q1 *Romeo and Juliet* similarly have characters' functions where the longer text has names: the "2. Seruing-men" of the opening stage direction of *Romeo and Juliet*, reduced to "1" and "2" in the speech prefixes, are called Sampson and Gregorie in the stage directions and the speech prefixes of the second quarto. Similarly, "Peter" in the speech prefixes of act four, scene five is simply a "Seruingman" in Q1. In *Hamlet*, finally, Bernardo and Francisco of the long texts are "two Centinels" in the first quarto, and the second quarto introduces the King as "Claudius," a name that is absent from the first quarto. Mysteriously linked to one's identity, indicative and constitutive of personal identity and individuality, the names in the long texts suggest "life-like" characters favored by a culture of literacy where the short texts suggest functions or types indicative of orality.

The following variant passages in Q1 and Q2 *Romeo and Juliet* provide a specific example of how a text constructs, or does not construct, a "round" character. At the beginning of the play's second scene, Paris asks Capulet to give him Juliet in marriage. Q1 reads:

> [PARIS.] [...] what say you to my sute?
> CAPU[LET]: What should I say more than I said before,
>   My daughter is a stranger in the world,
>   Shee hath not yet attainde to fourteene yeares:

---

[36] Ibid., 151–53.

Let two more sommers wither in their pride,
Before she can be thought fit for a Bride.
PARIS: Younger than she are happie mothers made.
CAP[ULET]: But too soone marde are these so early maried:
But wooe her gentle *Paris*, get her heart,
My word to her consent is but a part.   (B2ᵛ)

The corresponding passage in Q2 substitutes a few words, but basically
provides a line-for-line equivalent with the exception of two verses that are
added to Capulet's last speech:

CAPU[LET]. And too soone mard are those so early made:
Earth hath swallowed all my hopes but she,
Shees the hopefull Lady of my earth:
But wooe her gentle *Paris*, get her hart,
My will to her consent, is but a part.   (B2ᵛ)

The rest of the play does little or nothing to develop Capulet's allusion
to his former loss, and he largely remains a "flat" character. Nevertheless,
the two lines provide the kind of information – "deeply interiorized in
motivation, powered mysteriously" – from which a Bradleian character
analysis might take off. Even though a loose end in terms of the intrigue,
they provide a psychological detail that makes Capulet a more interesting
and somewhat "rounder" character. Arguably, the lines go some way toward
constituting a round character *because* they form a loose end, fulfilling no
immediate function, thereby suggesting that the character is not confined
to the dramatic text in which he figures.

Bradleian character analysis dominated Shakespeare criticism in the early
twentieth century, but was subjected to mockery by L. C. Knights as early
as 1933 in his essay "How many children had Lady Macbeth?"[37] It fared
badly both with New Critical and more recent postmodernist approaches.
As Heather Dubrow has pointed out, "character has virtually become a dirty
word, quite as taboo in many circles as frank glosses on Shakespeare's sexual
wordplay were to an earlier generation of editors."[38] A better understanding
of the cultural contingency of characterization might change such a state
of affairs. Specifically, an assessment of Shakespeare's characters that does
not teleologically take for granted the superiority of the "round" character

---

[37] L. C. Knights, *How Many Children Had Lady Macbeth? An Essay in the Theory and Practice of Shakespeare Criticism* (Cambridge: Minority Press, 1933), often reprinted, for instance in L. C. Knights, *Explorations: Essays in Criticism Mainly on the Literature of the Seventeenth Century* (New York University Press, 1964).

[38] Heather Dubrow, *Captive Victors: Shakespeare's Narrative Poems and Sonnets* (Ithaca: Cornell University Press, 1987), 17.

which a culture of literacy has brought about might profitably be included in a more extended treatment of the theatrical and literary features of Shakespeare's playtexts.

This chapter has explored some of the implications for the variant texts of *Romeo and Juliet*, *Henry V*, and *Hamlet* of the argument I developed in Part I of this study: to a degree that has not been fully recognized, Shakespeare became a dramatic author during his own lifetime, writing drama for the stage *and* the page, to be published in performance *and* in print. The two media, I have argued, have left traces in some of the variant playtexts: the literariness of the long texts contrasts in certain ways with the theatricality of the short texts, reflecting respectively an emergent culture of increasing literacy and an enduring culture of orality. I have thus tried to complicate our understanding of the "bad" quartos, whose designation has often been lamented but perhaps not yet been properly historicized and redefined. According to the literary logic with which Shakespeare's plays were approached for most of the nineteenth and twentieth centuries, the long variant playtexts are indeed better than the short. Yet, if we restore them to the early modern culture out of which they grew, it seems less useful to consider them as bad than as simply different. This difference, as this chapter has tried to show, records crucial traces of both the plays Shakespeare and his fellows performed and of Shakespeare, literary dramatist.

The plays of Shakespeare and his contemporaries in print, 1584–1623

Table 1 contains a summary of all publications of works by or attributed to Shakespeare from 1593 to 1623. I underline all editions that advertise Shakespeare's authorship on the title page. I use a dotted line when the title page contains Shakespeare's initials, when an edition was printed with two title pages of which only one contains Shakespeare's name, or when the title page or the entire edition is lost. The three columns in the center and to the right list the various publications divided into "Plays," "Poetry," and "Other." "Other" includes miscellanies that contain Shakespearean verse as well as plays and poetry that have been wrongly (or doubtfully) ascribed to Shakespeare. For want of space, the stationers, in the second column, are mentioned by last name only. For further information, the reader is referred to McKerrow's *Dictionary of Printers and Booksellers*, still an indispensable reference work. For abbreviations of Shakespeare's works, I follow the MLA *Handbook*. For all other titles and for a number of Shakespearean editions, I provide explanatory glosses below.

Table 2 provides a summary of all plays performed on the commercial stage that appeared in print between 1584 and 1623. It complements and illustrates some of the points I make above, especially in Part I. While many title pages make clear whether a play had been written for the commercial stage, not all of them do. In cases of doubt, I have based my choice of in- or exclusion on Chambers' *Elizabethan Stage*, Bentley's *Jacobean and Caroline Stage*, and Harbage's *Annals*.

I use the numerical system in Greg's *Bibliography* to refer to the plays: "82a" thus designates the first edition of *Sapho and Phao*, published in 1584; "389a" refers to the first edition of *The Duchess of Malfi*, published in 1623 (see Greg, *Bibliography of the English Printed Drama to the Restoration*, 1.160, II.535). Greg assigned numbers to all printed plays, starting with the earliest. He further added letters to designate editions, "a" for the first, "b" for the second, and so on. I have also observed the following conventions: bold for Shakespeare plays, underline for playbooks that identify the playwright, dotted underline for initials only, and double underline for plays that are attributed to more than one playwright. In this and the following table, I add a question mark to undated or lost editions whose approximate dating is based on conjecture.

For easy reference, I here provide a brief summary of some information contained in this table. The total number of plays published in quarto or octavo format is exactly 200. Only 17 plays were published in the first ten-year period from 1584 to 1593. The following fifteen years (1594–1608) saw a significant rise (133 plays) followed by a significant drop in the final fifteen years from 1609 to 1623 (50 plays). As for the publication of Shakespeare's plays, 14 out of 57 of the plays published in the period from 1594 to 1600 are Shakespeare's, that is nearly one in four or 25 percent. In contrast, only five out of the 111 plays published in the period from 1601 to 1616 are Shakespeare's, that is less than 5 percent.

As for the gradual emergence of dramatic authorship, the title pages of 112 of the 200 plays attribute the play to one (99) or several (13) authors. Of these, 17 identify the playwright by initials only. Of the 60 plays published before the turn of the century, 42 (70%) do not identify the playwright(s) on the title page. In contrast, of the 140 plays published after the turn of the century, only 47 were published anonymously (34%).

Table 3 provides a summary of all editions of the plays listed in Table 2. The 200 quarto or octavo playbooks published from 1584 to 1623 appeared in a total of 347 editions during those same years. Insofar as Shakespeare is concerned, what is particularly noteworthy is that, while 25 of the 84 editions printed in the period from 1594 to 1600 are Shakespearean, that is about 30 percent, that percentage drops to a mere 11 percent for the period from 1601 to 1616 (20 out of 183).

Table 4 provides the total number of extant printed playbook editions and of extant titles for the period from 1584 to 1623. For the number of extant titles, I am indebted to Alain Veylit's website at http://cbsr26.ucr.edu/ESTCStatistics.html, which presents "Some Statistics on the Number of Surviving Printed Titles for Great Britain and Dependencies from the Beginnings of Print in England to the year 1800." It is noteworthy that the fraction of printed playbooks in the trade in English books is significantly higher during the years of Shakespeare's active involvement with the Lord Chamberlain's and King's Men (1594 – c. 1613) than in the ten-year segments before or after this period.

Table 1 *Notes*

The 1595 quarto edition of *Locrine* is said to be "By W. S." Considering Shakespeare's name did not appear on a title page for another three years, it seems unlikely that the initials were used to induce the reader to think that Shakespeare wrote the play. I therefore do not include this edition in the table.

O1 *Ven.*, 1595 (?): the only extant copy of this edition lacks the title page.

Q/O1 *LLL*, 1597: the first edition of *Love's Labour's Lost* is lost, yet its date, as has recently been discovered, is mentioned in the library catalogue of Edward, 2nd Viscount Conway (1594–1655): "Loves Labours Lost by W. Sha: 1597." See Arthur Freeman and Paul Grinke, "Four New Shakespeare Quartos?," *The Times Literary Supplement*, April 5, 2002, 17–18.

O1, O2, O3 *PP*, 1599, 1599, 1612: *The Passionate Pilgrim* (*STC* 22341.5, 22342, 22343). Of the first edition of *The Passionate Pilgrim*, only an undated fragment survives. For the date 1599, see John Roe, ed., *The Poems*, New Cambridge Shakespeare (Cambridge University Press, 1992), 294.

O *Parnassus*, 1600: *England's Parnassus* (*STC* 378). The dedicatory sonnet is signed R[obert]. A[llot].(?). This anthology contains a large number of excerpts from Shakespeare's plays and narrative poems; the excerpts are attributed to Shakespeare.

O *Belvedere*, 1600: *Bel-vedére, or the garden of the muses*, by John Bodenham, ed. by A[nthony]. M[unday].(?). (*STC* 3189). This anthology contains a large number of excerpts from Shakespeare's plays and narrative poems; the excerpts are not attributed to Shakespeare.

Q, O *Helicon*, 1600, 1614: *England's Helicon* (*STC* 3191, 3192). This miscellany, edited by John Bodenham or L[ing]. N[icholas].(?), contains one poem by "W. Shakespeare" – Dumain's address to Kate in *Love's Labour's Lost* (previously included in *The Passionate Pilgrim*).

Q *Love's Martyr*, 1601: (*STC* 5119). This miscellany, "by R[obert]. Chester," contains the poem commonly referred to as "The Phoenix and the Turtle" by "W. Shakespeare." It was reissued in 1611 with a cancel title page as "The anuals [*sic*] of great Brittaine" (*STC* 5120). Note that Chambers (*William Shakespeare*, 1.549) mistakes the 1611 reissue for a new edition.

Q1, 2 *Cromwell*, 1602, 1613: *Thomas Lord Cromwell*, "Written by W. S."

O5 *Ven*, 1602 (?), O6 *Ven.*, 1607 (?), O7 *Ven.*, 1608 (?), O8 *Ven.*, 1610 (?): the only extant copy of O5 *Venus and Adonis* lacks the title page. O6, O7, and O8 *Venus and Adonis* are falsely dated 1602. For the dating of these editions, see Harry Farr, "Notes on Shakespeare's Printers and Publishers, with Special Reference to the Poems and *Hamlet*," *The Library*, 4th series, 3 (1922–23), 225–60, esp. 229–45. The dating in the *STC* and the *ESTC* follows Farr's article.

Q2 *Ham.*, 1604: some copies of Q2 *Hamlet* are dated 1605 rather than 1604.

Q1 *London Prodigal*, 1605: "By VVilliam Shakespeare."

Q1 *Puritan*, 1607: "Written by W. S."

Q1, Q2 *York. Tr.* 1608, 1619: *A Yorkshire Tragedy*, "Written by VV. Shakspeare" (1608), "Written by W. SHAKESPEARE" (1619).

Q3 *Per.*, 1611: the format of this edition is what is called an "octavo-in-fours," i.e., it was printed on double-sized octavo paper that had been divided into two halves. The book's chain lines, contrary to those of a quarto, are therefore vertical.

Q2, 3 *Tr. Reign*, 1611, 1622: *The Troublesome Reign of King John*, "Written by W. Sh." (1611), "Written by W. SHAKESPEARE" (1622).

Q *Fun. Elegy*, 1612: "A Funeral Elegy in Memory of the Late Virtuous Master William Peter" (*STC* 21526) "by W. S." G[eorge]. Eld [for Thomas Thorpe], 1612.

Q2 *Oldcastle*, 1619: *Sir John Oldcastle*, "Written by William Shakespeare."

Q4 *Rom.*, 1622 (?): the fourth quarto of *Romeo and Juliet* is undated. George Walton Williams ("The Printer and Date of *Romeo and Juliet* Q4," *Studies in Bibliography*, 18 (1965), 253–54) suggested 1622 as the publication date, but Lynette Hunter ("Dating of Q4 *Romeo and Juliet* Revisited") has convincingly argued that the edition may have been published in any year between 1618 and 1626. Note that Q4 *Romeo and Juliet* was printed with two title pages, one anonymous, one "by W. Shakespeare."

Q4 *Ham.*, 1622 (?): the fourth quarto of *Hamlet* is undated. Harold Jenkins (*Hamlet*, The Arden Shakespeare (London, 1982), 17–18) argues that the edition appeared in 1622. Note though that the *STC* suggests 1625 as date for Q4 *Hamlet*.

Table 1 *Shakespeare and Print, 1593–1623*

Year	Stationers' Register	Plays	Poetry	Other
1593	4/18 Field, *Ven.*		Q1 *Ven.*	
1594	2/6 Danter, *Tit.*; 3/12 Millington, *2H6*; 5/9 Harrison, *Luc.*	Q1 *Tit.*, Q1 *2H6*	Q1 *Luc.*, Q2 *Ven.*	
1595	12/1 Burby, *E3*	O1 *3H6*	O1 *Ven.* (?)	
1596		Q1 *E3*	O2 *Ven.*	
1597	8/29 Wise, *R2*; 10/20 Wise, *R3*	Q1 *LLL*, Q1 *R2*, Q1 *R3*, Q1 *Rom.*		
1598	2/25 Wise, *1H4*; 7/22 Roberts, *MV*	Q1, Q2 *1H4*, Q2 *LLL*, Q2, Q3 *R2*, Q2 *R3*	O1 *Luc.*	
1599		Q2 *Rom*, Q3 *1H4*, Q2 *E3*	O3, O4 *Ven.*	Q1, Q2 *PP*
1600	8/14 Pavier, *H5*; 8/23 Wise, Aspley, *2H4*, *Ado*; 10/8 Fisher, *MND*	Q1 *H5*, Q2 *2H4*, Q1 *Ado*, Q1 *MND*, Q2 *2H6*, Q1 *3H6*, Q2 *Tit.*, Q1 *MV*	O2, O3 *Luc.*	O *Parnassus*, O *Belvedere*, Q *Helicon*
1601				Q *Love's Martyr*
1602	1/18 Busby, *Wiv.*, 7/26 Roberts, *Ham.*	Q1 *Wiv.*, Q3 *R3*, Q2 *H5*	O5 *Ven.* (?)	Q1 *Cromwell*
1603	2/7 Roberts, *Tro.*	Q1 *Ham.*		
1604		Q2 *Ham.*, Q4 *1H4*		
1605		Q4 *R3*		Q1 *London Prodigal*
1606				
1607	11/26 Butter, Busby, *Lr.*		O6 *Ven.* (?), O4 *Luc.*	Q1 *Puritan*
1608	5/20 Blount, *A&C*, *Per.*	Q1 *Lr.*, Q4 *R2*, Q5 *1H4*	O7 *Ven.* (?)	Q1 *York. Tr.*
1609	5/20, Thorpe, *Son.*	Q1 *Tro.*, Q1, Q2 *Per.*, Q3 *Rom*	Q *Son.*	
1610			O8 *V&A* (?)	
1611		Q3 *Tit.*, Q3 *Ham.*, Q3 *Per.*		Q2 *Tr. Reign*
1612		Q5 *R3*		Q3 *PP*, Q *Fun. Elegy*

1613	Q6 1H4		Q2 Cromwell
1614			O Helicon
1615	Q5 R2		
1616		O5 Luc.	
1617		O9 Ven.	
1618			
1619	Q3 2H6, Q2 3H6, Q4 Per., Q2 Wiv., Q2 MV, Q2 Lr., Q3 H5, Q2 MND		Q2 Oldcastle Q2 York. Tr.
1620		O10 Ven.	
1621	10/6 Walkley, Oth.		
1622	Q1 Oth., Q6 R3, Q7 1H4, Q4 Rom. (?), Q4 Ham. (?)		Q3 Tr. Reign
1623	F1		

Table 2 *Print Publication of English Stage Plays, First Editions, 1584–1623*

Year	Editions published as designated in Greg's *Bibliography*																		No. of editions published
1584	82a	83a	84a	85a															4
1585																			0
1586																			0
1587																			0
1588																			0
1589	92a																		1
1590	93a	94a	95a																3
1591	99a	101/2a																	2
1592	105a	106a	107a	109a	110a														5
1593	112a	113a																	2
1594	114a	115a	**117a**	118a	119a	120a	121a	122a	123a	124a	125a	126a	127a	128a	129a	130a	131a	133a	18
1595	134a	136a	137a	**138a**															4
1596	139a	**140a**																	2
1597	**141a**	**142a**	143a	144a	**150aa**														5
1598	**145a**	146a	148a	149a	151a														5
1599	153a	154a	155a	156a	157a	158a	159a	160a	161a										9
1600	162a	163a	164a	**165a**	166a	**167a**	**168a**	169a	**170a**	171a	**172a**	173a	174a	175a					14
1601	176a	177a	178a	179a	180a	181a	182a												7
1602	184a	185a	186a	**187a**	188a	189a	190a	191a	192a	195a									10
1603	**197a**	198a																	2
1604	203a	204a	205a	206a															4
1605	210a	211a	212a	213a	214a	215a	216a	217a	219a	220a	221a	222a							12
1606	224a	226a	228a	229a	230a	231a	234a	235a	236a										9

Year																				Count
1607	241a	242a	243a	244a	245a	246a	247a	248a	249a	250a	251a	252a	253a	254a	255a	256a	257a	258a	259a	19
1608	262a	263a	264a	**265a**	266a	267a	268a	272a	273a	274a	275a	276a	277a							13
1609	**279a**	281a	**284a**	283a	285a															5
1610	286a	287a	290a																	3
1611	292a	293a	294a	296a	297a	298a														6
1612	299a	300a	301a	303a	304a?	305a	306a	307a												8
1613	313a	315a	316a	317a																4
1614	321a	323a																		2
1615	327a	328a	329a	333a																4
1616	334a	336a	337a	FI JONSON																3 + F
1617	352a																			1
1618	356a																			1
1619	357a	360a																		2
1620	362a	363a	364a																	3
1621	368a																			1
1622	**379a**	380a	382a	384a																4
1623	386a	388a	389a	FI SHAKESPEARE																3 + F

Table 3 Print Publication of Stage Plays, 1584–1623

Year	Editions published as designated in Greg's *Bibliography*	No. of editions published
1584	82a 82b 83a 84a 84b 84c 85a	7
1585		0
1586		0
1587		0
1588		0
1589	92a	1
1590	93a 94a 95a	3
1591	82c 84d 99a 101/2a	4
1592	85b 105a 106a 107a 109a 110aa 110a	7
1593	94b 112a 113a	3
1594	110b 114a 115a **117a** 118a **119a** 120a 121a 122a 123a 124a 125a 126a 127a 128a 129a 130a 131a 133a	19
1595	134a 136a 137a **138a**	4
1596	120b 139a **140a**	3
1597	94c 95b **141a** **142a** **143a** 144a **150aa**	7
1598	118b 125b 129b **141b** **141c** **142b** **145a** **145b** 146a 148a 149a **150a** 151a	13
1599	107b 109b 110c 112b 123b **140b** **143b** **145c** 153a 154a 155a 156a 157a 158a 159a 160a 161a 161b	18
1600	**117b** **119b** **138b** 153b 154b 162a 163a 163b 164a **165a** 166a **167a** **168a** 169a **170a** 171a **172a** 173a 174a 175a	20
1601	176a 177a 178a 179a 180a 181a 182a	7
1602	110d 118c **142c** **165b** 184a 185a 186a **187a** 188a 189a 190a 191a 192a 195a	14
1603	110e **197a** 198a	3
1604	114b **145d** 163c? **197b** 203a 203b 203c 204a 204b? 205a 206a	11
1605	95c **142d** 153c 154c 191b 204c 210a 211a 212a 213a 214a 215a 216a 217a 217b 217c 219a 220a 221a 222a	20
1606	94d 151b 215b 224a 226a 228a 229a 230a 230b 231a 234a 235a 236a	13
1607	120c 241a 242a 243a 244a 245a 246a 247a 248a 249a 250a 251a 252a 253a 254a 255a 256a 257a 258a 259a	20
1608	**141d** **145e** 191c 215c 262a 263a 264a **265a** 266a 267a 268a 272a 273a 274a 275a 276a 277a	17

Year	Entries	Count
1609	**143c** 205b 224b 273b **279a** 281a 283a **284a** **284b** 285a	10
1610	118d? 151c 175b 215d 255b 286a 287a 290a	8
1611	101/2b 110f **117c** 151d **197c** 205c 247b 249b **284c** 292a 292b 293a 294a 296a 297a 298a	16
1612	129c **142e** 256b 264b 299a 300a 301a 303a 304a? 305a 306a 307a	12
1613	**145f** 151e 153d 154d 189b 212b 215e 313a 315a 316a 317a	11
1614	191d 234b 273c 321a 323a	5
1615	110g **141e** 151f 204d 255c 327a 328a 329a 333a	9
1616	205d 262b 315b 334a 336a 337a FI JONSON	6+
1617	118e 148b 258b 264c 352a	5
1618	110h 151g 171b 175c 356a	5
1619	**119c** **138c** 151h 153e 154e **165c** 166b **170b** **172b** **187b** 205c **265b** 272b **284d** 357a 360a	16
1620	205f 304c 362a 363a 364a	5
1621	151i 191e 212c 368a	4
1622	101/2c 129d **142f** **143d?** **145g** **197d?** 323b 352b 357b 363b **379a** 380a 382a 384a	14
1623	110i 215f 224c 234c 386a 388a 389a FI SHAKESPEARE	7+

Table 4 *The Fraction of Printed Playbooks in the Trade in English Books,*
1584–1623

Year	Number of extant printed playbooks	Number of extant printed titles	Percentage of printed playbooks	Average percentage
1584	7	280	2.5	
1585	0	328	0.0	
1586	0	230	0.0	
1587	0	237	0.0	
1588	0	247	0.0	1584–1593: 0.9
1589	1	296	0.3	
1590	3	353	0.8	
1591	4	302	1.3	
1592	7	299	2.3	
1593	3	210	1.4	
1594	19	261	7.3	
1595	4	324	1.2	
1596	3	313	1.0	
1597	7	279	2.5	
1598	13	291	4.5	1594–1603: 3.4
1599	18	316	5.7	
1600	20	402	5.0	
1601	7	254	2.8	
1602	14	325	4.3	
1603	3	443	0.7	
1604	11	418	2.6	
1605	20	382	5.2	
1606	13	407	3.2	
1607	20	442	4.5	
1608	17	402	4.2	1604–1613: 3.2
1609	10	471	2.1	
1610	8	419	1.9	
1611	16	414	3.9	
1612	12	461	2.6	
1613	11	500	2.2	
1614	5	447	1.1	
1615	9	542	1.7	
1616	7	483	1.5	
1617	5	429	1.2	
1618	5	535	0.9	1614–1623: 1.4
1619	16	504	3.2	
1620	5	606	0.8	
1621	4	581	0.7	
1622	14	607	2.3	
1623	8	568	1.4	

Heminge and Condell's "Stolne, and surreptitious copies" and the Pavier quartos

Building upon recent textual scholarship, I have argued in chapter 8 that Pollard's identification of Heminge and Condell's "stolne, and surreptitious copies" with what he termed the "bad" quartos has been of crucial importance for our understanding of Shakespeare's texts. I have further suggested that the traditional understanding of the "bad" quartos is in need of refinement and revision. If these texts were legitimately put together by players who transcribed (approximations of) what they had acted – as Moseley implies – and are not the result of theatrical pirates as Pollard thought, then it may legitimately be asked whether Pollard's identification "of the stolne, and surreptitious copies" with the "bad" quartos was correct. I believe it was not. But what then *were* Heminge and Condell referring to?

What may have been important about these "copies" from the point of view of the people involved in a risky business venture in the 1620s was not that non-authorial manuscripts with what scholars several centuries later were to call "corrupt texts" had been printed late in the sixteenth or in the first years of the seventeenth century. Q1 *Hamlet* and *Romeo and Juliet*, it may be well to remember, had been published twenty and twenty-six years ago and had long been superseded by several "good" editions. Rather, it was that they belonged to a bibliographical project recent enough to affect the market when the First Folio appeared.

A collection of ten plays, generally referred to as the Pavier quartos, had appeared in 1619 in what may have been an aborted attempt to publish an even larger collection of Shakespeare's plays.[1] The credentials of the collection, published by Thomas Pavier and printed by William Jaggard, were

---

[1] On the Pavier collection, see W. W. Greg, "On Certain False Dates in Shakespearian Quartos," *The Library*, n.s., 9 (1908), 381–409; Pollard, *Shakespeare Folios and Quartos*, 64–80; Chambers, *William Shakespeare*, I.133–37; Greg, *Bibliography*, III.1107–9; Greg, *First Folio*, 13–15; W. S. Kable, *The Pavier Quartos and the First Folio of Shakespeare* (Dubuque, Iowa: W. C. Brown, 1971); Gerald D. Johnson, "Thomas Pavier, Publisher, 1600–25," *The Library*, 6th series, 14 (1992), 12–50, esp. 35–40, 48; Berger and Lander, "Shakespeare in Print," 403–5; and Andrew Murphy, *Shakespeare in Print* (Cambridge University Press, forthcoming), ch. 2. The possibility that Heminge and Condell's "stolne and

rather mixed: apart from the five plays mentioned above, it included reprints of *A Yorkshire Tragedy* (first published in 1608 and wrongly attributed to Shakespeare), *1 Sir John Oldcastle* (first published in 1600 without authorship attribution), *A Midsummer Night's Dream*, *The Merchant of Venice*, and *King Lear* (formerly printed in 1600, 1600, and 1608 respectively). That a collection was planned is suggested by the fact that the first three plays (*1 Contention* and *The True Tragedy*, renamed *The Whole Contention*, plus *Pericles*) were printed with continuous signatures. A letter dated May 3, 1619, from the Lord Chamberlain to the Stationers' Company demanding "That no playes that his Ma^tyes players do play shalbe printed wth out consent of som*me* of them" has generally been understood as an indication of opposition to the Pavier collection.[2] It may well indicate that the Shakespeare Folio was projected by that time.[3] The seven remaining Pavier quartos were not printed with continuous signatures and, more importantly, all but one of them were printed with fake imprints, suggesting that the Lord Chamberlain's intervention made Pavier and Jaggard change their plan while printing was in progress.

It seems unlikely, however, that the Stationers' Company opposed the printing of the plays or the fake imprints. Even though Pavier seems to have complied insofar as the collection was not *advertised* as a collection, several bound copies of the ten quartos survive from the seventeenth century, suggesting that the Pavier quartos were nevertheless bound and sold together. Among the "Records of the complete collection," Greg lists two extant copies in seventeenth-century bindings and evidence of at least four more collections that had once formed a single volume.[4] It therefore does not seem entirely accurate to claim that Pavier decided to "issue the texts individually with falsely dated title-pages."[5]

When promoting the Folio of Shakespeare's plays in 1623, what Heminge and Condell therefore needed to cry down in order to praise their own edition was the 1619 Pavier collection. That the Folio contained better texts

surreptitious copies" may be a reference to the Pavier collection has occasionally been mentioned in passing, though it has not, to my knowledge, been fully explored. See, for instance, Irace, *Reforming the "Bad" Quartos*, 168.

[2] See Jackson, *Records*, 110.

[3] Note, though, that the Pavier quartos were not the only editions the King's Men may have objected to. As Ernst Honigmann has pointed out: "it is a curious coincidence that the Lord Chamberlain's letter was considered by the Stationers on 3 May 1619, that *The Maid's Tragedy* was registered on 28 April – and that this same play was reissued in 1622 in an augmented, improved text" (Honigmann, *Stability*, 25–26). *A King and No King*, another King's Men's play, was also published in 1619, and seems to have been set up from a private transcript. The King's Men may have felt that there were rather too many publications of their own plays over which they had no control.

[4] Greg, *Bibliography*, iii.1108.   [5] Kastan, *Shakespeare After Theory*, 84.

of some plays than the earlier editions may have been one, though hardly the chief, of their considerations. The Lord Chamberlain's intervention in 1619 suggests that Pavier's venture was perceived by Heminge and Condell as an illegitimate threat to the projected Folio edition. It seems therefore plausible that, when Pavier still went ahead and flooded the market with playbooks by (or falsely attributed to) Shakespeare, Heminge and Condell thought of them as "stolne, and surreptitious," that is, published in contravention to the Lord Chamberlain's express order.[6]

David Scott Kastan has recently come up with a different interpretation of Heminge and Condell's "stolne, and surreptitious copies." He argues that Shakespeare's fellow actors tried to suggest that *all* early printings were "unauthorized or defective" while fully knowing that some or most of them were not.[7] It is true, of course, that some publishers tried to cry down earlier editions with rhetoric that bore little relationship to the truth. Nevertheless, we *know* that there had been an attempted collected edition of Shakespeare's plays only a few years earlier to which the King's Men objected. Is it likely that Heminge and Condell were trying to lie in a situation in which they could truthfully refer to earlier publications which they considered surreptitious?

My interpretation is supported by the context in which Heminge and Condell refer to the "stolne, and surreptitious copies":

It had bene a thing, we confesse, worthie to haue bene wished, that the Author himselfe had liu'd to haue set forth, and ouerseen his owne writings; But since it hath bin ordain'd otherwise, and he by death departed from that right, we pray you do not envie his Friends, the office of their care, and paine, to haue collected & publish'd them; and so to haue publish'd them, as where (before) you were abus'd with diuerse stolne, and surreptitious copies, maimed and deformed by the frauds and stealthes of iniurious impostors, that expos'd them: euen those, are now offer'd to your view cur'd, and perfect of their limbes. (A3ʳ)

Heminge and Condell do not mention the "stolne, and surreptitious copies" in the context of previous Shakespearean playbook publications in general.

---

[6] The point, it may be worthwhile stressing, is not that the Pavier quartos *were* published surreptitiously, but that Heminge and Condell thought they were. The Lord Chamberlain's/King's Men and the Stationers' Company may not have agreed on the rights the players claimed to have over "their" plays. While the Lord Chamberlain's letter and, I argue, Heminge and Condell's "surreptitious" imply that the players felt entitled to have a say, the Stationers' Company would naturally have considered it their own business. The faked imprints may well have been the result of a compromise: the Company may have urged Pavier to abandon the collection, but the easily detectable differences between genuine and fake imprints suggest that Pavier made no effort to hide from the publishers of the genuine editions or from the Company at large (see Johnson, "Thomas Pavier, Publisher," 39–40, see note 1 above).

[7] See Kastan, *Shakespeare After Theory*, 87–91.

Rather, the reference occurs more specifically in the context of his friends' task to collect and publish Shakespeare's plays after his death. The only Shakespearean playbooks published between Shakespeare's death and early 1622, when work on the Folio began, were the Pavier quartos. The passage on which our understanding of the so-called "bad" quartos was long based may thus well have more to do with the Pavier collection than with the textual quality of a group of Shakespearean quartos; with non-respect of the Lord Chamberlain's order in 1619 rather than with memorial reporters around the turn of the century; with economics rather than with textual integrity.

Shakespeare and the circulation
of dramatic manuscripts

In the main part of this study, the possibility that Shakespeare's plays circulated in manuscript during the playwright's lifetime has been briefly touched upon. In particular, I have argued that small-scale manuscript publication might have been a reason for the delay with which Shakespeare's plays appeared in print (see chapters 3 and 4). In this appendix, I intend to survey what evidence there is for such a practice.

Richard Dutton has recently devoted several pages arguing for manuscript circulation of Shakespeare's plays.[1] Most of the apparent evidence he adduces seems to me of doubtful value, however. *Troilus and Cressida*, as I have argued above (chapter 4), is less likely to be based on a private transcript than on a manuscript Shakespeare and his fellows sold to James Roberts before the play was entered in the Stationers' Register in February 1603. That "Chettle implies...that 'divers of worship' have access to written texts" by Shakespeare at a time when none of his plays had appeared in print depends on the questionable belief that Chettle's apology in *Kind-Hartes Dreame* was to Shakespeare.[2] Dutton further thinks that manuscript circulation "would help to explain just how so many quartos based on 'foul papers'...found their way into print."[3] A more economic explanation, as I have argued above, is that Shakespeare and his fellows themselves sought publication.

Nevertheless, it may well be that some private transcripts of Shakespeare's plays existed during the author's lifetime, circulating in manuscript "among his priuate friends" as his poems did, according to Francis Meres's *Palladis Tamia*. It would indeed seem surprising if the practice had suddenly arisen out of nowhere after Shakespeare's death. There is no extant private transcript of any play that can be dated to Shakespeare's lifetime. But, while absence of material evidence dictates scholarly caution, it is not necessarily

---

[1] Dutton, "Birth of the Author," 99–111.
[2] Ibid., 108; for Chettle's apology, see Erne, "Biography and Mythography."
[3] Dutton, "Birth of the Author," 103.

evidence of absence. Greg downplayed the possible existence of manuscript circulation during Shakespeare's lifetime, writing that he was "not aware that any private transcript can be dated before 1624, when the scandal over *A Game at Chess* created a sudden demand."[4] Yet there is evidence for two earlier instances, suggesting that the practice was of some standing in 1624. The manuscript that served as copy for the 1619 quarto edition of Beaumont and Fletcher's *A King and No King* was – as the publisher's epistle "To the Right Worshipfull and worthie Knight, Sir Henrie Neuill" makes clear – a private transcript the publisher had obtained from Nevill.[5] In addition, according to the conventional protestations in the printer's address prefacing the 1620 quarto edition of *The Two Merry Milk-Maids*, the play would not have been published "had not false Copies trauail'd abroad (euen to surbating)."[6] However truthful this claim may have been, it would barely have made any sense if the manuscript circulation of plays had been an unknown phenomenon in 1620.

It may well be, then, that a number of private transcripts of Shakespeare's plays circulated in manuscript, among a private circle of friends and patrons and occasionally beyond, prior to their print publication. One piece of evidence that seems to point to such a practice is Gabriel Harvey's note added on a blank half-page in his copy of Speght's edition of Chaucer. It reads in part: "the younger sort takes much delight in Shakespeares Venus, & Adonis: but his Lucrece, & his tragedie of Hamlet, Prince of Denmarke, haue it in them, to please the wiser sort."[7] It is difficult to imagine that Harvey – who had apparently retired to Walden after 1593 – thinks of *Hamlet* as a play he saw in performance rather than as a reading text, like Shakespeare's narrative poems.[8] The context of Harvey's comment makes clear, however, that his entry must have been written before the Earl of Essex was executed in 1601, so well before *Hamlet* appeared in print.[9]

---

[4] Greg, *Editorial Problem*, 45.
[5] See *Beaumont and Fletcher Canon*, gen. ed. Bowers, 11.169.
[6] See T. H. Howard-Hill, " 'Nor Stage, Nor Stationers Stall Can Show': The Circulation of Plays in Manuscript in the Early Seventeenth Century," *Book History*, 2 (1999), 32.
[7] Moore Smith, ed., *Gabriel Harvey's Marginalia*, 232. See also L. L. Schücking (*Zum Problem der Überlieferung des Hamlet-Textes* (Leipzig: S. Hirzel, 1931), 34–42) and, more recently, in Melchiori, "Acting Version," 195–210, and in Dutton, "Birth of the Author," 105–6.
[8] For Harvey's retirement to Walden, see Virginia F. Stern, *Gabriel Harvey: His Life, Marginalia and Library* (Oxford: Clarendon Press, 1979), 130.
[9] Stern, *Gabriel Harvey*, 125–29. Lewis Theobald's much later mention of private transcripts of the lost play *Cardenio* is not normally accorded much credibility:

There is a Tradition (which I have from the Noble Person, who supply'd me with One of my Copies) that it was given by our Author, as a Present of Value, to a Natural Daughter of his, for whose Sake he wrote it, in the Time of his Retirement from the Stage. Two other copies I have (one of which I

While it is thus possible to make a tentative case for the circulation of some Shakespearean play manuscripts, it is important to stress that all the available evidence suggests that it was not nearly as widespread as the circulation of "Beaumont and Fletcher" manuscripts before 1647. If we believe with Blayney that at least some of the "bad" quartos were set up from some kind of private transcript, this would suggest that a still relatively improvised practice of producing private transcripts may have been emerging (see chapter 8). According to his theory, "performance texts [were] written down by actors who took part in them," sometimes copying from the allowed book, on other occasions reconstructing the text "partly or wholly from memory."[10] Moseley's address in the 1647 "Beaumont and Fletcher" Folio suggests that the practice was well established. This is corroborated by the survival of several material witnesses, manuscripts of "Beaumont and Fletcher" plays which seem to be among the very private transcripts Moseley refers to.[11] Nothing similar is extant in the case of Shakespeare. It would thus be unwise to suppose that the circulation of Shakespeare's plays in manuscript was a well-established practice that existed on a large scale.

was glad to purchase at a very good Rate), which may not, perhaps, be quite so old as the former; but One of Them is much more perfect, and has fewer Flaws and Interruptions in the Sense.

(I quote from the preface to *Double Falsehood* (1728), Theobald's adaptation of *Cardenio*. The preface is printed in Chambers, *William Shakespeare*, 1.540.) The "Natural Daughter" sounds distinctly like a piece of gossip which post-Restoration antiquarians liked to perpetuate. Private transcripts of *Cardenio* may well have existed, but it does not seem possible to accept Theobald as a reliable witness.

[10] Blayney, "Publication of Playbooks," 394.
[11] See Bald, *Beaumont & Fletcher Folio*, 50–102; and chapter 6 above.

Select bibliography

Adams, Joseph Quincy, ed., *The Dramatic Records of Sir Henry Herbert, Master of the Revels, 1623–1673* (New Haven: Yale University Press, 1917).

Albright, Evelyn May, *Dramatic Publication in England, 1580–1640: A Study of Conditions Affecting Content and Form of Drama* (London: Oxford University Press, 1927).

Alexander, Peter, *Shakespeare's "Henry VI" and "Richard III"* (Cambridge University Press, 1929).

Allen, Don Cameron, ed., *Francis Meres's Treatise "Poetrie": A Critical Edition*, University of Illinois Studies in Language and Literature (Urbana: University of Illinois Press, 1933).

Allen, Michael J. B. and Kenneth Muir, eds., *Shakespeare's Plays in Quarto* (Berkeley: University of California Press, 1981).

Allot, Robert, comp., *England's Parnassus*, ed. Charles Crawford (Oxford: Clarendon Press, 1913).

Arber, Edward, ed., *A Transcript of the Registers of the Company of Stationers of London 1554–1640*, 5 vols. (London: Privately Printed, 1875–94).

Ayres, Philip, "The Iconography of Jonson's *Sejanus*, 1605: Copy-text for the Revels Edition," in *Editing Texts: Papers from a Conference at the Humanities Research Centre, May 1984*, ed. J. C. Eade (Canberra: Humanities Research Centre, Australian National University, 1985), 47–53.

Bald, R. C., *Bibliographical Studies in the Beaumont & Fletcher Folio of 1647* (Oxford: Printed at the Oxford University Press for the Bibligraphical Society, 1938 [for 1937]).

Baldwin, T. W., *Shakespeare's "Love's Labor's Won": New Evidence from the Account Books of an Elizabethan Bookseller* (Carbondale, Ill.: Southern Illinois University Press, 1957).

Barish, Jonas, *The Antitheatrical Prejudice* (Berkeley: University of California Press, 1981).

Barroll, Leeds, *Politics, Plague and Shakespeare's Theatre: The Stuart Years* (Ithaca: Cornell University Press, 1991).

Bartlett, Henrietta C. and Alfred W. Pollard, *A Census of Shakespeare's Plays in Quarto* (New Haven: Yale University Press, 1916).

Baskerville, Charles Read, "A Prompt Copy of *A Looking Glass for London and England*," *Modern Philology*, 30 (1932–33), 29–51.

Bate, Jonathan, "Shakespeare's Tragedies As Working Scripts," *Critical Survey*, 3 (1991), 118–27.

Bennett, H. S., *English Books & Readers, 1558 to 1603* (Cambridge: At the University Press, 1965).

Bentley, Gerald Eades, *The Jacobean and Caroline Stage*, 7 vols. (Oxford: Clarendon Press, 1941–68).

The Profession of Dramatist in Shakespeare's Time 1590–1642 (Princeton University Press, 1971).

Berger, Harry, Jr., *Imaginary Audition: Shakespeare on Stage and Page* (Berkeley and Los Angeles: University of California Press, 1989).

Making Trifles of Errors: Redistributing Complicities in Shakespeare, ed. Peter Erickson (Stanford University Press, 1997).

Berger, Thomas and Jesse Lander, "Shakespeare in Print, 1593–1640," in *A Companion to Shakespeare*, ed. David Scott Kastan (Oxford: Blackwell, 1999), 395–413.

Bevington, David, *From "Mankind" to Marlowe: Growth of Structure in the Popular Drama of Tudor England* (Cambridge, Mass.: Harvard University Press, 1962).

Bevington, David, ed., *The Complete Works of Shakespeare*, updated 4th edn (New York: Longman, 1997).

Troilus and Cressida, The Arden Shakespeare (Walton-on-Thames: Thomas Nelson, 1998).

Bland, Mark, "The Appearance of the Text in Early Modern England," *TEXT: An Interdisciplinary Annual of Textual Studies*, 11 (1998), 91–154.

"William Stansby and the Production of *The Workes of Beniamin Jonson*, 1615–1616," *The Library*, 20 (1998), 1–34.

Blayney, Peter W. M., *The Texts of "King Lear" and Their Origin: Nicholas Okes and the First Quarto* (Cambridge University Press, 1982).

The First Folio of Shakespeare (Washington DC: Folger Library Publications, 1991).

"The Publication of Playbooks," in *A New History of Early English Drama*, eds. John D. Cox and David Scott Kastan (New York: Columbia University Press, 1997), 383–422.

Bowers, Fredson, "The Publication of English Renaissance Plays," in *Elizabethan Dramatists*, ed. Fredson Bowers, Dictionary of Literary Biography, 62 (Detroit: Gale Research Company, 1987), 406–16.

Bowers, Fredson, gen. ed., *The Dramatic Works in the Beaumont and Fletcher Canon*, 10 vols. (Cambridge University Press, 1966–96).

Bradley, David, *From Text to Performance in the Elizabethan Theatre* (Cambridge University Press, 1991).

Brady, Jennifer and W. H. Herendeen, eds., *Ben Jonson's 1616 Folio* (Newark: University of Delaware Press; London and Toronto: Associated University Presses, 1991).

Brooks, Douglas A., *From Playhouse to Printing House: Drama and Authorship in Early Modern England*, Cambridge Studies in Renaissance Literature and Culture, 36 (Cambridge University Press, 2000).

Brown, John Russell, *William Shakespeare: Writing for Performance* (New York: St. Martin's Press, 1996).

Bullough, Geoffrey, ed., *Narrative and Dramatic Sources of Shakespeare*, 8 vols. (London: Routledge, 1957–1975).

Burkhart, Robert E., *Shakespeare's Bad Quartos* (The Hague: Mouton, 1975).

Carroll, D. Allen, ed., *Greene's Groatsworth of Wit, Bought with a Million of Repentance (1592)*, Medieval & Renaissance Texts & Studies, 114 (Binghamton, New York: Medieval & Renaissance Texts & Studies, 1994).

Carson, Neil, *A Companion to Henslowe's Diary* (Cambridge University Press, 1988).

Chambers, E. K., *The Elizabethan Stage*, 4 vols. (Oxford: Clarendon Press, 1923).
The Disintegration of Shakespeare (London: Published for the British Academy, 1924).
William Shakespeare: A Study of Facts and Problems, 2 vols. (Oxford: Clarendon Press, 1930).

Chartier, Roger, *Cultural Uses of Print*, trans. Lydia G. Cochrane (Princeton University Press, 1987).
Publishing Drama in Early Modern Europe, Panizzi Lectures, 14 (London: The British Library, 1999).
"Texts, Printing, Reading," in *The New Cultural History*, ed. Lynn Hunt (Berkeley and Los Angeles: University of California Press, 1989), 154–75.

Clayton, Thomas, ed., *The "Hamlet" First Published (Q1, 1603): Origins, Form, Intertextualities* (Newark: University of Delaware Press; London: Associated University Presses, 1992).

Clegg, Cyndia Susan, "The Stationers' Company of London," in *The British Literary Booktrade 1475–1700*, eds. James K. Bracken and Joel Silver, Dictionary of Literary Biography, 170 (Detroit: Gale Research, 1996), 275–91.
"Liberty, License, and Authority: Press Censorship and Shakespeare," in *A Companion to Shakespeare*, ed. David Scott Kastan (Oxford: Blackwell, 1999), 464–85.

Cloud, Random (Randall McLeod), "The Marriage of Good and Bad Quartos," *Shakespeare Quarterly*, 33 (1982), 421–31.

Coursen, Herbert R., *Shakespearean Performance as Interpretation* (Newark: University of Delaware Press; London: Associated University Presses, 1992).
Reading Shakespeare on Stage (Newark: University of Delaware Press; London: Associated University Presses, 1995).

Cox, John D. and David Scott Kastan, eds., *A New History of Early English Drama* (New York: Columbia University Press, 1997).

Crawford, Charles, *"Belvedere, or The Garden of the Muses,"* *Englische Studien*, 43 (1910–11), 198–228.
"Appendix D: J. Bodenham's *Belvedere*," in C. M. Ingleby, comp., *The Shakespeare Allusion-Book*, 2 vols. (London: Chatton & Windus, 1909, rpt. by Oxford University Press 1932), 11.489–518.

Cressy, David, *Literacy and the Social Order: Reading and Writing in Tudor and Stuart England* (Cambridge University Press, 1980).

de Grazia, Margreta, *Shakespeare Verbatim: The Reproduction of Authenticity and the 1790 Apparatus* (Oxford: Clarendon Press; New York: Oxford University Press, 1991).

Dessen, Alan C., "Weighing the Options in *Hamlet* Q1," in *The "Hamlet" First Published (Q1, 1603): Origins, Form, Intertextualities*, ed. Thomas Clayton (Newark: University of Delaware Press; London: Associated University Presses, 1992), 65–78.

Dillon, Janette, "Is There a Performance in This Text?," *Shakespeare Quarterly*, 45 (1995), 74–86.

Dobson, Michael, *The Making of the National Poet: Shakespeare, Adaptation and Authorship, 1660–1769* (Oxford: Clarendon Press; New York: Oxford University Press, 1992).

Downes, John, *Roscius Anglicanus, or an Historical Review of the Stage* (London, 1708).

Duncan-Jones, Katherine, *Ungentle Shakespeare*, The Arden Shakespeare (London: Thomson Learning, 2001).

"Was the 1609 *Shakespeares Sonnets* really unauthorized?" *The Review of English Studies*, 34 (1983), 151–71.

Duncan-Jones, Katherine, ed., *Shakespeare's Sonnets*, The Arden Shakespeare (Walton-on-Thames, Surrey: Thomas Nelson, 1997).

Duthie, George Ian, *The "Bad" Quarto of Hamlet* (Cambridge University Press, 1941).

Elizabethan Shorthand and the First Quarto of "King Lear" (Oxford: Blackwell, 1949).

"The Quarto of Shakespeare's *Henry V*," in *Papers Mainly Shakespearian*, ed. G. I. Duthie (Edinburgh: Published for the University of Aberdeen by Oliver and Boyd, 1964), 106–30.

Dutton, Richard, *Ben Jonson, Authority, Criticism* (Houndmills, Basingstoke: Macmillan, 1996).

"The Birth of the Author," in *Elizabethan Theater: Essays in Honor of S. Schoenbaum*, eds. R. B. Parker and S. P. Zitner (Newark: University of Delaware Press; London: Associated University Presses, 1996), 71–92, reprinted and revised in *Texts and Cultural Change in Early Modern England*, eds. Cedric C. Brown and Arthur Marotti (London: Macmillan, 1997), 153–78, and in Dutton, *Licensing, Censorship and Authorship in Early Modern England: Buggeswords* (Houndmills, Basingstoke; New York: Palgrave, 2000), 90–113.

Edmond, Mary, *Rare Sir William Davenant: Poet Laureate, Playwright, Civil War General, Restoration Theatre Manager*, Revels Plays Companion Library (Manchester University Press, 1987).

Erne, Lukas, *Beyond "The Spanish Tragedy": A Study of the Works of Thomas Kyd*, Revels Plays Companion Library (Manchester University Press, 2001).

"Biography and Mythography: Rereading Chettle's Alleged Apology to Shakespeare," *English Studies*, 79 (1998), 430–40.

Eisenstein, Elizabeth L., *The Printing Press as an Agent of Change: Communications and Cultural Transformations in Early Modern Europe*, 2 vols. (Cambridge and New York: Cambridge University Press, 1979).

Evans, G. Blakemore, "New Evidence on the Provenance of the Padua Prompt-Books of Shakespeare's *Macbeth, Measure for Measure,* and *Winter's Tale,*" *Studies in Bibliography*, 20 (1967), 239–42.

Evans, G. Blakemore, ed., *Shakespearean Prompt-Books of the Seventeeth Century*, 8 vols. (Charlottesville, Virginia: Bibliographical Society of the University of Virginia, 1960–96).

Evans, G. Blakemore, gen. ed., *The Riverside Shakespeare*, 2nd edn (Boston and New York: Houghton Mifflin Company, 1997).

Farley-Hills, David, "The 'Bad' Quarto of *Romeo and Juliet,*" *Shakespeare Survey*, 49 (1996), 27–44.

Farmer, Alan B. and Zachary Lesser, "Vile Arts: The Marketing of English Printed Drama, 1512–1660," *Research Opportunities in Renaissance Drama*, 39 (2000), 77–165.

Febvre, Lucien and Henri-Jean Martin, *The Coming of the Book: The Impact of Printing 1450–1800*, trans. David Gerard, eds. Geoffry Nowell-Smith and David Wootton (London: NLB, 1976).

Foakes, R. A., "Tragedy at the Children's Theatres after 1600: A Challenge to the Adult Stage," in *The Elizabethan Theatre*, 2, ed. David Galloway (Toronto: Macmillan of Canada, 1970), 37–59.

Foakes, R. A., ed., *King Lear*, The Arden Shakespeare (Walton-on-Thames, Surrey: Thomas Nelson, 1997).

Foakes, R. A. and R. T. Rickert, eds., *Henslowe's Diary* (Cambridge University Press, 1961).

Foster, Donald W., *Elegy by W. S.: A Study in Attribution* (Newark: University of Delaware Press; London and Toronto: Associated University Presses, 1989).

Foucault, Michel, "What Is an Author?," trans. Catherine Porter, in *The Foucault Reader*, ed. Paul Rabinow (New York: Pantheon Books, 1984), 101–20.

Freeman, Arthur, ed., *Palladis Tamia: Wits Treasury* (New York: Garland, 1973).

Gaskell, Philip, *A New Introduction to Bibliography* (Oxford: Clarendon Press, 1972).

Goldberg, Jonathan, " 'What? in a Names that which we call a Rose': The Desired Texts of *Romeo and Juliet,*" in *Crisis in Editing: Texts of the English Renaissance*, ed. Randall McLeod (New York: AMS Press, 1994), 173–202.

Graves, R. B., *Lighting the Shakespearean Stage, 1567–1642* (Carbondale and Edwardsville: Southern Illinois University Press, 1999).

Gray, H. D., "The First Quarto of *Hamlet,*" *Modern Language Review*, 10 (1915), 171–80.

Greenblatt, Stephen, *Shakespearean Negotiations: The Circulation of Social Energy in Renaissance England* (Oxford: Clarendon Press, 1988).

Greenblatt, Stephen, gen. ed., *The Norton Shakespeare* (New York and London: W. W. Norton & Company, 1997).

Greg, W. W., *Two Elizabethan Stage Abridgements: "The Battle of Alcazar" & "Orlando Furioso"* (Oxford University Press, 1923).

Dramatic Documents from the Elizabethan Playhouses, 2 vols. (Oxford: Clarendon Press, 1931).

A Bibliography of the English Printed Drama to the Restoration, 4 vols. (London: Bibliographical Society, 1939–59).

The Editorial Problem in Shakespeare: A Survey of the Foundations of the Text, 3rd edn (Oxford: Clarendon, 1954).

The Shakespeare First Folio: Its Bibliographical and Textual History (Oxford: At the Clarendon Press, 1955).

A Companion to Arber (Oxford: Clarendon Press, 1967).

"Prompt Copies, Private Transcripts, and 'the Playhouse Scrivener,'" *The Library*, 4th series, 6 (1926), 148–56.

"*The Spanish Tragedy* – A Leading Case?," *The Library*, 4th series, 6 (1926), 47–56.

"The Rationale of Copy-Text," *Studies in Bibliography*, 3 (1950–51), 19–36, rpt. in Greg, *Collected Papers*, ed. J. C. Maxwell (Oxford: Clarendon Press, 1966), 374–91.

Greg, W. W., ed., *Henslowe Papers: Being Documents Supplementary to Henslowe's Diary* (London: A. H. Bullen, 1907).

Shakespeare's "Merry Wives of Windsor," 1602 (Oxford: Clarendon Press, 1910).

The Spanish Tragedy (1592), Malone Society Reprints (London: Oxford University Press, 1948).

Guibert, Albert-Jean, *Bibliographie des oeuvres de Molière publiées au XVIIe siècle*, 2 vols. (Paris: Centre national de la recherche scientifique, 1961).

Gurr, Andrew, *The Shakespearean Stage 1574–1642*, 3rd edn (Cambridge University Press, 1992).

Shakespearian Playing Companies (Oxford University Press, 1996).

"Maximal and Minimal Texts: Shakespeare v. The Globe," *Shakespeare Survey*, 52 (1999), 68–87.

Gurr, Andrew, ed., *The First Quarto of King Henry V*, New Cambridge Shakespeare: The Early Quartos (Cambridge University Press, 2000).

Haaker, Ann, "The Plague, the Theater, and the Poet," *Renaissance Drama*, n.s. 1 (1968), 283–306.

Hackel, Heidi Brayman, "'Rowme' of Its Own: Printed Drama in Early Libraries," in *A New History of Early English Drama*, eds. John D. Cox and David Scott Kastan (New York: Columbia University Press, 1997), 113–30.

"The 'Great Variety' of Readers and Early Modern Reading Practices," in *A Companion to Shakespeare*, ed. David Scott Kastan (Oxford: Blackwell, 1999), 139–57.

Halio, Jay L., "Handy-Dandy: Q1/Q2 *Romeo and Juliet*," in *Shakespeare's "Romeo and Juliet": Texts, Contexts, and Interpretations*, ed. J. L. Halio (Newark: University of Delaware Press; London: Associated University Presses, 1995), 123–50.

Hammond, Anthony, "Encounters of the Third Kind in Stage-Directions in Elizabethan and Jacobean Drama," *Studies in Philology*, 89 (1992), 71–99.

Harbage, Alfred, *Annals of English Drama, 975–1700*, rev. by Samuel Schoenbaum (London: Methuen, 1964).

Harrison, G. B., ed., *Kind-Hartes Dreame*, The Bodley Head Quartos, 4 (London: John Lane, 1923).

Hart, Alfred, *Shakespeare and the Homilies and Other Pieces of Research into the Elizabethan Drama* (Melbourne University Press, 1934).

    Stolne and Surreptitious Copies: A Comparative Study of Shakespeare's Bad Quartos (Melbourne University Press, 1942).

    "The Number of Lines in Shakespeare's Plays", *Review of English Studies*, 8 (1932), 19–28.

    "The Length of Elizabethan and Jacobean Plays", *Review of English Studies*, 8 (1932), 139–54.

    "The Time Allotted for Representation of Elizabethan and Jacobean Plays," *Review of English Studies*, 8 (1932), 395–413.

Helgerson, Richard, *Self-Crowned Laureates: Spenser, Jonson, Milton and the Literary System* (Berkeley and Los Angeles: University of California Press, 1983).

Heltzel, Virgil B., "The Dedication of Tudor and Stuart Plays," *Wiener Beiträge zur Englischen Philologie*, 65 (1957), 74–86.

Heywood, Thomas, *The Dramatic Works of Thomas Heywood*, ed. R. H. Shepherd, 6 vols. (London, 1874).

Hirschfeld, Heather, "Early Modern Collaboration and Theories of Authorship," *PMLA*, 116 (2001), 609–22.

Holland, Peter, "Measuring Performance," in *Performance*, ed. Peter Halter, Swiss Papers in English Language and Literature, 11 (Tübingen: Gunter Narr, 1999), 37–53.

Honigmann, E. A. J., *The Stability of Shakespeare's Text* (London: Edward Arnold, 1965).

    The Texts of "Othello" and Shakespearian Revision (London and New York: Routledge, 1996).

    "The Date and Revision of *Troilus and Cressida*," in *Textual Criticism and Literary Interpretation*, ed. Jerome J. McGann (Chicago and London: University of Chicago Press, 1985), 38–54.

Honigmann, E. A. J., ed., *Othello*, The Arden Shakespeare (Walton-on-Thames, Surrey: Thomas Nelson, 1997).

Hoppe, H. R., *The Bad Quarto of "Romeo and Juliet"* (Ithaca: Cornell University Press, 1948).

Howard-Hill, T. H., *Ralph Crane and Some Shakespeare First Folio Comedies* (Charlottesville: The University Press of Virginia, 1972).

    "The Author as Scribe or Reviser? Middleton's Intentions in *A Game at Chess*," *TEXT: An Interdisciplinary Annual of Textual Studies*, 3 (1987), 305–18.

    "Modern Textual Theories and the Editing of Plays," *The Library*, 6th series, 11 (1989), 89–115.

    " 'Nor Stage, Nor Stationers Stall Can Show': The Circulation of Plays in Manuscript in the Early Seventeenth Century," *Book History*, 2 (1999), 28–41.

Howard-Hill, T. H., ed., *A Game at Chess*, The Revels Plays (Manchester University Press, 1993).

Hunt, Arnold, "Book Trade Patents, 1603–1640," in *The Book Trade and Its Customers: Historical Essays for Robin Myers*, eds. Arnold Hunt, Giles Mandelbrote, and Alison Shell (Winchester, Hampshire: St. Paul's Bibliographies; New Castle, Delaware: Oak Knoll Press, 1997), 27–54.

Hunter, G. K., "Were There Act-Pauses on Shakespeare's Stage?," in *English Renaissance Drama: Essays in Honor of Madelaine Doran and Mark Eccles*, eds. Standish Henning, Robert Kimbrough, and Richard Knowles (Carbondale, Ill.: Southern Illinois University Press, 1976), 15–35.

Hunter, Lynette, "The Dating of Q4 *Romeo and Juliet* Revisited," *The Library*, 7th series, 2 (2001), 281–85.

Ingleby, C. M., comp., *The Shakespeare Allusion-Book*, 2 vols. (London: Chatto & Windus, 1909, rpt. by Oxford University Press, 1932).

Ioppolo, Grace, *Revising Shakespeare* (Cambridge, Mass.: Harvard University Press, 1991).

Irace, Kathleen O., *Reforming the "Bad" Quartos: Performance and Provenance of Six Shakespearean First Editions* (Newark: University of Delaware Press; London: Associated University Presses, 1994).

   "Reconstruction and Adaptation in Q *Henry V*," *Studies in Bibliography*, 44 (1991), 228–53.

Jackson, William A., *Records of the Court of the Stationers' Company* (London: The Bibliographical Society, 1957).

Jewkes, Wilfred T., *Act Division in Elizabethan and Jacobean Plays, 1583–1616* (Hamden, Conn.: Shoe String Press, 1958).

Johns, Adrian, *The Nature of the Book: Print and Knowledge in the Making* (Chicago and London: University of Chicago Press, 1998).

Jones, John, *Shakespeare at Work* (Oxford: Clarendon Press; New York: Oxford University Press, 1995).

Jonson, Ben, *The Works of Ben Jonson*, eds. C. H. Herford and Percy and Evelyn Simpson, 11 vols. (Oxford: Clarendon Press, 1925–52).

Jowett, John, "Jonson's Authorization of Type in *Sejanus* and Other Early Quartos," *Studies in Philology*, 44 (1991), 254–65.

   "Henry Chettle and the first Quarto of *Romeo and Juliet*," *Publications of the Bibliographical Society of America*, 92 (1998), 53–74.

   "After Oxford: Recent Developments in Textual Studies," in *The Shakespearean International Yearbook, 1: Where Are We Now in Shakespearean Studies?*, eds. W. R. Elton and John M. Mucciolo (Aldershot: Ashgate Publishing Limited; Brookfield, Vermont: Ashgate Publishing Company, 1999), 65–86.

Jowett, John and Gary Taylor, "The Three Texts of *2 Henry IV*," *Studies in Bibliography*, 40 (1987), 31–50.

Kastan, David Scott, *Shakespeare after Theory* (New York and London: Routledge, 1999).

   Shakespeare and the Book (Cambridge University Press, 2001).

Kastan, David Scott, ed., *A Companion to Shakespeare* (Oxford: Blackwell, 1999).

Keenan, Siobhan, *Travelling Players in Shakespeare's England* (London and New York: Palgrave, 2002).

Kehler, Dorothea, "The First Quarto of *Hamlet*: Reforming Widow Gertred," *Shakespeare Quarterly*, 46 (1995), 398–413.

Kermode, Sir Frank, *Shakespeare's Language* (New York: Farrar, Straus and Giroux, 2000).

Kerrigan, John, "Shakespeare as Reviser," in *English Drama to 1710*, ed. Christopher Ricks (New York: Peter Bedrick Books, 1987), 255–75.

Kidnie, M. J., "Text, Performance, and the Editors: Staging Shakespeare's Drama," *Shakespeare Quarterly*, 51 (2000), 456–73.

Kirschbaum, Leo, *Shakespeare and the Stationers* (Columbus: Ohio State University Press, 1955).

"Is *The Spanish Tragedy* a Leading Case? Did a Bad Quarto of *Love's Labours Lost* Ever Exist?," *Journal of English and German Philology*, 37 (1938), 501–12.

Kirwood, A. E. M., "Richard Field, Printer, 1589–1624," *The Library* 4th series, 12 (1931), 1–39.

Klein, David, "Time Allotted for an Elizabethan Performance," *Shakespeare Quarterly*, 18 (1967), 434–38.

Klotz, Edith L., "A Subject Analysis of English Imprints for Every Tenth Year from 1480 to 1640," *Huntington Library Quarterly*, 1 (1937–38), 417–19.

Knowles, Richard, "Revision Awry in Folio *Lear* 3.1," *Shakespeare Quarterly*, 46 (1995), 32–46.

Knutson, Roslyn L., *The Repertory of Shakespeare's Company, 1594–1613* (Fayetteville, Ark.: University of Arkansas Press, 1991).

"The Commercial Significance of the Payments for Playtexts in *Henslowe's Diary*, 1597–1603," *Medieval and Renaissance Drama in England*, 5 (1991), 117–63.

"The Repertory," in *A New History of Early English Drama*, eds. John D. Cox and David Scott Kastan (New York: Columbia University Press, 1997), 461–80.

"Shakespeare's Repertory," in *A Companion to Shakespeare*, ed. David Scott Kastan (Oxford: Blackwell, 1999), 346–61.

Lee, Sir Sidney, *A Life of William Shakespeare* (London: Smith, Elder, & Co., 1898).

Leech, Clifford, "The Plays of Edward Sharpham: Alterations Accomplished and Projected," *Review of English Studies*, 11 (1935), 69–74.

Leishman, J. B., *Themes and Variations in Shakespeare's Sonnets* (London: Hutchinson, 1961).

Levin, Richard, "Performance Critics vs Close Readers in the Study of English Renaissance Drama," *Modern Language Review*, 81 (1986), 545–59.

Loewenstein, Joseph, *Ben Jonson and Possessive Authorship* (Cambridge University Press, 2002).

"The Script in the Marketplace," *Representations*, 12 (1985), 101–15.

Long, William B., " 'A Bed / for Woodstock': A Warning for the Unwary," *Medieval and Renaissance Drama in England* 2 (1985), 91–118.

"Performing Texts: Shakespeare's Players and Editors," *TEXT: An Interdisciplinary Annual of Textual Studies*, 8 (1995), 377 86.

"Perspective on Provenance: The Context of Varying Speech-heads," in *Shakespeare's Speech-Headings: Speaking the Speech in Shakespeare's Plays*, ed. George Walton Williams (Newark: University of Delaware Press; London: Associated University Presses, 1997), 21–44.

"'Precious Few': English Manuscript Playbooks," in *A Companion to Shakespeare*, ed. David Scott Kastan (Oxford: Blackwell, 1999), 414–33.

Love, Harold, *Scribal Publication in Seventeenth-Century England* (Oxford: Clarendon Press, 1993).

Lull, Janis, "Forgetting *Hamlet*: The First Quarto and the Folio," in *The "Hamlet" First Published (Q1, 1603): Origins, Form, Intertextualities*, ed. Thomas Clayton (Newark: University of Delaware Press; London: Associated University Presses, 1992), 137–50.

Maguire, Laurie E., *Shakespearean Suspect Texts: The "Bad" Quartos and Their Contexts* (Cambridge University Press, 1996).

"The Craft of Printing (1600)," in *A Companion to Shakespeare*, ed. David Scott Kastan (Oxford: Blackwell, 1999), 434–49.

Marcus, Leah S., *Puzzling Shakespeare: Local Readings and Its Discontents* (Berkeley and Los Angeles: University of California Press, 1988).

Unediting the Renaissance: Shakespeare, Marlowe, Milton (London and New York: Routledge, 1996).

Marlowe, Christopher, *The Complete Works of Christopher Marlowe*, ed., Fredson Bowers, 2 vols. (Cambridge University Press, 1973).

Tamburlaine the Great Parts 1 and 2, ed. David Fuller, and *The Massacre at Paris with the Death of the Duke of Guise*, ed. Edward J. Esche (Oxford: Clarendon Press, 1998).

Marotti, Arthur, *Manuscript, Print, and the English Renaissance Lyric* (Ithaca: Cornell University Press, 1995).

Masten, Jeffrey, *Textual Intercourse: Collaboration, Authorship, and Sexualities in Renaissance Drama*, Cambridge Studies in Renaissance Literature and Culture, 14 (Cambridge University Press, 1997).

"Authorship and Collaboration," in *A New History of Early Modern Drama*, eds. John D. Cox and David Scott Kastan (New York: Columbia University Press, 1997), 357–82.

May, Steven W., "Tudor Aristocrats and the Mythical 'Stigma of Print,'" in *Renaissance Papers 1980*, eds. A. Leigh Deneef and M. Thomas Hester (Durham, NC: The Southeastern Renaissance Conference, 1981), 11–18.

McKenzie, D. F., "Printers of the Mind: Some Notes on Bibliographical Theories and Printing-House Practices," *Studies in Bibliography*, 22 (1969), 1–75.

"Printing in England from Caxton to Milton," in *The Age of Shakespeare*, ed. Boris Ford, The New Pelican Guide to English Literature, 2, rev. edn (Harmondsworth: Penguin, 1982), 207–26.

McKerrow, Ronald B., *An Introduction to Bibliography for Literary Students* (Oxford: Clarendon Press, 1927).

McKerrow, Ronald B., gen. ed., *A Dictionary of Printers and Booksellers in England, Scotland and Ireland, and of Foreign Printers of English Books 1557–1640* (London: Printed for the Bibliographical Society, 1910).

McManaway, James G., "The Two Earliest Prompt Books of *Hamlet*," *The Papers of the Bibliographical Society of America*, 43 (1949), 288–320.

"Additional Prompt-Books of Shakespeare from the Smock Alley Theatre," *Modern Language Review*, 45 (1950), 64–65.

McMillin, Scott, "Casting the *Hamlet* Quartos: The Limit of Eleven," in *The "Hamlet" First Published (Q1, 1603): Origins, Form, Intertextualities*, ed. Thomas Clayton (Newark: University of Delaware Press; London: Associated University Presses, 1992), 179–94.

"The *Othello* Quarto and the 'Foul-Paper' Hypothesis," *Shakespeare Quarterly*, 51 (2000), 67–85.

McMillin, Scott and Sally-Beth MacLean, *The Queen's Men and Their Plays* (Cambridge University Press, 1998).

Melchiori, Giorgio, "*Hamlet*: The Acting Version and the Wiser Sort," in *The "Hamlet" First Published (Q1, 1603): Origins, Form, Intertextualities*, ed. Thomas Clayton (Newark: University of Delaware Press; London: Associated University Presses, 1992), 195–210.

Shakespeare's Garter Plays: "Edward III" to "Merry Wives of Windsor" (Newark: University of Delaware Press; London and Toronto: Associated University Presses, 1994).

Melchiori, Giorgio, ed., *King Edward III*, The New Cambridge Shakespeare (Cambridge University Press, 1998).

Melnikoff, Kirk, "Richard Jones (fl. 1564–1613): Elizabethan Printer, Bookseller, and Publisher," *Analytical & Enumerative Bibliography*, 12 (2001), 153–84.

Miller, Stephen Roy, "*The Taming of a Shrew* and the Theories; or, 'Though this be badness, yet there is method in't,'" in *Textual Formation and Reformation*, eds. Laurie E. Maguire and Thomas L. Berger (Newark: University of Delaware Press; London: Associated University Presses, 1998), 251–63.

Miola, Robert S., "Creating the Author: Jonson's Latin Epigraphs," *Ben Jonson Journal*, 6 (1999), 35–48.

Moore Smith, G. C., ed., *Gabriel Harvey's Marginalia* (Stratford-upon-Avon: Shakespeare Head Press, 1913).

Mowat, Barbara, "The Theater and Literary Culture," in *A New History of Early English Drama*, eds. John D. Cox and David Scott Kastan (New York: Columbia University Press, 1997), 213–30.

"The Reproduction of Shakespeare's Texts," in *The Cambridge Companion to Shakespeare*, eds. Margreta de Grazia and Stanley Wells (Cambridge University Press, 2001), 13–29.

Murray, Timothy, *Theatrical Legitimation: Allegories of Genius in Seventeenth-Century England and France* (New York and Oxford: Oxford University Press, 1987).

Murphy, Andrew, *Shakespeare in Print* (Cambridge University Press, forthcoming).

Nashe, Thomas, *The Works of Thomas Nashe*, ed. Ronald B. McKerrow, 5 vols. (London: Oxford University Press, 1904–10).

Neill, Michael, ed., *The Tragedy of Anthony and Cleopatra*, The Oxford Shakespeare (Oxford: Clarendon Press, 1994).

Newton, Richard C., "Jonson and the (Re-)Invention of the Book," in *Classic and Cavalier: Essays on Jonson and the Sons of Ben*, eds. Claude J. Summers and Ted-Larry Pebworth (University of Pittsburgh Press, 1982), 31–58.

Ong, Walter J., *Orality and Literacy: The Technologizing of the Word* (London and New York: Methuen, 1982).

Orgel, Stephen, "The Authentic Shakespeare," *Representations*, 21 (1988), 1–25.

"Acting Scripts, Performing Texts," in *Crisis in Editing: Texts of the English Renaissance*, ed. Randall McLeod (New York: AMS Press, 1994), 251–94.

Patrick, D. L., *The Textual History of "Richard III"* (Stanford University Press; London: Oxford University Press, 1936).

Patterson, Annabel, *Shakespeare and the Popular Voice* (Oxford: Blackwell, 1989).

Patterson, Lyman Ray, *Copyright in Historical Perspective* (Nashville: Vanderbilt University Press, 1968).

Peters, Julie Stone, *Theatre of the Book, 1480–1880: Print, Text, and Performance in Europe* (Oxford, New York: Oxford University Press, 2000).

Plant, Marjorie, *The English Book Trade: An Economic History of the Making and Sale of Books* (London: George Allen & Unwin Ltd., 1939).

Pollard, Alfred W., *Shakespeare Folios and Quartos: A Study in the Bibliography of Shakespeare's Plays 1594–1685* (London: Methuen, 1909).

Shakespeare's Fight with the Pirates and the Problems of the Transmission of His Text (London: A. Moring, 1917).

Pollard, Alfred W. and J. Dover Wilson, "The 'Stolne and Surreptitious' Shakespearian Texts," *The Times Literary Supplement*, January 9, 1918, 18; January 16, 1919, 30; March 13, 1919, 134; August 7, 1919, 420; August 14, 1919, 434.

Pollard, A. W. and G. R. Redgrave, comp., *A Short-Title Catalogue of Books Printed in England, Scotland and Ireland, and of English Books Printed Abroad*, 1475–1640, 2nd edn (London: The Bibliographical Society, 1976–1991).

Pomeroy, Elizabeth W., *The Elizabethan Miscellanies: Their Development and Conventions* (Berkeley: University of California Press, 1973).

Price, H. T., *The Text of "Henry V"* (Newcastle-under-Lyme: Mandley & Unett, 1920).

Rabkin, Norman, *Shakespeare and the Problem of Meaning* (University of Chicago Press, 1981).

Radaddi, Mongi, *Davenant's Adaptations of Shakespeare*, Studia Anglistica Upsaliensis, 36 (Uppsala: Almqvist & Wiksell International, 1979).

Randall, Dale B. J., *Winter Fruit: English Drama, 1642–1660* (Lexington, Kentucky: University of Kentucky Press, 1995).

Rasmussen, Eric, *A Textual Companion to "Doctor Faustus,"* The Revels Plays Companion Library (Manchester and New York: Manchester University Press, 1993).

"The Revision of Scripts," in *A New History of Early Modern Drama*, eds. John D. Cox and David Scott Kastan (New York: Columbia University Press, 1997), 441–60.

Rhodes, R. Crompton, *Shakespeare's First Folio* (Oxford: Blackwell, 1923).

Robinson, Benedict Scott, "Thomas Heywood and the Cultural Politics of Play Collections," *Studies in English Literature*, 42 (2002), 361–80.

Rollins, Hyder Edward, ed., *The Passionate Pilgrim* (New York and London: Charles Scribner's Sons, 1940).

Rose, Mark, *Authors and Owners: The Invention of Copyright* (Cambridge, Mass., London: Harvard University Press, 1993).

Saunders, J. W., "The Stigma of Print: A Note on the Social Bases of Tudor Poetry," *Essays in Criticism*, 1 (1951), 139–64.

Schoenbaum, Samuel, *William Shakespeare: A Compact Documentary Life*, rev. edn (New York: Oxford University Press, 1987).

Shakespeare's Lives, new edn (Oxford: Clarendon Press, 1991).

Shakespeare, William, *The Complete Works*, gen. eds., Stanley Wells and Gary Taylor (Oxford: Clarendon Press, 1986).

Sheavyn, Phoebe, *The Literary Profession in the Elizabethan Age*, 2nd edn, rev. by J. W. Saunders (Manchester University Press; New York: Barnes & Noble Inc., 1967).

Smidt, Kristian, *Iniurious Imposters and "Richard III"* (Oslo: Norwegian Universities Press; New York: Humanities Press, 1964).

Memorial Transmission and Quarto Copy in "Richard III": A Reassessment (Oslo: Universitetsforlaget; New York: Humanities Press, 1970).

"Repetition, Revision, and Editorial Greed in Shakespeare's Play Texts," *Cahiers Elisabéthains*, 34 (1988), 25–37.

Smidt, Kristian, ed., *The Tragedy of King Richard the Third: Parallel Texts of the First Quarto and the First Folio with Variants of the Early Quartos* (Oslo: Universitetsforlaget; New York: Humanities Press, 1969).

Smith, Emma, "Author v. Character in Early Modern Dramatic Authorship: The Example of Thomas Kyd and *The Spanish Tragedy*," *Medieval and Renaissance Drama in England*, 11 (1999), 129–42.

Sorelius, Gunnar, "The Smock Alley Prompt-Books of *1* and *2 Henry IV*," *Shakespeare Quarterly*, 22 (1971), 111–27.

Spencer, Hazelton, "Seventeenth-Century Cuts in Hamlet's Soliloquies," *The Review of English Studies*, 35 (1933), 257–65.

Stephen, Sir Leslie, and Sir Sidney Lee, eds., *The Dictionary of National Biography*, 22 vols. (Oxford: Smith, Elder, & Co., 1885–1901).

Styan, J. L., *The Shakespeare Revolution: Criticism and Performance in the Twentieth Century* (Cambridge University Press, 1977).

Taylor, Gary, *Three Studies in the Text of "Henry V,"* in Stanley Wells, *Modernizing Shakespeare's Spelling*; with Gary Taylor, *Three Studies in the Text of "Henry V"* (Oxford: Clarendon Press, 1979).

"The War in *King Lear*," *Shakespeare Survey*, 33 (1980), 27–34.

"Revising Shakespeare," *TEXT: An Interdisciplinary Annual of Textual Studies*, 3 (1987), 285–304.

"Shakespeare and Others: The Authorship of *Henry VI, Part I*," *Medieval and Renaissance Drama in England*, 7 (1995), 145–205.

Taylor, Gary and Michael Warren, eds., *The Division of the Kingdoms* (Oxford: Clarendon Press, 1983).

Taylor, Gary and John Jowett, *Shakespeare Reshaped, 1606–1623* (Oxford: Clarendon Press, 1993).

Thomas, Sidney, "Shakespeare's Supposed Revision of *King Lear*," *Shakespeare Quarterly*, 35 (1984), 506–11.

"*Hamlet* Q1: First Version or Bad Quarto?," in *The "Hamlet" First Published (Q1, 1603): Origins, Form, Intertextualities*, ed. Thomas Clayton (Newark: University of Delaware Press; London: Associated University Presses, 1992), 249–56.

"The Integrity of *King Lear*," *Modern Language Review*, 90 (1995), 572–84.

Thompson, Ann and Neil Taylor, " 'O That This Too Too XXXXX Text Would Melt': *Hamlet* and the Indecisions of Modern Editors and Publishers," *TEXT: An Interdisciplinary Annual of Textual Studies*, 10 (1997), 221–36.

Thomson, Leslie, "A Quarto 'Marked for Performance': Evidence of What?," *Medieval and Renaissance Drama in England*, 8 (1996), 176–210.

Urkowitz, Steven, *Shakespeare's Revision of "King Lear"* (Princeton University Press, 1980).

"Reconsidering the Relationship of Quarto and Folio Texts of *Richard III*," *English Literary Renaissance*, 16 (1986), 442–66.

" 'Well-sayd olde Mole': Burying Three *Hamlets* in Modern Editions," in *Shakespeare Study Today*, ed. Georgianna Ziegler (New York: AMS Press, 1986), 37–70.

"Good News about 'Bad' Quartos," in *"Bad" Shakespeare: Revaluations of the Shakespeare Canon*, ed. Maurice Charney (Rutherford, N.J.: Fairleigh Dickinson University Press; London and Toronto: Associated University Presses, 1988), 189–206.

" 'If I Mistake in Those Foundations Which I Build Upon': Peter Alexander's Textual Analysis of *Henry VI Parts 2 and 3*," *English Literary Renaissance*, 18 (1988), 230–56.

"Back to Basics: Thinking about the *Hamlet* First Quarto," in *The "Hamlet" First Published (Q1, 1603): Origins, Form, Intertextualities*, ed. Thomas Clayton (Newark: University of Delaware Press; London: Associated University Presses, 1992), 257–91.

Van Lennep, William, "Thomas Killigrew Prepares His Plays for Production," in *Joseph Quincy Adams Memorial Studies*, eds. James G. McManaway, Giles E. Dawson, and Edwin E. Willoughby (Washington, DC: The Folger Shakespeare Library, 1948), 803–8.

Van Lennep, William, ed., *The London Stage 1660–1800: Part 1, 1660–1700* (Carbondale, Ill.: Southern Illinois University Press, 1965).

Velz, John W., "From Authorization to Authorship, Orality to Literature: The Case of Medieval and Renaissance Drama," *TEXT: An Interdisciplinary Annual of Textual Studies*, 6 (1994), 197–211.

Veylit, Alain, "Some Statistics on the Number of Surviving Printed Titles for Great Britain and Dependencies from the Beginnings of Print in England to the year 1800," http://cbsr26.ucr.edu/ESTCStatistics.html.

Vickers, Brian, *Counterfeiting Shakespeare: Evidence, Authorship, and John Ford's "Funerall Elegye"* (Cambridge University Press, 2002).

"Review of William Shakespeare, *The Complete Works* and *A Textual Companion*, ed. Stanley Wells and Gary Taylor (Oxford, 1986–7)," *The Review of English Studies*, 40 (1989), 402–11.

Vickers, Brian, ed., *English Renaissance Literary Criticism* (Oxford University Press, 1999).

Wall, Wendy, *The Imprint of Gender: Authorship and Publication in the English Renaissance* (Ithaca and London: Cornell University Press, 1993).

Warren, Michael, "Quarto and Folio *King Lear* and the Interpretation of Albany and Edgar," in *Shakespeare: Pattern of Excelling Nature*, eds. David Bevington and Jay L. Halio (Newark: University of Delaware Press, 1978), 95–107.

Warren, Michael, ed., *The Complete "King Lear," 1608–1623* (Berkeley: University of California Press, 1989).

Warren, Roger, "The Folio Omission of the Mock Trial: Motives and Consequences," in *The Division of the Kingdoms*, eds. Gary Taylor and Michael Warren (Oxford: Clarendon Press, 1983), 45–57.

"The Quarto and Folio Texts of *2 Henry VI*: A Reconsideration," *The Review of English Studies*, 51 (2000), 193–207.

Webster, John, *The Works of John Webster*, eds., David Gunby, David Carnegie, and Anthony Hammond, one volume published (Cambridge University Press, 1995).

Weimann, Robert, *Author's Pen and Actor's Voice: Playing and Writing in Shakespeare's Theatre*, eds. Helen Higbee and William West, Cambridge Studies in Renaissance Literature and Culture, 39 (Cambridge University Press, 2000).

Weis, René, ed., *"King Lear": A Parallel Text Edition* (London and New York: Longman, 1993).

Wells, Stanley, "Revision in Shakespeare's Plays," in *Editing and Editors: A Retrospect*, ed. Richard Landon (New York: AMS Press, 1988), 67–97.

Wells, Stanley and Gary Taylor, with John Jowett and William Montgomery, *William Shakespeare: A Textual Companion* (Oxford: Clarendon Press, 1987).

Werstine, Paul, "Folio Editors, Folio Compositors, and the Folio Text of *King Lear*," in *The Division of the Kingdoms*, eds. Gary Taylor and Michael Warren (Oxford: Clarendon Press, 1983), 247–312.

"The Editorial Usefulness of Printing House and Compositor Studies," in *Play-Texts in Old Spelling: Papers from the Glendon Conference*, eds. G. B. Shand and Raymond C. Shady (New York: AMS Press, 1984), 35–64.

"The Textual Mystery of *Hamlet*," *Shakespeare Quarterly*, 39 (1988), 1–26.

"Narratives About Printed Shakespeare Texts: 'Foul Papers' and 'Bad' Quartos," *Shakespeare Quarterly*, 41 (1990), 65–86.

"Plays in Manuscript," in *A New History of Early English Drama*, eds. John D. Cox and David Scott Kastan (New York: Columbia University Press, 1997), 481–97.

"A Century of 'Bad' Shakespeare Quartos," *Shakespeare Quarterly*, 50 (1999), 310–33.

"Post-Theory Problems in Shakespeare Editing," *The Yearbook of English Studies*, 29 (1999), 103–17.

West, Anthony James, *The Shakespeare First Folio: The History of the Book, Volume I, An Account of the First Folio Based on Its Sales and Prices, 1623–2000*, with a Foreword by Stanley Wells (Oxford University Press, 2001).

Wheatley, Henry B., "Post-Restoration Quartos of Shakespeare's Plays," *The Library*, 3rd series, 4 (1913), 237–69.

Williams, George Walton, *The Craft of Printing and the Publication of Shakespeare's Works* (Washington, DC: The Folger Shakespeare Library; London and Toronto: Associated University Presses, 1985).

"The Publishing and Editing of Shakespeare's Plays," in *William Shakespeare: His World, His Work, His Influence*, ed. John F. Andrews, 3 vols. (New York: Charles Scribner's Sons, 1985).

Williams, Gordon, *Shakespeare, Sex and the Print Revolution* (London and Atlantic Highlands, N.J.: Athlone, 1996).

Worthen, William B., *Shakespeare and the Authority of Performance* (Cambridge University Press, 1997).

"Deeper Meanings and Theatrical Technique: The Rhetoric of Performance Criticism," *Shakespeare Quarterly*, 40 (1989), 441–55.

"Drama, Performativity, and Performance," *PMLA*, 113 (1998), 1093–107.

Woudhuysen, Henry R., ed., *Love's Labour's Lost*, The Arden Shakespeare (Walton-on-Thames: Thomas Nelson, 1998).

Yamada, Akihiro, ed., *The First Folio of Shakespeare: A Transcript of Contemporary Marginalia* (Tokyo: Yushodo Press, 1998).

Index

CPSIA information can be obtained at www.ICGtesting.com
Printed in the USA
BVOW040432021211

277250BV00004B/9/A